7-16-2011

John,

I hope you enjoy this trip
back in time to the days
of WWII.

Robert Lovell

UNLIKELY WARRIOR,
A SMALL TOWN BOY'S VIEW OF WORLD WAR II

UNLIKELY WARRIOR,
A SMALL TOWN BOY'S VIEW OF WORLD WAR II

ROBERT C. LOVELL

TWO HARBORS PRESS
MINNEAPOLIS, MN

Two Harbors Press
212 3rd Avenue North, Suite 290
Minneapolis, MN 55401
612.455.2293
www.TwoHarborsPress.com

ISBN - 978-1-936198-20-7
ISBN - 1-936198-20-7
LCCN - 2010920569

Cover Design and Typeset by Nate Meyers

Printed in the United States of America

DEDICATED TO:

THAT LITTLE BROWN HEADED GIRL,

BILLIE DOLORES BULLARD LOVELL

THANKS TO:

My three sons: Rusty, Bill and John, for inspiring me
to write this story; Rev. Robyn Goggs for pushing me
to keep going; Jennifer O'Steen, JD (part of my extended family)
and Christine Reid, JD for helping me get it ready to publish;
and my mother, Charlotte Shades Lovell, for saving all
of my letters home. They were lacking in
content, but were invaluable for establishing a time line
for the story.

PROLOGUE 1

UNLIKELY WARRIOR
A SMALL TOWN BOY'S VIEW OF WORLD WAR II

November 2007

About a year ago, while I was attending a gun show, I saw a table covered with books. Most of them were related in some way to guns and I noticed one of them had a picture of a pontoon bridge on it. I picked it up and saw that the book was one of the Time-Life books on World War II and this particular book was called "Across the Rhine." I opened the book and saw that the picture on the cover had been taken three days after I had crossed the same bridge in 1945. I purchased the book, took it home and started reading it. I was reading about the battle to take Limburg, Germany and one sentence caught my attention: " A combat command of the U.S. Ninth Armored Division knifed through the German's defenses and had driven fifteen miles beyond by nightfall." It suddenly dawned on me that they were talking about something I had been involved with. I thought about this for some time and decided maybe someone would be interested in an account of one person's view of the war.. I have been reading that the public broadcast station is encouraging veterans of World War II to tell their stories, before it is too late. My sons and others have also encouraged me to tell what I remember. Therefore, I have decided that I will set down my view of World War II. I hope that it will not be boring. I do intend put in a lot of detail of the things I remember that happened back then and try to give an idea of what life was like.
Robert C. Lovell

PROLOGUE 2

November 2009

It has been over two years since I started writing my book. It has taken much longer than I thought. All of the stories contained herein are true, but some names have been changed for different reasons. It has been my intention to show what life was like from 1937, when World War II was just beginning, until 1946 when the war ended. During that time, the war touched every aspect of everyone's life. My part in the war was so much easier, than it was for many, but each person had his part, whether he was in the front lines or supplying those that were.
Robert C. Lovell

Chapter I

You will hear of wars and rumors of wars, but see to it that you are not alarmed.
Such things must happen, but the end is still to come. Matthew 24:6

January, 1937, the Lovell family has moved to Hennessey, Oklahoma. The Lovell family consists of Byron J. Lovell, his wife, Charlotte and their three sons, Donald 15, Robert 10, and Tommy 4. Gooden Hardware has opened a John Deere dealership in Hennessey and Byron "Barney," has been sent to manage it. They are able to find a house to rent and although it is small, it is the nicest house they have ever lived in.

Hennessey is about 65 miles northwest of Oklahoma City. At the time it is on the edge of the dust bowl. The hottest year ever has just ended, and things seem to be getting better. The Great Depression is also gradually ending. The population of Hennessey is about 2500 people and the major industry is agriculture. The town has five grocery stores and a meat market. It has two drugstores, two banks, two clothing stores, two variety stores, four restaurants, five filling stations, three doctors and a dentist. In addition, there are three automobile dealers and three implement dealers. To serve the farm community, there are two blacksmith shops, two grain elevators, two cotton gins, a flour mill, three feed stores, and three produce houses. There are three bars (beer), one newspaper, post office, phone office, movie theater and numerous other businesses. It is a great small town in the heart of America. People leave their doors and cars unlocked. Most people pay their bills and almost everyone knows those that do not. There are numerous churches and the school is known as a solid institution.

We move on a weekend and the following Monday I report to school and enroll in the fifth grade. I have no sooner arrived when two boys come forward and welcome me. One says, "My name is Charles Baker and this is Jack Wells." I immediately feel like this is my home; something that has not happened for some time.

We walk to school and then walk home for lunch. For some reason, we walk the alleys. Maybe it is because the alleys are more interesting. Charles lives the closest, one-third of a mile, I live two-thirds of a mile and Jack lives a mile from school. There's no school lunch program and if for some reason we do not go home to eat, we have to carry our lunch and eat on the school ground or if it is bad weather, in the class room.

The week goes fast and the following Sunday, we go to the Methodist Church. (Church attendance, at my house, is not optional.) Several of the members of my school class are there too. The church provides many of our social activities.

My father transfers his American Legion membership to the local post. They have an organization known as Sons of the American Legion. This allows us to be a part of the organization and to learn patriotism and respect for the flag. They have small tin copies of World War steel helmets for us boys to wear. I wonder what part each of the veterans has played in the war, but they seldom tell of their adventures in front of us boys.

I have not been in Hennessey more than a couple of weeks, when my mother helps me get a job. Every Friday evening after school, I go to the local newspaper and pick up sales ads for one of the grocery stores and deliver one to every house in town. With five grocery stores in town, competition is strong. For this I receive the huge sum of fifty cents. This provides me with spending money and allows me to learn more about the town. Segregation is in effect and I find that there is a large Negro population in one section of town that I really did not know about. I am even more surprised to find that there is another school for those children.

Even though we do not have much money, we always subscribe to a daily newspaper and the local weekly paper. We also take the Saturday Evening Post, which allows us to read short stories. We have a radio and listen to entertainment and news programs, in the evening. The local theater is our most desired entertainment and there we are exposed to the latest newsreel. All of these, in 1937, tell of wars around the world. But in this small town, the price of wheat and the weather are more important topics. But we do hear of the Spanish Civil War and Germany's participation in it; Italy's invasion of Ethiopia and Japan's march into Manchuria. But we are used to hearing about other countries having war and do not suppose that it has any effect on us.

We boys make sling shots and rubber guns; fly homemade kites and make little model airplanes out of small blocks of wood. These planes copy the latest war planes of the U.S. and other countries. We have chores to do and mine are mowing the yard and drying the dishes. We do not have much money, but we are better off than before, and we enjoy the life that we are living.

1938 comes with more changes. The owner of the business that my dad is managing has a heart attack and decides to close that store. He tells my dad that he will have to move to another store. My dad says that he is through moving. He starts doing odd jobs, repairing about anything that needs repairing. At this time, the Rural Electric Administration is extending electric lines to many rural areas and he gets some jobs wiring houses. Sometimes, he will take me to help him with the wiring jobs. These are simple systems, usually consisting of one light and one outlet in each room. The hardest part is getting the wire through the house when the walls are already en-closed. He develops ways to work around that, but they sometimes require more than one person, even if it is only a small boy.

My older brother gets a job with the local newspaper, so he has some income coming in too. He had previously worked at different papers, but when we moved to Hennessey, there was no opening. He would ride a bicycle thirteen miles to another little town to work on the newspaper on weekends. But this year, he is able to work locally and get in more hours in the evening after school.

In March, I have a birthday and reach the magic age of twelve. My brother gives me a "store bought" kite and a cap gun and caps. Twelve is an important milestone because I can no longer get in the picture show for a dime. It is now a quarter. I am small enough to pass for much younger, but my school teacher takes tickets at the show and she knows how old I am. The other thing about getting to be twelve is that I can now join the Boy Scouts. Charles and I both join, but Jack is not able to, as he has to work. His family is large and his dad does not make much as Town Marshall. His mother does laundry and it falls to Jack to pick up and deliver the clothes every evening. Our principal at school is the scoutmaster, so we are able to work on requirements during recess.

Scout meetings are held on Monday nights in the basement of the Christian Church. Our favorite game is "hide the belt." We all go back in a small room and close the door and someone hides a belt in the big room. When it is hidden we all go into the big room and the one that finds it can whip anyone he can reach in the room. This forces a mad rush back into the little room. He then hides it again and it starts all over. It is not much fun to get hit, but it is worth it, if you can find the belt and get to hit several of the other boys.

This summer I get to go to my first Boy Scout camp. It is held in the Wichita Mountains National Wildlife Area near Fort Sill, Oklahoma. It is my first time to be away from home by myself for more than one night. It takes about all the money I have to pay my way. I do not have a swimming suit. I find a used suit for fifty cents. I gather together what things I think I might need. I later find that I do not have enough with me, to live up to the Scout motto of "Be Prepared." Our scoutmaster cannot go with us because he is an officer in the Army Reserve and has to attend summer camp. Several of the parents take cars and even stay at the camp for the whole week. I am a new boy and the smallest one here. I am often the brunt of jokes, but I am determined to be a part of things. I cannot swim and no one takes it upon themselves to try to help me learn, so I am left out of several of the water activities. One area that I excel in is that I am a great shot with a sling shot. They have contests and put up a row of small candies and we shoot at them. If you hit one you can have it. I get several, but most of mine are badly damaged from direct hits. We also shoot dragonflies off of rocks and limbs near the creek that runs through camp. I am able to hit many of them. It is later that we find out that it is against Federal law to kill anything in a Wildlife Area. The whole week is quite an experience for me.

Later in the summer, I mow yards and spend a lot of time playing under the big tree on the vacant lot back of our house. It's all right to play there in the day time, but we do not like to go there at night. When we do cross it at night, since it is a short cut to town, we always run as fast as we can. The former owner of the house died, when he tried to burn the house and the flames got him. We are sure his ghost is still there.

In the fall, I go back to school and enter the seventh grade. I still have the same teachers, just a different room.

The newspapers and the newsreels at the movie theater tell of war around the world. Hitler's troops have arrested many Jews. They have marched on Austria and have been greeted by many of the people. When Hitler announces that they are going to protect the Germans living in or near Czechoslovakia, other European countries protest, but he reaches an agreement with them not to go further. Chamberlain makes his famous speech about "Peace in our time" and shortly after that Hitler takes the rest of Czechoslovakia. In the far east, Japan tries to get China to surrender, but the Chinese vow to keep on fighting and Japanese forces expand their conquest.

CHAPTER II

The year 1939 brings about a number of changes. My father has gone to work for the local hardware store and although it is not a big paying job, at least it is a steady paycheck. My older brother has graduated from high school and is working full time at the local newspaper. My father has traded our old Whippet car for a later model Chevrolet. Financially, we are much better off.

I am older now and my range and activities have expanded. I build a tree-house in the big elm on the lot, back of our house. I make the platform and then a neighbor man helps me to pull a refrigerator box up into the tree. I put a door on it and have a nice hideout. My dad has a set of climbing tools and I put his safety belt on and hang from a limb like a monkey. There is a pond about a mile away and some of us boys go there to swim. It is not really much of a pond. More of a mud-hole; surrounded by willow trees. We call it the "Willow Patch." It is not more than three feet deep, so swimming is limited. I cannot swim, but I am not in much danger. We come home and slip into the bath to get the mud off of us. Sometimes, we find a leech that has found a home on one of us.

One time we are in the Willow Patch and when we get out, we find that our clothes are missing. We look and some boys have taken our clothes and placed them on fence posts along the road, beginning about a quarter of a mile away. All we wear are overalls and shirt, so they make sure that our overalls are the furthest away. We start running down the road as hard as we can, keeping one eye open for cars. We get dressed without anyone seeing us and, from that time on, we hide our clothes when we go swimming.

To the west are the canyons, red shale bluffs overlooking the red shale land below. Along the top of the bluffs, there are two or three places where the shale has eroded leaving small caves. We get in these caves and pretend to be fighting Indians. Later on, we get to stand on these bluffs and watch a re-enactment of the massacre of Pat Hennessey, the man for whom the town was named.

One day in June, a truck pulls up to the house and the driver gets out and says he has a shipment for Lovell. My dad insists that he has not ordered anything. But the driver unloads this large box. My brother steps forward and said that he has ordered it. Inside are fireworks. My dad is not happy with the idea. He says that we have to keep them in the garage, because the car is insured and the things in the house are not. He also says that they will all be gone before July 5. The neighbors must love us. We start shooting firecrackers that day and continue until late in the night on the Fourth of July.

But that is not the end of the fireworks. About a week later, my younger brother, who is six, finds one of the firecrackers that we had missed. He decides that he will get in on the fun. He had watched us shooting them, so he finds a piece of punk and lights it in the kitchen stove. He goes outside, lights the firecracker and throws the punk. The firecracker explodes in his hand cutting and bruising his fingers. He is taken to the doctor and has to get a tetanus shot. Of course, my older brother and I get the blame and our punishment lasts longer than the bruise on his fingers. And the story makes the local newspaper.

About this time, I start my campaign to get a BB gun. I ask my parents if I can get one. They tell me that I have to check to see if it is legal for me to have one in town. I ask the Town Marshall and he tells me that if I will be careful, not break any windows or shoot anyone, not shoot any song birds and only shoot sparrows, that he thinks it would be ok. The next thing is to save the money. It seems that every time I get some money saved that something comes along to take it. I cannot even save enough for the cheapest single shot.

In the summer, the town decides to have a celebration in honor of Pat Hennessey. They have many kinds of events including horse racing, a parade, rodeo and topped off by a pageant depicting the massacre of Pat Hennessey. The Boy Scouts sell cold soda pop at the events. Most of the boys are doing other things, but I am there for everyone, carrying a heavy bucket full of ice and bottles of pop. After the event, I gather all of the empty bottles. The acting scoutmaster tells me that by working so hard I have earned enough money to pay for my scout camp the next year.

By the time fall gets here, I have changed my strategy and start asking for a BB gun for Christmas. As Christmas gets closer, I increase my efforts to make sure that everyone knows just what I want. Christmas morning, as we load the car to go to my grandmother's house, I watch closely and there are no packages that could hold a BB gun. I am disappointed, but still keep hoping that there might be one under the tree when we get to Grandma's house. When we arrive, I quickly look and see nothing that would hold what I want. We all open our presents and although I get some nice things, I am disappointed. After all have been opened, my brother goes back in another room and comes out with a package and there is no doubt in my mind what it holds. But I am even more surprised because it does not hold the single shot that I asked for, but it holds a Daisy Golden Eagle. The Daisy Golden Eagle is the fanciest gun that Daisy has ever made. It is copper coated to look more like gold and has a black stock with a golden emblem on it. The gun has been made to celebrate the fiftieth anniversary of Daisy guns. It is more than I ever could have hoped for.

The newsreels, the radio and newspapers tell of war around the world. Spain falls to Franco, with the help of Germany and Italy. Italy increases its hold in North Africa; Germany invades Poland;

Russia invades Finland and Japan pushes deeper into China towards Burma.

CHAPTER III

The news tells of the invasion of Denmark and Norway by German forces and Japanese armies move deeper into China, but in Hennessey, Oklahoma, this still seems far away and of little importance. I now have a new job burying dead dogs and cats for the city. I get fifty cents for each dog and twenty-five cents for each cat and pup. I know that my mother is horrified at this, but she so encourages us to work that she does not say anything. When I get a call of a dead animal, I take my little red wagon and shovel and head out. I load up the deceased and off we go to the junkyard for the burial. I have always had a weak stomach, but this does a lot to cure it.

I gather up bicycle parts from junk piles and put together my own bike. This greatly increases my mobility and range. By now, I am going beyond the canyons west of town and on to Turkey Creek. This is a great place to play. My older brother helps me make a long bow and some arrows. I am never very good with it, and rabbits do not have much to fear, but several frogs meet their end skewered by an arrow.

As soon as school is out in the spring, we get ready to go to scout camp in Arkansas. The temporary scout master, whom I worked for last summer selling soda pop, has died suddenly from a heart attack.

When it comes time to pay the money for camp, I tell them that he said I had made enough to pay my way. But it seems that they never found the money or any bank account. No one knows if he had put the money where it could not be found or if he had spent it. One of the women organizing the trip says that I can't go unless I pay the money. I explain that I do not have the money and am counting on the work I have done for the scouts to pay my way. Two of the other women say that they know I worked for it and should not be punished because he died. So I get to go by the vote of two to one.

I might be better off if I had not been able to go. We ride to Arkansas in the back of a lumber truck and it is a long, hard trip. When we get there, nothing is organized. We are to camp at an abandoned farmyard. You can see why it is abandoned; it is nothing but rock. It is close to the White River and we find a jon boat and push it up and down the river for about a half of a mile. I get so sunburned that I cannot sleep. If the ride over was bad, the ride back is terrible. My sunburn is hurting and I cannot find a place to lay that I do not hurt. There is no relief from the sun all the way home. I have learned some valuable lessons.

About this time, a big change occurs in our lives. One evening, our next door neighbor comes over to the house and tells my parents that the bank has foreclosed on a house and that my folks should buy it. My dad protests that he just does not have the money, but the neighbor insists that they talk to the bank; he thinks that they can work something out.

My parents mortgage everything they have, except us kids, and are able to close the purchase. The house is a two-story house just a block and a half from the center of town. It has enough room so that my older brother can have a room of his own and just my little brother and I have to share one. The house takes a lot of work and my dad spends most of his "leisure" time making repairs and remodeling the house. It soon feels like home. In addition, I can go out the back door and walk only one and a half blocks down the alley to my friend Charles Baker's house. It is not long before I am spending more time there than at home.

Charles and I have a lot of adventures together. We go hunting, Charles carrying his .410 shotgun and I carrying his .22 rifle. His dad, Mark Baker, takes us different places to hunt rabbits.

The Boy Scouts decide to build a log cabin for the scout meeting place. We get permission to cut logs on a farm southeast of Hennessey. One of the assistant scoutmasters has a truck and we load up on it and spend the day in the woods. We cut down the trees using a two man crosscut saw and then take axes and trim all of the limbs off of them. We work hard for every log we get. The logs are then loaded onto the truck for the trip back to town. We have to burn all of the limbs, so we always have a fire going. At noon, we eat our lunch.

One time I learn a valuable lesson. I have a can of pork and beans for lunch and I punch a hole in the top of the can and put it in the coals to heat. In a little while, the can explodes and there is no one there, who doesn't have some beans on him someplace. I guess one of the beans covered the hole in the can and blocked the release of the steam. From then on, I always punch more than one hole in the top of a can before heating it.

The news now is the German invasion of France, Belgium and the Netherlands. People are becoming more concerned, but to most of us, it still seems far away.

I change jobs. No more trips with my little red wagon to the dump to bury a dead dog. I am now the janitor of the Methodist Church. The hardest part of the job is in the winter, when I have to go over early and light the furnace. The furnace is a converted coal furnace. All they did was to take out the grates and install two gas lines, one small and one large with a gate valve on each. To light the furnace, you take a sheet of paper, set fire to it and throw it into the furnace, close the door and then open the small valve. There is a small explosion as the gas catches fire. Then you open the larger valve a little and wait for the second larger explosion. This is a scary thing. Of course, there is no way that you can regulate the temperature; you just do the best that you can. I notice that everyone who comes into church goes to look at the thermometer to see how cold it is. I learn how to make the church feel warmer. Just before church starts, I take a match and hold it under the thermometer and run the mercury up to one hundred degrees, so that by the time anyone looks at it, they will notice a nice balmy reading. No one ever mentions the black soot at the base of the thermometer.

One day when I am cleaning the church, Charles comes over and joins me. There is an aluminum collection plate there and I ask Charles to bring it to me. Instead, he turns it upside down and throws it to me. Instead of just tumbling through the air, it takes off and sails down the aisle and I have to run and jump to catch it. So I turn around and sail it back to him. We do this every chance we get. We have invented the "Frisbee," but do not dare to tell anyone about it, for fear that they will not approve of using the church property in that manner.

I receive nine dollars a month as janitor of the church and the first month, I go to the drugstore and buy a Westclock wristwatch so I will know when it is time to ring the church bell. It costs seven dollars and fifty cents, which leaves me very little to spend the rest of the month. A couple of months later, I take my money and buy a used wood lathe. I take an old electric motor that my dad has, and set up the lathe on the back porch. It is not long until I have saturated the local market for candlestick holders, ash trays and nut bowls. When my mother is asked what I am making, she says that as near as she can tell, shavings.

This is a great time and place to be a boy growing up. We get a group of boys together and go to the livestock sale building for rubber gun fights. They only use the building one day a week, so there is no one to bother us and there are lots of wooden pens to run through and climb over. The building has a loft where hay is kept, so there are lots of hiding places and places for an ambush. The rubber guns are made from a board with a clothes pin fastened to it. The rubber band, cut from a tire inner tube is stretched from the clothes pin out over the end of the gun. To fire, you just squeeze the clothespin. Sometimes a knot is tied in the rubber band to make it go farther.

We spend more time at Turkey Creek. We follow one of the different draws leading to the creek and usually take a different route back to town. We hunt along the creek, go fishing or just take off our clothes and wade along the creek. We never feel much danger as we travel around. If you do something that you shouldn't have, word of it usually gets home before you do. This "jungle telegraph" is amazing.

The radio and newspapers tell of the evacuation of the British forces at Dunkirk. The newsreels at the movies make it more graphic, as we watch the British soldiers hanging on for dear life as the Nazi Stuka dive bombers pound them. Later, we get to see pictures of Hitler goose-stepping down the street in Paris. Italian forces have entered Egypt. The pictures of the German bombing of London are frightening. About the only good news on the war front is the attack of the British against the Italians in North Africa; and that the price of farm products is rising, but war still seems far away.

The eighth grade: we are the big kids now. Charles, Jack and I are the only boys in the class. All of the other boys have moved away. We still have the same teachers that we have had for the last two years, but by now, we know what to expect from them and they know our strengths and weaknesses. We will be the last class to graduate from this building. Next year the building will be torn down and a new grade school will be erected. It is none too soon, as the ceiling has already fallen down in parts of our room and we are in danger of being hit by those parts remaining.

I am still spending a lot of my time with the Boy Scouts. I have completed my second class requirements and am working on my first class badge. I have completed a merit badge and have done over twenty-five hours of service.

In February, the Scouts hold a banquet in honor of the birthday of Scouting. We decorate the City Hall and many dignitaries show up to present the awards. I receive my merit badge and a certificate for the twenty-five hours of service that I have put in for the community. The newspaper prints a story about the program. I am proud to be a part of it.

Suddenly, in the spring before school is out for the summer, the war seems to be getting closer to home. One afternoon, our principal calls me to come into his office. This is not the fear that it once was, because by now, he has been my scoutmaster for over two years and I consider him to be my friend. He shows me the telegram that he has just received. It orders him to report the next morning for active duty. No reserve summer camp this time; he will be serving full time. He asks me if I will go with him to help him pack up his things, so he can get away.

I spend the evening helping him box up the few things that he has. He is single, and since he lives in a small apartment, it does not take long to get him ready to leave. When we get done, I go with him and he drives to the house of another reserve officer, Dr. C. K. Bennett, a veterinarian. Dr. Bennett has also received his orders and is packing to leave in the morning. It is not so easy for him. He is married and he has his clinic to close, but both are ready to do their duty. We finish out the eighth grade minus one teacher and principal.

We listen to the news of the German attack on England and wonder when the Germans will try to invade and if the British forces can hold out.

CHAPTER IV

No Scout camp this summer. We have no adult leader to help organize it. But there is plenty to do. I mow yards, and then I get a job working at the drug store. I think that it will be great. All you have to do is to make fountain drinks and serve them to the people coming in. And you can have all the ice cream you want. I am in for a surprise. My job is to wash the dishes and wait on the cars that park in front and honk for curb service. If you want any ice cream, you have to pay for it. The hours are long and the pay is low. I never once receive a tip for serving someone at the curb. I do not last long. I leave by mutual agreement. I am sick of the place and they are tired of me.

This summer, I am among several boys that are initiated into the Sons of the American Legion. It is an important event and the District Commander of the American Legion comes to conduct the ceremony. We feel proud and are ready to do our part when called upon. The American Legion is very active.

The draft is instituted and all men from the ages of 21 to 35 have to register. There is a drawing to see who will be called first. As soon as the draft is announced, several local boys enlist. The

National Guard is also asking for recruits to help fill vacancies in their ranks, when they go on active duty.

When fall comes, we go from being the big kids to being low-life freshmen. We are joined by several students coming in from the country schools. Charles, Jack and I are no longer the only boys in the class.

Over at the grade school, Asbury Smith has been hired as principal and teacher to replace Maury Banks, who has been called to active duty. Mr. Smith becomes our scoutmaster and once again, we have an active program.

I join the band and since I do not have an instrument, I am given the bass drum to play. I can beat the drum okay, but I have difficulty keeping in step. It is not often that the drummer is the only one out of step, but I seem to have that talent. It is not long until they substitute cymbals for the drum. They seldom let me crash them together, but will let me ding the edges together during the loud numbers. I do little for music, but I do serve the purpose of filling a space whether marching or in concert.

We still have time for other activities. Charles and I make a few trips to Turkey Creek with the intention of seeing if we can live off of the land. Even though we are Boy Scouts, we still have not learned the principle of being prepared. One time, the only thing we can find to kill is a crow. We dress it and get ready to build a fire. That is when we find that we do not have any matches. There is no flint in the area, it is cloudy so we cannot use a watch crystal and there is no suitable wood to make a fire by friction. So we try to open cartridges, put the powder on the tinder and then shoot into it. We try several times but are not successful. Luckily we do not have to eat crow this time. Another time, we shoot a rabbit and this time we have the material to make a fire. We cook the rabbit to a nice brown, but we find that it needs salt to make it suitable fare. On one trip to Turkey Creek, we come back up through one of the waterways and find a pool of water that has several leopard frogs frozen in the ice. We chop them out, lay them in the sun to thaw and when they start hopping, we kill them and dress out the legs.

We take them to Charles' place and cook them. When I tell my dad about it, he says that they were probably toads. We know they were not, but it makes us think, anyway.

About this time is when my hormones begin to kick in. The other boys have been thinking about such things for some time, but I am a "late bloomer." When we graduated from the eighth grade, I was the smallest one in the class, boy or girl. I could not expect one of the girls in my class to want to go out with me when she towered over me. I notice a girl a year younger than me in the eighth grade and she seems to pay attention to me. She also pays attention to all of the other boys, but that does not make a difference to me. The main event of the year is the senior class play, which is held in the spring of the year. It is a reserved-seat-only event and you have to buy your tickets at the drugstore and pick them out of a big board that is fitted, like the floor plan of the auditorium. I get up nerve enough to ask if she will go with me to the play. My heart is pounding and I worry that she will laugh at me, but she says yes, she would like to. I hurry to the drug store and purchase two tickets on the left side about four rows from the front. They are rather choice seats.

When the night comes for the play, I walk to her house and pick her up at the door. She only lives a block from the school, so it is not a long walk. We enter the auditorium and all the other students turn to see who is coming in next. Then they began to whisper when they see who it is. I feel grown up and am very grateful to her for going with me and making me feel so good. At that moment, I fall madly in love with her. She is only my girl for a couple of months, because her parents move to Arkansas. But in those two months, I am living in the clouds. When I get word that she is moving, I am not as devastated as I would think, because I know that I am not the only boy that she has eyes for. I am still grateful for the experiences that she has given me.

Defense bonds and stamps go on sale. The local newspaper, The Hennessey Clipper, runs ads encouraging people to buy them to finance the defense of the country. Our former principal and scout-master, Lieutenant Banks, comes to Hennessey on leave. He tells us that he is working in the Quartermaster Department and that his term has been extended to two years. Every issue of the Clipper has recruiting ads in it, urging young men to join. There is a story about the practice bombing range on the Salt Plains to service the planes from Oklahoma City and the new airfield at Enid. The local Lions Club organizes a scrap metal drive and urges farmers to bring in their old machinery to be made into arms. The Boy Scouts join the drive and collect aluminum. I take my little red wagon and go from door to door collecting old aluminum pots and pans and anything else they have of aluminum that they can spare. Congress passes an excise tax on almost everything to raise money for the defense fund. This excise tax hits everyone. For me, it means paying a tax on every ticket I buy to go to the movies, a sacrifice indeed. Mass amounts of goods are being sent to England under "lend-lease."

The National Commander of the American Legion urges Legion members to register to aid in the defense of America. My mother is president of the local Legion Auxiliary and takes over the job of registering all of those who volunteer. They urge everyone to re-member all of the boys at camp and to send them letters and gifts. Letters appear in the Clipper thanking the people back home for the gifts. The letters from the boys at camp are light hearted and cheer-ful. To many of these boys, it is the first time that they have had new clothes and all they want to eat. The work is no harder than what they were used to on the farm and there are free movies and a trip to town a couple of times a month. By fall, notices appear wanting people to volunteer to be aircraft spotters. The war is getting closer all the time.

I am still janitor at the church and during the summer, I mow yards. We still have time to go to the creek and one of our favorite things is to get a box of .22 short rifle shells for fifteen cents and take the single shot rifle with us. We pick out a small twig and sit down and carefully shoot off just the very tip. We keep doing that until there is nothing left of the twig. It takes a keen eye and steady hand, but on a lazy summer afternoon, it is just the thing to do.

When school starts in the fall, I decide to go out for football. I have been eating everything that I can to try to put on weight, but nothing seems to work. My parents are not thrilled at the thought of me playing football, but they do not stand in the way and sign the permission slip. I start doing exercises ahead of time, but they do not prepare me for the rigors of practice. We only have about seventeen boys show up for football. The uniforms and equipment are next to nonexistent. After running short of funds at the end of last year, the school is not going to spend much on athletics. We are able to get a few rolls of tape and that is about it. The older boys get the better pieces of equipment, and after all of the others have been fitted out, the coach tells me to go in the room and pick out my outfit. I find an old jersey, pair of broken shoulder pads, hip pads and a pair of pants that are many sizes too big for me. When I put them on, the knee pads are down on my shins and the thigh pads cover my knees. I find an old pair of shoes and like everything else, they are too big and the cleats are worn all the way down. I do not get a helmet; there are not enough to go around. They do have one, but it is so big that when I put it on, it covers my eyes. These are not high impact helmets, but the old style made of leather with a strap inside to go around your head. When I get all of my equipment on, they weigh me and I weigh ninety pounds.

I am faithful to football practice and go every day and work as hard as I can, but no matter how hard I work, I am still just a scrub. I sit on the bench at every game and watch our team get beat to a pulp. Our biggest player is six feet tall and weighs one hundred eighty pounds. The team averages about one hundred thirty pounds. Finally it is getting near the end of the season and I have not been in a game. We are playing another team that is worse than we are, if that is possible. Anyway, with two minutes to go in the game, we score and are leading 33 to 6. The coach turns to me and tells me to go into the game. The only helmet that I can find is the huge one that covers my head like a fish bowl. I put it on and run on to the field. The fans cheer to see this little guy with the big helmet get in the game. We kick off and I start running down the field, I can't see, so I throw off the helmet, run down the sideline and tackle the ball carrier. My first time to play football and on the first play, I get a tackle. I get to stay in the game until the end, but the referee makes me keep my helmet on, so I can't see to make another play. That ends the season. The coach will not be here the next year.

CHAPTER V

It is Sunday afternoon, December 7, 1941, and I am returning from the church. I have straightened up the church and checked to see if it is warm enough for the evening services. As I walk down the alley towards home, one of my friends comes out of his house and asks if I have heard the news. I tell him that I have not and ask why. "The Japanese have bombed Pearl Harbor."

"Where is that?"

"I don't know. Dad is on the ham radio now, trying to find out."

I run home and tell my folks to turn on the radio. We listen until bedtime to the news, most of which is just a repeat from before. But the part that makes the situation more tense is the announcement that all military personnel are to report to their duty stations immediately. We learn that Pearl Harbor is a U. S. Naval Base in the Hawaiian Islands and that there is severe damage.

The next morning I go to school and everyone is talking about what happened the day before. They make an announcement that we will be going into the auditorium shortly before ten o'clock. to listen to the President's speech.

We file into the auditorium and everyone is real quiet. No talking now. On the stage, the superintendent has placed his large cabinet radio from home. The President comes on the air and makes his famous speech: "Sunday, December Seventh, 1941, a day that will live in infamy." He outlines the attack on our forces and asks Congress to declare war on Japan. After it is over, we file out to go back to our classrooms. I am the last one in line and the superintendent, Mr. Hart, falls in behind me. He says to me, "After today, your life will never be the same." He is a veteran of World War and he knows how much change this will make. Later in the day, Japan, Germany and Italy, declare war on the United States. And on December Eighth, the United States declares war on Germany and Italy.

The government has been urging farmers to plant less wheat and produce more milk and eggs, but with the outbreak of war, they urge them to raise as much food as they can. This is a change from the policy of just a few years ago, when farmers were paid not to raise food.

The American Legion runs ads urging the farmers and others to gather up their old iron and turn it in. The Agricultural Department even sends out notice that they will help the farmers get their scrap iron to market. Some of the smaller steel mills are running out of material and industry is needing all of the steel that can be produced. The Boy Scouts are collecting scrap paper and are even offering to buy it, but no one charges for it. Everyone is glad to donate for the war effort and what little profit is made on the sale should go to the Scouts. There is a side benefit to the scrap paper drive. The drug stores give the Scouts their scrap paper, including the unsold magazines, which have the top of the covers removed. Included are many comic books. We read these as we sort out the different types of paper. Once in awhile, an adult magazine is included. They are considered to be very racy. We gather and sell paper for about three years and we barely cover expenses, but hopefully it helps the war effort.

After Pearl Harbor, censorship is extremely tight. About two weeks after the attack, the War Department sends out notices to a large number of families. Clifford Hill and Loren Beaman, Jr., are listed as missing. Shortly after receiving their notice, the Beaman family receives a letter written by Loren and dated December 11, 1941. Their hopes rise but of course the question remains, is the date correct. Shortly after that, they receive notice that he has been found and is okay. The Hill family is not so lucky. Their next telegram confirms the death of Clifford. The war has come to Hennessey for sure.

The attack spurs enlistments and the papers are full of the names of those who have volunteered to serve. Two of my friends who are only a couple of years older than I am volunteer for the Army Air Corp and leave for training camp. The American Legion agrees to provide assistance in filling out papers for those wanting to enlist. A drive is held to obtain books to send to the many camps, so that the boys will have something to read. There are drop off points set up for the "victory books." The Red Cross is raising money to aid in their services to the boys. Many of the members of the Red Cross are meeting to knit and sew articles to be included in the kits that the service men are given at camp. The ages for registration are extended to include all of those from twenty to forty-five and more and more men are being called up to serve.

In church on communion Sunday, they read a list of those in the service and as each name is read, someone comes forward and takes communion in honor of that person.

The Boy Scouts are planning to go to camp. Asbury Smith has been our scoutmaster for nearly a year now, but during the time we were without a leader, the number of scouts dropped and we only have eight scouts who will go to camp. Charles and I are the oldest, so we are delegated to get the camp ready. We go to Mr. Smith and start making plans. We ask who is going to do the cooking? Mr. Smith immediately tells us that we are and not only that, but we will have to make up all the menus, determine the cost and purchase the food. We have never done anything like this before, and some of our meals are not very elaborate, but they are things we know how to cook and do not cost much. We make arrangements to camp at

Boiling Springs State Park near Woodward. We arrange for transportation and nine of us go to camp; Mr. Smith and eight boys.

This is the best camp we have ever had. The park is nearly deserted because of the war and we have the run of the place. We have games and work on passing scout requirements. Every boy there is able to advance or pass requirements for at least one merit badge. I am able to pass the swimming requirement for my first class badge and another boy and I go on a fifteen-mile hike to satisfy another requirement. We hike from the camp into Woodward and back. The shoes that I usually wear are slick, so I put on my tennis shoes for the hike. By the time we get to Woodward, I have blisters on my feet and walk the last half of the hike barefoot. I just do not have proper equipment, partly because I do not know what is required, and partly because I cannot afford to buy what I should have.

It is a tradition that on Wednesday evening during scout camp, that the drug stores take turns bringing ice cream to camp as a treat for the boys. This year, it is Dinkler Drug's turn. On Wednesday evening we wait and wait, but no one shows up, so most of the boys go to sleep. Charles and I are still up, planning for the next day's activities when finally George Dinkler arrives bringing two-and-one-half gallons of strawberry ice cream. We try to wake up the other boys, but they are so sound asleep, we cannot get them awake. This is the first time in our lives that Charles and I have had all the ice cream we can eat. And for some reason, we do not get sick. After we get back, Mr. Smith leaves and we are without a scoutmaster again.

The home front is starting to feel the war more. Tires are now rationed and the names of those who have been approved by the rationing committee, for a new tire or tube, are printed in the paper, setting out what they are allowed to purchase. This leads to speculation by the public on which of these people really should be entitled to a new tire. To take advantage of sunlight, all clocks are ordered to be moved ahead one hour. This is called "war time." Most places honor this and move their clocks ahead, but the nearby Town of Lacey, made up mostly of farmers, never does change its clocks.

For the rest of the war, notice of every meeting has to specify if it is war time or standard time.

Preparation is made for the rationing of sugar. Ration books are given to the students at school to take home to their parents. Those without children in school are asked to go to the city hall and get their books. A drive for rubber is held. The service stations are authorized to pay two cents a pound for the rubber. If you do not want the money, it will be used for some charity. We Boy Scouts go door to door collecting rubber for the drive. The county holds air raid maneuvers to be ready in case we are attacked. Those included in the draft are given notice of their number. My older brother Don, is number 815, one of the higher numbers.

There are tragedies too. One of the planes from the flying school at Enid crashes west of Waukomis, killing one and injuring the other. A farmer living west of Hennessey receives his draft notice. He appeals the induction and his appeal is denied. He goes home and takes a gun and kills himself. He leaves a wife and young child. Another man living near Hennessey, receives his notice of induction. He is unable to read and write, and does not really understand what is happening, but is so upset, that he takes a shotgun and tries to kill himself, his wife grabs the gun but it fires blowing off his arm. We get news that Bataan has fallen after a heroic stand. It is a long time after the surrender that we find out how really horrible it has been. Most of the news from overseas has not been good. Our forces are putting up a brave fight, but with few supplies, all they can do is to try to delay the enemy until we are strong enough to go on the offensive. The draft ages are extended from eighteen to sixty-five.

CHAPTER VI

The war has moved much closer to home. My older brother Don, enlists in the army. He is sent to Fort Sill for induction and then is sent to Camp Roberts, California, for his basic training. He will be there for the next thirteen weeks.

When Don leaves, I get to inherit his bedroom. For the first time in our lives, my younger brother, Tommy, and I have a bed all to ourselves. I not only inherit Don's room, but I also get his .22 rifle. It is an old Winchester, octagon barrel, hammer, pump. It has been shot so much that the barrel is shot out and you can drop a shell in the barrel and it will go all the way to the rim. It is .22 short only, but is so loose that you can also shoot longs or long rifle shells by using it single shot. I love to shoot it, even though it is almost impossible to hit anything with it. I sometimes lay back and pretend that I am shooting at Japanese dive bombers with it.

Tommy is in the band now. I am sure that he has much more to offer the band than I did. He plays a horn and can even make music with it. At least, he can probably stay in step better.

On the home front, the local news paper, The Hennessey Clipper, now has a column called "Follow the Flag," which has items of news about local boys in the service and often prints some of their letters to home. To start with, there are only a few small items, but in just a few months, it grows to two or three columns and spills over from the front page to the back page of the paper. The local furniture store hangs the hat of one of the boys, who has joined the service, on a nail on the wall of the store and tells him he can have it back, when he comes safely home. Soon others have their hats there and the collection grows as more and more boys leave home. Sugar rationing is joined by coffee, tea and cocoa. The choice of drinks is being shortened. Some people buy lemon drops to dissolve in their ice tea to sweeten it some and give it a lemon taste. I feel that it is a poor substitute for sugar and lemon. My mother has for a long time made me hot cocoa for breakfast every morning, but I have to cut back on the number of times that I can have it. Gas rationing is instituted next and it proves to be probably the hardest, of the different items rationed, for the people to accept. The shortage of gasoline is not that great, but since almost all rubber shipments to the United States have been halted, it is done to save tires. Also along with that, a national speed limit of thirty-five miles an hour is ordered.

The supply of items for sale in the hardware stores has dwindled to almost nothing. The owners are glad to have my dad leave to go work in the war effort. Dad gets a job working to help build the Enid Flying School, where they train pilots. He only works a short time when he has a disagreement with the foreman. Dad is one of the easiest persons in the world to get along with, so I suspect he is right when he says that the man is a tyrant. Dad tells him that he is going to quit and the man is furious and threatens to have Dad blacklisted from anything to do with defense. Dad leaves and within an hour he has a job working in a machine shop, a part of Stearman Aeronautics, making parts for planes. He and two other men who work there car pool from Hennessey, going back and forth at thirty-five miles an hour.

Not long after Dad goes to work in Enid, our old alarm clock gives out. Dad goes looking for one to replace it. The only thing he can find is a war time replacement. The works are metal, but the housing is made of pressed paper and wood. When the alarm goes off, it sounds like a giant woodpecker pecking on the house. No worry about not hearing it; it raises you out of bed.

I am old enough now to get a driver's license, but I have no opportunity because the car must be saved for Dad to go back and forth to work. It must last until the end of the war. I am limited to walking or riding my bicycle. Most of the time, I just walk. Some of the boys have access to cars but joy riding is frowned on. The farm kids usually have some form of transportation and the supply of tractor gas is often raided to provide them a way to have a date. For the rest of us, a girl must be willing to walk if she wants to go out. Since the only entertainment, other than church and school activities, is the local movie theater, it does not entail a lot of walking. I am a little taller now, still the shortest boy in the class, but I am now taller than some of the girls. One of the girls either decides that I am tall enough so that she will not get laughed at or takes pity on me, but she agrees to go to the movie with me. We go out three or four times to the movies. Nothing romantic here, more like going out with your cousin. Our class has been together for so long, that we have all become very good friends. Not only are we together all day in school, but most of our social events are with the same people.

In school, I enroll in shop class. It is almost a joke. There are no mechanical tools at all. Only a few old hand tools. There are a few saws that are so dull that it takes forever to cut a board; a drill brace, but only a few odd size dull bits. It does have one sharp countersink bit. A couple of old planes that need sharpening. I am sure that the teacher wonders what he has done to get here. There is no money to buy anything. All of we boys (girls are taking home economics) pick out some small project. I choose to make a foot stool. Good lumber is very hard to find and expensive. I am able to get enough lumber for my project, but it is not quality material. I do the best I can with the tools we have, but the result is a stool that works much better than it looks. We still have a lot of time left in the year when our projects are finished, so one of the boys asks if we could work on model airplanes. At first the teacher refuses permission, but when he takes a look around and begins to try to think of something to keep us busy, he gives the O.K. This is not hard for me because I am already working on a model at home and just take parts to school to work on. I make several of these models from balsa wood and tissue paper and hang them from a wire stretched across my bedroom. A light breeze will make them fly around.

At the end of his basic training, Don comes home on ten-day leave before going on to his next assignment which is Infantry Officers Candidate School at Fort Benning, Georgia. It is good to see him. He seems much older now and stands straighter. The ten days goes by fast and he is gone again.

And once again war hits close to home, when the family of seventeen-year-old George Iven get a telegram from the Navy Department saying that he died in action and was buried at sea. Not much to show for a boy who had only been in the Navy a few weeks. The news now includes a few victories and they are heralded with much fanfare, but all in all, we are still losing ground on both fronts. In Africa, Allied Forces move back and forth against the Germans and Italians. The Germans advance across Russia and most of the rest of Europe is already under German control. In the Pacific, the United States has a few successes in naval engagements but Japan continues to capture more and more territory. The United States stages a surprise raid on Tokyo, by B-25 bombers, led by Colonel Doolittle, but at the same time, the British surrender Singapore.

For years, my mother has made candy at Christmas time and even sold some to help cover the expense of all that she gives away. With sugar rationing, it does not look like we will have any this year. She goes to the grocery store to get the usual groceries and one of the clerks asks if she is making candy this year. She tells them that without sugar, she is not going to make very much. When she gets home and unpacks, she finds a couple of five pound sacks of sugar in the bottom of her sacks.

More of my friends, who are only a year or two older than I am, are enlisting in the service. When they come home after basic training, they are excited about what they have been doing and eager to get to their duty station. Local boys are scattered all over the world.

I am anxious to get in the service and be a part of that. No use thinking of that now because you have to have your parents' consent to enlist if you are under twenty-one and there is no way that my parents will consent before I graduate from high school.

I go out for football again this year. I am a little taller and weigh about twenty pounds more. Still I am the smallest one on the team. I get to play very little and we never win a game this year. However, I am awarded a letter in football.

CHAPTER VII

The war is a little more than a year old for the Americans. Congress passes the five percent "Victory Tax" on wages. For the first time, employers will have to withhold tax from wages. The law provides that after the war, a portion of this tax will be refunded. For the first time in their lives, many people will have to file an income tax return. The newspapers run articles showing how to fill out a tax return.

Word is received that another Hennessey boy, Ernest Huffman, has been killed in the southwest Pacific. And Ernest Havlik, from Bison, is listed as missing in North Africa.

The Christian Church pastor agrees to become scoutmaster and the Scouts are reorganized with twenty-eight boys enrolled. I am elected patrol leader. We no sooner get reorganized, when the pastor leaves and the organization folds up again. I stay active as best I can. I pay my dues to the Council and work on my merit badges. The merit badge requirement books are in the school library, so I have access to them and when I have completed the requirements, I go to one of the former committeemen to have him sign off for me. I hitchhike to Enid and present my paper work to the District office and then receive my merit badge by mail. It is not easy, but I am able to get enough merit badges to be eligible for my Star rank. No presentation awards banquet for this one, I receive it by mail. I work on my Life rank, but am not able to complete it because the required merit badges take more equipment and instruction than I can get on my own.

Canned goods and shoes are now rationed. Keeping track of the number of coupons, necessary to buy food stuffs is a nightmare. Checking out at the grocery store requires doing it twice: once for the money and the second time for the ration stamps. One thing that helps is that the stores do not have near as many products available as they did before.

A couple of student pilots from the Enid Flying School have fun diving at a straw stack in a field east of town. As they fly over it, the straw flies up in the air and scatters over the field. The farmer watches and waves at the planes. When the pilots land back at the base, the commanding officer is waiting for them. It seems that the farmer was not only waving, but he was writing down their numbers. It takes several days, with rakes and pitchforks for the boys to get the straw stack put back together.

My brother Don comes home from Fort Benning, a brand new second lieutenant. While he is home, he marries Catherine "Cappy" Edwards. This is the first time I have ever been to a wedding. He is spending his honeymoon at Enid, and we see very little of him. When his leave is over, he leaves his wife at Enid for the time being and goes to his next assignment at Florence, Arizona. There is a large prisoner of war camp there, housing Italians and Germans captured in North Africa. Don is made range officer and is responsible for keeping the guards proficient with their arms. The duty is not hard and they have prisoners to take care of all of the menial tasks. Most of the prisoners to start with are Italians and they are glad to be in the United States. Most of them work in the valley around Florence, working in the fields helping the farmers. Don makes friends of a lot of them and they are glad to go help him take care of the ranges.

When summer comes, I get a job working at the local Ford dealership. My dad has talked to the owner and asked him if I can do some work there and learn how to be a parts man. He puts me to work dusting the parts and parts bins. It is about the most boring job that I have ever had. It is not long before I am going out into the repair shop and working on brakes and other things that do not take much skill. My dad does not like it when he hears this. He says that the reason that he wanted me to learn about parts was so I would not have to work with my hands. After about two weeks, I get an offer to go work on a farm. I jump at it. The car dealer is not too happy at me leaving, but I tell him that I want to get out into the country. Dad figures that it will be better for me to be running a tractor than working in a repair shop, so he does not object.

When I arrive at the farm, I am as green as green can be. I have never even driven a car. First thing they do is to put me on a tractor to bring a plow a half mile around to the other side of the section. I get almost a quarter of a mile and just short of the corner, when the hitch comes loose and I lose the plow. When the plow comes loose, the trip rope on the lift for the plow is still tied to the tractor, so it trips the plow and the plow shears hit the road. I find reverse and back up to try to hitch the plow up again. It takes me several times to get close to the hitch. I cannot see the hitch when I am on the tractor. I back a ways, get down to look and then back up some more. When I get close, I find that I cannot lift the tongue of the plow. After several tries, I get it hitched up again. When I start forward again, the plow is plowing the road. I pull the trip rope, and the plow comes out of the ground and then dives right back in. The second time I pull it, the plow stays up and I am able to go the rest of the way to where they are waiting for the tractor and plow. They want to know what took me so long and I tell them about my experiences. The road will remain rough until the next time the county grader comes by.

The farmer is unable to hire regular farm laborers so he has four of us high school boys from town out here. He tries to get what help he can out of us. I think that he earns all that he gets. We get three dollars a day, plus three meals and a cot on the screened in porch. The meals are probably the best part of it. For breakfast, we have homemade sausage, eggs fried in the grease, homemade bread or biscuits, gravy and all the milk we want. For dinner, it's fried chicken or chicken fried steak or pork chops with mashed potatoes and gravy, home canned green beans or fresh peas and carrots. Pie for desert and fruit jars full of ice tea. Supper is often roast beef or pork, vegetables, pie or cake and more ice tea.

My next job at the farm is to drive the tractor and pull the binder, while we harvest the oats. I take off and am doing fine until I reach the first corner. The tractor is an old tractor on steel wheels. When I turn the corner, I can't get the steering wheel to go back the other way and we go around in a circle. I finally get it turned and we start cutting again. I look back at the guy sitting on the binder tying the bundles and he is laughing so hard he has to hold on to the binder to keep from falling off. After awhile, I find that I have to stand to the side of the steering wheel in order to have enough strength to turn the wheel.

My next experience on the farm is probably the worst. They show me how to hitch up two giant work horses. They then hitch them to the hay rake and tell me to start raking the alfalfa. I am scared to death of these gentle giants and they know it. I am able to drive them because they know what needs to be done better than I do. I never have to use them again and that is okay with me.

In less than two weeks, I am driving a tractor and pulling a large combine cutting wheat. When we work during the harvest, we work from dawn until after dark or until the wheat gets too tough to cut. In the afternoon, we get a snack to carry us through. After supper, it does not take long for us to get to sleep. After everything is cut, it comes time to plow. For this, we get two dollars a day. But knowing how boys are, he announces that he will dock us a quarter every time he finds us off of the tractor playing around. That means that we can't get off and chase those rabbits that get caught in the furrows. While plowing, we do not start until after the sun is up and we quit about dark. It's hot, dirty and dangerous work. We have to fight to keep from going to sleep. Fall asleep and you will fall off under the plow. I work there until school starts.

When school starts, I get a job working at the Safeway store. There are four of us boys working on Saturday. We go to work at seven in the morning and work until close to midnight. We sack groceries and carry them out to the cars and when we are not doing that, we have to stock shelves and candle eggs. You are expected to move with a gait somewhere between a walk and a run. If you slow up, the assistant manager will put his shoe to your butt. For this we receive seventeen cents an hour.

I go out for football again. We have a new coach and he seems to know what he is doing. For the first time, we get real instruction on how to play. I get to play in the first two games and we win them. This is exciting since we had not won a game the year before. The third game, I do not get to play and the game ends in a tie.

The boy that was assistant produce man at Safeway leaves when his folks move to another town. I am surprised when I am asked to take his place. It means that I will have to give up football and I hate that, but that is not really a factor. What does matter, is that not only will I get more hours of work, but I get a raise to twenty cents an hour. I need the money more than I need football. I go to work every morning at seven and work until eight-thirty when I leave for school. At three, I go back to work and work until six-thirty. On Saturdays I work the same hours as the others. Now that I am an important employee, I have to wear khaki pants, dress shirt and tie, with my official apron over that. I also get to carry a large curved banana knife, which is sharpened razor sharp by the butcher. With my dressy clothes, all the kids in school know what my job is.

CHAPTER VIII

Ernest Havlik from Bison, who is serving as a tank driver in North Africa and was listed as missing, is now listed as being a prisoner of war in Germany. The parents of Ernest Huffman who was killed in the Southwest Pacific, receive his Purple Heart medal. J. Ernest Trojan who was listed as missing over Germany is now listed as a prisoner of war in Germany. Southeast of town, a twin engine bomber crashes, but the pilot bails out and lands not far from his burning plane.

The flyers at the Enid Flying School have put out a request for rags to be used in the maintenance of the airplanes. The Lions Club sponsors a rag drive and we Boy Scouts go door to door and collect them.

War Dads are organized. They are men who have some relative in the service. Their object is to do anything to help those in the service and to aid in the war effort. They gather scrap iron and the proceeds are sent to supply cigarettes to those overseas. Later, the War Moms is organized. You can tell where they live because if they have a child in the service a little flag with a blue star is in their window. If their child is overseas a silver star, and for those poor mothers who have lost a son, a gold star.

We receive a letter from Don saying that he is not at the prison camp right now. He is setting up another smaller camp Northwest of Tucson. He has with him fourteen enlisted men and twenty-five Italian prisoners. Every one of the Italians is a skilled worker. Their job is to construct facilities for five hundred prisoners and one hundred twenty guards. When completed and occupied, the prisoners sent there will work on a twenty-five-thousand-acre ranch.

With fall approaching, notice is given that gas ration stamps are not to be used to purchase gas to go hunting or to football games. It causes wonder at just how they think that people can get there. This is one regulation that is frequently violated.

We are seniors now and school is more fun than it has ever been before. Maybe it is because we know that in a few short weeks, we will be breaking up and spreading out over the world. We work on the senior play and instead of being work, it is a lot of fun. And instead of sitting in the audience with a girl for the first time, I will be on the stage. I have a different girl now. She is a couple of years younger than I am and works at the library in the evenings. I go by and pick her up after the library closes and walk her home or sometimes we go to the movie and see the last part of it. It is nothing serious, but she does like to kiss and she will even let me cop a feel once in awhile, just to keep me happy.

I am really busy now. Work at the grocery store and school take six days of the week. Sunday mornings are for church. Sunday afternoons are for doing projects for school and after that, my time is free. Sometimes we still get a chance to go to the creek and play on Sunday afternoon. It is easy to see that we are already drifting apart more. I am named Junior Lion and get to attend Lions Club for lunch one day. Being named Junior Lion is another one of those rites of passage. I know all of the men in the Lions Club and it makes me feel older to be able to meet with them.

January, 1944, my brother Don is home on leave. He is on his way to Camp Swift, Texas, to be part of the newly formed One Hundred Second Infantry "Ozark " Division. He will help organize it and train the men as they are assigned to the division. We have an idea what this will mean, but no one says anything about it.

March 27, 1944, my eighteenth birthday. I get on the bus and ride to Kingfisher where the draft board office is located. I fill out the necessary paperwork and am given a registration identification card. I then return home on the bus. I think that is probably the most interesting birthday present I ever received. And it does give me an excuse to skip school and work for a day.

It seems now that almost every week the paper lists someone who has been wounded or killed. Most of those killed are from nearby towns. The letters from those in the service come from even more different places. The tone of most of them is the same. They are not allowed to write what they would like to and what they can write about is boring. But they all request letters from home. There is nothing more valuable than that.

I hitchhike to Enid and go to the recruiting office to see what my options are. It is a wasted trip, because if I enlist, I have to go in immediately, but since I am in the last semester of high school, they will not draft me until I graduate. I want to get that diploma and just as well because I know that my parents are not about to give their permission for me to enlist before that. Since my dad goes back and forth to Enid every day, I can hitchhike up there and then go to where he works and get a ride home.

It is time for the social event of the year, the Junior-Senior Banquet. Every one of both classes will be there and the sophomore girls will do the serving. Somehow, they get enough ration points to put together a very nice meal. There are a lot of jokes told on the seniors and it is a nice evening. This is no prom. No dancing. After the dinner, a few of the families throw a party for the kids and they dance there. I am not invited to any of them, but it is ok, because I have a long day at work the next day.

A few days later, I get very ill and vomit for a couple of days. They figure that I have stomach flu. The doctor comes and says that she thinks that I have had a gall bladder attack. After a few days,

I am able to go again. I remain in not the best of health, but I still keep up my busy schedule.

I receive notice from the draft board that I am to report for a physical on May 1, 1944. I catch the bus that morning to Kingfisher and go to the board office for my paperwork. They give me tickets for the bus and a meal ticket for lunch. I catch another bus to Oklahoma City and report to the building where they give physicals. They go over my paperwork and hand me a small bag, with a string on it to go around my neck. I go into another room and take off everything, put it in a locker and put my valuables and the key to the locker in the little bag. I feel funny with nothing on but the little bag. I have been naked a lot of times with other boys, but this is different. I feel so vulnerable and, well, naked.

I start moving from room to room as they check me over. I have never really had a physical before. Oh, I had to go to the doctor before I went out for football, but he just listened to my heart, had me move around and that was it. This time they listen to my heart, take my blood pressure. In the next room, they open my mouth and check my teeth and throat, nose and ears. The next room, they stick me with a needle and take my blood and send me off to pee in a bottle. Next room, they have me move around and jump up and down and walk across the room and back. Then the doctor has me walk over to where he is sitting and he tells me to turn my head and cough. I know why he has me turn my head, because if I knew what he was going to do, I would have jumped back. Then he has me turn around and bend over. If I had known what he was going to do that time, I am sure I would have jumped back. The last room has a doctor sitting at a desk and, he calls me and has me stand before him at the desk. He takes a quick look and reaches over and picks up a stamp and slams it down on my papers, leaving a big 1A. I am accepted for service.

A few days later, I get a new registration card listing my 1A status. On May 15, I get notice to report for induction on June 15.

The next couple of weeks go by fast and then it is time for final exams. If you are a senior and have at least a C average, you do not have to take the exams. That means that we have a couple of days off. The last day of school, three of us, Nathan Armstrong, Charles and I grab our fishing tackle, Nathan buys a six pack of beer (he looks at least twenty-one.) and we head to Skeleton Creek. We each have a couple of beers, my first. We don't catch any fish, but have a great afternoon, just taking it easy.

May 19, 1944. School is over and we seniors go to Baccalaureate and then Commencement. It is both joyful and sad. The girls are all crying. I am glad to get my diploma. The next couple of weeks I try to get all of my loose ends taken care of, including going to Scout camp.

When I get back from camp, I take care of some of the things I need to do before I go to the army. I give the old Winchester to an old friend to use as parts for his. I almost immediately regret it, but tell myself that I will get another when the war is over. I write thank-you notes for the graduation gifts I have received. My uncle sends me money to buy a watch. I hitchhike to Enid and find a small jewelry store right off of the square. I look over the watches and pick out one that looks good and is in my price range. I ask the old man in the store if the watch is guaranteed. He replies that he personally guarantees it. I make my purchase, walk around looking at the different stores and then walk a few blocks to the place where Dad has parked the car and wait for him to go home.

June 6, 1944, and the radio is spreading the news. The Allies have landed in France. There are heavy casualties and the results of the operation are unknown yet. Troops in Italy have taken Rome, but the news is over shadowed by the invasion. It is hard to keep up with the news because of the many places we have never heard of before. I only have a few days before I go.

CHAPTER IX

At last the day arrives, June 15, 1944, the day for me to report for induction into the army. My parents are up early and of course, I awake early too. My mother fixes me my breakfast, as she has for many years. A cup of cocoa, made from scratch, and toast with jelly. I already have my things ready to go. A small bag suitable for shipping my civilian clothes back home, a tube of Ipana toothpaste and a new toothbrush. Spare underwear and handkerchief to satisfy my mother, and that is all. No need for a comb or hair oil, because I have already had my hair cut as close as you can get with clippers. No razor or saving cream, because I do not have to shave yet. I have my orders and my bus voucher in my pocket. A few dollars and two twenty-dollar traveler's checks for emergency, in my billfold. I am set to go.

After breakfast, we try to think of things to say. My mother telling me to be good and this and that, but also trying to not act too protective. My dad listening in. Finally it is time to go catch the bus. Mother kisses me good-bye and then turns her head. I know she is crying, but she is good at covering it. Dad picks up my bag and we walk out of the door. We will walk to the bus stop, because it is only a block-and-a-half away. On the way Dad tells me not to gamble.

We stand on the corner waiting for the bus, not another person to be seen all the way up and down Main Street. He sets my bag down at my feet and we stand silent. A little dog comes around the corner, walks up to my bag, lifts his leg and decorates my bag. I do not know it at the time, but this is the highlight of my day. The bus pulls up, I grab my bag, my dad shakes my hand, I climb aboard and I am on my way to the army.

I hand the driver my voucher and find a seat. It only takes a few minutes until we get to Dover and when we stop there, two more guys get on the bus. I can tell from the actions of the people seeing them off, that they too are going to be inducted. When we get to Kingfisher, it is less than a block from the bus station to the draft board office. We get checked in, one at a time and we sit and visit about what we think is ahead for us. One of the guys from Dover is Jack Webber. More guys check in from Kingfisher. After they get everyone checked in and make sure that they have their paperwork, they send us off to the Blue Moon Café for an early lunch. The clerk hands me a voucher to give to the café to pay for our lunch. After lunch, we return to the draft office, where the clerk hands me a large folder, containing the papers for all of the men and tells me to get them to Fort Sill.

When we get to Fort Sill, we get off of the commercial bus and get on a school bus painted OD (olive drab) color. At that time, I hand over the papers to the man in charge. Ours is not the only bus to arrive. Several buses come in about the same time and the smaller buses are busy shuttling the men to the Replacement Center.

When we get off the bus, we are told to line up in the street in two lines with our bags beside our left leg, and face the front. There must be a hundred men lined up. In front of us is a private first class, acting corporal, giving orders like they are coming direct from God. He shouts in a loud voice and tells everyone to be quiet and pay attention. His next order is a little different. "Take out your dicks and when I step in front of you, skin it back and milk it down."

There is nothing quite like standing in the middle of the street with ninety-nine other guys, at four PM, on June 15, 1944, in the blazing sun, with your dick in your hand. For some reason, this is not how I thought wars are fought, but I soon find out how wrong I am.

As our names are called out, we are assigned to different barracks. I get separated from the rest of those from Kingfisher County and put across the street. Jack Clements, who is stationed in headquarters here, sees my name go through and comes to visit me. I am glad to see someone because I am already lonesome. Jack visits for a little bit and promises to come back and see me again. I do not have a uniform yet. In fact I have not received anything yet. They say to listen, so if my name is called I can report to where ever they say. I hear a bell ring and figure that it must be chow call, because everyone seems to be moving toward the mess hall. I fall in behind some guys that have uniforms on and figure they know what to do.

I have always been finicky about my eating, but I decided before I got here that whatever they put out, I am going to eat it. I get in line and watch what the other guys do. I get a tray and some silverware and move down the line. Guys behind the line with big long handled spoons wait for you to tell them if you want what is in front of them or not. If you indicate that you want something, they scoop up a big spoonful and slap it on your tray. They are not always careful about where they put it and your meal is often mixed before you eat it. The meal tonight is beef stew for the main course, with peas and carrots, apple sauce, bread, butter and ice tea to drink. The stew is nothing to rave about, but is edible and filling. The peas and carrots were canned and taste like it, but not unlike the store-bought ones we get at home. The applesauce tastes good and I am glad to get the ice tea. I watch the others as they finish and follow them to scrape my tray and turn it and my utensils in to be washed. When I finish, I go back to the barracks and lie down and rest.

The barracks is filling up and I listen as the guys talk about what is in store for us next. Of course, there are rumors. This is my first experience with rumors and I find that rumors are a way of life in the army. Then there are those old timers, guys that have been in the army for two days, who tell you what to expect. They love to tell about how bad the shots are. After awhile, I go to the latrine and take a shower. I do not have any soap yet or towels or wash cloths, but I find a piece of soap and wash off and then stand around, shaking the water off. In the dry heat of Fort Sill, I dry very quickly, put on my underwear and go in and lay on my bunk. No sheets here. Each mattress has a mattress cover on it and one blanket. There is a pillow case for the pillow. I lie down but do not need the blanket in the warm building. The guys are still talking and the lights are still on when I go to sleep. Tomorrow will be a busy day.

I wake up the next morning, wash up and get ready for breakfast. When the bell rings, I walk that way. Not bad, scrambled eggs, bacon, toast, potatoes, grapefruit juice and coffee. I eat up and then go back to the barracks and put my blanket over my bed, as near as I can to how I think it should be. It is not long before I hear my name called and I go report to the office. A guy goes over my paperwork and then explains some things to me and has me sign a bunch of papers. I am given copies and told to send them home. He then gives me a paper showing my serial number, 38 711 637. Then I am told to go back to the barracks or day room where I can hear them call me. I go back to the barracks and lie down. It is bright sun-shiny day, but it sounds like thunder. The big cannons are firing over on the range. Once in awhile I can hear the sound of a machine gun firing.

In a little while, I am called to fall out in the street. There are a bunch of other guys there too. This time it is a corporal, acting sergeant, who addresses us. He tells us that it is now time to be sworn into the United States Army. He says that it does not make any difference if we take the oath or not, because under the law, we are in it anyway. With that, he asks everyone to raise their right hand and to repeat after him. Every one of the guys takes the oath. When he is finished with it, he says, "as I call your name, take one step forward." He calls off all the names and everyone is now one step in front of where they were. He now says "with that step, you just stepped into the United States Army. You are now a soldier." It is

11:40AM, June 16, 1944. He tells us to go wait until we are called for further processing. I spend part of the time in the barracks and the rest in the recreation hall. They have newspapers there and I read the war news. The news of the invasion sounds encouraging, but not much mention is made of the casualties. Pictures from Rome show a joyful greeting of the American troops by the Italians. Hard to believe we were enemies a short time ago. I am not called, so after supper, I go to a movie and then take another drip dry shower and go to bed. I am now in the army, but still do not have a uniform.

CHAPTER X

It is Saturday morning and after breakfast, they call my name and I am sent to the barber shop. Not much he can do, because my hair is already as short as you can cut it with clippers, but he makes an effort. When I leave there, I go to a small room and hand the guy there my papers. He puts a couple of small metal plates in a machine and then types information and it is stamped on the metal plates. He takes them out, fastens them together with a beaded chain and hands them to me. I now have my dog tags. I am then sent to the supply building to draw my uniform. I get in line and one guy measures me. They hand me my clothing and two bags to put it in. Not a white thing in the bunch.

I go back to the barracks and sort everything out. I put on a set of suntans and shorten the belt so that it will fit me. I look in the mirror and I look a little like the barracks bag myself, with the big clothes gathered in the middle, with my belt. The socks fit ok but the shoes will take getting used to.

They call out a bunch of names, including mine, and we go for a lecture. The first part is about military courtesy and how to salute. Then they read the Articles of War to us. By the time they get through telling us what they can do to us, I am afraid to do anything.

We go back to the barracks to get washed up for dinner. I start to the mess hall and meet the first officer of my military career. I straighten up and salute. He returns my salute as we pass. I think that I did a pretty good job for the first time. Just then it dawns on me that I have just given the Boy Scout salute, but I have been in the Boy Scouts for six years and the army for one day. I pack up my civilian clothes and take them to the place designated for shipping them home. They will take care of that for me.

Sunday morning is very quiet. I write a letter home, telling my folks what has happened so far. I am waiting for the Chaplain to come to the recreation center for services. They announce services and I go over for church. The Chaplain is very nice and I enjoy the service. After the service, I go back and practice memorizing my serial number.

Monday morning, right after breakfast, I start taking tests. IQ test, general knowledge test and Morse code test. I feel that I am too slow and that I have not made a good grade. In the Morse code test I am supposed to hear two sounds and just tell if they are the same or different. I can't tell them apart, so I just guess what they should be. After the tests, I go in for an interview. It appears from all that I am able to tell them, that I am only suitable for the infan-try. After the tests, we go for shots. I am standing in line and I see ahead, that when they stick one guy, he hits the ground like a sack of potatoes. A couple of guys pick him up and carry him into another room. Then when the guy in front of me gets there, they stick him and he starts to wobble all around and they have to catch him and guide him into the next room too. Now it is my turn. One guy grabs my right arm and shoves a needle into it and I turn to see what he is doing and a guy shoves a needle in my left arm. I turn that way and I get another in the right arm. Tetanus, typhoid and small pox, just like that.

After we get our shots, we are sent to the movie theater to see some films on the evils of venereal disease. I learn that no matter how good looking the girl is, she may cause you big trouble and you should stay away from her. But if you can't stay from her, you should use a rubber and then a pro kit. The movie shows the proper way to use each. But to make sure that we get the message, they show pictures of penises that have been infected. Big sores that have split open and are oozing pus out of them. It is sure an impressive message.

As soon as the movie is over, we go out of the back door of the theater and into the front door of the mess hall. There are two guys in line ahead of me in the mess hall and when the first one gets to the serving line, he suddenly ducks his head, grabs his mouth and runs for the door. The second guy does the same thing. I move up and look into the big fifteen gallon kettle and find it is full of large frankfurters that have been boiled until they split open. I am not going to let that bother me, I tell the guy to give me two.

As soon as dinner is over, I am put on a work detail cleaning the barracks. It is really hot and I sweat so much that not only my socks are soaked but my shoes too. I work at that job until four P.M. (1600 hours, military time, but I will probably always use the other) Then I am told to go clean up and change into my class A uniform to go on another detail. I find out that I am to clean up headquarters. I clean the C.O.'s office and when I finish, I am so tired that I just go by the PX and get some ice cream instead of supper. They come by and tell me to hang a towel on the foot of my bed because they will be in at four A.M. to get me up to go on KP. I have just realized that I should not have griped about not having a uniform. At least when I did not have a uniform, I did not have any details. I take another shower and go to bed. My shoulder is so sore that I can hardly lie down.

Just before four in the morning, someone wakes me up and tells me that I have fifteen minutes to get to the mess hall and report for KP. I am still tired and sleepy and my shoulder hurts, but I show up at the mess hall. The mess sergeant, who is a corporal, acting sergeant, gathers us around and tells that we are working for him today and that we are to do what we are told and not to take a break unless he tells us to. My first job is to clean some pots and pans. I am watching one guy break eggs into one of the fifteen gallon pots. He is taking eggs out of the case and cracking them on the edge of the pot and dropping them in. I see a piece of shell fall in and tell him that he has dropped some shell in. He reaches into the case of eggs and takes a whole hand full of eggs and drops them whole in the pot, and says, "The hell I did." I work at cleaning pots for awhile and then the mess sergeant comes over and tells me and one other guy to go with one of the cook's helpers and to do what he says. We go and unload supplies. We get the first batch unloaded and the cook's helper tells us to go outside and wait until he is ready to unload the next load. We no sooner get outside, when the mess sergeant sees us and starts yelling at us for taking a break without his permission. He is furious. The cook's helper stands there watching what is going on. I tell the sergeant that we were just doing what we were told to do, but he would not listen. The cook's helper does not say a word, he just turns and walks away. Right then, I know that the army does not care anything about being fair.

He put us to cleaning out the empty garbage cans. We wash them until I would not be afraid to eat out of them. We spend the whole day cleaning pots, pans and garbage cans. When it comes time to get off of KP, we are told that since we did not obey the rules we have to stay and work. We are put to work shelling black-eyed peas.

Jack Clements goes to the barracks to see me and asks the guys there where I am. They tell him I am on KP. He asks when I went on KP and they tell him four in the morning. Jack says that it is after eight-thirty in the evening and I should not be still on KP. But they tell him that I am. Jack goes to the mess hall and finds the mess sergeant and asks him how come I am still there. The mess sergeant tells him that I am being punished for disobeying orders. Jack, who is a T/4 (technician fourth grade), out ranks the mess sergeant and tells him that he does not have the authority to punish me, and that he is taking me out of there. The mess sergeant says, "You do not have any authority here."

Jack says, "No, but I know a lot of people that do."

The mess sergeant gets the message and says "Take him I don't want him here anyway." Jack and I go back to the barracks and I explain what happened. I guess if Jack had not come to my rescue, I might have been there forever. Jack visits for a little bit and brings me a couple of letters from home. I had not been able to make mail call for the last two days and he picked up my mail for me. He sees how tired I am and does not stay long. I get a shower and fall asleep fast.

The next morning, I am so sore that I can hardly move, but I get up and go for breakfast. I remember the egg shells, but I go ahead and eat eggs anyway. After breakfast, I make my bed and straighten up my things before falling out for details. There is a butt can every few feet, all through the area, for soldiers to dispose of their cigarette butts. Previously, I watched one guy that had the job of cleaning them. He would make the rounds every hour, emptying them and washing them out. It only took about ten minutes to make the round and the rest of the time he got to spend in the recreation hall. It seemed to me that was a pretty good job. I also knew that he had shipped out the day before. When we fell out for duty assignments, and the guy in charge asks who all have jobs to do, I hold up my hand. He asks where I am working and I tell him I am supposed to clean the butt cans. He tells me to go ahead and get started. I have not been in the army a week, but I am already learning how to survive.

I go out every hour and clean out all of the cans. It only takes me ten minutes to make the rounds. So instead of working fifty minutes out of the hour and having a ten-minute break, I work ten minutes and have a fifty-minute break. I go back to the recreation hall between rounds. Then I make a tour through the barracks and back to the rec. hall. I try to keep moving around so that no one will get the idea that I should be doing something else.

It is Thursday now and I have been here a week. After breakfast this morning, when we go for details, I tell them again that I have a job of cleaning the butt cans and they tell me to go get with it. It is not all that pleasant, but sure a lot better than most of the other jobs around here. It does give me a chance to keep up with the news.

It is Friday, and after breakfast, they call my name to report. I thought they might have discovered that I had not been assigned to the butt can clean out. But instead, they tell me to get all of my stuff together, turn in my blankets, mattress cover and pillow cover, because I am shipping out. I can't hide the smile on my face. I take a shower and change from my fatigues into my suntans. I pack all of my things into the two barracks bags and wait to be called. I am still here at noon, so I go eat dinner and hope that it is my last meal here.

CHAPTER XI

It is the middle of the afternoon before I am called out. We line up in the street in some semblance of order. Our names are called and we have to answer with our serial numbers. It is a good thing that I have mine memorized. We load up in the shuttle buses. There are twenty-five or thirty of us being shipped out. We go down to the train station and get on the railroad coach that is setting there. As we get on, they hand each one of us a sack lunch to eat for evening meal. The coach is just that; hard wooden benches that you can flip over to seat either way. Most are set so that you are facing the front, but a few of the guys turn theirs the other way, so they can face the other guys and talk. It seems like a long time before we feel the coach jolt. We have been hooked onto a train. I am sure someone knows where we are going, but so far, no one has said anything. The train is not very fast. It stops at every town to drop off and pick up passengers and freight, as well as the mail. As long as the sun is up, I can tell that we are going north, towards home. I open my sack to see what I am having for supper. I find an orange, peanut butter and jelly sandwich and an oatmeal cookie. I can't eat oranges, so I find someone with an apple and make a trade. Not very much to eat, but I guess I will get by. My canteen is packed in my duffle bag, but it is empty. There is a water cooler in the corner of the car with some little paper cups, so I use it. When we get to El Reno, I see the name of the depot and am sure that we will be going through Hennessey.

We go through Dover. Jack Webber is on this car, but I do not see anyone at Dover to greet him. On to Hennessey, and we stop to pick up the mail and express packages; too bad they kept our route secret, because my folks just live three and one-half blocks away and I would love to see them.

I wake up in the morning and it is not long before the train stops and unhooks from our car. Someone gets on the car and tells us that we can get off of the car, but not to leave the station area; we will have a couple of hours before we go on. They tell us that the USO has space in the depot and they and the Red Cross have coffee and doughnuts for us. I go into the station and get a cup of coffee and a cake doughnut. I prefer the other kind, but I am sure thankful for what I get. I buy a postcard and a stamp from the news stand and write home. I can even mail it right here and it will be there tomorrow morning. Not too much to see at the train station, but several soldiers are waiting to board the train. You can tell them from those of us, who have only been in for about a week. They call for us to board the train and we are off again, heading west this time.

It is not too long before we arrive at Junction City, Kansas. We get off of the train and there is an army truck for us to climb into. It is only a short drive until we see the sign, "Welcome to Fort Riley." At least now we know where we are going. The truck takes us to a bunch of tar-paper shacks. This is the transient area. We go into the barracks and it looks better on the inside than it does on the outside. Still, it is nothing to brag about. No latrine here; that is a half a block away. The mess hall is a block away. We each pick out a bunk and lay down to rest. Someone comes in and tells us that the mess hall was not prepared for us, but if we go over there in about fifteen minutes, they will have something for us. We wait about ten minutes and go get in line. We have not had much to eat the last twenty-four hours. They open the doors and we march in. There is bread and they have taken some roast beef and sliced it so we can make sandwiches. There is both catsup and mustard for it. They have also made some lemonade out of the powdered mix. And from someplace, they have come up with a couple of sugar cookies for each of us. Not a big meal, but we are hungry and it tastes really good. They promise more for supper.

After we eat, we all go back to the barracks. I feel bad and I think I am running a fever from the shots. I lay down and am soon asleep. I wake up and I am sitting up on the bunk and the guys are all staring at me. It seems that when one guy walked by my bunk that I said, "Don't touch that bed." He stopped dead in his tracks. When the others realized that I was talking in my sleep, they started to laugh and that is what woke me up. I apologize and the one guy feels free to move on by me. I think that my fever may have broken and I feel somewhat better.   Jack Webber and I visit about people back home, that we know in common. It helps keep us from being so homesick. I go to the latrine and wash up some and then come back to the barracks to wait for supper.

We are early at the mess hall and get in line. The line is longer this time because guys that were already here and some more newcomers are in line too. The evening meal consists of green salad, pork chops, mashed potatoes with gravy, green beans and sheet cake for dessert. There is coffee and milk to drink. The pork chops are rather greasy, but all in all, not a bad meal, or maybe it is just that I am hungry.

After supper, I decide to get a shower and get ready for bed. It is hot and I have not had my clothes off or a shower for two days. I realize this business of having a latrine a half block from the barracks is not very convenient. I go get my shower, but I have to dress again before I return to the barracks, since it is broad daylight. I feel much better after the shower and again lay down on my bunk. I promise those around me that I will try not to attack anyone this time. They get a laugh out of it, including the guy that I scared so much before. Sometime in the night, I wake up and have to go pee. This is another adventure. I slip on my shoes and I go walking outside with just my shorts, undershirt and shoes. The trip goes without a hitch, but I feel funny with my feet slipping around in those big shoes.

In the morning, I wake up early and go to the latrine and get washed before most of the others get there. I am close to the front of the line at the mess hall and ready for breakfast. They open the door and almost instantly the word goes back along the line "SOS." I ask, "What is SOS?" and someone replies, "shit on a shingle." I still do not know, but when I get inside the door, I see the menu for breakfast and it says "creamed beef on toast, bacon, apple juice, coffee and milk." The toast is oven toasted and the pieces hit the tray like ceramic tiles. Then comes the creamed beef. It is hamburger mixed in gravy. The grease swims across the top of it. The guy serving is happy to slop a big scoop of it across the toast and most of the rest of my tray. I live up to my promise and eat the whole thing. It is not so bad once I get into it. But I do drink my carton of milk, and when the guy next to me just pours a little out of his into his coffee, I ask him if I can have the rest.

We have been told that we will be leaving here this morning, so I get my things all packed up and wait to be called. About nine, the truck comes and several of us are told to get on. Jack Webber and I, along with some others, climb aboard. We go over to another part of Fort Riley and are greeted by a sign that says "Cavalry Replacement Training Center. Fort Riley, Kansas." I know one thing, I do not want to be riding a horse. We go a ways and the truck stops and I and three other guys are told to get off and report to the orderly room. The sign over the door says "Troop H - 1st Regiment." I have arrived where I will take my basic training.

CHAPTER XII

We check in and they give us an address. Barracks 2056. Troop H - 1ˢᵗ Regt., C.R.T.C, Ft. Riley, Kansas. We are given a card with the address on it, so we can mail it home and our families can write to us. Then we are told to go next door to the supply room and draw our equipment. I get another set of fatigues, a steel helmet, leggings, pack harness, a couple of wool blankets, and a shelter half with pole and pegs. I exchange my pistol belt for a rifle belt with a first aid packet on it. And last, but certainly not least, I am handed a M1 Garand rifle.

When everyone in the group has received their equipment, we are led to our barracks. We are placed on the second floor of the building and my bunk is the first one on the bottom on the left side. One of the cadre men is there to show us how to place our things. We each have a foot locker to hold most of our small things. But each item must be folded just so and placed in one certain place in the chest. Our packs are fastened to the end of our bunks. The rifles are placed in the rack at the end of the barracks, where they can be locked. The cadre man then tells us that we must button our uniforms and hang them on hangers on the rack behind the bunk. Of course, we do not have any hangers. He suggests, however, that he does have a few spare ones that he can let us have for twenty cents apiece. Every one of us gives him two dollars and gets ten hangers for our clothes.

Each of us works to get our things put away as we are supposed to. We are shown how to make a bed. No matter how hard I try, I am not able to get it as tight as it should be. More guys keep coming into the barracks and the cadre man shows them how to stow their things. And, of course, picks up another two dollars for hangers. Upon advice, we each write down the number of our rifle, and are told to memorize it. Mine is 2447683. There is sure a lot to learn in a short time. The intercom in the barracks, or the "bitch box" as the guys call it, is constantly calling for different ones to go to the orderly room to complete papers or to the supply room to pickup or exchange something. Before too long, the bitch box announces that chow is ready. Those of us who got here earlier, take off immediately, but some of the others are still trying to get their things put away.

We line up for chow and start through the line. Today's menu is ham with pineapple, mashed potatoes and gravy, cole slaw, peach cobbler and ice tea. The best food that I have had since I got in the army. Maybe this place will be OK, after all. More and more guys filter in to eat. After we eat, we go back to the barracks and some of us get out our rifles and look them over. It is a lot heavier than I thought it would be, not much like the little .22's that I am used to. It is not two minutes before one of the guys lets out a yell. He is the first victim of the famous "M1 thumb," caused when you let the bolt close before you have your thumb out of the action. I had heard about this from some place and am extra careful about closing the bolt on mine.

While we are sitting around the barracks, a large number of guys come in who look miserable. They are dressed in winter, OD, uniforms. Their faces and hands are black. They tell us that they have spent more than three days coming from Fort Lewis, Washington. The train they were on did not have any kind of air conditioning, so once they got away from the cool air of the mountains, they had to open the windows of the coach. The train was pulled by a steam locomotive and the black soot had drifted into the windows. By the time they got to Kansas, they were burning up, tired, dirty and hungry. We tell them to go ahead and leave their stuff and put it up later. So they can grab a shower, put on some cooler clothes and get to the mess hall before it closes. They hurry around and the mess sergeant stays open later so they can get something to eat. After they go to eat, we look up and here comes a guy with an armed MP on each side of him. They take him to a bunk and set him down on it and then remove the handcuffs from his wrists. The MPs then leave. He is an older guy, probably in his late twenties. I guess that he knows that we are staring at him, because he says, "Don't any of you get too close to me, I am a criminal." We just laugh and then one of the guys asks him what the deal is. He tells us that he is single, does not have much family and that when he got the first notice to report for induction, he just laid it aside for awhile. Then he got another notice to report, and on the day he was to report, he was doing something else, so he thought he would wait a couple of days to go in. But the next day after he was to report, these two big MPs show up at his door, handcuff him and bring him all the way from Utah to Fort Riley.

Another guy walks in and walks up to where I am sitting. He said that if it was OK with me, he would take the bunk over me. He is an old guy. I find out that he is thirty-one and married, with four kids and that he has been a rural mail carrier in Missouri. I ask him if he would not rather have the lower bunk and he tells me that he definitely wants the upper. The barracks is filling up with guys coming in to start their basic training. The cadre man is kept busy showing everyone how to arrange his things and, of course, he just happens to have a few extra hangers for sale. By now, I have figured out that every word in the army is either preceded or followed by a profanity. I am already picking up the habit and I have only been in for about ten days.

Some of us go ahead and line up at the mess hall to wait for the evening meal. When we get inside, we find that since it is Sunday evening, they are not cooking. The menu is cold cuts. There are potato chips and ice tea or coffee to wash it down. To me, it is a great supper. I have always liked sandwiches.

When we get back, I get my soap and towel and head for the showers. It feels good to get the grime and sweat off of me. I lay out the clothes that we will be wearing in the morning and then lie down on my bunk. I am tired and I know tomorrow will be a hard day, so I go to sleep with the lights on and everyone moving about and talking.

CHAPTER XIII

At four-thirty in the morning, someone turns the lights on and yells for everyone to get up and get dressed. The uniform is fatigues, shoes, leggings and helmet liner. Fall out at five o'clock. There is a rush to the latrine to get cleaned up. Since I do not need to shave, it does not take me as long. Then it is back to get dressed. The fatigues go on easy and the shoes do not take long to get laced up, but the leggings are a struggle to get laced and then tied. Almost everybody has finished by the time they yell for everyone to fall in outside.

It is a ragged bunch that gathers. They yell to form two lines and then yell at the guys that are straggling to join us. Straighten up the line and put your arm up and touch the shoulder of the person beside you, to get the correct distance. The command is then given for attention and most seem to know what that is. The next command is left face and it takes a little bit for everyone to figure out which direction that is. At the command of forward march, we move out. As soon as we all get going at a rather smooth pace, the command is given for double time and everyone takes off running.

We only go a little over a half a block, when in front of me a guy suddenly goes flying towards the ground and hits rolling. Then another guy goes down and then a third. Right behind me, another guy goes down and hits my heel as he falls. It takes a little bit to figure out what is happening and then someone says that they have put their leggings on wrong. I am glad it was not me, but several of them have laced the leggings up on the inside of their legs instead of the outside and when we started running, the hooks caught. With their feet tied, down they went. We keep running and the guys on the ground are taking their leggings off and putting them on right.

We run for about fifteen minutes and we are back at the area. Then we start doing physical training. This is not my favorite thing to do and I do not see many others that seem to enjoy it. Pushups, side straddle hop, bend over and touch your toes among the others. The only way I can touch my toes is to spread my feet wide. That is okay until they catch me and then make me put my feet together. After about a half an hour, they tell us to wash up for breakfast.

The latrine is crowded again. Breakfast is at six o'clock but most of us are already tired by the time we get in line for chow. They start us out right. Juice, fried eggs, (you can ask for how you want them cooked), thick bacon, little boxes of cold cereal, milk and coffee to drink. The eating is rather slow; everyone is winded and sweaty. After breakfast, we go back to the barracks and make our bunks and get ready for the day's work. The uniform is the same as this morning, except, we put on our rifle belts with canteens and first aid pouches.

We fall out at seven o'clock and get back in line again. The cadre look us over and of course find that we all have our canteens and first aid pouches in the wrong places. After that, they name a couple of guys as squad leaders. My bunkmate is the squad leader for my squad. Then we start close order drill. It is very ragged at first. I do very well because of my training in band and the Scouts, other than not being able to keep in step. We practice the different movements for fifty minutes and then get to take a ten minute break. Most of us head for the side of the barracks in the shade.

When the break is over, we are ordered back into formation and we march over to the day room. They have us move into the day room for orientation lectures. They explain that we will begin with basic training and after six weeks, we will also go to classes on radio operation. They also tell us that one of the platoons will be mechanized cavalry and the other platoon will train with horses. I sure hope that God is listening to me and that I get a truck instead of a horse. They explain some of what is in store for us and set out what we are expected to do. They anticipate questions and the first answer is that we will not be able to leave the post for three weeks. At that time we will receive our class A passes which are good from Saturday afternoon until Monday morning. They are also good for up to 175 miles. We are told about going on sick leave, mail and keeping our quarters clean. When the fifty minutes are up, we get a ten-minute break.

The next hour is spent teaching us about pulling guard. They tell us what is expected and then show us the General Orders. We are supposed to memorize them so that if the Officer of the Day asks, we can repeat them. It seems that it will take a long time to remember them, but they come quicker than I thought. By the time we get our break, we are all repeating them out loud for each other. The next hour they show us a movie about the M1 rifle. Then they bring out an oversized model of the M1 showing all of the parts. Dinner is at eleven, so this gives us ten minutes to go clean up before we get in line to eat. After I eat, I go back to the barracks and lay down on my bunk, but I am very careful not to mess it up. Then I hear mail call, so I go downstairs to see if I have any letters yet. There are only two letters for the same guy. They could have just called out his name and saved the rest of us the trouble of going to mail call.

This time when we fall out, we take our rifles with us. We drill and learn how to do the manual of arms. We stand and go through the different commands until most are doing it together. A couple more guys get their thumbs hit when they try to close the action after inspection arms. Then we start marching around the area carrying our rifles this time. The sun is straight over head and it is blistering hot. The sweat is pouring off of us. When the hour is over, we all head for what shade we can find. When the ten minutes are up, we get into formation again and march down the road to another building.

There are tables in this building and we proceed to take our rifles apart. They tell us what we can disassemble. This is a lot better than marching in the sun. It is not long before they are all apart and then we start the process of putting them back together. This is harder than taking them apart. There are little tricks to doing it the easy way. We are told how to clean the rifle and take care of it. This takes a couple of hours and we are glad to have the time inside. When the two hours are over, we march out away from the buildings to a grassy field.

When we arrive, we are taught how to stack rifles. Then we start physical training again. It is so hot, that I think I am going to pass out. When one of the other guys passes out, I am sure of it, but no such luck. The only good thing about it is, that the grass is not as hot as the dirt, but with the heat, there is not much moisture left in the blades. When the hour is over, we put our things back on, shoulder our rifles and march back to the barracks. We have an hour to clean up and change into our class A uniforms, before we fall out for retreat.

It gets crowded again with everyone trying to take a shower at the same time. We get cleaned up and put on our suntans, rifle belts and helmet liners. We will need our rifles this time too. When we are called out, we fall in and look much better than we did this morning . Can it be possible that it was just this morning, when we fell out for the first time? It seems like it was a week ago. We present arms, holding our rifles up and down in front of us. Retreat does not last that long, but standing at attention under the sun has brought sweat out again and our suntans show the stains. We are dismissed for chow. We run back into the barracks and put our rifles, rifle belts and helmet liners away before we hurry to get in line at the mess hall. No short line this time; everyone is here at the same time. The menu is beef stew, peas and carrots, apple sauce, cantaloupe and ice tea. The cantaloupe and ice tea sound good after a hot day, but you can't fuel this kind of activity on that, so I take some of everything and eat it all.

After supper, we change back into our fatigues so we can clean up our equipment. We all have out our M1's and get in little groups of three or four guys and practice taking them apart and putting them back together. At the same time, we take smelly bore cleaner, a brush and patches and clean every part of the rifle. My rifle already has some slight pits in the bore from not having been cleaned properly sometime before. After we get it clean, we oil the working parts and put a thin film of oil over the rest.

I go take a quick shower and slide into my bed. The lights are still on and some of the guys are moving about. I am sunburned, sore and so tired I can hardly move, but I have made it through the first day of basic training. That is the last thing I remember before falling asleep.

CHAPTER XIV

Someone is yelling to get up. I open my eyes and there is light shining in them. I try to move something else, and nothing will move. I try again and every single muscle screams in pain. I know that I must overcome the pain and get up. I slowly move my head and then a hand, an arm and I am on my way. I roll out on the floor and then take hold of the bunk and pull myself to my feet. Not all of those sounds are coming from me. Everyone else is crying out of a sore body. I get down to the latrine, pee and wash my face and hands and I am awake but moving very slow. Back upstairs I pull on my pants and slip into my fatigue jacket. They are both stiff and coated with salt. And they smell too. I sit down to put my socks, shoes and leggings on and I have trouble reaching the laces to tie them. I stand back up, grab my helmet liner and head downstairs and outside.

We start PT again, and my muscles protest but I have to override them. After a little bit they seem to loosen, but with each different exercise, another set complains. We get through it and it does not seem as long as it did yesterday, but it may be because I am too numb to know. We head for the chow line. Today we have boiled eggs, thick bacon, oatmeal, milk and coffee and orange juice. My boiled egg is hard, but that is okay with me. The oatmeal will stick with me more than anything else.

After breakfast we get our bunks made and all of our gear stowed, and fall out for some more close order drill. We march to the day room and have classes on how to sight the M1 until eleven o'clock when we go to eat. After dinner, I head back to the barracks and lay down to try to get a few minutes rest. From downstairs the sound of "mail call" comes, and I get up and go down just in case. This time I luck out. I get two letters from my mother, that were forwarded from Ft. Sill. My day gets brighter. Even though it is old news, it does not matter; they came from home.

In the afternoon, we hike down to the Republican River bottom and practice creeping and crawling through the rough ground, pretending to sneak up on the enemy. It is hot, hard, dirty work. There is little wind down here in these trees and we suffer. I do not drink any water, because they make us put salt tablets in our canteens. This is supposed to keep us from having heat exhaustion, but the effect is that we are not getting the water we need to keep going. Later in the afternoon, we march back to the barracks and get ready for retreat. I load up on water when I get back. I swallow a couple of the salt tablets and drink several cups of tap water.

After supper we change back into our fatigues for an evening hike. Our fatigues have not had time to dry and they are wet and sticky with sweat. We put on our equipment, head out for a march out into the field, have a session of PT and then back to the barracks. We have just time to clean our rifles and equipment before lights out. My eyes are closed when my head hits the bed.

The next sound I hear is "hit the deck." It can't be morning yet, but it is. I try again to get out of my bunk and my muscles revolt again. I fight back and am able to pull myself to my feet. The fatigues have gotten stiff in the night. I do not know how long I can wear them, but I am going to have to wear them the rest of the week. I can't send in any laundry until next Monday. I only have one other set, so I will need them next week. We do our run and then PT. I am not as stiff as I was yesterday, but they add more exercises, so I end up with just as much pain. Breakfast is more of a chance to rest than it is to eat. Today we are having grapefruit, corned beef hash, cold cereal and of course, coffee and milk. After breakfast, I hurry back to the barracks and get my things straightened out.

We fall out today with our rifles and march out into the field again. We go about a mile and a half away from camp and find a place in the trees to have lectures on cover and concealment. We practice creeping and crawling again and on using cover. The weather is hot, but we are in more of a breeze today, so is not as bad as yesterday. The morning goes rather quickly and then we march the mile and half back to the barracks.

After lunch, I head back to the barracks to get as much rest as I can. I start a letter to Mom. Mail call comes and I get a card and a letter from my mother and a letter from a girl, who goes to the same church I do. I check the bulletin board and see my name for KP in the morning. Oh no, I hate to see that. I still remember KP at Ft. Sill. I go back upstairs and read my mail. It makes me feel much better but gives me a touch of homesickness again. I finish my letter home and put it in the mail box.

All too soon, we have to fall out. This time, we police the area before we go back to class. A long line of guys, side by side, moves through the entire area, picking up anything that is out of place and that can be seen with the naked eye. After class, we have another session of PT. After supper we have a chance to clean our equipment for tomorrow. I clean up things as fast as I can and then, before I slide into my bed, I hang a towel over the end of my bunk, so that they will know to wake me up for KP at four o'clock in the morning.

It seems like I barely get to sleep when I get shaken and a light shines in my eyes. A voice says that it is time to go on KP. I have everything laid out, so it does not take long for me to get ready, and I go over and report at the mess hall. I am told to set the things on the tables; salt and pepper, sugar, butter and catsup. I get all of them put out and then I am told to help set up the serving line. I make sure that the burners under the steam table are working, so that the food will be hot. The menu today is scrambled eggs, sausage, canned pears, tomato juice, milk and coffee. I get to work the serving line dishing out pears. After breakfast, I get to clean up. The table waiters clean the tables, but I help clean out the pots and pans. The garbage truck comes and after it leaves, I get the job of cleaning the garbage cans under the watchful eye of the mess sergeant. I scrub them with hot soapy water and a brush and then rinse them and dry them, just like you would one of the pans. When I get through, I would not hesitate to eat out of them.

By the time I get through, it is time to serve the noon meal. I get the steam table going and help carry the pans and set them in place. I guess I am doing a good job, because the cook asks me if I want to help him cook for the evening meal. What we are making is dessert. We have this big stack of bread that I take out of the sacks and tear into pieces and put it in three big loaf pans. He has the recipe in front of him and he tells me what to add. Then I put in sacks of sugar, boxes of cinnamon, nutmeg, some salt and gallons of canned cherries. We stir it up and add some milk and work it in and then put it into the oven to bake. Then we take lemon juice and sugar and cook up a sauce to pour over the pudding. It really looks good.

Then it is time for the evening meal. It is not bad, but the bread pudding does not taste as good as I thought it would. Another guy dishes it out and I get to ask if they want sauce on it and if so, I put a small ladle of sauce over the top. Some of the guys elect to put milk on it. When I eat, I put both on mine. When the meal is over, we start cleaning up again and it is nearly eleven o'clock when I get back to the barracks.

That was really a short night. I can hardly get awake. I do my running and the PT that follows in a daze. By the time breakfast is over, I am finally starting to wake up. They did a lot of marching and hiking yesterday, so I probably did not miss much, but I would have rather been doing that than KP. Today, it is more of the same. We march out of the camp and then start hiking out into the country. We stop a couple of times for lectures before heading back to the camp for dinner. After dinner, I start a letter to Mom again but am interrupted by mail call. I get a letter from her and one from the preacher. I go back and finish the letter home before we are called out again. It is really hot this afternoon again, but we are lucky and get to stay inside of a building, where we are taught how to set the sights on the rifle.

After supper is our first "GI party." The GI party is cleaning the barracks. We move everything, sweep the floor, then scrub and mop the floor. We wash the window screens and the windows and dust everything. When the floor is dry, we replace all the furnishings. It takes a couple of hours to do the whole thing, including the latrine. When we get that done, I then get to work on cleaning my rifle and equipment for inspection in the morning. After that, I have time to write to my brother, Don, before it is time to go to sleep.

It is Saturday morning and after breakfast, we stand inspection. We are lined up and the lieutenant, followed by the first sergeant, goes from man to man looking them over and checking their rifles and their appearance. Any deficiencies are noted by the first sergeant. When they get through with us, they proceed through the barracks looking for anything they can find that is not just right. We get through inspection with only a few exceptions and then we do an hour of close order drill. We are so much better than when we started that you would not know it is same group. I am able to stay in step and we all think that we look very sharp. At noon, we are dismissed for the day. After dinner, I walk to the PX to see what is there. A couple of women are working there, the first that I have seen for a couple of weeks. They look like they have heard about everything. I buy a pint of ice cream, the first since I left Fort Sill. They hand me a little wooden spoon to eat it with and I go outside and find a shady spot to eat. I also pick up a couple of candy bars to take back to the barracks with me. The ice cream was fifteen cents and the candy bars cost three cents each. At some tables back behind the PX, a lot of guys are busy drinking beer.

I am stopped when I step outside of the PX. I look up and there is a funeral procession. The mounted color guard followed by the horse drawn caisson with the casket. Behind that is the horse with the empty saddle and empty boots in the stirrups. Following them is the entire company of mounted cavalrymen. This is very impressive with all the horses moving together. I had heard a rumor that a guy picked up an unexploded rocket and was showing it to another guy, when he dropped it. One man was killed and the other wounded. I guess it is true. When I get back, I lay down on my bunk and am soon asleep.

I wake up later in the afternoon, in time for supper. Since we are not allowed to leave the post, most of the guys are back for supper too. After supper, one of the guys has a radio and we get to listen to the evening news. American forces are still battling in the hedge rows in France after taking Cherbourg. In the Pacific, American carrier planes shot down 220 Japanese planes while losing only 20 American planes. A few of us gather around and work on assembling our M1 rifles. We practice taking them apart and putting them back together again, while blind folded. Of course, when you start to put it back together, there is always a part missing. If you recognize that it is missing, it will reappear. I write another letter home while I have time.

Sunday morning. We do not have to get up this morning. I wait until it is time for breakfast and then race over to the mess hall. After breakfast, a guy is going through the area selling Sunday papers. I buy the Topeka paper and take it back to the barracks and read the news and comics. Then I go over to the chapel for church. Not too many there, but the service is good and I feel better. In the afternoon I go back to the PX and get some more ice cream and pickup a magazine to read. After supper, I walk to the post theater and see a movie. I go back and get my things ready for morning and go to bed. I have just completed my first week of basic training.

CHAPTER XV

Monday morning. Not quite as hard to answer the call to "hit the deck." The rest over the weekend has eased some of those tired muscles. I put on clean fatigues this morning. The ones I wore all last week are in my laundry bag, with my other dirty clothes. Last night I checked to see that they were all marked with my identification, L637, the last letter in my name and the last three digits of my serial number. I will turn in the laundry after breakfast. We fall out and are told that we will not be doing our morning run or PT before breakfast. It seems that some doctor told the army that it is hard on the men's digestion to exercise so hard just before breakfast. But do not worry, we are not going to do without it; they will just postpone it until later in the day. Instead, we will do close order drill for an hour. This is not so strenuous and will not upset our digestion as much. After breakfast, we get our things ready for the day. Then we fall out with our rifles, rifle belts with canteen and first aid pouch. We march outside of the area and then start a route march to the Republican River bottom again. We spend the morning practicing sneaking up on the enemy. We take mud and smear it on our faces and hands to camouflage our appearance. It is extremely hot down in the river bottom and crawling through the brush saps our strength fast. We do not worry about snakes or ticks; we do not think they can live in these conditions. We use our helmet liners as sun helmets, but with their dark color, they get so hot that you can't lay your hand on them.

After dinner, only a brief time to lie down in the barracks before mail call sends me back downstairs. I get a package from Mom. It is full of cookies and they are wrapped in the funny papers. I share them with some of the other guys and we all enjoy the cookies and reading the funnies. The chocolate cookies are especially good. The mail I get is the only thing that keeps me going. I think if it wasn't for that, I would just give up. I do not get all the way through the funnies and cookies before we are called out. It is time to make up for the running and PT we missed this morning. We go through all of the exercises. The sun is blazing down. When we finish the exercises, we start our run. Like the first day, one guy goes down, another and then the third hit the ground. Not from the leggings this time; they have just passed out from the heat. When the third one goes down, they call it off and move us into the shade and in whatever slight breeze there is. We sit there and the sweat rolls off of us. It takes a long time before we get cooled down enough to do anything. They march us to some covered bleachers for lectures the rest of the afternoon.

We go back to the barracks to get ready for retreat. It is great to get a shower and cool off for a few minutes. We fall out for retreat and I guess the word has gone up to headquarters about what happened this afternoon, because retreat is cut short this evening. We go to supper and it is a regular meal, but I notice that they have pitchers of both ice tea and lemonade. After supper, most guys are just lying on their bunks. The heat has done its work. They announce over the bitch box that we will fall out at seven o'clock in the evening. We still have to make up that PT we missed before breakfast. Hopefully it will be a little cooler by then.

Once again it is time to hit the deck. We are going to have breakfast earlier today and then do our running and PT after breakfast before it gets quite so hot. Today is July 4th, Independence Day, but it is a working day for us. After breakfast and our exercises, we get our things put away and get ready to go to the field. We go out to the rough area near the river and are divided into two groups. The one group will take positions near the top of the hill and conceal themselves there, while the rest of us will attack the hill and try to take it. The exercise is supposed to teach us how to advance against the enemy. I am glad that it is not real, because I do not think many of us would be able to reach the top. They are firing blanks. It is hard crawling and then running up the hill. At last we reach the top. Then we change sides and we get to defend the hill. Defending is easier. We are given some blanks to fire. Some of the other guys do not want their blanks, so they give them to me. I am having a good time shooting them. At least I am getting to celebrate, if not with fire crackers, then with something else that makes a bang.

They are having mail call as I come out of the mess hall and I get a letter from Mom and one from a girl that I have known for a long time. I have time to read them both and start one of my own before we are called out. We go to a building and they have lectures about attacking or defending a position and show us some training films about it. This is a lot easier than having to actually do it, but I am sure that we are not done with that either. We still have our running and PT to do before the day is over. I wish it were a little cooler so we could do it earlier. After supper, we change back into our sweaty fatigues and get ready to go do PT. We run out into the field area, do our exercises and then run back.

I start to get my things cleaned up from the day's activities. Now I find out why the guys gave me their blanks. The powder residue from those blanks is hard to get off. I work hard on it and then finish the letter that I started at noon before I take my shower and crawl into bed.

I crawl out of bed again and get dressed to go eat breakfast. After breakfast, we have PT again. It is cloudy and starts to drizzle a little. They tell us to fall out in our rain coats with rifle belts, canteens, first aid pouches and helmet liners. We start marching out to the field. We take off our rain coats, fold them and then loop them through the back of our rifle belt, something else to add weight and get in the way as we crawl around through the brush again. The temperature is cooler, but with the high humidity we suffer more than before.

This afternoon, we practice the different positions for shooting the rifle. We take turns being the coach and the shooter. We check each other's alignment with the target. Then we are taught the commands we will be using on the range, and are also warned of the dangers of not obeying every order. This is easier than what we have been doing lately. After we finish our lessons, we run out to a field and do our PT again. It is not as hot today, and the ground feels cooler after the little shower this morning, but it is still more humid and we suffer from the heat. No one passes out, so I guess it is not as bad as it was or we are getting used to it.

Tonight they are telling us about the hike that we will be taking tomorrow night. We will be carrying full packs with rifles and steel helmets on this one. It is to get us used to the helmets because we will have to wear them all next week at the rifle range. I am glad when it is over so we can eat supper.

After supper, we get a lesson on fixing our packs. We lay out our shelter halves, then put our blankets on them, lay the tent pole pieces and stakes and the tent rope on it and roll it in a tight roll and hold it in place by rolling it into the envelope formed by the shelter half. We then strap it tightly into our pack harness. Our mess kits and other articles go into the pouch on the back, which is strapped down over the shelter half. The straps go over our shoulders and fasten to our rifle belts. It is heavy, when it is all put together. I try it on, together with the rest of my equipment and I realize that all of it together weighs half as much as I do. This is going to be a load for such a little guy.

Up in the morning and fall out for formation. Then it is time for breakfast. After breakfast, we do our running and PT then back to the barracks to get ready for the lessons of the day. We learn about the signals from the leaders. How to move up and how to stay where we are. When to fire and when to hold our fire. These are important if we are going to act as a unit.   After dinner, we go back to the woods to practice what we have learned. The problem is, we are mixed up with another unit and different people are in charge of the squads. I do not know the others and am not sure what they mean by their signals. And when it is my turn to lead, I have little luck getting them to go where I want them. I think we would have a much better exercise, if we were using our regular squad leader. Then we eat supper and get ready for the night hike.

We take off with full packs, steel helmets and rifles. We have not gone far before I start feeling it pressing down on my shoulders and the steel helmet rocks back and forth on my head. I need to adjust the straps on the helmet liner now that I have the extra weight. I will do it as soon as we take a break. My fatigue jacket is soaked through under the straps and the wet cloth rubs on my skin, and I slog along.   We take a break and I start to sit down, but the weight of my pack pulls me over backward and instead of sitting, I am lying down on top of my pack. I roll over and sit back up. I take off my helmet and adjust the straps on the helmet liner so that it rides higher on my head and I can even see further ahead now. We go in a loop out of camp so that we come back in from a different direction. We have been five miles and this is one of our required hikes, so at least I get that out of the way.

It is Friday and after breakfast, PT and running, we go to classes on how to do scouting. Then after dinner, we put on full pack, steel helmet and rifle and hike out into the country. Then we drop our packs and go on a scouting mission. We bend over low so we will not be seen and then as we get closer, we crawl up to where we can see what is there. It is a scouting trip of about two miles. Then we go back to where we dropped our packs and they have a critique on how we did. They have a lot of corrections, but all in all, we did okay. After that, we hike back to the barracks and do PT before supper. After supper, we all get busy with GI night. We scrub everything and get the barracks ready for inspection in the morning.

Saturday morning after breakfast, we have regular PT and then get ready for inspection. Everything passes and we are free until

Monday morning, except for those guys who are assigned to details, such as KP. I take the time to write a letter home. My brother left a couple of pair of old fatigues at home and I ask Mom to send them to me. They are not fit to wear, but when I get them I will go to the supply room and trade them in on new ones. If I have twice as many sets, I will not have to wear them so long. I go over to the day room and catch up on the news. The marines have invaded Saipan in the Pacific, and in Europe, the American troops are slowly moving north in Italy, and in France they are still trying to get through the hedgerows.

After dinner, I walk down the street to where Jack Webber is stationed. I visit a little while and compare what we are doing. So far, it is about the same thing. Then I go back to the barracks and lie down to read the Reader's Digest, but fall asleep before I get very far. I wake up in time for supper and after supper, I walk over to the theater and watch a movie.

I get up in time to make it to breakfast and on the way back I find the guy who sells papers and get a copy of the Topeka Capitol-Journal. I read the paper until time to go over to church. Quite a few are attending church services, because a lot of us still can't leave the post yet. I enjoy the service; it reminds me of home. I am not as home sick as I was at first, but would still like to be home.

CHAPTER XVI

Monday, July 10, 1944, we are starting on the third week of basic training. It is very much like last week. Today we learn how to sight the .22 rifles, on the thousand-inch range. We each take turns, as coach and shooter, but without any ammo yet. It is difficult for me to get into the sling and get a good position and still be comfortable enough so that I do not put stress on my body and get to shaking. I have trouble relaxing with people crowded around me and they make such a big issue out of everything. I wish that I could just take it easy and relax and shoot it. Tomorrow we will fire the .22's at small paper targets one thousand inches away. This simulates the M1 out on the rifle range. At mail call, I get a letter from Mom and a box of chocolate chip cookies from my aunt. I pass them around and most of them are soon gone. They are delicious and we are able to eat them, even if we did just come back from dinner.

In the afternoon, we go out on another scouting problem and are out in the brush until time to come back in for afternoon PT. We get ready for retreat, and after it is over, we eat supper, change clothes again and are called out to make a march of three miles. No steel helmets or packs this time; just a light load for a walk out into the country. A couple of the guys are on stable duty tomorrow. They will get out of shooting the .22's and PT tomorrow, but I think I would rather do a couple of hours of PT than shovel horse manure all day.

Tuesday, is a busy day. We get our things put away and fall out for PT, before we march over to the thousand-inch range to fire the .22's. We take turns shooting and coaching. It takes quite a bit of time and not everyone gets through shooting in the morning. On the way back to the barracks, we stop and do the afternoon PT before we have to get ready for retreat. At retreat, they announce that after supper, we will go to the day room to have our pictures taken for our class A passes. The cost is a dollar. We already have our class A uniforms on, so we are ready for our pictures to be made. This is one time that everyone will show up.

After I get my picture taken, I go back to the barracks and pass the bulletin board and see that my name is on it. I have latrine orderly duty for tomorrow. I have never done it, but I have an idea what I will have to do. It is only a half a day, but will get me out of some other things. I have time to write a couple of letters, before I have to get to bed.

After breakfast when the others fall out, I remain behind. As soon as I have my things arranged, I go to the latrine and start to work. I sweep the floor, and scrub and mop it before I move on to clean each lavatory. I clean each toilet and the urinal before I go into the shower. I clean each soap dish. I clean each window and then wipe down all the surfaces with a damp cloth to get any dust. When I get through with that, I take Brasso and polish every faucet, shower head, drain pipe and handle that is made of metal. By now, the whole place shines like the pictures of bathrooms in the Montgomery & Ward catalog. After that, I go and make sure that everyone has their things lined up in order and their beds properly made.

I have been coached about how I am to report when the inspecting officer comes in. I practice what I am going to do. "ATTENTION!" "Barracks Orderly reporting, Sir." "Barracks is ready for inspection, Sir." And then I follow him around and answer any questions he may have and note anything he may tell me. I wait by the door for the officer to appear. I wait all morning and no one appears. Then the other guys are back, pouring into the latrine and barracks messing them up. They then leave to go to dinner and I follow them. After dinner and mail call, I wait until everyone has gone back out, I give the latrine a quick once over and then fall out to join them for the rest of the day. I have time to go on one of the problems, get one session of PT and then get ready for retreat. After supper, we go to a class on pulling guard. We are taught about using passwords, with sign and countersign. I go to take my shower and the latrine does not look like it did when I finished with it this morning, but that is another guy's problem now.

Thursday and the training continues. This morning after drill, breakfast and PT, we go to another class on pulling guard. We go over the General Orders for Sentries and then pair off to work on memorizing them. We say them over and over until we have them memorized and can recite each, when asked the number.

After dinner, we have another class on what to do when we are on guard in a combat situation and when it is over, we go and run a physical training course. This takes us up to retreat and after supper, we change back into our fatigues, put on full pack, and steel helmet and, with our rifles, we fall out for another five-mile hike. This one is not as bad because it is cooler in the evening. When we get back, I get my things cleaned up and put away and as soon as I shower, I slide into bed.

Friday morning after PT, they tell us that we are going to move. We are moving from barracks 2056 to 2055, right next door. That is not so bad. We just switch things. Two of us pickup a foot locker and carry it next door and carry an empty one back. We pick up the mattress and blankets off of one bunk and move it over and carry the other mattress back. It looks kind of like a string of ants moving things, but we take turns and it moves rather smoothly. No one seems to know why we are moving; I guess it is just the army way. Now I have to change my mailing address, so that I will not have to go next door for mail call. Then it is PT again, retreat and supper, followed by GI night. It is a job; the last ones to live in this barracks left it dirty and we must get it cleaned so it will pass inspection in the morning. There are no brooms or mops, so we have to go back and get the ones from our former barracks. It takes longer, but we get it cleaned up.

Saturday morning, we fall out for drill and after breakfast we fall out for inspection. When it is over, we change into fatigues with rain coats, because it looks like rain. It is humid, but we start marching towards the rifle range, to get a view of it before we shoot next week. We do not go far when it starts to pour. We put on our rain coats and keep on going. I do not like the lightning, and am glad I do not have my rifle to act as a lightning rod. It rains harder and harder and the ground gets covered with water. It stops raining and we are able to see where we will be working in the target pits and also the shooting positions. We march back to the barracks, and before we are dismissed, they announce that the class A passes are available in the orderly room and that we can pick them up when we are ready to leave the post. We cheer and then are released until Monday morning.

I go into the barracks and start taking my wet clothes off. I wring them out and hang them where they can get dried out, before I put them into the dirty clothes bag. I put on one of my extra sets of fatigues to lie around in. I will have to change into class A uniform before I can leave the area, but right now, I do not plan on going anywhere. Most of the guys are getting dressed to leave. Not too many guys are left here for dinner. After dinner, I go to mail call and get a couple of letters and then settle down on my bunk to read the letters and answer them. When I am done, I take a nap. After supper, I change clothes and go to the PX and then to the movie. I get back and have not been in bed long before the guys that went on pass start returning. They tell what it was like and then start telling about the carnival that is in Junction City. They have a "girlie show." It seems that most of these young guys were impressed. I decide to go tomorrow. I am ready to be corrupted.

I wake up on Sunday morning and the first thing I think of is going to the girlie show. I eat breakfast as usual and get a copy of the Sunday paper to read. I am not going to go into town until afternoon. I go ahead and get dressed, but decide that maybe I should go to church, before I go sinning. To save money, I eat dinner before I go to town. After dinner, I go by the orderly room to pick up my pass and to sign out. There is a box of condoms and pro kits on the counter and I am reminded by the Charge of Quarters to take one with me, when I go on leave. I pick up one of each, but do not plan on using them. He admonishes me to be careful off of the post and I go to the PX where the bus stop is located. While I am waiting for the bus, I look at my pass. It is a light-orange-colored, thick paper, with my picture fastened to it. I look at my picture and I see a skinny guy with a pointed cap perched on top of his head. My ears stick out and there is a white stripe across my face down over my chin, where the chin strap of my helmet liner has prevented my face from getting burned. Certainly not the handsome soldier that I imagine myself to be.

The bus comes and I get in line to board. The bus fills up and takes off. When we reach the gate, the bus stops and the MP gets on and tells us to hold up our passes. He then walks through the bus and looks to see that each soldier has a pass and then gets off and we are on our way. It's the first time I have been out of camp, other than when I was traveling on the train, for over four weeks. We get into Junction City and the bus stops and we all pile off. I walk down the street and see very few people that are not soldiers. It is Sunday, but most of the stores are open. There are pawn shops and stores selling souvenirs of the army or Fort Riley, cheap, shoddy merchandise. And, of course stores are selling insignia for the uniforms. Many of the businesses have signs that say "off limits to military personnel." For some reason the commanding officer thinks that we should not do business there.

I work my way down the streets and notice that a lot of guys are going off towards the east side of town. I walk that way too and, in a little bit, I see the carnival. It is not much of a carnival; a few rides for little kids and some booths where you can try to use your skill to win a prize. The prize is not worth what it costs to try, but it does not seem to bother a lot of guys. I keep walking and when I get to the far side, there is a tent with a sign on it advertising "Fatima and her seven veils." I decide that must be what I am here for. I move closer to the crowd. There is a sign that tells the times of the show and I notice that it is only fifteen minutes until the next show. I get in line to buy a ticket and the price is two dollars. It is a lot of money, but I guess sin is not cheap. I get my ticket and move closer to the tent. I only have to wait about ten minutes before a guy comes out and pulls back the flap of the tent allowing us to go inside. We start pushing into the tent and more and more guys are coming in. We are just packed. They get every possible person into the tent before they close the flap back up. Only two of the guys here are not in uniform. Most have the telltale sign of being in basic training. We wait for the show to start and we are pressed tight against each other. It is humid and the sun is bearing down on the tent. Sweat is pouring from everyone. There is the smell of hot canvas and of body odor. I hope that it starts soon.

After what seems like a half hour, but is only about ten minutes, a guy comes out on the small stage and winds up a record player and starts a scratchy record playing what is supposed to be a Mid-eastern song. As the music plays, a woman enters from the side of the stage. She is wrapped in several silk scarves. She dances across the stage and turns and goes back, the scarves flying. I look up at her face and she is about my mother's age, and her body has seen much better days too. As she races around the stage to the sound of the music, she casts off the scarves one after another, until there she is, in all of her naked glory. Nothing on but a pair of high heeled shoes. The first naked female I have ever seen. My eyes get big and I feel the sweat pouring off of me and not all is because of the temperature. She then moves about the stage swinging her ample breasts and shaking her hips to the scratchy music. She then faces away from the audience and bends slightly at the hips and begins to shake her butt. She shakes it rapidly side to side and then when she gets it going real good, she moves one leg so that it throws that side of her butt out of time and the two cheeks of her ass smack together, with a loud noise, just like someone clapping their hands. Everyone cheers to the sound, including me. I have never seen anything like it. We do not applaud because we are pressed in so tight we can't get our arms up, but she knows that we enjoyed the show.

I move out of the tent and find my way back to the bus stop. I am ready to go back; I have seen enough for one day. I stop at the PX and get a pint of ice cream to eat on the way back to the barracks. When I get back, the other guys are waiting to hear what I thought of the show. And I am only too glad to give my impression. I have finished my first three weeks of basic training; only fourteen more to go.

CHAPTER XVII

Week four is to be spent on the rifle range. We get up at five-thirty and breakfast is at six. No drill this morning. We hike out to the rifle range right after breakfast. We will be eating in the field at noon. I draw target pit duty first. We march along side of the range until we reach the pit area. Then we are each assigned to a target. We will be sitting on this ledge, while they shoot over our heads. The targets are in a wooden frame and are attached to weights, by cables that go over pulleys, to raise and lower the targets. We have patches for the targets and also a black disc on a pole, so we can hold it in front of the target and show the shooter where they hit. If they miss the whole target, we have a red flag that we wave, known as "Maggie's drawers."

The firing lines are earthen pads, raised a couple of feet above the surface of the ground. The rifle range is located on a large flat area that at one time was the bed of the Republican River. The river has since moved about a mile south and left this flat plain bounded by the river on the south and by a cliff, about a hundred feet high, on the north. Down in the pit we can look behind us and see the cliff and the gouged out areas on the face of it where bullets have impacted. In front of the pit, dirt has been pushed up for several feet, to form a protective barrier for the pits.

The guy down at the end, on the telephone, hollers that they are going to start shooting and to listen for hits. I start to hear the sharp crack of bullets going through the air but I can't tell which target they are on. I finally realize that my target has been hit, so I pull it down, patch the hole and run it back up. I take my marker and hold it over the bullet hole, which is down in the right hand corner. It is not long before another bullet hits it. This time, I can tell from the sound that it is my target. He is closer to the black this time. We keep this up for some time as they are sighting their rifles in.

As one group finishes sighting in their rifles, another group takes their place. We are busy, but the work is not that hard and the morning goes fast. At noon, we gather up our things and go out to the firing line for chow. The food has been brought out in insulated metal cans holding about fifteen gallons each. As we go through the line, we have to learn for the first time how to use a mess kit. Open it up, take out the knife, fork and spoon and put them into your pocket. Slide the tab on the lid over the handle, leaving it flat on top of the handle and with the bottom part out in front of you. This makes the lid kind of a second plate. They take ladles and slap the food into your mess kit. You better have a good hold or it will fly out of your hand. Some of the guys find that their lid goes to the ground when the first spoonful hits it. We carry the mess kit in one hand and our canteen cup in the other. I get my stew and vegetables in my mess kit and my bread and sheet cake on the lid. Ice tea goes into my cup. I go to find a place to eat. There is no shade, since we are out on the range. It is hot and I realize how lucky we were in the pits in the morning when it is mostly shady. I eat my food and then go to wash my mess kit. This is another lesson. You turn the lid around and again put the tab over the handle so that it slides down along side of the other part. Then you use the holes in your knife, fork and spoon to slide them down the handle too. There is a garbage can to put any leftover food in. There are two garbage cans with heaters in them. The first has soapy water in it and a brush hanging there. You take the brush in one hand, dip the mess kit into the soapy water and scrub it clean. Then you go to the other can which at one time had clear water in it and rinse off your mess kit. You can shake it to get most of the water off, but the hot sun soon takes care of the rest.

Then it is time for my group to sight in our rifles. We open the bolt and approach the firing point. We each have a coach with us. The coach draws ten rounds of ammunition. Again, they give us our instructions about what we are supposed to do and about safety. We then take the prone position at our firing point and check to see which is the right target. I move my sight up the number of clicks for the starting point at two hundred yards. I load one round, sight at the target and pull the trigger. I did not know it would be this loud. I am right at the bottom of the target, but in the middle. The coach tells me to raise my sight. I raise the sight four clicks to get it up higher. This time, I am at the bottom of the four ring and just a little right. I keep shooting and adjusting my sight. It takes six shots before I get one into the black. I loosen the knob on my sight and move the two hundred yard mark next to the mark on the other side of the sight and then tighten it back down. My rifle is zeroed in.

After supper, we take off our good clothes and start working on cleaning our rifles. Someone yells "Mail call" and I have a letter from Mom and one from Don. Then it is back to cleaning the rifles. We are careful not to mess up the sight setting. After mine is clean, I read my letters and then take time to answer them. They will both be surprised to receive an answer so quick.

The next day starts off just like the day before. We get through the morning and then go to the firing line for chow again.

By now, the guys do better with their mess kits. I get mine out and it feels greasy from yesterday. No one has washed their mess kits today, so I walk over and wash mine again. The water is clean and hot now. I would rather have it wet than greasy. In this temperature, the food is still nice and hot even though it was cooked a couple of hours ago. The ice tea does not have any ice in it, but it is still cool. When we finish, we get ready for the next turn at shooting.

We draw our ammo and move to the firing point. I do very well following up from where I was shooting yesterday. Next is five rounds sitting. This time I feel I am uncomfortable and have a hard time holding the rifle still. My score is not as good either. The next is kneeling. I do better here. The final off hand position is comfortable for me, but the rifle seems awfully heavy and it does not have to move much to get out of the black.

When everyone finishes, we all hike back to the parade ground again and get in our day's PT before we go back to the barracks. They bring our mail when we get back, and I get a letter but do not have time to read it before we have to fall out for retreat. Of course, after supper, we have to clean our rifles for tomorrow. If it were not for the sun and the heat, the last two days would have been really easy. I have a little time so I write a letter to my aunt and uncle. I thank her for the chocolate chip cookies and tell her how much we enjoyed them. Then I slide into bed and know nothing until morning.

Another day at the range. After dinner, it is our turn to shoot. I take coach first and let my partner shoot. Then I get to shoot. It goes fairly smoothly. Then we move back to the three hundred yard line. The target gets a lot smaller from here. He shoots and when it is my turn to shoot, he gets called away to do something, so I am on my own. I am shooting prone and have shot all but eight rounds, which are in an M1 clip. One of the cadre men is watching me shoot, and he reaches down and takes the clip and pushes it into my rifle and the bolt closes. I know that we are supposed to be loading just one round at a time, but I do not want to say anything. I shoot a couple of rounds and then I notice a lieutenant walking along the line. He stops behind me. I do not want him to know that I have a whole clip in my rifle, so I wait to shoot. I wait and wait, but he just stands there. Finally I feel I can't wait any longer to shoot and so I fire and hope he will not notice. "What in hell are you doing? You know you are supposed to be loading single shot." I am not about to get the cadre man in trouble, so I do not say anything, I just pull the bolt back and hit the clip release and all the cartridges pop out. I put in one and fire and he seems satisfied and walks away.

We move back to the five hundred yard line. We start shooting and there are a lot of Maggie's drawers. It is easy to miss the whole target. I settle down and get my sight adjusted and start hitting the target, but not a great score. I am disappointed. I think that I should be able to do a lot better than I am doing. We finish up and the day ends just like the previous day.

It is Thursday and today we will shoot a practice round which is the same thing we will shoot tomorrow, when it is for record. The day is much like yesterday. I am not shooting bad, just not shooting good. The sun is hot and when I start to shoot, my rifle gets so hot that oil drips out of the stock. The heat waves come up off of the barrel and when you look across the range, the heat waves blur the target. It is not as noticeable on the two hundred yard position, but the three and particularly the five hundred are very bad. But I get through the day and can only hope for a better score tomorrow.

Today we shoot for record. The score we shoot today will be entered in our service record and will be there for everyone to see. I must try to do as good as I can. After dinner, our group gets to shoot. I shoot well on the two hundred yard line. Not so good on the three hundred, but still in line to make expert. But when I get to the five hundred, I just can't seem to find the bullseye. My rifle shimmers in the heat and the heat rising from the range makes the target appear wavy. I do the best I can but I am disappointed to find that I have only shot one hundred seventy three out of possible two hundred ten. It is good enough for sharpshooter, but I had my heart set on shooting expert. One guy shot two hundred one. He shot early in the morning. I notice that almost all of the higher shooters fired in the morning. Maybe that was the problem. Anyway, it is over now. After supper, it is GI night and after we get the barracks scrubbed down, I clean my rifle and equipment for inspection in the morning.

Sunday morning after breakfast, I go to the orderly room and pick up my pass and go catch the bus to Junction City. When I get there, I catch the bus to Manhattan. Fare is a dollar each way. I had heard that it is nicer than Junction City, and find that is right. It is a nice clean town. It has a university, so there are people other than soldiers to see. They have a public swimming pool and the next time I go, I will take my suit and go swimming. There is also a USO for the military. It has a large room with a pool table and then there is a kind of a barracks behind that with bunks where you can stay the night. I make up my mind to come back here before long. I spend a lot of time just sitting in a park and enjoying a quiet time alone. I get a hamburger for dinner, walk around some more, then catch the bus back to Junction City. I am back at the barracks in time for supper. Cold cuts again, but unlike a lot of the guys, I like cold cuts. I go to the movie after supper and stop at the PX for a pint of ice cream on the way back. I have now completed four weeks of basic.

CHAPTER XVIII

Monday morning after breakfast, we go to an area and sit around and they tell us about hand grenades. They show how they work and explain how to throw them. The grenades are nothing new to me, because Don brought home a deactivated one, when he came home from Camp Swift. I had played with it many times. They have stories about recruits getting nervous and dropping grenades. This makes me more nervous than the grenades themselves. Then they start talking about rifle grenades. I am not familiar with them. They have two kinds. The first is just a metal frame that you put a regular hand grenade in. Then you put it on the rifle grenade launcher and, using a special blank, fire it up into the air, so that it will lob into enemy territory. When fired, it causes the lever to fly off and activate the grenade. In effect, it just extends the range that you can throw one.

The next hour, they show us anti-tank rifle grenades. They look like a little round nose rocket, but they slip on to the rifle grenade launcher and are shot with a special blank. They have a shaped charge in the head that is detonated when it hits a solid object. It will blow a hole through several inches of armor plate.

The next session is about anti-tank rockets. They are fired through a tube which is known as a "bazooka." The rocket itself works like the anti-tank grenade, but the head is pointed and it has longer fins. The launcher is just a hollow metal tube with wooden handles. The tube is placed on the shoulder and you look through a metal sight on the side of the tube. To fire, you pull the trigger, which closes the circuit and sends a current into the rocket, igniting the propelling charge. The shooter can expect to have a ball of fire come back at him when the rocket leaves the tube. It sounds exciting; I am anxious to shoot it.

After dinner, we go to a class on map reading and compass. I do not have trouble reading the map, but I do not understand the different things we are supposed to do with a compass, to find where we are going. I check the bulletin board and find that I am on duty as a table waiter tomorrow. I will have to get up at four o'clock. I also notice, that the whole platoon is on emergency guard tomorrow night. We did not have to do that before we all qualified with the rifle. I write a letter and then get my things ready. The last thing I do is to hang a towel on the end of my bunk, so they will wake me up in the morning.

It is hard to get awake at four o'clock, but I get washed up and go to the mess hall. As table waiters, we are required to put things on the table that will be used for breakfast and help get the food ready to serve. Then while the troops are eating, we keep the coffee pitchers filled and make sure that there are ample supplies on each table. After breakfast, we empty the pitchers, put things away and then put hot soapy water in a pitcher and use it to scrub the tables with a brush. When I get through, I hurry to join my unit before it goes to the field. We march out into the field and after a rain last night, it is humid and hot. We really feel the heat. We practice looking at objects and then finding them on the map and figuring the compass route. I can see that this is going to be hard to do, especially at night. We march back at noon and I have to hurry to the mess hall and get my tables ready for the others to eat. About the only good thing about being table waiter is, you don't get to eat until the others finish, but you can have anything you want that is left over.

When I get through cleaning up, I follow them to where we were yesterday and we have additional lessons on grenades and rockets. We go back for PT, but I go and clean up and go to the mess hall. I work until seven-thirty cleaning before I get to go back to the barracks. I sit down on my bunk to take my clothes off, but before I can even untie my boots, we get the command to fall out for emergency guard. We grab our rifle belts, helmets and rifles and race outside. When we are all in formation, they tell us that we are too slow, and that we will be called out later.

When we are dismissed, I race back, take a shower and put my clothes back on and lay down on my bunk, resting before our next alert. I do not have to wait long. This time I have all my things where I can grab them as I run for the stairs and then out the door and get into my spot. We are a lot faster this time and they tell us that we have done okay and if we are called out again tonight, it will be for real. I do not know what they really expect, but we will be ready. I put my things beside my bunk and lay down on top of my blankets with my clothes on. I am soon asleep.

Today we march out into the field to study how to shoot at targets at unknown ranges. On the way out, we have to move off of the road to make way for twenty light tanks. Even though it rained yesterday, it has all dried out and the tanks make so much dust that we can't see.

At dinner time, I go to mail call and get a letter from Mom and one from Richard Gritz. It is good to hear from home. Then in the afternoon, we go out in the field again and practice throwing dummy hand grenades. I am fairly accurate, but do not have enough body strength to throw them very far. But, of course, I am a lot stronger than I was when I got here. I get to find out just how strong I am, when we finish with the grenades. We go to a long obstacle course and have to run it. They have all kinds of things to go over, under, or through. A few of them are designed for team work and we have to help each other.

After supper, there are a half dozen little boys standing around the barracks with their shoe shine kits. Almost everyone has at least one pair of shoes they want shined. The boys are good at it and can shine a pair in just a few minutes. At a quarter for each pair, they make as much as we soldiers do. I have them shine two pair.

After I get my clothes off to go to bed, I check my right leg right above my ankle. The rivet on my legging has rubbed on my leg and at first it was a blister. Then it broke, but now the scab has come loose and black blood is coming out. I clean it off and one of the guys has some Vaseline and I put some of that on it before I go to bed. If you have something wrong, usually it is better to just tough it out. I have not been on sick call yet, but those that have, usually say that they did not get any help.

Today we study the 1911A1 pistol. We learn to take it all apart and to put it back together. The ones they have for us to use have been used a lot and are badly worn, but I guess they will still shoot. I haven't fired a pistol very many times and never one as big as a .45, but I am anxious to get to shoot it.

We go back to the area early for dinner and line up for payday at the orderly room. They have instructed us on how to act, when we get paid. "Step in front of the paymaster, identify yourself with name and serial number. Then present your pay book. You will sign the payroll and they will count out your money to you. You step away and count it again before leaving." I go through the line and am paid $35.60, after deductions for insurance, laundry and savings bond.

After supper, we change back into our fatigues and then fall out with full packs, steel helmets and rifles. We are going on a seven-mile hike. It is hot to start with and the straps rub through the sweat soaked fatigues, but after the sun goes down it cools off enough so that it is not too bad.

This morning after breakfast, we march down to the Republican River bottom among the trees. We have a class on explosives. They demonstrate how to prepare them. They show us some of the different kinds of explosives that we will be using. They have TNT and nitrostarch.   The nitrostarch is not as powerful, but safer to use. They show us primacord which is like cord but is made up of explosive. You can light it with a match and it will just burn like any other cord, but if you fasten a blasting cap to it and set it off, the primacord explodes at a rate of 23,000 feet per second. It can be wrapped around something that you want cut, such as a beam or tree, and then fired.

We go back in for dinner and after dinner we return to the river so that we can make our own explosive charges. We take a piece of fuse and crimp an igniter to one end and then a blasting cap to the other, being careful when we crimp the cap to hold it behind us so if it explodes, it will get our butt instead of our face. We then punch a hole into a quarter-pound block of nitrostarch and stick the cap into it. They examine our work and if it is okay, we get to light the fuse and throw it into the woods. It is the loudest bang that I have ever made. Later they set off one pound blocks fastened together with primacord. When we are through with our lesson, we go for PT and then retreat. After supper, it is GI night.

Saturday morning after breakfast, we have inspection and when it is over, we are released for the weekend. Most of the guys take off but a few of us stay. I have my Readers Digest and I read it and take a nap in the afternoon.

I spend Sunday like most Sundays. After breakfast, I read the paper and go to church. In the afternoon, I take another nap and try to get rested up. But this Sunday is different. I have guard duty to-night. I report to the guardhouse after supper with my rifle and get my instructions. I am to guard the road leading into our area. After ten o'clock at night, we are to challenge anyone entering or leaving the area. There are two other guys that have the same area that I do and we will take turns of two hours on and four hour hours off. When we are off, we sleep in our clothes, because we are on call. For the first time, we are issued live ammunition, a clip with seven rounds, so that we have ammo in our rifles but the chamber will be empty. It only takes a second to pull back the bolt and load a round into the chamber. The night is uneventful.

CHAPTER XIX

This morning after breakfast, we have follow-up instruction on the .45 pistol. After dinner, we march out to the pistol range and get ready to shoot. They hand each shooter a pistol and each coach a magazine. The coach then picks up eight rounds of ammo and we move up to the firing line. The targets are life-sized silhouettes of a man. They are not very far away. In fact, I can see the large heads of the nails that hold them to the stake. I am to shoot first. I aim at the nail head. I figure that if I can hit both nail heads, the target will fall down and everyone will get a laugh out of that. I shoot and do not see a hole, so I must have hit the nail. I shoot at the other nail and again I do not see a hole, but the target did not fall. I fire another shot at each of the nail heads and the target remains standing. I aim right at the middle of the target and shoot and a hole appears down in the lower right hand corner. The next two shots hit the right and left shoulders. I do not know where the final shot goes. We score our targets and I have three out of eight. I can't believe it.

We shift positions and the other guy shoots. I warn him about trying to hold right in the middle and he is able to get four of his in the target. The next time we shoot, we each get five hits. I can see that this pistol is going to take some getting used to. We clean all of the pistols and turn them in. We then find that we have qualified. We are notified that we will have to stand inspection in the morning. The sergeant tells everyone to be sure and shave in the morning. I ask if that means me too and he says "No, but wash your face." That means after supper, we will have to GI the barracks again and get all of our things cleaned.

After breakfast, we are called out for inspection. The captain shows up and goes over everything. Almost everything is okay. A few of the guys get gigs. The first sergeant makes note and I am sure that they will be on one of the work rosters. After inspection, we attend class and review the procedure for throwing live hand grenades. After dinner, we march out to the grenade range. Most of us are back behind a big bunker and the guys who will be throwing, each go to a small bunker, which is manned by one of the cadre. Each bunker has a hole in the floor for the cadre to either throw or kick a loose grenade into. And of course, someone will be telling about some recruit that let the lever go on the grenade and just stood holding it, frozen with fear. That is almost enough to make you drop one.

When it is my time to go into the bunker, I walk in and the cadre man hands me a grenade out of the box. He says "Lovell, don't be nervous, just follow the commands and you will be okay." I tell him that I am okay with it. I follow the commands and throw it. They do not have to tell me to duck down. I get down below the wall fast. It takes longer than I thought it would to go off. He tells me that I did okay, but to try to get it out further this time. We go through it again. By the third time, there is nothing to it. I could take one and play catch with it. This is great for my confidence. I then throw my last grenade as far as I can.

We march back and do PT on the way back in. We get ready for retreat and at retreat they announce that we are going on a hike after supper. We are traveling light this evening, no steel helmet, pack or rifle. It will just be a five-mile hike around the area. It is a good thing because it is so hot. We are already worn out from the day's activities. The hike goes fairly quickly and we are back to the barracks.

The barracks are hot; there is not much air coming through the windows. I do get some air because of the natural draft coming up the stairs, but just that many men creates a lot of heat. The afternoons are so hot and the strong wind is like a blast furnace. My face is burned so badly, it is hard to find a way to lay my head without it hurting. I am sitting on my bunk lacing up the shoes I wore today and unlacing the ones I will wear tomorrow, when a there is a loud commotion down at the other end of the barracks. Then here come five guys, dragging another guy, through the barracks. He is struggling with them, but they have him in their control. They go down the steps and I can hear yelling. I ask someone what is going on and he says that they are going to give the guy a GI bath. That he has not been taking baths and they have had all of it they can stand. Some of the guys come back upstairs and tell us that they put him in the shower, turned it on and stripped his clothes off. They then took GI soap and a brush and scrubbed him down. The soap is harsh lye soap and the brush is very stiff, used to scrub down the floor. In a little while the five guys come back up and start changing out of their wet clothes. After that, the bath recipient comes up and he now has a rosy complexion and leaves no doubt that he is squeaky clean. I bet he takes baths from now on.

I talk to one of the guys that did the scrubbing and he says it finally got so bad that they told the first sergeant about the guy not bathing. That the first sergeant said for them to take care of it and that he did not want to know anything about it. Well, they did.

Today we are out in the field doing a problem with live ammo. We are working as a squad. We start out and go around to a dry creek and follow it, until we are in range of the targets. When the targets pop up, we open fire on them. After that we go back and they tell us what we did wrong.

They bring food out in the field and we eat and then they try an experiment. They give us salt water to drink. Someone got the crazy idea that if we had salt water in our systems that we would not get so exhausted. Then we start on the afternoon problem. We go a different direction this time and go up a hill, where we can fire down on the targets. Everyone is feeling sick. I fall down to shoot at the targets and start vomiting. The rocks we are laying on are so hot they burn our bare skin. We all go back and there are guys laying everywhere. They bring out some water with lemon juice in it and half of us get to drink it. The other half just get plain water. Then we start the march back to our area. All but one of us who got the water with lemon in it make it back, but none of the guys that only got plain water make it. They have trucks going along and picking them up and hauling them in. I hope they quit using us to experiment on.

When they call us to fall out for retreat, over half of the guys are not able to make it. A half dozen of the guys had to be taken to the infirmary. I guess I am lucky because I have bounced back some. We go to supper and most do not eat much. I am hungry because I did not keep my dinner down, so I eat. But we all drink ice tea and water as fast as they can fill our glasses.

Today we go to the building where we will study communications. They show us around and show some of the equipment that we will be using. Then we watch a movie before going back for dinner. At least we have cold ice tea today instead of salt water. I think all of the guys are okay today, but it is a wonder that we did not lose some for good yesterday. After dinner, they divide us up with the guys in horse cavalry going to one place and the rest of us going to the motor pool to look over the vehicles that we will be using in our training. I assume that the horse guys are doing the same thing at the stables.

After supper, it is GI night and when we go to clean up, we find that all of our brooms and mops are missing. We have to wait until the barracks next door get done, so we can borrow theirs. Some of the guys want to go out right then and steal back some mops and brooms but I tell them to wait until tomorrow night.

Saturday morning after inspection, we are free for the weekend, except those assigned to duty. I write some letters and catch up on the news.   In the afternoon, I lie down and take a nap and try to get my tired body ready for next week.

After supper, I gather some of the guys and make plans for our raid.   There are nine of us and I tell them to wait until just as it is getting dark.   Then we will split up and everyone will go to a different area.   We each will walk along the area behind the barracks and when we see a barracks with no one around, take only one thing, either a broom or a mop.   Then we will walk alongside the barracks to the street and, carrying the broom or mop over our shoulder, just walk slowly back to our barracks.   If someone catches you, just say that you need to borrow it for a few minutes to clean up a mess.   If he raises a fuss, just give it to him and say that you will find someone else that will loan one to you.

We sit around the barracks visiting until it is time to go on the raid.   Then we go out and spread out.   I go five barracks down on the other side of the street.   I grab a mop off of the rack and walk to the street and back to the barracks.   Within fifteen minutes, we are all back with four mops and five brooms; just the right amount.   Maybe our training is paying off.   We carried that raid off without a hitch.

Sunday, I intend to go to church, but I lie down after I read the paper and go to sleep and never wake up until someone asks me if I am going to chow.   I intend to rest today, because I have stable guard tonight.   After supper, I get dressed for guard and go to the guard house and report for duty.

When the Officer of the Day shows up, he issues me a .45 and holster.   He then hands me a clip of ammo with seven rounds.   I get the first shift, so I walk to the stable that I am to guard.   Most of the stalls have horses in them and they watch me as I walk up and down the building.   I move to the next building and then the third.   When I complete a round, I go back to the first and when I enter, there is a horse loose.   I try to get him to go into his stall, but he runs right past me to the other end of the building.   I go down to that end and he runs to the other end.   He does this five times before he goes into his stall.   But at least my two hour shift goes fast and I get to go to the guardhouse for four hours. I pull all of my shifts and then head back to the barracks to change clothes and get ready for the next week.

CHAPTER XX

Today we start communications training. We learn about continuous wave or CW. The signal is sent out by an AM radio and the message is transmitted by breaking the wave in long and short breaks. Some call it Morse Code, but it is a different version. We just call it code. After an introduction, we start lessons on writing block letters, which are used for messages. They show the way to make each letter the fastest. We practice writing messages, using this type of writing. Then we learn the signals for each letter. We call them dots and dashes.

In the afternoon, our platoon goes to the motor pool and we see a film about driving the army way. The horse platoon goes to the stables and I guess they learn which end of the horse is which. Since the only thing that I have driven is an old slow tractor, I will have a lot to learn. Then we go over the vehicles that we will be driving, and they show us the different instruments and equipment. After supper, we have another class on communications, this time, the use of the field telephone.

This morning, the horse platoon goes to the stables and we go to the motor pool. We get into the vehicles and drive them out to the driving range. We take turns driving around the course and up and down hills. I am surprised at how steep a hill they can climb. I take my turn first on a three-quarter truck. This is really one of the easiest times we have had, because if you are not driving, you are just riding around. I am glad I am doing this instead of trying to ride a horse.

After dinner, we all go to the communications building. Today we put headphones on and listen to a recording of code. It is very slow and gives you a chance to figure out what the letter is. We start with the most used letters and learn them. My trouble is hearing the letter and writing at the same time.

After supper, we get our equipment ready for tomorrow. Tomorrow night we will hike out into the country and spend the night in camp and then return the next day. It will be our first night out of the barracks.

Today we continue our communications instruction by learning how to string wire and how to splice wire. We learn the best places to lay wire, so that it will not be damaged, and how to tie it to different objects to keep it in place. Then we are shown how to make an "all weather" splice.

After supper, we fall out with full equipment ready to go on an overnight hike. They check to see if we have what we need and then we move out. We go about five or six miles out to a grove of woods and they mark out an area for us to pitch our tents. I am bunking with my squad leader, Burkemper, and so we button our shelter halves together. We scrape the ground down inside of our tent to make sure we have all of the sticks off of it and then lay out our blankets to sleep on. I use my pack, with what is left in it, for a pillow. It has been a couple of months since I have slept in one of these tents. Some of the guys are still trying to figure out how to put theirs together. Three other guys are detailed to go dig a slit trench latrine, some distance from the tents.

We will have to pull guard tonight. Two hours on and four off. We have enough guys and small enough area that we will each only have to do one shift. I elect to do the first shift. I would rather do that than have to get up in a couple of hours. Before I start guard duty, I go to the latrine. I am standing on the side urinating, when the bank where I am standing, caves in, dropping me into the ditch. There are several guys standing around and it is not long before they are all kidding me about falling into the latrine.

I start guard and it is not even dark yet, but it is by the time my shift is over. I take off my shoes and leggings and my fatigue top but leave my pants on. No need to cover up because it is still hot even after dark.

They wake us up at daylight and tell us to get ready to move out. The last thing is to cover up the latrine. The lieutenant laughs and says that I do not have to help, since I filled up most of it, last night.

Today we go to the communications building and practice on our code. I have a hard time learning it. It seems that I can't get the letters and write them before the next letter comes. I keep thinking about that test I took at Ft. Sill and how I guessed at those sounds. Maybe if I had not guessed so many right, I would not have to do this. But then I remember if I were not here, I would be in the horse cavalry. I am determined to learn these.

In the afternoon, we split up and the horse platoon goes to ride horses and we go to drive vehicles on a road march. We take turns driving and each of us drives about three or four miles. We are in convoy, but do not cover much territory, because we stop so often to change drivers.

It is Friday again and I am a table waiter. They get me up at four and I go to work before four-thirty. When I get off at noon I go to join the class on the .30 caliber machine gun, then back to the mess hall. It is ten o'clock at night before I get off. After that I have to get my things ready for inspection in the morning. At least I did not have to GI the barracks tonight.

After Saturday morning inspection, I decide that since I do not have anything until Sunday evening, that I will go to Manhattan. I am already in my class A uniform, so I get my swimming suit and a towel, pick up my pass at the orderly room and sign out. In Junction

City, I catch the bus to Manhattan. I go to the public swimming pool when I get there and go swimming.

The water feels so good on my body. I just relax and slowly swim around the pool. I stay a couple of hours. When I get out, I go to the little snack stand and get a hotdog for my late lunch. I walk towards the center of the city and the location of the USO. I ask the woman working there to reserve a bunk for me. She says, "Honey, we do not have any left. They have all been taken." I thank her and then go out to look around. I go to the parks and sit and watch the little kids playing. I meet a couple of other soldiers in the park and we go look around at the business district. There is not much for a soldier to buy. And it is a good thing because we do not have much money. In the evening we go to a café for supper.

We go in and sit at a table and after awhile the waitress brings us water and a menu. In most restaurants these days, it takes a long time to get waited on because of the shortage of help. But here in Manhattan, the university provides an ample supply of labor and the waitress is soon back to take our order. One of the guys orders fried chicken, the other orders veal cutlet and I order the chicken fried steak. We all three order Cokes. Even though it is Saturday night, we get our food quickly and it tastes good after a diet of army chow. The chicken fried steak is a dollar and the coke is a dime. Tax is two cents and I leave a fifteen-cent tip.

We walk around some more then head for the USO. One of the guys had got there in time to get the last bunk. We play pool and keep asking the woman if they have anybody not show up. The one guy leaves us and goes to his bunk and we keep playing pool. The woman closes the counter and goes home. It is all quiet except for the click of the pool balls. After a little bit, we look at each other and he says, "Hell, yes." We put all the balls in the pockets, rack the cue sticks and he takes one side of the table and I take the other. My suit and towel have dried, so I use them as a pillow and we are soon asleep.

We wake up before anyone else in the morning and get up and sit in the chairs waiting until someone comes and makes the coffee and gets out the doughnuts. A different lady shows up and she makes the coffee and brings out the doughnuts. She asks if we have been here all night and we say yes. I am sure that she meant in the chairs, but we did not tell her any different. I was going to go swimming today, but the pool does not open until two o'clock, so I decide to go back to the post. I make it to dinner and then take a nap in the afternoon. My bunk, as hard as it is, is still softer than a pool table. I wake up in time for supper and head over to the mess hall for cold cuts, buns, ice tea and watermelon. Then I check to make sure that my rifle is clean and that I look okay and I go report to the guard house for guard duty. I have to take my rifle, but when I get there, they issue me a .45 to carry again. I hope that there are no problems tonight.

CHAPTER XXI

It is a good thing I took a nap yesterday afternoon, because I only got two hours and five minutes sleep all night, on guard duty. I get back to the barracks in time to change clothes and go to breakfast. Then we go to school and work on learning code. It is such a struggle for me; I am so sleepy that I can hardly hold my head up. It will take a long time at this rate to learn what I need to know.

After supper, we go on another hike. Just a four-mile hike this time, with full equipment. I do okay while we are marching, but when we stop to rest, I doze off and they wake me when it is time to go. When we get back, it does not take me long to get into bed.

Today we have school in the morning and in the afternoon we have a class on the .30 caliber machine gun. Of course, we have PT in the evening and after supper, we go back to the communications building for a couple of hours of code. We will have one hundred and fifteen hours of code, total. During that time, I will have to get to where I can take it and write it down at the rate of thirteen words a minute. I am on table waiter again tomorrow. I hang a towel on my bunk and go to bed early.

They get me up at four o'clock again, I clean up and head for the mess hall. I have been on table waiter enough that I know what

to do without being told. We finish breakfast cleanup and then I
march out to the machine gun range. I get to fire the .30 caliber, but
they take the fun out of it. We have to practice shooting using the
knobs to adjust the gun and then they make us just bump the trigger
to fire. We can only fire one or two shots at a time. I would love to
hold down the trigger for a little bit, but they are standing right over
me and they would kill me if I tried to. When we finish shooting,
we march back to the area and clean machine guns. We have to be
careful taking them apart. If you let the spring get loose, it could kill
someone. As soon as they are clean, I have to go back to the mess
hall again.

I finish table waiting at noon and then go to study code until
three. It is PT for an hour, then stand retreat until time to go to the
mess hall. I get off of table waiter duty at ten o'clock and then have
to get my things ready for the next day. It has been another long
day.

Today we have class at the communications building all day.
Then PT and retreat and after supper, we go on a twelve-mile hike.
We travel light this time. It cools off after sundown and the heat
does not bother so much. We are late getting in and by the time we
all get cleaned up bed is mighty welcome. But before bed, we get
the mops and brooms and put them in the latrine. We are not going
to have to do without them, tomorrow night.

Everyone is talking about the news. Mickey Rooney is in the
army and is taking basic training right down the street. Some of
our guys have friends in the same unit that Mickey is in. They have
been talking to them and it seems that things are not all fun. Their
story is that when Mickey is put on some duty, that he hires some
other guy, for big bucks, to do it for him. This makes the cadre mad,
not that someone else is doing his duties for him, but that they are
not getting the money. The story makes some of our guys furious
that he should be able to pay his way out of doing what we have to
do. They say that the public should know what is going on. Three
or four of them decide to write to Walter Winchell and tell him about
it. They spend some time getting the letter written.

Today we go out in the field for some squad problems. Our squad is made up of eight men. Two squads practice locating an objective using a map and compass and then advance on it following hand signals. It works much better if we know each other well. We spend the morning doing this and then after dinner we go back out to another area and do it again. We have our daily PT on the way back in. After retreat and supper, we GI the barracks. I tell the guys to take off the window screens and I will clean them. I take off all of my clothes and gather up all of the screens and take them to the latrine and get in the shower. I wash them good and then take them back and hang them up to dry. Of course, while I am washing them, I am also getting my shower as well. By the time I get through with them, the rest of the barracks is clean, I put my clothes on and I am that much ahead of all the others.

Saturday morning after breakfast we stand inspection and then go to the communications building and take code. Since this is not dirty work, we will not have to change back into our fatigues. When class is over, all who do not have duty over the weekend are free until Monday morning. Some go ahead and leave to get ahead of the rush at the bus stop, but most save some money by eating dinner before they go.

I decide to go to Junction City just to get off of the post for awhile. I look around in town for a little while, but there is not much difference here than on the post because everywhere you look there are soldiers. I catch the bus back and I am in time for supper.

Sunday I get a paper after breakfast and read it before I go to church. In the afternoon, I write letters to several people. My father's half brother sent me a beautiful hand tooled leather billfold and I write a letter thanking him. I finish reading my Reader's Digest before supper. After supper I walk to the PX and get a pint of ice cream for dessert.

The guys turn on the radio to listen to Walter Winchell to see what he says about Mickey Rooney. They are disappointed that he has nothing to say about it. Someone points out that he probably did not have time to get it in this week's news, but that he will probably have it in next week. Then I get my laundry ready and lay out clean clothes for the next week before going to bed.

CHAPTER XXII

We start the week out by going to a lecture on poison gas. They describe the different kinds and their effects. They issue each of us a gas mask and show us how to put it on and use it. Then we go out and they line us up and shoot off samples of diluted gases, so that we can learn the odor of them. They shoot off the sample of phosgene, right in front of me and the gas goes right to me and the half a dozen guys next to me. When we smell it, we can't help it, we have to get away from it. They keep yelling at us to get back in line, but it takes a few minutes, before we can get ourselves turned around and get back, where we are supposed to be. It is easy to see how this gas could be used to break down an enemy's defense.

Next, we are introduced to the gas chamber. Today it is filled with tear gas. A group of us are herded into the chamber and the door is closed. We then take out our gas masks, put them on and clear them. We stay in the chamber for a little while, and then they open the door and we go outside. There we take off our masks and let the air clear the tears from our eyes. I have tears running down and dripping off of my chin, by the time I get my mask off. That is just from the tear gas I got before I could get my mask on.

After everyone has gone through, we let our masks get aired and dried out and pack them away. Then we march back to the area in time for dinner. We have mail call and I get a letter from Mom. In the afternoon, we go to the communications building and work on code. It is not ventilated very well and with all of us in there, the residue from the tear gas that is in our clothes starts coming out. It gets so bad, that they let us take our break early so we can get outside in the wind and get aired out. Then we go back inside and I do well enough on the code to move up to the ten words per minute table. I still have a ways to go to get to thirteen, which is required to graduate.

After class, we do our PT, get cleaned up for retreat and then eat supper. After supper, we go back and study code for a couple of hours. Before I go to bed, I write a couple of letters. I have to buy the paper and envelopes that I use, but to mail a letter, I do not need a stamp. I just write "Free" in the corner, where the stamp would go. This is a help because it would be hard for us to get stamps.

It is Tuesday and today we will get to know the M1 carbine. In the morning, we go to a classroom and they pass out one carbine for each two guys.

We learn to take them apart and put them together. They seem real small compared to the M1 rifle. They are not hard to take apart, except for the slide that has to be lined up just right before it will come loose. The sight is a little "L" shaped piece with a hole in each end.

After dinner, we hike out to the range and take turns shooting the carbine. We fire it at both one hundred fifty yards and three hundred yards. After shooting the M1 rifle, it is more like a toy. But with the sights as they are, no one does very well. But it is obvious that some carbines shoot better than others. The one I have is neither the best nor the worst.

We march back in and then get the job of cleaning the carbines before they are turned in. When we finish, we go for PT, retreat and supper.

We spend the whole day at the communications building. They introduce us to a couple of radios that we will be using. The first is a portable set that is carried on the back. It is powered by a generator that is turned by hand. The generator is carried by another person. The second radio is one that is large and mounted in a vehicle. They tell us that it cost the army thirty-five hundred dollars. I guess they tell us that so we will know how much we will have to pay if we ruin it. It would take me eight years to pay for one at my rate of pay. Come to think of it, soldiers are about the cheapest thing that the army has to pay for.

They have a bicycle at the communications building and they explain that if we are sent to deliver a message to someone in the camp, we can ride the bicycle and that when we are riding it, the procedure is just like when riding a horse. You stay on the right side of the road and observe all traffic signs and rules. If you meet an officer, you sit up straight and salute as you pass.

When we get through with the radios, we spend the rest of the day on the code tables. After supper we fall out with full equipment and head out in the country. As soon as we are out of our area, we go into route step and in a little over two hours we are back. Then we clean equipment and ourselves before going to bed. Tomorrow, I am on duty as latrine orderly.

After breakfast, the men march off without me and I go to work cleaning up the latrine. By now, I know pretty well what needs to be done and I get it done. At noon, the guys come back in from their problem and I am off latrine duty. After noon, my platoon is to go to the communications building and the other platoon is to go out in the field for the problem. I ask the lieutenant if I can go on the problem instead of school and he says I can if I want to. So I get my rifle and load up in the trucks with the other platoon.

We get out in the field and we are issued tracer ammo. Then we form up in a couple of squads and are sent to attack an enemy position. The enemy is located in a wide draw with higher ground on two sides and a dry creek on another. We work our way around and then get into the dry creek and travel in it until we are about one hundred fifty yards from the enemy, which is represented by silhouette targets. When we are all in position behind some logs, the command is given to fire and we open up on the targets as fast as we can shoot, and you can see the tracers ripping into the targets. We are being observed by some high ranking brass and that is the reason for the tracers, to show how well we are shooting.

We then go back and they gave high praise for the way we did the problem. However, the tracers have set the prairie on fire. They have a garbage can full of wet burlap bags to use in fighting a fire and we each grab one and head out to fight the fire. The wind is blowing and it is close to one hundred degrees. We get ahead of the fire and beat it with the wet sacks but it is not long before our sacks are dried out and instead of putting the fire out, they are spreading it. We have the fire about contained, when we run out of water and it starts up again.

I notice a low place where the grass appears greener than the rest and go there and there is a small seep hole. I put my sack in the hole and stomp on it and it gets wet. I yell for the others to come and get their sacks wet too. We are able to attack the fire on the side and work it toward a bare draw and get it put out. We are exhausted and only when it is over, do I realize just how dangerous that was being in front of the fire. We ride back to the barracks and we get praise for how we did on the problem and also for how we fought the fire. We go in and when I look in the mirror, I can't believe how black I am from the smoke and ash. A shower really feels good.

Today we go back to the gas chamber. This time it is filled with chlorine gas. And they remind us that it is deadly poison. Six of us will go into the chamber at a time. As we go in, we will hold our breath and take out our gas masks and put them on. We will clear our masks and signal the cadre man that we are okay and then stay in the room for two to three minutes until he releases us. Then we will go outside, in the air and remove our masks. We go in and everything seems to be going just as it should, except the guy beside me has not signaled that he is okay. The cadre man notices something is wrong and goes to him. He is having trouble clearing his mask.

It seems that the valve is stuck. The cadre man works on the mask and he gets it cleared. By then, the guy is getting wobbly. Soon as he starts getting air he is okay. They open the door and we all go outside and remove our masks. We have now completed our training in chemical warfare.

After supper, it is GI night and once again I volunteer to wash the window screens. This way I get my shower and I can dress while the other guys are trying to get into the showers. We do not have school tonight, but we have to go all day tomorrow. It is unusual that we do not get Saturday afternoon off. I check the bulletin board and find that I have guard again tomorrow night.

Saturday after inspection, we go to the communications building and work on code and after dinner we go back again and work on it. It makes my brain tired straining to get the letters right, but I need the practice, if I am going to graduate. I get ready to go on guard and after supper I head for the guard house. I hope I get more sleep this time than I did last time.

Guard is quiet tonight and I get the late shift. But I am able to get a couple of hours of sleep before I go on and I get four more hours of sleep before I have to go out again. Six hours is about all the sleep we usually get, so I am okay.

I go back to the barracks and have time to wash up before breakfast. I get a paper and lay down to read it and I wake up just in time to get to the mess hall, before they close up from dinner. I go back and write some letters and then after supper, a bunch of us guys are sitting around the barracks listening to the radio and waiting for Walter Winchell's program. He is known for his truthful and accurate reporting.

When the Walter Winchell show comes on, it is completely quiet in the room, as everyone listens to see if he will say anything about Mickey Rooney. We all listen as he gives the weekly news. Then just before the end of the program, he starts telling about Mickey Rooney. He tells about how Mickey is in the army now, in basic training at Fort Riley, Kansas, and how he is going through the training, just like everyone else and is a model for others in the service, and how proud he is of Mickey. The guys are stunned. They feel their hero, Walter Winchell, has let them down.

CHAPTER XXIII

My watch gave out on me today. My sweat caused corrosion and the cover no longer fits tight. The pins that hold the strap on rusted until they were stuck and today the winder came out and the strap broke. The second hand came off some time ago and I lost it.

We went to the communications building this morning and I got to move up to the thirteen words per minute table. It is after dinner now and I am using the time to write a quick letter to Mom to send my old watch to me and I will send this one back home.

This afternoon, we go to the motor pool and drive out to the driving course and get some practice driving over rough ground. The guys say that I am really doing good driving, considering that I just learned. Then instead of PT, we run the obstacle course again. Then it is back in to get ready for retreat. After supper, we go back to the communications building and practice code for a couple of hours.

Today we spend the morning taking code again, and after dinner, we go back to the motor pool and drive the difficult driving course. After we finish that, we go on a thirty-five mile drive. We take turns driving and switch to different types of vehicles. After supper, it is back to the communications building and work on the code tables for a couple of hours.

Today we learn about the encoding machine. It looks a lot like a kid's toy typewriter. It is small machine made out of stamped metal. You raise the cover and there are a lot of bars and little tabs to set on them. To use it, you set the tabs on the bars according to the setting provided for that twenty-four hour period. Then you turn the knob to show the first letter of your message and press the lever. It prints an entirely different letter on the strip of paper that goes through the printer part of the machine. You continue doing that, until the entire message has been encoded. The message that comes out is radioed to another location and when they get it, they put it into another encoding machine that is set the same and when the tape comes out this time, it is with the original message. These machines can create millions of different code combinations.

We practice encoding messages and then sending them to another person who takes it down and runs it through another encoder and they check to see that the message is the same. These machines are "secret" and each machine must be accounted for. We are told that in combat that it will be our responsibility to destroy the machine if we see that we are going to be captured.

Today we go out into the field all day on squad problems. We try to use as many of the skills that we have been taught as we can. We get the objective, with the location coordinates, then have to find it on the map, use the topographic map to find the best way to go there and then use the compasses to follow our course. The squad leader uses signals to get us to move or stay, as we get closer. Since this is a scouting trip instead of an attack, we make notes of what we see and then send a runner back with the information, while we go on to the next location. It takes until afternoon to get it completed so we are late in getting back to our starting place for chow. No salt water this time. I guess they learned before what it would do. We have hamburger patties, fried potatoes, corn on the cob, a vegetable salad, bread and a lemon drink with a cookie for dessert.

It is hot where they have set up and the vehicles do not give much shade at this time of the day. The lucky ones grab what shade they can and the rest of us have to eat, sitting in the sun. When we are through, we get set to go out on another problem, going the other direction from this morning. We can't use the same settings. We do it all over again this afternoon. We are lucky that part of the route goes through some timber and we get some shade. And of course, since it is Kansas, the wind does blow and that helps keep us cooler.

Today we study at the communications building all morning working to get our speeds up. Then we go back early because today is payday. We get paid and I still have some money left from last month. I guess I am doing okay. After dinner, we go back to the communications building. When we get out of class, we do our daily PT and then get ready for retreat. It seems really hot and humid as we stand there in formation. After supper, we start to GI the barracks and, as usual, I volunteer to do the screens. I hope no one catches on to why I always do them. We just start to work and a front comes through with a huge dust cloud. We can hardly see in the barracks. And just as fast as it comes, it leaves, depositing another coat of dust on everything. Not a drop of rain, but it is not as humid afterwards.

Saturday morning we stand inspection, and when it is over, we are free until Monday morning, except for me and a few other unlucky guys. I have guard tomorrow afternoon and night. I go buy a money order, write a letter and get it mailed.

Sunday morning is like other Sundays. After breakfast, I get the Topeka paper and read the news and comics. I get through it and decide since I have to put on my class A uniform to go on guard duty, that I will go to church. When I get out of church, I hurry to the mess hall to eat so that I can get to guard duty.

I run back to the barracks, exchange my cap for my helmet liner, put on my rifle belt and grab my rifle and walk to the guardhouse. After we are inspected, I get to put my rifle in the rack, take off my rifle belt and the OD issues me a pistol belt and holster. He then hands me a .45 pistol and a magazine with seven rounds in it. It is a good thing that I rested this morning, because I got first shift today in the stables. The stables are usually a good place to pull guard. Not likely you will have anyone around, until late in the evening, when they come to water the horses.

When my two-hour shift is over, I go back to the guard house and visit with the other guys. It is too early to go to bed now. But I probably will after my next shift. That will be eight o'clock tonight. I make it through the night with no problems and get back to the barracks in time to change clothes, before we fall out for reveille.

CHAPTER XXIV

Monday morning we go to class on the Thompson submachine gun. We watch a film on it and then we learn how to take it apart and put it back together. Then they show us how to shoot it, how to load the magazines, hold the gun for shooting and how to sight it. It is a solid piece of equipment. I think every guy is anxious to shoot one, but that will have to wait until tomorrow.

In the afternoon, we go back to the communications building and work on the code tables some more. I am on the thirteen word per minute table. I will be glad when I can take thirteen, because then I will be fast enough to graduate. If I do not make it, I will either have to take basic over again or get shipped to something else.

It is Tuesday and after breakfast, we go out to the ranges and they bring out a bunch of Thompsons. While the first group is firing, the rest of us are practicing to shoot them. Before we get to shoot, they give each of us a magazine and a box of shells. We go ahead and load up the magazine. At first it is clumsy to load it, but in a little bit, I get thirty rounds in it. I hand the rest of the box of shells to the next guy.

We move up to the firing line and they have silhouette targets at twenty-five and fifty yards. We get the command to lock and load and then wait for the command to commence firing. They have made it clear that we are to only shoot short bursts of three to five rounds. No holding down the trigger. I wish I could, but I am not ready to get chewed out by the range master. On the commence firing command, I aim at the twenty five-yard silhouette and fire a burst. I do it right, because there were either three or four rounds in that burst. I was too nervous to tell. I fire a couple of more bursts and then adjust the sight and fire at the fifty yard target. The gun climbs when you shoot it and I see why they insist on the short bursts. Only too soon, do I go through the whole magazine. Then I remove it, clear the gun and hand it off to one of the next group to fire. It is a lot of fun. Makes me think of Dick Tracy or Melvin Purvis of the FBI.

We get through in time for dinner and after that, we go work on code again. I do better today, but it is still going to be hard to get a perfect message, at this speed. We get through early and have to go dress up for a parade that the general wants to have. We put on our class A uniforms and march to the parade grounds. We then march around the grounds and pass the reviewing stand, where the general is. After that, we stand in formation in the hot sun, while the general pins good driving medals on three WACS. After about an hour, guys start passing out right and left. It is so bad that they give the order that only the guy on the left of the one that passes out shall take care of him. I don't know what happens if you are the last one in the line and there is no one to help you. I watch to see if the general tries to feel up the WACS when he pins on the medals. After supper, we go back to the communications building and work on our code some more.

We spend the morning in class on establishing a radio net and then we practice around the room just as if we were talking on radios. We also learn the newer method of sending, so that the identity of the net command is not revealed.

We go back for lunch and at mail call, I get a letter and a package from my mother. She sent a package of cookies and inside the package is a small box with my old watch in it. I pass around some of the cookies and then eat one, as I read the letter. I feel bad, because she says that my dad had been wearing my watch and now he is going to have to try to find one. If I had known, I would not have asked for it. Watches are just not available now. The military is taking all of the production and the stores have run out.

In the afternoon, we go out to the range where we fired the Thompson submachine gun and they give us instruction on the M3 submachine gun, better known as a grease gun. It is called a grease gun, because it looks like one. It is made of stamped metal, except for the bolt and the barrel. It uses magazines similar to the Thompson. It is an ugly gun, but it is cheap to make and at close range, it is effective. It has a couple of pieces of thin stamped metal for sights and they can only be adjusted by bending them with something.

I get to be in the first group to shoot them. I take my place and when it is time to fire, I start with a burst of three rounds. It does not fire as fast as the Thompson and I find it is easier to hold on the target. I even try a couple of bursts of five rounds before I shoot up the rest of my magazine. I find that I do even better than I did with the Thompson. We clean them after we all get through shooting and then start marching back. As usual we stop on the way back in and have PT. We clean up for retreat and after supper, we change clothes again and get ready for another hike. This will be a seven-mile hike with full equipment.

We start out and, as usual for the first couple of miles, it is still very hot and the straps rub on my shoulders. After the sun goes down, it is not so bad and we keep up a fairly fast pace. But when we stop, everyone hits the ground to rest their shoulders from the packs.

This morning we are back at the communications building setting up a net and we are using the portable radios this time. That means that someone has to crank the generator, while the other uses the radio. The guy on the generator has to really work when they are talking, because it pulls a lot of electricity, when they are using voice. The generator man always urges the operator to make short sentences. We go back for dinner and after dinner, we go back out to one of the ranges. It has been some time since we studied rifle grenades and rockets, but today we are going to fire them, so that we can qualify on them.

We split into two groups, with one group using the rifle grenades and the other firing the rocket launcher or "bazooka." I go with the rifle grenade group first. The instructor fires one first, at an old tank hull. He hits it and then we go out to the target to see the damage. Of course, it has been hit many times, but you can tell the fresh mark from this shell. It blew a hole completely through the side.

We then take turns firing them. However, the ones we get are practice grenades and do not have an explosive charge. He shows me just how to aim it and it looks like I hit the tank, because it bounces. The recoil is tremendous from shooting such a heavy object. After everyone has shot one, we exchange groups and we go to shoot the bazooka.

The Army calls it the 2.36 anti-tank rocket launcher, but everyone refers to it as a bazooka. It is heavy enough that we fire it from a kneeling position. They make it easier for me by telling me the approximate distance to the target. My loader goes to get a rocket and brings it back. It is a practice rocket, without an explosive warhead. He pulls the safety pin, slides the rocket into the launcher, until the clip catches the fin and then wraps the wire around the spring on top of the launcher. He taps me on the shoulder to signal that it is ready to fire. He then gets around to the side of me, so that he is not back of the tube. I pull the trigger and there is a loud boom, a swoosh and a ball of fire coming back at me. I can't see where the rocket went, but my loader says that I hit the target. We change positions and I load for him. He fires and he does not hold high enough, because his rocket hits right in front of the tank hull.

When everyone has had a chance to fire a rocket, we head back, but of course, we stop for PT on the way. When we get back, we change and fall out for retreat. They announce that we will be having an artillery demonstration on Saturday afternoon.

It is Friday and today we are going to be driving all day. We march to the motor pool and then climb into one of the vehicles that we will be using. We drive out to a rough part of the post and take turns driving each of the different vehicles over the rough ground. Up and down hills, into creeks and right down the middle of the creek. Whatever they can see, they have us drive over it. It is hard to steer over such stuff, but there is no rest for the riders either. We take them back to the motor pool and have to service each one before it is put away.

The obstacle course it not too far from the motor pool, so they have us go through it instead of PT. We get back and clean up for retreat and then eat supper. After supper, it is GI night again.

Saturday morning we go to school and work getting our speed up on the code. After dinner, we march out to the top of a hill. We sit down, facing another hill. Then they fire 105mm shells over our heads into the hill we are facing. We have a very good view of the shells exploding. One boy gets hit with a piece of shrapnel and it goes through his shoe into his heel. One of the guys close to me gets hit in the elbow, but it does not penetrate. He says that it is like getting hit by a baseball. I guess they sent word back to the artillery, because the shells now are hitting further away on the other hill. The demonstration is really exciting.

I go to the mess hall and of course they are having cold cuts again. I like them, even though a lot of the guys gripe about it. But the cooks do not want to make a bunch of food and then have no idea how many will show up to eat. With the cold cuts, it is not a problem, they just put back what we do not eat. This evening we have cantaloupe too and I like it. After I eat, I walk over to the PX and stand around watching, until it is time for the movie.

Sunday I read the paper before church and then in the afternoon I go to the day room and listen to the radio and read some magazines. Nothing exciting, but I need the rest. In the evening I get my things ready for the next week.

CHAPTER XXV

Today, we go on a one-hundred-mile road trip in the vehicles. This will be to teach us to drive in convoy. I get into one of the trucks to ride, as we start out. When we take the first break to shift drivers, the lieutenant in charge tells me to get into his jeep and drive. We get all of the vehicles moving out again and we drop in behind them to see how they are doing. In a little bit, the lieutenant tells me to pass everyone and get up at the head of the column. I am uneasy about having to pass all of these trucks, since I have never done that before. I get around a couple and then have to pull back in, because we are meeting a vehicle. I keep passing until we are in the lead and then I am the one to set the pace. With wartime regulations, thirty five miles per hour is the speed limit. He tells me to hold right on the speed limit and to hold it steady, so that the others can follow. I lead the convoy until we get to the place to pull over for the noon break.

While we are eating, the colonel drives up in his jeep. He says that he has come out to see how well we are learning to drive. He visits with the troops and then when it is time to move out, the lieutenant tells the colonel that I had never driven before we started training and that he can check me out and see how the training is working. So the colonel tells me that I will be his driver the rest of the way.

I am very nervous, but I start driving the jeep and we follow the column to see how well they hold their speed. I find out that the last vehicle has to adjust its speed a lot more than the others to stay in position. After awhile, he has me pass the other vehicles and go to the head of the column, just as the lieutenant did. This time it is easier. The colonel gives me pointers on how to drive and praises me for my driving skills, after such a short time driving. I guess he is satisfied as to the training we are getting.

We get back to the motor pool and then have to service the vehicles before we go to PT. Then we go back to the barracks and get ready for retreat. They announce that we are on alert tonight. Tomorrow we will move out on the lawn between the barracks and sleep in our pup tents, while they fumigate the barracks. As we go back in the barracks, I check the bulletin board and find out that I am on table waiter duty tomorrow. It looks like tomorrow is going to be very busy.

After supper, we have to remain in the barracks in case they call us out. We are already in our class A uniforms, so if we are called, we will have to grab our helmet, rifle belt and rifle and get outside fast. We do not have long to wait, until they have us fall out. It took thirty seconds for everyone to fall out. The lieutenant said we need to do better than that, if we are called out again.

We think it will be awhile before they call us out again, and one of the guys decides to take a shower. He has all of his clothes off, except his shorts, when they call us out again. He does not have time to dress, so he grabs his helmet, rifle belt and rifle and goes out with the rest of us. We make it in twenty seconds. The lieutenant laughs, when he sees him standing at attention, with just shorts, helmet, rifle belt and rifle. But he does not say anything, because the guy has everything they said to bring. We are fast enough this time and they say if we are called out again it will be the real thing.

I go back in, place the things I need where I can grab them and then hang a towel on my bunk so they will wake me at four in the morning. I lay down on top of my bunk in my clothes, but I will have to change to my fatigues, when they get me up in the morning.

Someone wakes me a little before four and I change my clothes and put everything back in its place, before cleaning up and heading to the mess hall. I work until after breakfast is over and then head back to the barracks, to get my things moved out to the yard. Burkemper has already moved some of the things I will need when I get there. We put the two halves of our pup tent together and pitch it, in line with the others. After we get everything set up, we go to the communications building for class until just before dinner and then I have to leave early to get to the mess hall to do my table waiter job.

At dinner, I tell Burkemper to get my mail for me and I will get it this afternoon. I finish up as table waiter and then go back to the communications building for the afternoon classes. Burkemper said that I got a package of cookies, but they ate them. I know he is kidding me, but he does have a letter for me. After class, we go for PT. I get to skip retreat to go to the mess hall, but I wish it was the PT I got to skip. I work all evening and it is after nine o'clock before I get off of table waiter duty. I get in the tent and take off my clothes. I am so tired that the ground feels good.

This morning we go to class on the .50 caliber machine gun. We take it apart and put it back together. We learn how to set the head space and how to use the sights. They are similar to the .30 caliber machine gun, only a lot bigger, so it does not take long. Instead of PT this afternoon, we move back into the barracks. We have to re-pack our equipment.

After supper, we go out on another hike, ten miles this time and it is with full equipment. It is not as hot today, so the walking goes a lot easier. At home, Wednesday night was church night, but it seems that here it is hike night. I make it okay, but my feet are tired by the time we get back.

Today we go out to the range to fire the .50 caliber machine guns. They have five of them on tripods, set up in a row and there is a metal roof to keep the sun off of them. We stand in back of the line some distance until it is our turn to fire. The noise is terrible when they are all five firing at the same time. They have a bunch of old vehicles and other things parked out on the range for targets.

When it is my turn to shoot, I go and sit down on the ground behind the gun. The other guy is the loader and he goes and picks up a belt of .50 caliber ammo. It is belted four rounds of ball and one round of tracer. He holds out the end of the belt to me and I open the cover on the machine gun and place the end of the belt in and close it. I work the bolt twice to put a round in the chamber. At the command to commence firing, I aim at an old truck body and press the triggers with my thumbs. The gun jumps as I send out a burst. I shoot about six rounds, enough that a tracer streaks toward the target. I keep moving to different targets and fire a burst at each one. The noise from the guns coming off of the tin roof is deafening. By the time I get through shooting the one hundred fifty rounds in the belt, I am unable to hear anything. The observer shouts that I really did well.

I then go and pick up a belt for the other guy and I act as his loader. I believe it is not as loud here, but it may be that I just can't hear any more. He shoots his belt and then we get to move back. They are supposed to be giving us instruction back at the rear, but none of us can hear anything and we are communicating by hand signals. We have dinner brought out to us and we eat in the field.

We get to run the obstacle course on the way back in instead of regular PT. We get back in time to clean up for retreat and supper. After supper, we go back to the communications building to study code. This is a almost a waste of time, since none of us can hear very well.

Today we go back out to a different range. We will be using the .50 caliber machine gun as an anti-aircraft gun. They have a couple of half tracks and two trucks and an armored car with ring mounted machine guns on them. We get set up and they tell us how far to track the target so that we do not shoot at something we shouldn't. The target is a small remote controlled airplane. The first group gets set up and they fly the plane over and they shoot at it. It doesn't look as though they get any hits. When the next group gets up, they open fire and the plane is hit and it stops and a parachute opens to bring it down. They try to get it fixed, but are unable to get it to fly again.

We have dinner while they are working on the plane and after dinner they announce that they could not get the plane to fly again. The rest of us will get our practice by pretending that an airplane is going over and we fire a few bursts into the sky. This is not very effective training, but at least we get to practice shooting from a ring mount, which is what most of us will have available in combat. PT on the way back, then after supper, we GI the barracks again.

Saturday morning after breakfast, we fall out for inspection. The captain is there for inspection and while we are in formation, he drops a bombshell on us. He tells us that the army has changed the standards and now you have to be able to take sixteen words per minute of code before you can pass the course. He suggests that since we only have four weeks of basic left and with two of them on bivouac, that we may want to start working on it. It just takes all of the wind out of me. I had to work so hard and I have almost got to thirteen, that I don't know how I can ever get to sixteen in only four weeks. I decide that I will spend the weekend at the communications building.

Sunday morning, I go to breakfast when it opens up, so that I can get down to the communications building, but I do stop to pick up the Sunday paper as usual. I am glancing through it, when some of the guys come in from breakfast. Neilson says "Lovell, there is a dog outside from Oklahoma."

"There is?" And I fall for the joke when I say "How do you know he is from Oklahoma?"

He says "Because he has an 'O' under his tail." Everyone breaks out laughing including me. I get along with all the guys and don't mind if they have a joke at my expense.

I tell the guys that I am going to go to the communications building and if anyone wants to work, to come on down. I go pick up the key and when I get there, I start up the machine on the thirteen word table. I have worked on it enough that I am close to completing this step. I decide to try to go forward and turn on the machine for the sixteen word table. It seems so fast that I am racing to write the letters. But the letters are coming so fast, that they no longer seem to be dots and dashes, they are just sounds, each letter having a different sound just like a foreign language.

I work on the table for awhile and then decide to go back to the thirteen word table and see how I do. It is easy now and I take down thirteen words a minute with little trouble. At least I can pass what we were originally supposed to take. Back to the sixteen word table and I am straining, but I now have hope that I will be able to pass and move out of basic. I feel much better than I did yesterday. No one else has joined me, so I lock up and go back. I get back just in time to go to church. Maybe a little prayer will not hurt anything either.

After dinner, I work a couple of hours and then my brain says it has had enough for one day and I leave. I go to the movie in the evening and get back to the barracks just as most of the other guys are getting back in. I am ready for bed.

CHAPTER XXVI

It turned cold last Friday and I put on the top to my long handles today. It is hard to believe, as hot as it has been here, that it could turn cold so quick. It does make the outside work much easier though. This morning, we go to the motor pool and get into some of the vehicles that have radios in them and practice setting up a radio network. We drive them out a little way and then send messages back and forth. We simulate combat conditions and the type of messages that we would send and receive then. We take turns using the CW radios and the FM radios with voice. When we send messages in code, we seldom send faster than ten words a minute, so I have little trouble receiving them.

We come back in for dinner and then in the afternoon we go to the communications building to practice code. I receive one message at the thirteen word table to satisfy the instructor that I can pass and then move up to the sixteen word table. I am coming along better on it than I thought possible. I am determined to pass. We go back for retreat and then after supper, we go back and work on the code tables for a couple of hours.

Today we go to another live ammo problem. This time it is pop-up targets. They are at different ranges and only stay up for a couple of seconds. You have to watch for the target to pop up and then recognize how far out it is and shoot, before it goes back down. It is more exciting than shooting at the plain paper targets. They bring out dinner and we continue shooting after dinner. Then it is PT, retreat, supper and two hours at the code tables before the day is over. I write a letter home, requesting cookies be sent a couple of times the next two weeks, while we are on bivouac. Every day is so long, but the weeks seem to fly by.

I am glad that I worked over the weekend. I start working on the sixteen word table and am doing fairly well. Not enough to pass yet, but enough to feel that I will make it. After dinner, we practice setting up communication nets and sending messages back and forth in code. We do not have PT this evening, because we are going on a hike after supper. We use the time to get our things ready for the hike. After supper, we fall out with full equipment and march out of the area. As soon as we get out a ways, we go into route march and move along at a good pace. At least the weather is cool and that makes it a lot easier to travel. We are late getting back in and as soon as I can put my things away, I get in bed.

It is Thursday and we will spend the whole day in class at the communications building. We study procedures and between the classes, we work on sending and receiving code. Several of the guys have already qualified at sixteen words per minute, but I am still struggling. We go to dinner and at mail call, I get a couple of letters.

In the afternoon, I am working on the sixteen word table and I have a good streak and take a whole message at sixteen words a minute. The instructor is there at the time and signs off on it. I have passed. I may never be able to take it that fast again, but I did once and that is enough to get out of here. The rest of the afternoon goes great and I am not too upset when I get back to the barracks and see my name on the KP list for tomorrow. After supper, we have a class on what we will be doing the next two weeks when we are on bivouac. As soon as it is over, I get ready for bed, hang a towel on my bunk and get to sleep.

It's four in the morning and I am trying to get awake. I clean up and get into my fatigues and make my way to the mess hall. I help prepare breakfast and get the serving lines set up and ready for the food. The menu today is scrambled eggs and sausage links, toast, cold cereal, grapefruit juice, coffee and milk. Getting it ready is the easy part. Cleaning up after is the hard part. But we do have time, after we serve everyone and they are gone, to sit down and enjoy breakfast ourselves, without the usual crowding at the table and the hurry to get through eating. I get a big serving of scrambled eggs and a half dozen sausages and I get the strawberry preserves out of the kitchen to have on my toast. I fix a cup of coffee with sugar and milk and take my time eating it.

When everything is clean, we start preparing dinner. I have been on KP enough that the cooks let me help with the cooking and the new guys get to do most of the cleaning. Today I will be helping to make meatloaf. We will have it with mashed potatoes, gravy and canned green beans. For dessert, there will be a cobbler made from canned apples. We get everything cooked and ready before time for the troops to get there. One of the cooks says that we really should test the food, before they eat it. This means that we get to eat early today.

We take a short rest after dinner and then get ready for supper. We are having pork steak for supper. They brown them in the big cast iron skillets and then put them in big loaf pans in the oven to bake. I help serve supper and after supper I supervise the table waiters in cleaning up the mess hall. I do not have to work as hard, but it is still nearly ten o'clock by the time I get back to the barracks. It has been another long day. At least I did not have to GI the barracks.

Saturday morning I run a patch through the bore on my rifle and take an oily patch and rub the metal down to get any dust off of it. Then I go to the mess hall. Everyone else is already there. I hurry to eat and then get back and make sure that my uniform is suitable for inspection. At inspection, they tell us that we will be changing to winter uniforms effective tomorrow. Not that it will make much difference to us, because we will be on bivouac on Monday. They will be picking details to load up the equipment and take it out to the bivouac area and set it up. They read off a list of names and mine is not on the list, I guess because I was on KP yesterday. We are already lined up, so we move over to the orderly room and go in for pay day. When I get paid, I take forty-five dollars and put it in an envelope with my name on it and have the first sergeant put it in the safe. I want to have it in case I get leave at the end of basic.

I spend the morning getting all of the things that I want to take with me for the next two weeks and finding a place in my pack for them. Most of the guys are at the supply building loading up equipment to haul out there. After dinner, they get on the trucks and drive out. I am taking it easy on my bunk, but I have it turned so I can watch out the window and see if anyone is coming down the street. Sure enough, I see a couple of the cadre coming down the street and I know that they must be looking for someone for a detail. I jump up, turn my bed around and go out the back door of the barracks. I watch them go into the barracks next door and I cross the street to the day room. I still have my class A uniform on from inspection, so I decide to play it safe and head out to the PX. As long as I am here, I go ahead and get a pint of ice cream and eat it. Then I head back to the day room and write a letter. By the time I get through, I figure the coast is clear and head back to the barracks by the back way.

Sunday morning I eat breakfast and then come back to try on my winter uniform. I have gained about eight pounds, so it fits better than it did when I got it. As soon as I am dressed, I take my Sunday paper and head for the day room. I know that they will still be looking for details and I do not want to be around. I stay in the day room, and I am early for church.

Sunday afternoon I take off my winter uniform and put my fatigues on. We will be wearing fatigues for the next two weeks. I am glad that I have an extra set. I would hate to have to wear the same pair for two weeks, out in the field. It does add weight to my pack though. When I have everything ready, I go to bed. It is the last chance I will have to get much rest for two weeks.

CHAPTER XXVII

Monday morning we fall out for reveille and are given the final instructions for bivouac. We then go for breakfast. This will be the last meal in the mess hall for two weeks. After breakfast, we fall out with full equipment and anything else that we think we will need in the next two weeks. We head out into the country. We go about six or seven miles to what was formerly some farmer's pasture, with a grove of trees in a lower area. Some large tents are already in position and house the supply, headquarters and mess. We are ordered to pitch our tents somewhere in the area close by. Burkemper and I get our tent up in short time. We pick a rather flat area just off of the road going through the camp. After our tent is put up, we dig a drain trench around it to carry off any rain water that falls on the tent. Everyone is required to dig a slit trench, like the one you would dig in combat, to protect you from bombs and shells. I move a couple of feet from the front of my side of the tent and dig mine. My idea is that we can sit on the sides of it and be more comfortable than sitting on the flat ground. A detail is sent out a hundred yards from camp to dig a latrine. It is a trench much like the ones we have dug for protection and then a canvas fly is stretched around some poles, giving it some privacy.

After everyone has their tents pitched and trenches dug, we go out a ways from the camp and work on a problem. We check out the portable radios and set up a network with them. We send and receive messages with the network control center, back in the head-quarters tent. It gives us practical training, except, I can't imagine carrying that radio or the generator, on my back in combat. Besides, it takes a lot of cranking to send just one message and you need to keep cranking in order to receive an incoming message.

At noon we get the message "close station-march order." We all move back to the camp for dinner. This is the first meal we have had that was all cooked in the field. I do not think the quality is as good as back at the mess hall, but it is better than the meals they used to bring out in the insulated cans. Burkemper and I get our food and move back to the tent and sit on the sides of my slit trench. It is much better than trying to eat while sitting flat on the ground. We are sitting up and have room to set our canteen cups beside us.

While we are out here on bivouac, we will have night problems until midnight every other night and every fourth night we will have to pull guard. This afternoon, we will have a problem in which our squad has been assigned to scout in advance of the main body. If we find the enemy, we will send back a message, giving the strength of the enemy and their location. We will do this by using the map and compass to locate them and then the radio to send back the informa-tion. We will take turns carrying the radio and generator. It takes all afternoon to finish the problem. Tonight we have guard duty. Some groups will be out on night problems. The camp has barbed wire around it, with only the road running through the camp open and it is the road that we are required to guard.

We do not have to start guard until almost dark. I get the first shift and I hide behind a fallen tree, where I can see the entrance to the camp. We were given the passwords earlier this evening. It is just getting dark, when a jeep comes toward the entrance. It has its headlights on and I can see the red flag with a white star on it, mounted on the fender. It is the general. I order them to halt and then give the sign. Of course, he does not know the password. So I give the command to advance and be recognized. I can see his face against the lights from the jeep. Then I tell them to proceed. The general wants to know how I know who it is, and I tell him that I have seen him before and recognize him. He says okay and has his driver move on. I did not want him to know that I cannot go over to where he is, because when I moved out of my hiding place, I got my leg caught in the barbed wire. Then just before my shift is over, part of one of the squads comes back to the camp. I get the proper response from them and let them in. I am glad to get relieved and go get into my bed.

Sleeping on the ground is certainly not as good as that bunk back in the barracks, but if you are tired enough, you can manage. We get a chance to use our steel helmets as wash basins today. The cadre tell us that when we get to combat, that we will use them not only to protect our heads but to eat out of, wash in, dig with and as a toilet. And not always in that order. We get our breakfast and after we eat, we clean our mess kits in the garbage cans provided.

Today is a repeat of yesterday, except we will not have guard tonight. Instead we will set up a communications net in the dark. It is very difficult to send and receive messages in the dark, when you are trying to operate under black out conditions. We use our rain coats to make a cover over the equipment and have someone hold the flash light.

Wednesday morning, we are out on top of a hill with the radio when a thunderstorm comes up. The sky gets black and we can see the lightning flashes and hear the thunder. We do not like this position and move down off of the hill, into a ravine. We do not try to set up in the ravine; we cover ourselves with our raincoats and close the covers on the radio. They may be watertight, but our rain coats are not. It pours rain and it is a good thing we did not go to the bottom of the ravine, because water is running down through it. We try to keep our rifles dry, but there is no way. We will have to dry and oil them when we get back to camp.

The storm moves through and we decide to go back to camp. When we get there, water is flowing down the road through camp.

My slit trench has turned into a lake. However, our ditching of the tent held and our beds are dry. The cooks had trouble getting dinner ready with all the rain, so dinner will be a little late. We store the radios in the supply tent, because we will not need them for the afternoon problem. We get ready to eat dinner and it starts raining again. Not hard this time, but enough to be uncomfortable. I get my food and the rain is splashing in my mess kit. Burkemper and I go back to the tent to eat. We sit down on our beds with our muddy boots outside of the tent. Not the easiest way to eat, but at least it keeps some of the water out of our food.

This afternoon, we run another problem as scouts. It is still drizzling rain and we slosh through the wet grass and mud. We skirt around the objective to a lower area, so that we will not have to crawl as far. As it is, we are all soaking wet and have mud all over us from what crawling we have had to do. Then we make our way back to camp. We are lucky. We do not have either school or guard tonight. We will be able to sleep, unless our beds got wet. After supper, we go to the supply tent and take our rifles apart and clean and oil them. We wrap them up to keep them dry and put them in our beds to protect them. Then we take off our leggings and shoes and slide into our blankets. Our wet clothes do not help any, but maybe they will dry some tonight.

This morning we have a class on malaria, and they explain by regularly taking Atabrine, that you can prevent it. They explain that it turns your skin yellow, but after you quit taking it, that the color will go away. To get us in the habit of taking it, they are giving us a small black tablet each morning. They explain that the pills are nothing but bicarbonate of soda, charcoal and peppermint, and will not hurt us, in fact may help our digestion. They hand each person one of the pills and tell us to take it. Of course, some of the guys decide that they are giving us salt peter. That is one of the constant rumors in the army, that they give you salt peter which suppresses sexual desire. After they pass out the pills, they give us each one C ration for dinner. This will show us what we will likely be eating in combat. The one I get is beef stew that comes in one can and the other can has some crackers, instant coffee, sugar, thee cigarettes, matches, a couple of hard candies, and a few sheets of toilet paper.

Bivouac continues to be about the same thing, long days and nights, with lots of hiking through the hills. When the weekend comes, training does not stop. However, for those that want to go, there is a church service Sunday morning at eight. I go, as much to see what it is like as anything.

The second week continues very much like the first week. But on Tuesday night we have a night mission involving a long scouting trip in the dark. We are to go to a certain point and then report what is there by sending a runner back to base. It is a terrible hike. We are following the road and the tanks and trucks have chewed it into sticky Kansas mud, a foot deep. Every step picks up more until you think that you will not be able to take another step. We get to the first point and the squad leader writes a message and we draw straws, to see who will go back. For once I am lucky and get to take the message back.

On Thursday, they call out my name to report to the headquarters tent. I do not know what I have done, but I figure it is something. But instead, the first sergeant has put me on a detail, to help load a truck with supplies The truck is driven by one of the cadre and I am along to help. We leave early in the afternoon and when we get there, he tells me that he will wake me up in the morning about five o'clock.

I go to the barracks and I am the only guy in the whole place. I take a long hot shower, and get my clean fatigues and put them on. Then I take my rifle apart and clean it. I even take apart things that we are not allowed to take off, and clean them too. My rifle is cleaner than any time since some time before I got it. The mess hall is not open, but I have a couple of C rations to eat. I eat one and then walk to the PX and get some candy bars, cookies and some ice cream. I go back and chow down on the sweets and then crawl into my warm dry bed.

He wakes me up in the morning and we load the truck with supplies. Mostly things for the mess tent: bread, fresh vegetables and a few canned goods. There will only be a few more meals, so this is to wrap up what they need. It is sure not hard duty and he could have handled it himself, but I am not complaining. We get back to the bivouac and I go out to join my squad in the field as they finish a communications problem. Then in the afternoon we attend a class on health and first aid. It is a summary of the classes that we have had earlier. They stress how important it is that each person takes care of his own health and that of his buddies. There may be times, in combat situations, when you will be the only medical help available. After supper we go out on the final night problem. At least it is not raining tonight and we are not going by the roads. Instead, we will go out across the hills, circle around and come back in from the other direction. We cover several miles using a map and compass. It is long after midnight before we get back to the camp. I am not as comfortable as I was last night.

Today we break camp. I am on the detail to pack up the supply tent and the things in it. We pack all of the radios in the truck first. They will go to another location. Then the rest of the supplies are loaded.

We are ordered to take our own tents down and make up our packs for the trip back. But before we can go back, we have to level off the ground, fill all holes and then police the area for anything that nature did not put there. When I get ready to fill my slit trench, I do not have enough dirt. The rain washed most of it away. I look around and see a large log lying a short distance away and I roll it into the hole and cover it with dirt. It looks perfect. I feel sorry for the next guy that has to dig a slit trench there.

When everything is ready, we put on our packs, sling our rifles over our shoulder and hike back to the barracks. When we arrive, we have to unload all of the equipment from the trucks and put it away. By the time we get done, it is evening. We will have tonight and tomorrow to get all of our things cleaned and ready for inspection on Monday morning. Mail call brings me a letter from Don. He is in France and they have not been in combat yet, but from the way it sounds, it will not be long.

CHAPTER XXVIII

This is the last week of basic training and will be a busy week. This morning, we march out to the infiltration course. This is to teach us about being under fire. We go single file down a ravine. When we are all lined up, along the ravine, we go up the side of the ravine and crawl under barb wire, stretched across above us. While we are crawling, they are firing machine guns over us. Of course, we have heard stories about guys getting excited and standing up and getting shot or about the bracket holding the machine guns, breaking and allowing them to fire into the soldiers below. Every so often on the course, there are small fenced areas, where they have planted explosives to simulate shells exploding. They set these explosives off as you crawl beside them. I crawl and take no chance. I hug the ground as tight as I can, rolling over on my back when I reach a low wire and holding it above me, with my rifle, as I crawl under. I am tired and dirty by the time I get to the end, crawl past the machine guns and get to stand up.

We go back out to the infiltration course for the night session. We crawl through as before. I am crawling along and get beside one of the fenced explosive areas, when I feel the wires going in to it. I take my hands and break the wires. I figure that I can lay there for awhile and rest. But about that time, there is a big blast covering me with dirt. I had broken the wrong wire. That is enough to get me to moving and I crawl on out. We get to go back to the barracks and get cleaned up.

Tuesday and today we go for the village fighting course. The buildings are just a shell, but inside are silhouettes to shoot at. When it is our squad's time, they issue us carbines instead of using our M1's. Our job is to take the town. We spread out and one half goes down each side of the street. We each have four practice grenades. They look like a regular grenade except they have a hole in the bottom, with a small bag of black powder inside. When it goes off, it makes a loud boom and a cloud of smoke comes out.

Burkemper and I are working as a team. We approach the first building and the other two guys cover us. We get tight against the wall and Burkemper throws in one of the grenades. As soon as it explodes, I stand up, lean in the window and try to see the targets in the smoke. When I locate them, I quickly fire a couple of rounds at each target. We move to the next building and Burkemper and I cover the other guys while they clear the building.

The next building, it is my turn to throw the grenade. We work our way through our side of the village. We get down towards the end and there are targets outside of the buildings which allow you to get rid of the remaining ammunition. While I am shooting at these targets, one of the lieutenants walks out onto the course. I do not know why, but he should not have been there. Burkemper grabs my arm and tells me not to shoot him. I was not going to shoot him and was not even pointing the gun at him. After we finish the course, Burkemper tells everyone that I was taking a bead on a lieutenant and he kept me from shooting him. He tells it with a straight face, but all the guys, including me, have a laugh.

After everyone has finished the course, we go back in and get our things ready for the fifteen-mile hike. This hike is required of everyone to complete basic. As soon as supper is over, we fall out with full equipment. We move out at a good pace and the weather is nice and cool enough to make the walking more comfortable.

We go about five miles and I start to feel sick. The further we go, the sicker I get. By the time we have gone about ten miles, I am vomiting. I drop out of the column and fall to my knees and vomit until my gut is hurting. I get back up and fall back into the column. I am doubled over with pain, but I keep going.

We stop for a break and I am laying on the ground doubled up. The lieutenant who was up at the front comes back to check on me. I guess that one of the cadre told him I was sick. He asks if I need to go back. I tell him that I want to finish the hike. It is required and I do not want to have to do this again. Besides if I have to take it again, some cadre will have to go with me to verify that I made it.

We start out again and as I struggle to my feet, one of the cadre grabs my rifle and another pulls my pack off and carries it. I keep going and I am not really conscious of much that is going on. I do notice that a couple of the cadre are taking turns with my pack. We get back to the barracks and I fall onto my bed.

I am almost asleep when the first sergeant comes in and tells me to not fall out for reveille, but to stay in bed and then come to the orderly room for sick call, and that I should not try to eat anything, until after I go on sick call.

I stay in bed in the morning and after everyone has gone off to class, I get up and go to the orderly room and sign in on sick call. They give me the admission slip and I walk to the infirmary. I have to get in the line of guys that are waiting. I don't think they question that I should be here today. I am pale and sick looking. I finally get to see the medic. I think he is supposed to be a male nurse. I tell him what happened, he takes my temperature, gives me two of those bicarbonate of soda, charcoal and peppermint pills. He then marks my slip "duty" and sends me back to my unit.

When I get back to the orderly room and tell the first sergeant what happened, he said "them sons a bitches." He said that since we were having class at the communications building for me to go there and take it easy and to see him at noon.

I start walking to the communications building with my head hanging down. I am feeling weak. I look up and here is the general riding down the road towards me on his horse. As he gets to me, I pull myself up as best I can and salute him. He gets past me and then turns his horse around and comes back. He says "That was not a very good salute, trooper. Let's see if you can't do better." He sits on his horse and gives me lessons on how to salute. I feel so bad, I can hardly hold my head up and I am standing beside the road learning how to give a better salute. Finally I get it to his satisfaction and he moves on. By the time I get to the communications building, I feel that I have had about all that I want for one day.

The session today is more to just practice code and let those guys that have had trouble passing get in some time so they can qualify. Since I got my qualification, I do not have to do anything. I sit at the table with the headphones on and pretend that I am working on it. I have the volume turned down and it is a good time to rest. When it is time for dinner, I go back with the rest of the guys. When I get there, I go to the orderly room and see the first sergeant and he tells me to go try to eat something. I go into the mess hall, but nothing smells very good. I drink some ice tea and eat some crackers. Then I go back to the barracks and lay down until time to go back to the communications building. Before we go, the first sergeant comes over and tells me to go back to class, but not to go to PT, but to come and see him instead.

I spend the afternoon sitting with earphones on and resting. Then instead of going to PT, I go back to the orderly room. The first sergeant tells me to go over to the mess hall and ask the mess sergeant for some bread and milk and then go lay down. I walk to the mess hall and go in and tell the mess sergeant that the first sergeant said for me to come over and ask him for some bread and milk. He says "The first sergeant is not running this mess hall, I am.' But unknown to us, the first sergeant had followed me over to the mess hall and was standing behind me, out of sight. When he heard this, he stepped inside, in front of me and said "You give this boy a quart of milk and some bread. It was probably you're damned old food that made him sick in the first place." The mess sergeant goes to the ice box, pulls out a quart of milk and grabs about a half a loaf of bread and hands them to me and says "Here, take these and get out of here." I grab them and head for the barracks. The first sergeant follows me out and tells me that if I need anything, to let him know.

I go to the barracks and take my canteen cup out, and break up some bread in it. I pour some of the milk over it and then dig in my foot locker, where I have some sugar hidden, and get it out. I pour some on the bread and milk. I dig out the spoon from my mess kit and proceed to eat. I am really hungry by now and it goes down really well. When I finish the first cup, I fix another. After I finish, I wash up my things and put them away. I take off my clothes and slide down into my bed. Hopefully I will feel better when I wake up.

I fall out with everyone else on Thursday morning. The first sergeant comes out to check on me. I tell him that I think that I am going to live. He tells me that if I get to feeling bad again to let him know. I thank him for what he has done for me. When I go to breakfast I go with the cold cereal, some toast with jelly and coffee with lots of milk in it.

Today we will be practicing what we have learned as radio operators. We go out in some of the vehicles that have radios mounted in them, set up a network and send messages back and forth. I am feeling well now, but still a little weak. A couple of the guys are going around assessing us each a couple of dollars, to pay for the end of basic party, tomorrow night.

After supper, we have our final problem. We do another night map and compass problem. I guess this is like a final exam, to see if we can go out in the dark and then find our way back. It is long enough that we are late getting back in. I check the bulletin board and there is a list of twelve names who are to report to the orderly room in the morning. My name is on the list. I presume it is to tell me where I will be going after basic.

The next morning after breakfast, I go to the orderly room with the rest of the dozen guys. They explain that every so often they will pick a dozen men from a group that is finishing basic and check to see how physically strong they are. We have been picked this time.

We will be measured as a group. Every one of us must finish. A couple of the cadre go with us and take us to the field and then we do so many of each of the exercises that we do during PT. Then we go and run the obstacle course. After that, we go back to the barracks and put on full field equipment. We will be running five miles. We start out with a slow trot and we keep it up for some distance and then we pick up the pace. We are in the last half mile and I notice that the guy in front of me is starting slow up. I move up beside him and take his rifle off of his shoulder and sling it on my other shoulder. I holler at the other guys that he needs help and a couple of them move along side of him and tell him to unfasten his pack. They each grab a strap and slide it off of his back. With the lighter load, he is able to pick up the pace again and we all go across the finish line in good time. They say that we did not break the record, but that we finished in the upper ranks. Back to the barracks in time to join the rest of the group for dinner.

After dinner, we start checking in those things that were issued to us for basic training. I say goodbye to my rifle and take it and the other things to the supply room. We get issued one of the new duffle bags to take the place of the two barracks bags. I pack what I will not need tonight into the bag and get ready. Tomorrow morning we will get our orders on where we will go next. They have already informed us that we will all be getting a ten-day pass, plus travel time to our homes.

We are all in our class A winter uniforms and we gather in the mess hall. They have brought out the cold cuts and we have those together with a bunch of chips and other snacks. The party committee has bought a bunch of pop and two beers for each person. Since the Mormons do not drink beer, there will be plenty for those that want it. We are all going around and shaking hands and wishing each other well. I dig into the food and while I am at it, I drink a couple of beers. Then I go with the cokes. Some of the guys are getting pretty high, but it will not matter, we are through our basic training. I go back to the barracks and some of the other guys are there too, getting their things packed up. Some of them will have a long trip tomorrow. I sit on my bunk and think about what all I have done, the last seventeen weeks. It has been tough, but I did it. I am now a soldier.

CHAPTER XXIX

We fall out on Saturday morning in our class A winter uniforms. We are a sharp looking outfit, not the ragged bunch, that started here seventeen weeks ago. We no longer have the white stripe running down our faces and across our chins. We got rid of that when we started wearing steel helmets. It is easy to see that we are trained soldiers. All of the brass is present to see us off. The colonel shakes hands with each of us, as we come up when our names are called. The first sergeant hands us an envelope containing our papers. We are at attention, so we can't open them at this time. We are all dying to know what is in there. As soon as we are dismissed, we all open up our envelopes and check our orders. I open my envelope and the first thing I look for is where I am to go next. I am coming back here to Fort Riley and am to report in twelve days to Troop I - Second Regiment, CRTC, Ft. Riley, Kansas. That does not mean much to me, but I guess I will be getting advanced training. The other guys are being assigned all over the country. This is probably the last time we will be in contact with each other, unless by accident.

I go through the rest of the things in my envelope. I have a travel voucher to go from Junction City to Hennessey; I have food ration stamps to take home to cover the food that I will eat while I am home. I will get paid for the meals for this twelve day period, when I get paid next. My pass is included in my orders to report back here. I go over to the orderly room and ask the first sergeant for the envelope containing my money, for my trip home. I thank him for all he has done for me, while I have been here. He shakes my hand and wishes me good luck. I think he really cared for me. Maybe because I looked so young, he felt that he needed to look after me.

Guys are rushing out, carrying their duffel bags with all of their things, trying to get to town to make connections with the bus or train that will take them home. I go into the barracks and sit down and watch as they all leave. I do not have to go yet since my bus leaves later and I do not want to get caught up in the rush. While I am sitting there, I look down the barracks and all of the bunks have mattresses folded up on them and it looks like it did when I got here seventeen weeks ago. Except for one thing, behind every bunk there are empty clothes hangers hanging, but not for long. While I wait, one of the cadre goes along and gathers up every hanger and takes them into his room, at the end of the barracks. I laugh to myself and imagine him selling them tomorrow, to the next group as they come in.

I shoulder my duffel bag and walk out of this part of my life. I head over by the PX, pick up a couple of candy bars and then go get on the bus.

I know from reading the Hennessey paper that the high school football team will be playing at Enid tonight. When we get to Enid, I get off of the bus and gather up my duffel bag and walk almost a mile out to the football field. I find the Hennessey people and ask if someone will give me a ride home after the game. Of course they are glad to.

They drop me off at the house and my mother meets me at the door, with my dad right behind her. It is after ten o'clock, but they are up waiting for me to arrive. I hug my mother and reach out to shake my dad's hand. I am sure that I have changed a lot since they last saw me. I am taller and by standing straighter and wearing my cap, I look even taller. I weigh about eight pounds more, and it is not just flesh, it is every bit muscle. I come into the house and set my duffle bag inside and we go into the living room and sit down. The house is warm and smells like home. They start asking questions about how I am and I try to answer them. They want to know what I will be doing next and all I know to tell them, is that I will be going back to Fort Riley and that I do not know what I will do there. I ask about my younger brother, Tommy, and she tells me that he worked at a grocery store that day. That he was tired and went to bed. She asks if I have eaten. And I tell her that I have only had a couple of candy bars since breakfast.

We all move out to the kitchen while she fixes me a sandwich and a glass of milk. I am almost finished eating when she says that she saved me a little of the homemade ice cream from supper. She still makes it every evening for my dad. While I am eating, I tell them about some of the things that happened in basic. Then she says that it has probably been a long day for me and that I would like to get to bed. I agree, go get my duffel bag and go upstairs to bed. The room looks almost like it did when I left. My model airplanes are still flying from the wire across the room. I run a bath and crawl into the first bathtub I have been in since June 14. It feels good. I go get in bed and lay there for a few minutes, remembering what home is like.

I wake up Sunday morning get dressed and go downstairs. I pass through my brother's room and he is still asleep. It seems late to me, but I realize that it is still early for them. I go out on the front porch and pickup the Sunday paper. I go back inside and sit down in the living room and read it. It is not long before my parents come out. My mother says that she did not think I would be up this early. I tell her that I thought it was late. I am just used to getting up early. She asks what I would like to have for breakfast and I tell her that I would like homemade cocoa and toast, if she can fix it for me again. But I would also like to have a couple of eggs. I am not sure she has cocoa powder or sugar to make the cocoa, but I know that she will have eggs, because they keep some chickens out in back and always have eggs.

She puts on the coffee pot for Dad and starts to make cocoa for me. The bread is in the toaster. She gets the skillet out and puts in four eggs. That will take care of Dad and me both. She fixes herself a bowl of cereal and some toast. While we are eating, Tommy comes down, sticks his head into the kitchen and says, "Hi." I say "Hi" and that is it. Pretty much how brothers communicate. After breakfast, I go back in and read the paper. My mother comes in and asks if I am going to church today. I tell her that I had planned on going. She says that she is glad, because she wants to show me off.

We go to church together, and I am greeted by everyone that I meet. They are probably surprised by how much older I look, than when I used to be the janitor. Mother introduces me to the new people in the church. The minister, Rev. Cartwright, greets me. He asks me if it was like going on scout camp and I tell him that some of it was, but most was hard work. Of course, during the service they recognize me.

When we get home from church, my mother fixes dinner. We have meat loaf, mashed potatoes and gravy, home canned green beans and pickled beets, hot rolls and for dessert, apple pie. I go to the kitchen and help by making the ice tea. She had made apple pie yesterday and mixed the dough for the rolls, so she would have it ready when I got home. I know that this took several ration stamps to prepare this dinner and I go get the stamps I was given, and give them to her, while I think about it. The dinner is great and we stay at the table longer than usual, talking about what has happened while I was gone. Of course they want to hear all about my experiences in the army. I have to be very careful with my language, they would not appreciate it if I let slip some of the words that I am used to using.

In the evening, some of my folks' friends show up to visit. I visit with them, but soon find that we do not have much in common. When they leave, I head up to bed.

Monday morning when I get up, Dad has already gone to work and Tommy is getting ready to go to school. I try to stay out of the way, until he gets off to school. Mother asks what I am going to do today and I tell her that I am going to go to town and walk around and visit. I eat my breakfast and then go to town. I go to the Safeway store, where I worked before I went in the army, and visit with them as they work. Four months ago, I would have been doing that. They all seem glad to see me, but they have to get their work done. I move to the different stores and say hello to the people that I know. I work my way through most of the stores and on down to the high school. I go in and talk to the superintendent. He seems glad to see me. I stay in his office until the bell rings to change class. He goes to check on things and I go visit my former teachers. They only have a few minutes before the next class. I say hello to the students that I know and then walk back up town.

I go to the pool hall, where I used to spend so much time. I visit with the owner a little bit, but it is still early in the day and no one else is there. After that, I go to the drug store and order a fountain coke. I sit at the counter and drink it. There are several people going in and out of here and I get to visit with them. I finish my coke and decide to go back to the house. My mother asks if I am home already. I tell her that there was not much doing and I go get the Reader's Digest and sit in the living room to read it.

Mother comes in and asks me what I would like to have for lunch. She says that she was going to have one of the leftover rolls with some homemade peach butter on it, but she also has peanut butter and thought I might like that with the peach butter on my roll. She says she will make us a pot of tea, if I would like. We sit at the kitchen table and take our time eating and visiting. I realize that this war is really hard on the people at home too. No one seems to complain, it is just something that has to be done. It was this way before I went into the army, but I just never noticed as much.

I read some more and then walk back up town. I go to the pool hall and pay to play a practice round on the snooker table. I go down the street a couple of doors to the drug store and order a chocolate malt. I get it and sit down at one of the tables. I can sit and watch people come and go from here. Most see me there and stop to talk to me. I haven't been home twenty-four hours, and already I am bored.

I wanted so much to come home, but it is no longer the same. I go back home, lay back on the divan and take a nap.

I wake up when Tommy gets home from school. This time, we do visit some. The next door neighbor comes in and we visit for awhile. She tells me some of the things that have been going on in town. It sounds like the way it was before, but this time I am not a part of it. When she leaves, Mom starts fixing supper. She likes to have it ready by six o'clock.

We visit at the supper table. Dad tells me about making landing gear for the Stearman training planes. The parts are made in Enid and shipped to Wichita where they are assembled. It is a steady job. Wages are frozen, so he does not make a lot of money, but there is not much to buy, so they are getting by okay. They do not travel except to work or an emergency. He is trying to make the old car last until the war is over. They do read a lot and take several magazines, as well as the daily and weekly newspapers. In the evening, the radio provides most of the entertainment. They are both active in the church and my mother spends a lot of time writing letters to boys in the service.

After supper, I go up town again. About the only thing open is the pool hall. The other businesses close early, because they do not have help. I go back home and sit and listen to the radio with my folks before I go to bed.

I get up later this morning and Dad and Tommy are gone again. At breakfast I tell Mom that I am going to go to Enid today and take my watch back to the jewelry store. A little before noon, I take the remains of my watch and go to the north end of the business district. The Lions Club has erected a covered bench there, as well as on the other end of town, where a service person can go for a ride. I am only there for a few minutes when a car stops and picks me up. They are going to downtown Enid and will take me right where I want to go. When I get to Enid, I walk to the jewelry store. When I get there, it is an empty building, with a for rent sign in the window. I go next door and ask if they know where the jewelry store moved to. They tell me that it closed and they sold off everything. They think that the old man that ran it has died. So much for the guarantee on my watch. I guess I will have to wear my old one.

I wander around the streets of Enid and go into some of the stores that I used to go to. There is not much to buy. Of course, there is not much that I need either. But I go into the Kress store and right in the front is the candy counter. It used to have so many different candies. But now, there are only a few different kinds, mostly hard candies. Not any chocolate that I can see. I go to the Coney island place and get one for lunch. After that, I go a few doors east to the theater and see that they are still having matinees.

After the movie, I walk over to the dairy store and get another chocolate malt. I go around the other side of the square and check out what they have in Montgomery & Ward and Sears. I slowly make my way down to where my dad is working and sit in the car to wait for him to drive home. On the way home, I get to visit with him and the other two guys that work with him.

CHAPTER XXX

Tuesday evening, I go to town and go to the library to see the girl that I went with some before I went into the army. Emma is still in school and working at the library in the evening. I ask her if she wants to go to the show after she gets off work and she says that she would. I tell her that I will be back about closing time and then I go to the pool hall to wait. I play a couple of games of snooker and visit with some of the younger guys until time to go back to the library. I meet her as she is turning out the lights. I kiss her and then we go to the show. It is not crowded and we sit in the back row. I put my arm around her and she puts her head on my shoulder, as we watch the show. After the show, I walk her home. When we get there, I kiss her goodnight. Things seem a little cool. I will wait a day or two, before I ask her out again.

On Wednesday, I do some work around the yard, raking some leaves, and even cleaning out the chicken house. I used to hate that job, but now that I do not have to do it, it is not so bad. I still have time to make a couple of trips to town to walk around and see if anything interesting is going on. When I get back from my afternoon trip, my mother says that the superintendent has called and invited me to Lions Club the next day. She says that she told him that she was sure that I would like to go.

On Thursday, I go to town and go to the city hall about eleven-thirty. The Lions meet above the city hall. I wait below until the superintendent gets there and then go up with him. He is the secretary, so he is busy, but he puts me with some of the other men that I know. I know most of the men, but I am soon introduced to those that I do not know.

The meeting starts and after the opening ceremonies, we sit down to eat. The food is good. They have a couple of women hired to fix the meal each week. Today they are having chicken fried steak, mashed potatoes with gravy, green salad, corn and apple pie, with ice tea to drink. I wonder how they can have all of this, with the rationing. I decide that they give some of their stamps to the club and that the steak was probably furnished by some farmer. Anyway, it is a great meal. After the program, they introduce me and ask if I will say a few words about what I have been doing. After the meeting, I thank them for having me and they thank me for serving in the army. It is really nice.

I spend the afternoon reading and napping on the divan. After Tommy gets home, he wants to play dominoes again. He smells blood, and he is right, he beats me every game. Dad gets home and we get ready for supper. Mother has made stew for supper and baked some cornbread. It is a great supper for a cool fall evening. I tell Dad about my trip to the Lions Club. He is excited that I got to go. Mother gets out the ice cream and we sit and talk as we eat it.

I visit awhile after supper and then I tell them I am going to town. I go to the library and ask Emma if she wants to go to the show. A new feature starts tonight. She says she will after she closes. I go back to the pool hall again. It seems that I am spending most of my leave in the pool hall. I go back and get her, when she closes the library. She turns out the lights and I take her in my arms and kiss her. She holds me close and I slide my hand into her blouse and slip inside of her bra. I squeeze her breast and rub her nipple. We are both breathing heavy. Then she says we better get to the show before we do something, that we shouldn't. I don't want to go, but I know she is right.

We go to the show and I hold her close during the show. We walk to her house and stop behind some trees before we get in sight of it. We kiss some more and this time, she takes my hand and puts it inside of her blouse. I take advantage and rub both breasts and nipples. I am so hard, she can't help but feel me pressing against her. She says that is enough for tonight, and pulls away and goes to the house. I follow and give her one last kiss on the porch. My heart is pumping, but not much of the blood is going to my brain. I go back to the house and everyone is already in bed.

I sleep late and Dad and Tommy are gone again by the time I get up. It gives me another chance to visit with Mom alone. We eat breakfast and are talking when the phone rings. It is Charles Baker. He is home on leave from navy boot camp and says he will see me after a while. I finish dressing and read the paper, while waiting for Charles. In a little while, he calls and asks if I will meet him at the drugstore. I tell him I will be there in about ten minutes.

We meet at the drugstore and since Charles used to work there, the druggist gives us each a fountain coke. We sit at the counter and there are a lot of people coming in and out today. Almost everyone stops to talk to Charles and I. In between, we talk about what we have been doing. He has just finished the six weeks boot camp and will be going back to San Diego for training in his specialty. I go with him to several of the stores to say hello. He is following about the same path that I followed Monday. The people at Safeway make a lot of wise cracks about having both of us back again. Charles wants to leave and go back to the house so that he is there when his mother gets back from delivering her rural mail route.

I get back to the house and Mom asks if some of the stew we had for dinner last night will be okay for lunch. I tell her that will be fine. While she heats the stew, I pour us a couple of glasses of milk. There are several dairies in the area so milk is not in short supply here and is not rationed. She has a little of the cornbread left too and I put my stew over a piece of cornbread. I am getting to spend quite a bit of time with my mother and I am sure she is glad of that. With Don about to go overseas, she is worried about him. I am sure she worries about me too. I have always been the one that does the things that she would rather I didn't, but she does not want to stand in my way. After lunch, she asks if I will go with her to the grocery store and carry home the groceries. We walk to town and go to Safeway. I get the basket and she selects the things to put in it. She has written down how many ration points she has, so that she will know what she can buy. With the coupons that I brought home, she will have enough to buy several things. She can even get some more sugar and meat. She has the basket full by the time we get to the checkout stand. They kid me about having to sack them and I take over the sacking, as they check the items, first for ration points and then for the money. Checking out is not easy any more. I pick up the sacks and we walk out of the store. Less than six months ago, I did this every day.

Tommy comes home and says that he has to get his band uniform on and get ready to go to the football game. Mother fixes him a sandwich and a glass of milk, while he is getting dressed. He eats and then takes his horn and leaves. Dad gets home and we have supper. I tell them that I told Charles that I would meet him at the football game. Since the game starts at seven, I only have a short time to visit. I go out to the stadium and start to buy a ticket, but they waive me on in. Charles joins me not long after I get there. We walk the sidelines, like most of the fans. Most of the team are guys that we played with last year. I only played for three games, but Charles played center and played the whole season.

Charles and I get to see a lot of people at the game. Almost everyone there comes by and shakes our hands and asks how we are. Hennessey wins the game and everyone is in good spirits. After the game, we walk home and Charles says he will see me tomorrow up town. I go home and Tommy comes in a few minutes later. We tell Mom and Dad about the ball game and I try to tell them who all I saw. Mom baked some cookies for us and asks if we want some before we go to bed. She brings out the plate of cookies and tells me to get the bottle of milk and some glasses. This is a great time, sitting around, eating cookies and milk and visiting.

I get up on Saturday morning and Dad has already gone to work. Tommy is still sleeping. I visit with Mom while we eat breakfast. She waits until I get up to eat, that way we get to visit in the kitchen. After we eat, I read the morning paper and then go to town. This is the day that the farmers come to town. It is the middle of the morning and already there are no parking spaces on Main Street. Those coming in now will have to park on the side streets. They drive up to the creameries to deliver a can of cream and a case of eggs. Some do not have cream to sell, and just drop off their eggs at one of the grocery stores. They will get credit for the eggs, when they buy their groceries. There are long lines at the barber shops. The women are shopping at the ten-cent stores and the dry goods stores. Some of the farmers are at the hardware stores getting repairs. Others are at the feed stores loading up. It is exciting to watch all the activity. Most of these people do not come to town more than once a week, unless it is an emergency, and some do not come but every two or three weeks. It is a great time to socialize.

I go into the drug store and it is crowded. I find an empty table and get a cherry limeade and sit down to wait for Charles. When Charles gets there, we go out and walk down the street. People notice us, since there is a soldier and sailor walking side by side. As it gets closer to noon, I tell Charles that Mom is fixing lunch for us and he is to come home with me. Mother fixes us sandwiches and ice tea and we have some of the cookies from last night. After lunch, we go back to town. We are walking down the street when we see Gloria Gramlich, one of the girls from our class. Charles and I both went with her. She was more like a sister than a girlfriend. She is working in Oklahoma City now and came home for the weekend. We walk around the streets looking in the stores and then we go back to my house. We visit awhile and Charles offers to walk Gloria home.

I lay on the divan and read until supper time. When Dad gets home, I help Mom get supper on the table. At supper, I get to tell what all I have done today. Today was interesting and I was not bored. Tommy wants to know if I will play checkers with him. I guess he is tired of beating me in dominoes and wants to move to another game. But this time, he is in for a surprise. I beat him every game. I stay up a little while longer and listen to the radio. I want to hear the ten o'clock news. After it is over, I go to bed too.

CHAPTER XXXI

I go to church on Sunday morning and both Charles and Gloria are there. I sit with them. I look around, but my girlfriend is not there. She had told me she might have to go to her sister's house and babysit for the weekend. Church is much like the week before, but this time, they acknowledge both Charles and I. After church, I join my folks and Tommy and we walk back home. I help mother get dinner on the table. She is fixing fried chicken, potatoes and gravy, harvard beets, cucumber pickles and pickled peaches. She has a gelatin dessert and some more of the cookies. I make the ice tea while she is cooking.

It is really a great dinner. When we get through with dinner, we put things away and stack the dishes to wash later. We all load up in the car and head for Waukomis, where my grandmother lives. It is only thirteen miles to Waukomis and we drive along at thirty-five miles an hour.

My grandmother is glad to see me. I have not seen her since about a month before I went into the army. She has something for me. It is a four leaf-clover, inside of a celluloid holder. I take it and attach it to my dog tag chain. She says that she hopes it will bring me good luck. We visit awhile and then I go outside and walk around the place. I have had a lot of fun here, playing with my brothers and my cousins.

I go back in the house and the folks say that it is time to go back home. They do not want to be out after dark and take the chance of having to fix a flat in the dark. We go home and get there in time to listen to our favorite radio programs. I have not heard them in a long time, but not much has changed. Bob Hope is broadcasting from one of the air bases. When the ten o'clock news is over, we all go to bed.

Monday morning, after I eat breakfast and read the paper, I help Mother with the wash. I go to town to the drugstore and meet Charles. We decide to go hunting. His mother has an old model A Ford that she drives when it is muddy. We get the guns and take off in the old model A. We go to one of the places where we used to hunt. We walk around through the trees along the creek. It has not been cold enough to kill all the vegetation and we do not find any rabbits. We do not care; it is good just to get out in the country. We come back in and I call my mother and tell her I will not be home for dinner. Charles and I are going to go to the café and eat. The service is slow. Just like every other business, they are short of help. We each order the plate lunch. It is hamburger steak today. It comes with a small salad, french fries and pudding for desert and ice tea to drink, all for a dollar.

After dinner, I go home and lay down on the divan with a magazine to read. I read awhile and then doze off. Mother wakes me up and asks me to help her bring the clothes in. By the time we get done, Tommy is home from school and he tells us what is happening there. While he talks, I help get supper ready. Mother is taking the leftover potatoes and making cakes out of them and we will have them with the rest of the fried chicken and the beets from yesterday. She has ice cream in the refrigerator and takes it out and whips Milnot into it and then puts it back in the freezing shelves.

When Dad gets home, we have supper and after supper, I go to town and go to the library. Emma is there, but she has her little niece and nephew with her. She is having to take care of them tonight, because her sister is still gone. She tells me that her sister will be back tomorrow and that she can see me tomorrow night. I tell her that is fine and remind her that I have to go back Wednesday.

I go back to the pool hall and Charles is there too. I ask him if he is bored, now that we are back home for awhile. He admits that he too, is used to being busy all the time and that even after such a short time, home is not the same. I say I will see him again tomorrow. He has to leave Thursday and go back to San Diego. We say goodnight and walk home. I visit with the folks until the news on the radio is over and then go to bed.

I get up earlier today and see Dad and Tommy off. Mother and I eat our breakfast together again. She has washed all of my dirty clothes and has them pressed and laid out for me to pack. I go ahead and pack all the things that I will not need into my duffle bag and have that much done. After that I go upstairs to clean up. I look in the mirror and I notice the fuzz on my face is getting thicker and that there are a couple of hairs growing out of my chin. I decide it is time to shave them off. I find Don's old shaving mug and brush, add a little hot water and lather up my face. There is a safety razor there too and a package of blades, so I put in a new one and give myself my first shave. It makes my face burn, so I look and find some Old Spice aftershave and put some of that on it. It stings. I know most guys like it when they get old enough to shave, but I hate to have to start.

Just before noon, I tell my mother not to fix lunch for me I will walk to town and eat. I go look around for Charles. He is at the barber shop getting a haircut. He is trying to get them to cut it close enough so that he will not have to get another when he gets to San Diego. I decide that I should get one too, before I go back. When I get in the chair, the barber asks me if I shaved this morning and I tell him that I did and ask why. He says that I missed a spot, but that he will get it when he shaves my neck.

After the haircuts, Charles and I go down the street to the little diner and get a hamburger and a piece of pie. They taste good. I used to stop in here and get a piece of pie when I went from school to work at the grocery store. After we eat, we walk two blocks east to Charles' house. His mother is home from her mail route. I am glad to see her. She has always been like a second mother to me. We visit for awhile and then I walk up the alley to my house and go in the back door.

Mom wants to know what I have been doing and I tell her all about it. We talk about what I may be doing when I get back. I really do not know, but do tell her what some of the things might be. I will not be far from where I was before. I know that I will miss home, but I will be glad to get back and get busy again. She is working on supper while we talk. Peeling the potatoes, carrots and onions to put in with the beef roast. She has made dough and will put rolls in the oven, with the roast. She has already made the ice cream and it is freezing in the tray. She will take it out later and beat it. I am sure that she has used up most of their ration points for this month and it will be slim eating for the rest of the month, but she wants my last meal at home to be memorable.

Tommy comes home from school and she sends him in to do his homework before supper. Of course he argues with her, telling her that he will do it later. She insists and he finally gives up and goes in and starts on it. Dad comes home and she tells him that by the time he gets cleaned up, supper will be ready. We move into the dining room for supper. Dad wants to know what the special occasion is and she says that she wants to have a nice dinner, before I go back. He knows that, but asks just to call attention to it. The dinner is wonderful. Everything tastes great. The meal is light spirited, but behind it is the knowledge that this may be the last time I ever eat here. They can't help but be worried about me.

After supper, I tell Tommy that I will play one more game of dominoes with him. He gets out the game and we start in. I get lucky and make some good draws and beat him two out of three games. We turn on the radio for the Tuesday night programs that the folks like. I listen for a while and then tell them I am going to go to town for awhile. They probably know that I am going to the library, but they do not say anything about it. I walk up to the library and tell Emma hello and ask if it's all right for me to wait there, until she closes up. She says that she would like that. I get a book and sit at one of the tables to read. At nine o'clock she turns out the lights and locks the door.

We start down the street towards the theater and she stops and says that she does not feel like going to the movie tonight. I figure that something is wrong and that she will want to go home. But instead she says, let's just walk around for awhile. That is fine with me. Instead of going down Main Street, we go east. Not many are out at this time of night. We walk along, hold hands and talk about things in general. Then she starts asking what I think I will do after I leave. I tell her that I am going back to Fort Riley for awhile and I suppose for advanced training, but that I will probably go overseas when that is finished. She asks if I will go into combat and I tell her that the type of job I have been trained for is needed in combat. As we talk and walk, we get close to the ball park.

We walk over to the stands and walk between the board fence and the stands. We are out of sight from anyone, but the streetlight across the street provides enough light so that we can see. I take her in my arms and kiss her. I hold her tight and when her lips part, I push my tongue into her mouth. This is a whole new sensation. We kiss that way for awhile and when I pull back some, she opens her coat, unbuttons her blouse and pulls her bra down, exposing her breasts. I reach out and take them and squeeze them and rub her nipples. I lower my head and press it against her breasts. I can hear her heart beating fast and feel her rapid breathing. I can see her dark nipples against her white breasts. I take my tongue and lick her nipples and then suck them into my mouth. I can smell the scent of a young woman who is aroused. My hand goes under her skirt and feels her thighs. I slide my hand up along her thighs, until I feel her cotton panties. They are damp. I rub the dampness and then try to slip a finger under the leg of her panties. She moves her leg to allow me access. My finger enters her. I can feel the warm, moist smoothness of it.

My heart is pounding and I am shaking. Every sense I have is stretched to the extreme, except for my common sense. Suddenly it comes to life, when she says "What would your mother think of this?" It strikes the right nerve. My mother is her Sunday school teacher. She knows what my mother would think, as much as I do. We are neither one ready to go any further. I help her get her clothes back together and we take hands again and I walk her home. I kiss her good night and goodbye and walk back home. When I get home everyone is in bed, so I go upstairs, run a bath, get in and masturbate.

I get up before anyone else today, pack up my things and carry my bag back downstairs. Mom gets up and starts breakfast. Dad comes in, in a few minutes. I will be riding with him to Enid and catch the bus there to Wichita. We do not say much. I hand Mom the part of my bus ticket that I did not use and tell her if she wants to take a trip to Enid and back to use it. Or take it to the drugstore and cash it in. I hug Mom and kiss her good bye, while Dad carries my bag out and puts it in the trunk. We get in the car and Dad goes to pick up the other two guys and we drive to Enid. He takes me to the bus station, shakes my hand and tells me to be careful. I say that I will. We both know that this may be the last time, that we will see each other. He drives off and I go in and present my ticket to the agent, so he will reserve me a seat on the bus.

CHAPTER XXXII

I get on the bus at Enid and head for Wichita. The bus is not full, so I get to sit by myself. This gives me more room to stretch out. We get to Wichita and I have about an hour layover before the bus leaves for Junction City. I go in the coffee shop and get a sweet roll and a cup of coffee. I was the only soldier on the trip from Enid, but about half of the passengers now are soldiers. I am sure that most are just like me and coming back from leave.

We get to Junction City and I board the bus back to the CRTC and go to the building, where I am to report. It is the temporary assignment office. They sign me in and assign me to a barracks to await my assignment to a unit. They tell me my barracks number and show me on a map where it is. I already suspect where it is, because it is in the same area as the barracks I was in, when I first came to Fort Riley. Sure enough, it is one of the single story, gray tar paper shacks, that I was in when I first got here. In June it was as hot as an oven and now it is as cold as a refrigerator.

The building is heated by a coal stove in the middle. The latrine is a block away and the mess hall about two blocks. I can only hope that I am not here long. My bunk is about halfway between the stove and the door, so the temperature may be as good as I can find.

I leave my things in my duffle bag, with the small padlock holding it closed. I have not been here long enough to know any of the guys and there are a lot of guys coming and going through here.

By the time I get my bed made up, it is time for supper and the guys start moving toward the mess hall. I fall in behind them. We have to wait awhile before we can go in and the wind is sharp. At last the door opens and there is a rush to get inside. As soon as the first part of the line is inside, it slows up. Once they are out of the cold, they are in no hurry to get their food. The line moves slowly and at last I am inside. They are serving some kind of stew, peas, bread and a flat cake without any icing. There are coffee and milk to drink. Nothing like the meals that we had during basic. I eat some of the stew and it is nothing like that my mother made, either. The peas are cold and taste like the can they came out of. I eat some bread and peanut butter, drink a glass of milk and a cup of coffee. Then I hurry back to the barracks.

As the others come in, we congregate on the bunks around the stove. We start to get acquainted. We are pretty much a mixture as to where we came from and what we do. We have one thing in common; we want to get out of here as soon as possible. We visit until nearly time for lights out and then everyone heads for the latrine. Then it is back to the barracks. One guy who has been here for a few days shows the rest of us how to bank the fire so that it will burn all night and we will not have to get up in the morning and build a new one. Then I take off all my clothes, except my underwear, and crawl between the blankets.

It is three-ten in the morning and I wake up and cuss myself for drinking that cup of coffee at supper. I get out of bed, put on my overcoat and slip my feet into my shoes and make the long trek to the latrine. There is a boardwalk leading to the latrine, but it has sunk into the ground and if you get off of it, you are in the mud. When I am done, I hurry to get back to the barracks. I step off of the walk a couple of times, so when I get to the barracks, I have to stop and scrape my shoes. I remind myself not to drink coffee in the evening any more, until I get out of this place.

Someone turns on the lights in the barracks and guys are scrambling around, getting clothes on and gathering their toilet articles for a trip to the latrine. I do not have to go as bad as some do, because of my trip in the night. I take off after most of the others. I get washed up and then go back to the barracks to wait. No one calls us out for reveille. Nobody knows who is here anyway. When we think it is about time for chow, we head for the mess hall. They even cook on coal stoves here. We get in out of the cold and find that they have SOS today. I am not opposed to it, and kind of like it, if it is prepared right, but this today has big pools of grease floating around on top of it. The toast is so hard they could use them for paving. I decide to go against my vow to eat everything, and pass up on it. I get a glass of grapefruit juice and grab a couple of small boxes of cold cereal. I eat the cereal and then drink the rest of the milk. I do drink coffee, but figure that it will be out of my system before night.

After breakfast, the sergeant comes into the barracks and starts handing out details. He sends me to the next barracks to sweep it out. This would be easy, if the barracks were warm. I decide that if they want it swept out, that they must plan on using it, and they will need heat. I go back to the other barracks and get some paper and kindling. I fill the coal bucket from the bin on the back of the building and proceed to build a fire. After I get the fire going, I finish sweeping out the barracks. I go back next door and find a magazine and bring it over and fix a place where I can read by the stove and still see out into the street, to see if anyone is coming.

We are back at the barracks and I look out of the window and see the sergeant coming. I know he is going to have more details. I tell everyone, "Here comes the sergeant, I better get back to work." With that, I go out the back door and head next door. I put a little more coal in the stove, pick up the magazine and sit down to read. I have only been in the army for a little over four months, but I am learning. I spend the afternoon there and go back to the barracks in the evening.

We are sitting there waiting for time to eat supper, when another guy comes into the barracks. He is from Broken Arrow, Oklahoma, and was in radio school at the same time that I was, but in a different platoon. He had a day longer leave than I had, because of the distance he had to travel home. We knew each other from school and he wants to know where we are going and what we will be doing. I have to tell him that I don't know any more than he does. He picks out a bunk next to me and I tell him to stow his things, until after supper. I hope that we get out of here soon.

The next morning after breakfast, I shoulder my broom and march next door. I have read everything there is to read here. I saw that there was a day room next to the orderly room, so I shoulder my broom again and walk straight past the orderly room and into the day room. No one is there and I grab a bunch of magazines, stuff them inside of my fatigue jacket, shoulder my broom and go back. I am able to spend the rest of the day next door reading, only coming out to eat or go to the latrine.

In the evening, I check the bulletin board and find that my days of leisure are over. I have table waiter duty tomorrow. I put the towel on my bunk in the evening and then crawl out when they wake me at four in the morning.

I have had table waiter duty enough to know what is required and also which jobs are the easiest. I work it so that I get those. After each meal, there is a time when we are not doing anything, so I slip off and go over to the day room and spend my time. For some reason, they do not have anyone keeping the day room. I mostly have it to myself. A few guys will drift in and out during the day. I decide that tomorrow, I will be in charge of the day room.

The next morning after breakfast, instead of putting on my fatigues, I put on my Class A uniform. The guys ask me if I have received my orders, but I tell them that I have another job. I walk over to the day room and start straightening it out. I get everything looking nice and then I sit behind the desk and read. About ten o'clock, the sergeant comes in and looks around. I ask him if I can help him with something. He says he is just looking for loafers. I tell him that there have only been a few guys in so far today. He seems satisfied and leaves. This is easier than working on some detail, but I am getting bored. Later in the afternoon, I put everything in place and go back to the barracks.

We go to supper and I am one of the few guys there with class A uniform on. One of the guys at the table asks why I am not in my fatigues. I tell him that they needed someone to supervise the day room and that I volunteered. Several of the guys say that they wish they could get a good job like that. I just tell them to watch the bulletin board when they put up notices and maybe there will be something else available.

Saturday morning, I go to the day room again. At noon, I go to dinner and catch the other radio operator, Gene, and ask him if he wants to go to town this afternoon. He wants to know how we are going to get a pass. I tell him to look in his orders for his pass from basic. We can use that. I tell him to go back, before the others get there and change into his class A uniform too. I meet him and we take off, before the other guys get back from dinner. We walk to the PX and catch the bus to town. At the gate the MP's come on to check passes and we hold ours up and they tell the bus driver to go ahead.

We walk around town for awhile and then go into an army-navy store. They have insignia and patches there. We each buy a radio operator's patch. We make our way back to the barracks and change out of our class A uniform. We go to supper and some of the guys ask where we have been. I tell them that we had to go get our radio operator's patches. I do not tell them where we went to get them.

Sunday is a quiet day. I walk over to my old area and go to the day room. I sit and read the paper and wait for church services. When the chaplain gets there, he says that he is surprised to see me. I tell him that I would do anything to get away from that other area and he says that he doesn't blame me.

After church, I go back and go to dinner. It is a little better today. They have ham with pineapple for the main course. I walk out and check the bulletin board to see if I am on duty tomorrow and I see that we two radio men and a mechanic are to report to the orderly room at eight o'clock tomorrow morning. It looks like we may be getting an assignment.

CHAPTER XXXIII

We report to the orderly room and are given our orders. We are to report to R-2, which is a replacement office. We move to another barracks in the same complex. The next day, we are assigned to Troop I - Second Regiment. We move to another of the brown tar paper barracks and the latrine is still a block away and the mess hall is almost as far as before. Everything is still heated by coal, including the cooking stoves. No one has really said yet what we will be doing. This unit is an assault gun outfit. They have light tanks with seventy-five mm howitzers mounted on a modified turret. As near as we can tell, the mechanic will be assigned to the weapons maintenance and we two radio operators will go with the unit and get our training, by operating radios while they are doing their training.

It is Wednesday and we are on detail cleaning out a barracks. At noon, we go to the mess hall and get in line. I may have misjudged this mess hall. It is in the same kind of building and they use coal stoves, but it is nice and clean and the food is about the best I have had in the army. I remark about it to one of the noncoms and he says that it is an award-winning mess, that everyone helps and that even the noncoms pull KP.

In the afternoon, we return to the barracks that we are supposed to be cleaning. When we see the men coming back in from training, we go back to our barracks. No one pays much attention to us. They fall out for retreat, but we just stay in the barracks. When it is chow time, we follow them and go eat. It is just as good as it was at noon. I have a feeling that nobody knows what to do with us yet. I make the trip to the latrine and shower before bedtime. It is really cold out and I hate having to walk back to the barracks with just my underwear and my overcoat on. But I don't want to have to dress either.

We do not fall out for reveille this morning when the others do. When the first sergeant gets through with them, he comes into the barracks and I figure that we are going to catch hell for not falling out. But he just says for us to come to the orderly room about eight o'clock, that he thinks he has finally found out what to do with us. This makes us nervous, but we go to breakfast and then wait at the barracks as the troops go out.

At eight we are at the orderly room waiting. The first sergeant is busy and they tell us to wait. After awhile, he calls us into his office. He says that he got the paperwork on us and all it says is that we are attached to his unit for meals and quarters. It does not say what we are to do. He says that he called headquarters and asked and they told him they would get back to him. Yesterday evening, they called and said that we were to help in the training of the trainees in using the radio. In addition, we would be getting advance radio training at the communications building. That means when the trainees go to the field, we will go with them and show them how to use the radios properly. On the days that they do not go to the field, we will go to the communications building and attend classes there. He says that since we are not really trainees, he is having us move into the cadre barracks and that we will live with them. He says that today, we can move our things and get set up and that tomorrow, we will be going out into the field with the platoon.

We gather up our things and move them into the cadre barracks. It is a little closer to the latrine and mess hall, but outside of that, there is not much difference. But here, we will not have to jump through the hoops, like the guys in basic. There is plenty of room in the building for us and we pick out a couple of bunks, leaving one bunk between us and the others; in case they feel we are moving in on them and crowding them.

After we get moved in, we decide that we will walk to the communications building and see if they know anything about what we will be studying. It is a long walk from where we are to there. We get there and ask the instructor what we will be studying and he says he does not know. But he says that we can spend our time practicing our code and working with the radios that they have there. He says that he will just leave it up to us. As long as we do not bother the other students, we can do just about what we want. We loaf around for awhile and then walk back to our area. We get there in time to go to dinner. After diner we just stay in the barracks. I figure that they will not be looking for details here and we can just take it easy. We both write some letters and then I look over and Gene is asleep on his bunk. I lay back and take a nap too.

We wake up when we hear the troops returning and get things straightened up before anyone comes in. No one even asks what we have been doing. However, I ask a couple of them what they are going to do tomorrow and tell them we are supposed to go with them in the morning. They tell us that we need to go to the supply room and check out a couple of tanker helmets. The supply sergeant gives us each an old helmet. They are like a football helmet except they have a place in the sides for ear phones.

After supper, we visit with some of the cadre. They ask what our job is. We tell them that when they go to the field, we are to go along and observe how the trainees use the radio and give them pointers, and on the days that we do not go to the field, that we are to go to the communications building and work there. I think that sounds better than to go study.

The next morning after breakfast, we fall out with the troops. I have on my regular underwear and my winter wool underwear, under my fatigues. I put my overcoat on over everything. I have the helmet with me. We march to the motor pool and everyone climbs into vehicles to drive out into the field. I am told to get into a halftrack. I watch as they turn on the radios and make contact with the other vehicles. They do not follow the procedure that we were taught, but I do not say anything. I think that it is better if I wait to make any corrections. We move out into the field with a jeep in front of us, a couple of halftracks and then the half dozen tanks. They are M24, heavy-light tanks. Only the army would label something like that.

We ride around all morning as the trainees take turns driving the tanks and halftracks. They take them over some of the roughest territory they can find. I am so cold, that I duck down in the half track to try to keep out of the wind. At noon, they drive back into camp for dinner. Fortunately, they have inside class in the afternoon, so I do not have to go out again today. We radio operators tell them we are going to the communications building and take off. We head to the PX. It is warm in there. We then decide it is not too safe there, and go to the communications building. We read the magazines that we got at the PX. Just before supper time, we head back to the mess hall. After supper, we decide to go to the movie. Bob Hope is starring in "The Princess and the Pirate."

The next day, the troop is not going to the field, so we wait until they move off to class and then we make our way over to the communications building. We go by our old day room and pick up some magazines on the way. When we get to the communications building, we go in and get ready to start taking code. There are a bunch of beginning students there, but we go to the sixteen words per minute table and we are not in their way. Our hands are cold and it takes a while to warm them up enough so that we can take code at that speed. We work about an hour, then we go back into the unused classroom, get comfortable and read our magazines.

About noon, we work our way back to the barracks. We both have our overcoats on, and the wind is really sharp and it is spitting snow and sleet. After dinner, we go back to the barracks and wait for mail call. I get one new letter and a couple of old ones. Everyone is off from now until Monday morning. Most everyone leaves for the weekend, except those who have duty. Gene goes into Junction

City, but there is nothing there for me. I will just stay in camp. I go over to the day room and pick up one of the books that I was reading while I had my job there, and bring it back to the barracks.

We go to the mess hall and do not have to stand long before they open the doors. The food is good and we take our time eating. They have peach cobbler for dessert, and since most of the guys are gone, we can have all we want. I would like to have some coffee to wash it down, but I have learned my lesson about drinking it in the evening with the latrine so far away. Later, we decide to go to the movie and walk over there.

Sunday morning, after breakfast, I go to the PX and get a paper and then go to the day room to read it. The same chaplain will be conducting services here this morning.   I am the only one there when he arrives, so I help him set up. After the service, I go back to the barracks and wait for time for Sunday dinner. There are only a few of us here. We walk over to the mess hall in a group. When we get our food, we go sit at the noncom table, with the cadre.

In the afternoon, I read and take another nap. Supper is the usual cold cuts, but they have sliced some of the cold meatloaf for sandwiches too. For dessert, they have some vanilla ice cream with strawberry preserves on top, another good meal. Next week is Thanksgiving.

CHAPTER XXXIV

Monday morning and we are back in the field with the trainees. I ride around in the halftrack and I huddle down in it, because it is so cold. They take a break to change drivers and they ask me if I would like to ride in a tank. I tell them that I would. I climb onto the top of the tank and then drop down through the hatch, into the interior of the tank. I will be sitting where the gunner would sit. I can't see out, I can only see the back of the driver and assistant driver, the legs of the tank commander and the loader sitting across from me. They take off and it jerks to a start. There is a lot of noise and I bounce around inside of the tank. Everything in there is steel and it hurts when you hit it. I have to hang on with both hands, to keep from flying out of my seat. I guess you get used to this, but it is a very rough ride. When they change drivers again, I climb out and make my way to the halftrack.

We come back in at noon for dinner and then we go back out for the afternoon. By evening, the fun is all over for me. I have all the rough riding that I want for awhile. When they get back in, the trainees start to clean up the vehicles, which are covered with mud and we head back to the barracks. They probably resent it, but no one said that we had to clean up vehicles. We are the radio operators.

We go to supper and sit at the cadre table. They treat us okay, but they are not overly friendly. One of them reminds us that everyone in this outfit pulls KP. We say that is fine, that we will be glad to. After supper, they have mail call and I get a letter and a package of homemade cookies from my aunt. I pass the cookies around and that does more for good relations with the cadre than anything else we could do.

Tuesday they have class, so we go to the communications building. We take magazines and books with us and spend the day there, only coming back to eat dinner. We take code, but you can only do that for so long before you have to do something else. We usually find some place to get in out of the weather. But we always find our way back in time for meals. Tonight they announce that the whole outfit is moving to another area.

No one seems unhappy about having to move. We start packing our stuff up, to get it ready to go. Some of the cadre have been here for several months, so it will take them some time to get their things all rounded up. Most of my things have not even been unpacked. I go to bed and hope that it is the last that I see of these barracks.

Wednesday morning after breakfast, we gather up our things and start the march to the new barracks. It is several blocks away, but is right next to the machine shop where they work on the equipment. The barracks are the newest ones on the post and the nicest that I have ever had. We bunk in the cadre barracks and put our things in there. We will be able to arrange them later. When the first trucks are loaded, we go with them to the new mess hall and help unload things. After that, we stay there and unload as the trucks keep making trips. We have a lot of it moved by noon, and the cooks are already working to get out some kind of dinner. It will be more of a lunch. We will have sandwiches and coffee or milk. After the mess hall has been moved, we help load up the orderly room. Most of the troops are working on moving the supply room.

We help get the equipment set up in the orderly room and get it operational. We stop for lunch and after that, we get a chance to unpack our things and make our beds and hang up our clothes.

There are a lot of little things to do. We now have a new address too. Everything is the same, except I am in barracks 2310. Since the whole unit moved, it should not make much of a problem with the mail.

The evening meal is stew and cornbread. It was something that they could fix without too much trouble. It is tasty and fill-ing. Tomorrow is Thanksgiving and they announce that because of the move, we will have the big meal in the evening. This gives the cooks time to fix everything. After supper, I go to the latrine, which is only a few feet away, on the same floor of this building. I take a shower and walk back to my bunk with just my shorts on. It is great to be in a warm building. The building is heated with a gas furnace.

Thanksgiving Day and it is not a holiday. The trainees go to class and we do the same thing. We come back at noon and they have a light lunch for us. We can smell the food cooking for the big evening meal. They have mail call and I get a couple of letters. The supply sergeant tells us to come over to the supply building and pick up our tankers outfits. We go with him and he issues us each a jacket, overalls and a hood, all wool blanket lined. Then we go back to the communications building and spend the afternoon, but we make sure we get back plenty early for dinner.

The troops are all in their class A uniforms. We wore ours today, so we are ready. When it is time for dinner, everyone lines up to go in, the trainees at one door and the cadre, including us, at the other. Tonight, we sit at the tables and the chaplain gives the Thanksgiving prayer and then we get up and go through the line. The trainees go first and then the cadre follow. It is probably the best meal that I have ever had. It starts off with grapefruit juice, tomato-mushroom soup, green salad, roast turkey with dressing, mashed potatoes and gravy, corn, green beans, cranberry sauce and on the tables are trays with apples, oranges, celery, pickles, olives, nuts and candy. To fin-ish it off, they have hot mince pie. All you want to eat. Since I do not have far to go to the latrine, I wash it down with a cup of coffee.

After supper, a bunch of us go to see a USO show at the theater. Then we come back to our nice barracks. I take a shower and go to bed. It has been a good Thanksgiving, even if I am not home.

The next day, we put on our tanker outfits and go with the troops out in the field. It is still cold and snowing some, but it would be worse, if I did not have this extra clothing. We come back in for dinner and we have mail call. I get a couple of letters. We go back out in the afternoon and ride around some more. This time, I make a few suggestions to the trainees on their radio procedure. They seem to be glad to get my suggestions. I think by waiting until now, and just making it as a suggestion, has had a good effect, not like I am trying to make them do something.

When we get back in, we stay in our fatigues, since we do not fall out for retreat. Then after supper, we are ready to help GI the barracks. It has been a while since these barracks have had a good cleaning, so it takes some time. But since these barracks are newer, they are easier to clean. When we finish, I get my shower and stay in the barracks. After riding around all day in the cold, I am tired and sleepy.

Saturday morning and the troops will have to stand inspection. We put on our class A uniforms, and as soon as we finish our breakfast, we two take off for the communications building. We would rather not be around when they are having inspection. Too much brass here. The communications trainees come in to work on their code. We go to the sixteen-word-per-minute table and work. When they take a break, we go into the unused class room and take it easy. Sometimes it seems that we are really working to keep from having to work. We go back in time for dinner. Not too many there. As soon as inspection was over, most of them took off.

I decide to just hang around and write some letters. I want to be sure to write to my brother, Don, and tell him what I am doing. He will wonder, since I have completed basic and they say that they do not send anyone under nineteen overseas. I figure that I had just as well stay here for the weekend. The barracks is warm and as comfortable as any place in the army. The food is excellent and I can probably even take in a movie sometime today or tomorrow. In the letter that I write to my mother, I tell her that I wish she would get with my relatives and make a schedule to send me my Christmas packages, so that I will not get them all at once. I also tell her that I can't think of anything I want, other than cookies and candy.

On Monday, we go back out in the field all day, just like Friday. It is colder and there is more snow on the ground. After being out in the cold all day, it is good to get back inside. But I get tired and sleepy when I get in where it is warm.

Tuesday, the trainees have indoor class, so we go to the communications building. The instructor asks us if we will monitor some of the nets they are setting up. We are glad to. It is something to do and does not take a lot of work. We spend the day there except for going back for dinner. After supper, one of the guys has a Montgomery & Ward Christmas catalog and he lets me look at it. I see some things that I would like to get for the kids in the family. There is a Montgomery & Ward store in Junction City and, as soon as I get paid, I want to go in and order some things.

When we come back in at noon, they have the pay table set up and we get paid. I have been waiting for this. We go back to the field in the afternoon. They are trying to get all of the trainees qualified on driving the tanks before they go on bivouac. After supper, I borrow the Montgomery & Ward catalog again and select things that I want to get.

The trainees have class today. My buddy and I put on our class A uniform and leave after everyone has gone to class. We go to the PX and catch the bus to Junction City. Since it is the day after payday, almost everyone wants to get to town. When the stores open, I head for the Montgomery & Ward catalog order store. I go in and pick out the things that I want to order for the kids. I place the order and have it shipped to my folks. I pay for everything and my Christmas shopping is done. My buddy, Gene, buys several things and has them sent home too.

We go back to the barracks and wait for dinner. While we are eating, the first sergeant comes over to us and says that he needs to talk to us. I think that some way he has found out about us going to town. But instead, he says that we are going to have to go on bivouac next week. They are going to be closing down the mess hall and barracks and we will have no place to stay. This is not the best news we have ever heard. He says for us to go to the supply room and pick up some things that we will need to stay in the field for a couple of weeks.

We head over to the supply building and tell the supply sergeant that we need enough equipment to go on bivouac. He issues us some heavy wool, knee-length socks, felt inner soles for our overshoes, mufflers, wool sweaters, wool mittens with mitten covers, steel helmet and a mosquito bar. Only the army would do that. He says that he does not have any sleeping bags, but to come back Saturday morning and he will see what he can do. Putting the felt inner sole in our overshoes and putting on the heavy socks is supposed to take the place of insulated boots.

Saturday morning we go to the supply room to get our sleeping bags. It is a mad house with them trying to load up what they will take to the bivouac site. The supply sergeant says that he could not get any more sleeping bags, but gives each of us another shelter half and an extra blanket. This is not what we wanted, but it looks like it is all we are going to get. We go back and get all of our things packed to take with us. Mail call brings a letter and a package from my mother. The package is just in time. It has cookies and candy in it. I am not sharing this package with everyone. My buddy and I will eat it while we are out in the field.

CHAPTER XXXV

Monday morning we load our things onto a truck headed for the bivouac area. At least we do not have to hike out, like we did when we went to bivouac in basic. When we get to the location, we see a bunch of tents set up in a clearing in a grove of trees. They point out an area, a little way away from the other tents, where we can pitch our tent. We pick a spot next to a clump of trees, where there is some taller dry grass. Of course, the ground is covered with snow. We scrape the snow away from a spot the best we can and pitch our tent. We take the four shelter halves and button them together, so that it makes one long, narrow, low tent. We each get in our side and take our blankets and make a bed. Our heads will be near the center, and our feet will be down in the tapered end of the tent. We will have to button and unbutton the flaps every time we want to go in or out.

We get all set up and then we go out to see what the rest of the camp is doing. The trainees are arriving in the tanks and halftracks. We watch as they go to the trucks and get their things and take them into the squad tents. We walk over to their tents and see that they are eight-man tents, with a canvas floor and a stove in the middle. They roll out their down sleeping bags on the floor of the tent. They have down sleeping bags and they are sleeping in a heated tent. It does not take long for us to realize that we are not considered part of this outfit.

When they get settled in, they have them fall out and go on tank maneuvers. We climb into the halftracks and go with them. It is really cold and spitting snow again. We go back to the tents at noon and they have the mess tent set up for the cooks. We get our mess kits out of the tent and get in line. We go to our tent and crawl inside and close the flaps, so that we can eat out of the wind and snow. I sit on my blankets and lean against my duffle bag, with my mess kit between my legs and eat. It is so cold that I drink some coffee. I will wish tonight that I hadn't.

In the afternoon, we go out with the tanks and halftracks again. Some places, the tanks break through the frozen ground and get into the mud. It fills the tracks and gets packed into the bogey wheels. When we go back to camp in the evening, we dismount and the trainees and cadre start taking anything they can find and cleaning the mud off of the vehicles. Gene asks if we are supposed to help them. "They are the ones in the down sleeping bags in the heated tents and we are the ones in the blankets in the pup tent, what do you think?" We go crawl into our tent and try to get our feet warm. I tell Gene that I don't think the mosquito net is going to help much to keep us warm.

We get our supper and head right for our tent and eat like we did at noon. When we finish, we go and wash our mess kits. I try to sling all the water off, but the drops that do not come off are soon frozen. It is starting to get dark and there is nothing that we can do, except go to bed. I take off all of my clothes, down to my wool long handles and slide into the folded blankets. It doesn't feel very warm. I curl up as much as I can, and pull my overcoat over the top of me. I shiver awhile and then go to sleep.

I wake up in the night and know that I am going to have to get up. I slide out of the blankets, slip my feet into my overshoes, unbutton the tent flap and crawl out. It is light out, the sky has cleared and the stars look so close that you could touch them. There is not much of a moon, but with the light shining off of the snow, it is easy to see. It is about seventy-five yards to where they have made a slit latrine and put a fly around it. I am not going to tramp over there. I go around the clump of trees and find a tree trunk that I can use, so that I will not leave a yellow spot in the snow. My urine steams as it hits the cold bark of the tree. I hurry back, open the fly on the tent and crawl back in. I get my overshoes off and slide back between the blankets again.

I wake up early in the morning. I go ahead and get out of the blankets and put my clothes on. It is hard to get everything on while sitting or kneeling on the blankets. When I am dressed, I head off for the latrine. When I get back to the tent, I lay back against my duffle bag, to wait until it is chow time. My buddy is awake now and going through the motions that I did to get dressed. We gather up our frozen mess kits and go to the chow line. They are serving sausage and pancakes today. The pancakes are cold, but the syrup is supposed to be hot and warm them up, when you pour it over them. Unfortunately, the syrup is not very hot either. The sausage is still warm when I get it, but has cooled off by the time I get back to the tent. I get a cup of coffee and pour in about a third milk. I won't worry about drinking it this morning, because there will be plenty of times when I can drain it out beside the halftrack or tank.

The troops get ready to go to the field, but there is a problem. They never got any of the tanks clean enough last night and with the cold air, the mud froze like concrete. They get the motors started, but they can't get the tanks to move. Of course, the cadre is telling them that they should have cleaned them better. The sun gets higher and shines on one of the tanks and that, together with the heat from the motor, allows it to break loose. Now that it is moving, they take it and hook it on to each of the other tanks and jerk them to break loose the frozen mud. The maneuvers are late today, but the lessons started early.

When we come in at noon, they call everyone together and tell them that this evening when they get in that everyone is to go to one tank and get it completely clean. Also, they say that they found a bunch of yellow snow in the camp this morning.

I get my dinner and instead of going to my tent to eat, I head out to one of the halftracks. I climb in and sit down on the seat, along the side. It is out of the wind and the heat of the engine and transmission has warmed the floor. I have a lot more room to eat than in the tent. I wash my mess kit and hang it up in the tent when I am through.

The afternoon is just a continuation of the maneuvers of this morning. When we go back into camp in the evening, they all go over to one tank and start to remove the mud. The two radio operators disappear. We are in our little tent, just waiting for supper. We eat our supper in the tent again and after we clean our mess kits, there is really nothing to do, but go to bed. It is another clear night and really cold.

This morning after breakfast, they take the tank that they cleaned well, start it and then pull the rest to get them going. They move back out into the field for more problems. I ride in the halftrack again. They do not say anything about me riding in one of the tanks, and I don't volunteer. For me, it is just more of the first two days. We come back in at noon and again I take my food and get in the halftrack to eat. Gene joins me today, after I told him last night about what I had done. It is warmer than the tent and more comfortable. I look to the north and there is a dark cloud bank building up.

This afternoon brings more riding around the Kansas prairie. It actually warms up a bit as the storm approaches. Just before they get ready to go in, it starts to snow. The flakes are bigger than what we had earlier in the week. When we get back to the camp, they all start to remove mud from one tank, and we head for our little tent. It is snowing harder now. We stay in there until time to go to chow. When we get in the chow line, it is snowing hard. We crawl into our tent and eat sitting on our beds.

When we finish eating, I dig out the box from home and share some of the cookies and candy with Gene. It is getting dark and some matches are our only light source. They do not last long, but give enough light to locate something. And of course, they do add a little heat to the tent. After a little bit, we make a run to the latrine and then back in the tent and get ready for bed. When I make my run to the tree in the middle of the night, it is still snowing.

When I wake up in the morning, I carefully unbutton the tent flap and pull the south side out so that the snow does not come into the tent. I slide on my overshoes and crawl out. There is about a foot of snow covering everything. Our tent is just a hump in the snow. Gene gets out too. We are both dressed only in our GI long handles and our overshoes. We run around and yell and throw snow balls at each other. The others are staring at us, like we have lost our minds. As long as we keep moving, we are not cold, but if we stop it gets cold quick. Then we go back in our tent and try to get dressed without bumping the tent overhead and knocking snow in.

We get dressed and go get our breakfast to take back to the tent to eat. It is not easy, because the top is much lower now. But the snow is providing insulation and it is warmer inside.   When we hear the tanks starting, we carefully open the flaps and crawl out. We each go pick out a halftrack to ride in for the day. Fortunately, they put the tops on them when it started to snow last night. I sit in the back next to the radio and turn it on. I can't see out, except by looking to the front and out the windshield. I am out of the wind and it is not as cold as it has been. Three of the trainees climb in the back with me and I turn the radio over to one of them to use. They are talking to me today. They start asking me questions about why we got sent to their outfit and about operating the radios. I tell them that no one seems to know why we were sent there, but we are determined to make the best of it. Maybe they are just waiting until they have a place where they need us. Then I tell them some of the things I have learned about making the radios work better.

When we go in at noon, I get in the chow line with them. They ask if I would like to go to their tent and eat with them. I tell them that I do not want to cause any waves and will just eat in the half-track. They decide to eat with me. I have made three friends, even if it did take running around in the snow like a crazy man.

When we get back to the camp, Gene and I go get into the pup tent that looks like an igloo. I tell him about making friends today and he said the guys he was with were more friendly too. We lay back and wait for supper to be ready. When it looks like they are serving, we get our mess kits and go get in line. The food is especially good considering where they have to cook it. But it does not help it to be placed in a frozen mess kit and eaten in the cold. We take ours back to the little tent, crawl in and lay back against our duffle bags to eat.

We decide to make our trip to the latrine. No doubt about it, this tent is a lot warmer tonight than it was the other two nights. The snow covering it makes a great insulation. I go to sleep but wake up in the middle of the night to make my tree trip.

CHAPTER XXXVI

Every day is much like the one before. We still go out with the troops every day and come back in to our snow-covered little tent. We are like a couple of animals, crawling down into our hole. Every few days, another layer of snow is added, to that covering our burrow. Sunday does give us a little break, when the chaplain comes out to conduct church services. Gene stays in, but I crawl out and go to where they are conducting the services. They have some of the vehicles pulled up in kind of a square and they set up a table for the chaplain to use. He gives the opening prayer, we sing a couple of songs, have a short sermon about always doing what is right, take communion and finish off with a closing prayer. All together, it takes less than fifteen minutes. Church services are a lot shorter out in the snow and cold.

The troops who stayed in for church services go out to catch up with those that are out in the field. For some reason, I miss the vehicle that I am to ride in, probably because I do not get out of the tent. I lay down on top of my bed and cover up with my overcoat. Gene wants to know what the service was like. I tell him and then tell him that the sermon was about always doing the right thing. He says "It did not stay with you very long did it?"

"I don't know, this seems like the right thing to me."

At noon, when we hear the vehicles coming into camp, we get out and go get in the chow line with everyone else. We get our chow and then go get in a halftrack and eat it. We decide not to push our luck, so in the afternoon, we go out again.

Each day is so long. It is boring, besides being uncomfortable. Wednesday night, the 13th of December, I am in bed, but Gene is out running around someplace. Gene opens the tent, crawls in and says, "We are going overseas."

I say, "Sure we are, but when?"

He says, "We are going to leave here tomorrow."

"How do you know that?"

"A couple of cadre told me."

"How do they know?"

"They said they heard the first sergeant talking."

"I don't believe it, but I don't care if we do. It couldn't be any worse than here."

The army has said that they will not send any eighteen-year-olds overseas. Neither one of us is over eighteen yet. Gene will be nineteen in January, but I will not be until the last of March. I get up in the night to go to the tree. I get to thinking that if I knew for sure we were leaving here tomorrow, I would sign my name in the snow for them all to see.

We go to breakfast in the morning and when we get through the chow line, one of the sergeants calls us over. He tells us to get our things together, that they are sending someone out to get us. It will be awhile before they get here because of the deep snow, but we are to get our things together so we are ready to go back when they get here.

We go to our tent and crawl in and roll up our blankets, drag out our duffle bags and pile our blankets and the rest of our things on top of them. Then we get inside of the tent and push up so that the snow slides off. It has melted and frozen many times, so it comes off in chunks. We dig down to find the tent pegs and work them out of the frozen ground. We unbutton the shelter halves, shake what snow we can off of them and then roll them up with the ropes, pegs and poles inside of them. We have everything stacked up, ready to go, in very little time.

We wait in the headquarters tent and finally someone comes in and says that someone is coming. We go out in time to see a weasel coming across the snow. It is a light tracked vehicle designed to cross snow or mud or even go in water.

It pulls up and we motion it over to where our things are piled up. We throw them on and get in the vehicle. When we are in, the driver turns it around and takes off for the post. When we get to the post, the driver does not go to the barracks. Instead, he goes to the brown tar paper shacks. He drops us off at the orderly room for the transit area.

We go check in and the sergeant says that we will have to stay there until we leave. We ask what we are to do about the things we have checked out and our things that are in the other barracks. He says that someone will be there tomorrow morning about ten to open the supply room and let us into the barracks to get our things. He gives us a barracks number where we are to stay until we leave. He also hands us a copy of our orders assigning us to Fort Meade, Maryland.

We take the copy of our orders, pick up our things and head for the barracks. We each find an empty bunk, dump our things beside it and start taking our clothes off. We get down to our underwear, put our overcoats on and head for the latrine a block away. It has been eleven days since we had a shower. It feels so good, we soak in it for a long time. When we get back, we have to put our fatigues back on because our class A uniforms are in the other barracks.

There are only a few guys staying in the barracks and they start coming in from details. I hope that we are not here long enough for that stuff again. I am not sure that I can get by as a day room orderly again. When it is time for supper, we make the long trip through the cold to the mess hall. The food is better than I remembered, but nothing to brag about.

The next morning after breakfast, we take the items that we have checked out to us, load them into our duffle bags and carry them to the supply room. We sit them down and I tell Gene to stay there with them, because I have to go the vehicle maintenance building and look for one of the mechanics. I gave him an empty .50 caliber shell to keep for me and I loaned him ten dollars. I find him and explain that I am shipping out and need my money. He says that he will get it and bring it to me either tonight or in the morning. I rather doubt that I will see it, because it was some time ago when we got paid. I ask him for the .50 caliber shell case and he digs it out of his tool box. I want it to make a cigarette lighter. He says again that he will see me either tonight or in the morning. I thank him and go back to the supply room.

It is almost ten-thirty before the supply sergeant shows up. We check in all of the items that we got to go on bivouac and the tanker suits and helmets. Then he locks up the supply room and goes with us to the barracks. He has the key and opens it so we can get in. He stays with us while we gather up our things. We pack them into the empty duffle bags, while he watches to see that we do not get anything we are not supposed to.

We change into our class A uniforms before dinner. As soon as dinner is over, we head for the PX and the bus stop. We go into Junction City and start to shop for some things for Christmas. There is not much to buy. I do find a couple of nice handkerchiefs for my mother. Then we go to an army store and I buy a small cigarette lighter that is shaped like a .50 caliber bullet. I talk the guy in the store out of a small box so I can mail some things home. Gene is like me; he can't find much to buy, but he picks up a couple of little things. We decide to go back to the camp.

When we get to camp, I go to the post office and buy a twenty-five-dollar war bond made out in my folk's name. We go to the barracks and I take the little lighter that I bought and take the base off, so that I can stick it into the neck of the .50 caliber shell case. It looks just like a complete .50 caliber cartridge. You pull on the tip and it comes off so that you can roll the little wheel and it lights.

This will be for my dad. I pack my extra fatigues and some other things that I want to send home, together with the lighter and the handkerchiefs and then tie it up so that I can mail it.

I get out my stationery and write a letter to my folks telling them that I will not be home for Christmas, that I am going to Fort Meade, Maryland, and likely overseas. I enclose the war bond and tell them it is the best I can do, under the circumstances. They can use it if they need the money, or keep it until after the war and then buy something for the house, when there are things to buy. I tell them Merry Christmas, that I love them and not to worry about me. As if that will keep them from worrying. I am glad to be going, but it is sad too. Then I walk to the post office and mail the package and my letter home.

Saturday morning, the first sergeant comes to the barracks and I figure that we will be on detail, but instead he calls out a bunch of names, including Gene's and mine. We are all shipping out Sunday morning, so we need to get our things packed and ready to go today. He says the uniform will be class A with loafers. Pack everything else with toilet articles on top in the duffle bag.

Almost everyone in the barracks is on the list to go in the morning. Every one of us is either eighteen or nineteen. Most are like me and have never really been anywhere before. I have given up on ever seeing my ten dollars again, when I look up and the mechanic is coming in the barracks. He says he is sorry it took so long, but it took him awhile to get the money. It makes me feel good that he did pay me back.

CHAPTER XXXVII

Sunday, December 17, 1944. I get up and dress in my class A uniform and go to breakfast. After breakfast, I go to the PX and get a Sunday paper. I go back to the barracks to wait for them to call us. They come over and announce that the train is supposed to be at Junction City at twelve-thirty and they will come and get us about eleven-thirty to go to meet the train.

About eleven-forty the trucks arrive and we throw our bags on and climb in. It is a cold ride to the train station, but it does not take too long to get there. We unload and go into the station to wait. Shortly after twelve-thirty, the train arrives. It is a troop train and has a bunch of guys on it already. Some have been on for almost three days. We load up and the train starts. The car is a coach but the seats are padded and very comfortable. We throw our duffle bags in the overhead rack until it is full and then put the rest under the seats.

We are not on long, before a sergeant comes into the car and says that anyone who has not had dinner yet should get out their mess kit and go back to the mess car. I am glad that I packed my mess kit in the top of my duffle bag. We take our mess kits and start walking back through the train. The mess car is six coaches back. We get in line and get our chow. They have some tables set up in one end of the car and we sit on benches and eat our food. When we get done, we wash our mess kits just like we did at bivouac, except they have some towels that we can use to dry them. The towels do not do much good and I just shake mine free of water.

We pull into Topeka and I remember that it's been almost six months since I came through here on the train going to Fort Riley.

We are entering eastern Kansas now and the scenery is changing some, but there is still a lot of snow on the ground. It feels good to be looking at it from the inside of a warm car, instead of a cold half-track. We travel on across Kansas and at supper time we take turns with the guys in the other cars in going to the mess car. It takes a long time for everyone to get fed.

Each car has a toilet in one end, and it is really not enough for this many men. There is usually a line waiting to get in there. By evening, we reach Kansas City. It is dark by the time we pull out. You can't see anything outside now, but a lot of lights from the city. Some of the guys have found a way to stack up some duffle bags to make a table and are playing cards. They come in and dim the lights in the coach and I tilt my chair back and go to sleep.

I wake up in the morning and we are in Illinois. I did not get to see the Mississippi River, but we are traveling through the lush farmland of lower Illinois, and even though it is covered with snow, you can see the well-kept farms. We travel northeast and we start seeing more factories as we go. We stop in Bloomington, Illinois, and women from the Red Cross and other organizations meet us with arms full of magazines and packs of cigarettes. We get to Chicago and they stop the train out in the rail-yard. They are re-supplying the train and they allow us to get off, but we have to stay close. They warn us to not get on any of the tracks because there may be trains traveling on them or even single cars that have been bumped to roll.

When the train has been re-supplied, they call for us to board and we load up again. The train pulls out and we get a look at the Chicago skyline in the distance, as we go out of the rail yard. I don't know how they know which set of tracks we are to go on, but I suppose it is controlled from some place. We travel southeast and there is more and more industry. We go by canals and see tugboats pushing barges. I think that, if I remember my geography correctly, we are going through Indiana and then into Ohio. I have never seen anything like this before. By afternoon, we are in Pennsylvania and going east. We have supper and by the time we are through, it is dark outside.

It is close to Christmas and a lot of us are a little homesick. Someone starts to sing Silent Night and the whole coach joins in. Then someone starts another Christmas carol and we sing that too. Before long, we are singing all the Christmas songs we know. They dim the lights and we go back to singing Silent Night again. When it is over, everything is quiet in the car. I feel lonesome, even with all the people around me. This is the most homesick I have been since I first got to Fort Riley.

The train keeps going and most of us get some sleep. Just before we arrive at Fort Meade, they come in the car and turn the lights back up and tell us to get ready to get off. It seems really late at night, but it is only eight-thirty in the evening when we arrive. We stand up, grab our duffle bags and start moving off of the train. They are waiting for us. We start going through processing. We go to this one big building and get a physical exam. It is the first one that I have had since I got to Fort Sill, six months ago. We have all of our clothes off, with a bag of valuables around our neck and our overcoats on to keep warm.

I get a little mixed up during the exam. I get checked for hernias and then I thought the next exam was for prostate, so when I get in front of the doctor, I turn around, bend over and pull my over-coat out of the way. Instead he is checking for abnormalities of the limbs. He slaps me on the butt and tells me to turn around and stand up straight. I am afraid to laugh, for fear he might think that I did it deliberately. When we get through the physical exam, they go over our paperwork with us and then assign us to a barracks. By the time I get to the barracks, it is one-thirty in the morning. I can't believe that all these people are working so late at night. But I guess they need to get everyone processed so we can ship out.

Tuesday morning, we have breakfast and then continue processing. We draw all new equipment. It does not matter if our old gear is still good, they want you to have new things. They said that is the best way of not having something fail at the wrong time. We get the new combat boots. They are like the shoes we had, but have a leather top on them that fastens with a couple of straps and buckles. When you put them on, it looks like you have on paratroop boots. The top of the boot is smooth leather, but the shoe is made with the smooth side in and the rough side out. It would be hard to polish these. It takes all morning to get our equipment. We get a pistol belt, harness and a musette bag.

When I get through with the equipment exchange, I go back to the barracks and finish writing a letter home. I started it on the train, but we were not allowed to mail anything until the train arrived here. I also fill out a change of address card to send home, showing my address here. I got separated from anyone that I know, but we are so busy, that we do not have time to do anything anyway.

In the afternoon, we are taken to a building where they go over our records and help us with our paperwork. They check to see that we have our dog tags, pay book, orders and if we want to make out a will. Then we get to change our pay allotments. I change from a ten-dollar war bond to a twenty-five-dollar war bond. I also make out a dependency allotment to my parents for forty dollars. I will get ten dollars more each month as soon as we leave the states and they say that you hardly ever need any money overseas.

While we are doing our paperwork, one of the boys tells them he is not eighteen yet, that he lied about his age and is only seventeen. He got this far, but the fear of going overseas caused him to admit it. They pull him out and say that they will check to see if that is true. If it is, he will be released from the service and sent home. One of the people helping with the paperwork, asks if I am eighteen. I guess because I look so young.

We spend the evening getting our new equipment ready to use. Every piece of clothing has paper manufacturing tags all over it. You have to pull them off. Many are stapled on. If you miss one on the inside of your clothes, it will stick you. Of course, all of the wool class A uniform parts are wrinkled, so we lay them out and try to get the wrinkles out. They smell strongly of moth balls.

The next morning, we have orientation courses on what we should expect, and what is expected of us. Then they show us how to make up a pack using the musette bag. You put most things that you need in the bag and then take your shelter half and roll it up with your blankets and make a bed roll, to go across the top of the musette bag and down the sides, like a horseshoe. The straps on the musette bag then hook on rings on the harness. It does not take long to realize that the hooks are in the wrong place. They cut into your shoulders.

After supper, we go on a hike. We have full field equipment on, except for a rifle. It snows some before we get back in, but it does not feel very cold. I guess it is because we are close to the ocean. We walk several miles following the roads through the countryside. We get back in and put our things away, get a shower and go to bed.

Today, most of us are on detail. I am working in the supply depot, unloading supplies and placing them on shelves. Also, we put the used things in big bins and they are loaded on trucks and hauled away. I guess they will be repaired, cleaned and issued to soldiers in the training camps. The rest will be sold as war surplus or destroyed. I work the whole day, but get time off for dinner and breaks every hour. We are all busy, but none of us is working really hard. We get off in time to put on our class A uniforms and stand retreat. Supper would rate as average.

They announce Friday morning that we will have a pass from Saturday morning until Tuesday morning. Then we get details again. I spend the day cleaning out several of the empty barracks. After supper, I get my things ready to go on leave in the morning.

CHAPTER XXXVIII

I put on my class A uniform and then decide to wear a pair of my new combat boots, to help get them broken in. I blouse my pants legs over the boots and look something like a paratrooper. I put the insignia on my coat. I use the US and the crossed sabers of the cavalry. I do not have any organization patch to wear on the sleeve. I do not know how cold it will get, so I put my overcoat on. It is bulky and heavy, but I am afraid that if I leave it, I will need it.

I walk to the orderly room, pick up my pass, which is good until Tuesday morning at six. I also pick up a couple of rubbers and a pro kit, which is mandatory when going on leave. I walk to where I can catch the bus to the train station. At the train station, I buy a ticket to Baltimore. I only have to wait about a half an hour before the train arrives. I get on the train and it is not too crowded on a Saturday morning, so I get to sit next to a window. I watch the scenery as we travel along the coast. It takes about a half an hour, before I arrive at the Baltimore train station.

There is a USO office in the train station and I go there and check about a place to stay. They give me a piece of paper with the name of a church and an address on it. They say that the church is providing places for GI's to sleep, and that I should go there tonight and give them the slip of paper and they will have a bed for me. With that, I take off to see the city. I walk around downtown Baltimore.

About noon, I find a Woolworth Drug store and go in and sit at the counter. I order a ham salad sandwich and a chocolate malt. The sandwich is OK, but the malt is not as thick as those at home and they do not leave the can with you either. I spend some time eating it. I make it last so that I can watch the other people coming and going. When I have finished, I go back out on the city streets again. It is cloudy, but it is not snowing. I make my way toward the docks. I want to see the Atlantic Ocean. I get down towards the docks and I am blocked. Wartime restrictions keep you away from where the ships are loading and unloading materials. I keep walking and get to a place where I can walk out on a dock that is not being used, so that I can see the harbor.

I work my way back toward town and walk around some more. In the late afternoon, I find a little bakery shop and go in and get a sweet roll and a cup of coffee. I finish just in time, because they are closing the shop. I had hoped to sit awhile inside, but have to leave. Everything is closing. I walk some more, waiting until it is time to go to the church for my bed. It is cloudy and since it is December 23, it gets dark quick. Here on the coast, they do not have the street lights on. The only lights are those of the bars. I need to piss and start looking for a place. There is nothing open but the bars and I am not old enough to go in there. I am walking on the street, when out of the dark comes two couples, heading into one of the bars. One of the women looks at me and says "Oh look, it is a little paratrooper." They all laugh as they disappear into the bar. I see an alley but I am afraid to go back into it. I do not know who might be waiting back in there. I still do not see any place to go, so I turn back to the alley and just step into it and hurry to get through my clothes. I throw back my over coat, move the tail of my coat, unbutton my pants, open my GI long handles and then my underwear, before I can go. I just get started, when a car swings around the corner and its lights hit me. I immediately stop and start to put my clothes back in place. I do not want to get arrested for indecent exposure. Of course, some of the piss goes down my leg. I hurry out of the alley and down the street.

I start looking for the church where I will be spending the night. It is not far from where I am. I go to the church and see a light burning by a door, on the side of the building. I go there and go in. It is stairs that lead to the basement. I walk into the basement and there are two older women and a younger girl there. They welcome me in and ask me if I have eaten. I tell them that I had a roll and coffee earlier. I take my overcoat off and put it on one of the canvas cots set up in a corner of the basement. Then I join them at the kitchen part of the basement. They have some sandwiches made and some hot cocoa. This is great. It reminds me of home. Since I am the only soldier there, they are interested in where I am from and what I am doing. I visit with them while I eat my sandwiches and drink my hot cocoa.

They tell me that there are three other guys that are supposed to show up tonight, but they will probably be in later. They have a couple of screens set up to close off the cots from the rest of the basement. The cots are close to the restroom. I decide that I will go ahead and go to bed. I am tired from walking around all day in the cold air. The younger woman hands me a small package that is wrapped in Christmas wrapping. I thank her and wish them Merry Christmas. I go to the restroom, then take off my coat and shoes and lay down on the cot. There is a quilt there and I put it over me. I can hear them talking at the other end of the room, but I can't understand them.

I wake up in the morning and there are three other guys on the other cots. I go to the restroom and wash up. By the time I come back out, there is a man in the kitchen. I go to the kitchen and he greets me. He says that the women gave him the job of serving breakfast. He sets out a tray with some sweet rolls on it and when the coffee is ready, he pours us each a cup and he sits down with me. I eat a roll and drink the coffee as we talk. When I finish the roll, he says that I might as well have another, because they have plenty.

Before I finish the second roll, another soldier joins us and not long after that, the other two get up.

I gather up my things, open my little package and find a small, hand-knitted scarf. I thank the man for the hospitality and ask him if he will give my thanks to the women. To tell them they really made me feel welcome. With that, I leave the church and walk to the train station. I buy a ticket to Washington, DC. Less than thirty minutes later, I am getting off of the train. I walk around in the station for awhile and then go out to see the city.

I walk towards the mall. I can see the capitol building at one end and the Washington monument at the other. I walk along the mall heading for the capitol. It is still early, but already there are some other tourists looking at the sights. I get to the Capitol building and it is huge, much larger than I imagined from the pictures. I walk up the steps, and when I get to the top, they are just opening the doors. I go inside and walk around the rotunda. It is way too early for a guided tour. Most of the area is closed off. All of the senators and congressmen have gone home for Christmas, as well as their staffs.

When I leave the capitol, I walk by the temporary buildings. They have been built to handle the large number of people who are working on things related to the war. The buildings are a contrast to the permanent buildings. These are just shacks. I continue on until I get to one of the buildings of the Smithsonian Institute. I go in and am amazed by all the things they have in there. I see the Library of Congress and decide to go there, until I see the line waiting to get in. I figure that my time will be better spent looking at other things. I decide that I better find the USO and get a bed reserved for tonight. I look at the address and start walking toward where I think it is. It takes me awhile to realize that the streets do not run square like they do in Oklahoma. A lot of them are on a diagonal running from the capitol out. I get to the address and there is no USO there. I look around and find someone and ask where it is. It seems that I am on northwest and I need to be on southwest. They tell me how to get there the easiest way and I am off again.

I get to the USO and get a cot booked for the night. They have doughnuts and coffee, so I stay there for awhile and eat a couple of doughnuts with my cup of coffee. They have some pamphlets about things to see in Washington and I look over them. Then I go back to the mall and walk to the Washington Monument. I get there and there are a bunch of people around it. I get in the line too. After awhile, one of the guards comes out and says that the elevator is broken and the monument is closed, and they can't get anyone to work on it before Tuesday.

I go along the mall and find another one of the Smithsonian buildings and go into it. This seems to be the best place to spend my time. It is comfortable inside and there are a lot of things to see, as well as not being crowded. I spend most of the day going from one Smithsonian building to another. I get a hot dog and Coke from a vendor for lunch. In the evening, I find a small café on a side street. I get a hamburger and a piece of pie. When I am done eating, I go to the address the USO gave me for a place to stay. I think it is the gym for some school. Anyway, there is a big room with cots set up and in the end of the building are restrooms.

The next morning, Christmas, I head for the USO. They have phones there you can use to make a call. The long distance lines are so crowded with calls, that the wait is about three hours from the time you tell the operator that you want to make a long distance call, until they have a line available. The USO have people to monitor the lines, so that when a line is available, they call the next person in line. I get my place on the call list and then get a doughnut and coffee. It is boring just waiting to call home. Finally after three hours, I get to make my call. I call collect of course and call to my grandmother's house in Waukomis, Oklahoma. The call goes through, but there is no answer. My folks must have decided to have Christmas at their house this year. I do not have the heart to wait another three hours for another call.

The USO has a list of people that have called in requesting a service person come to their house for Christmas dinner. I ask for one of the names. About that time, two other soldiers also come to the desk. The clerk says "Oh, I have one right here that has requested three soldiers for Christmas dinner." She hands the address to one of the guys and we go outside. The other two guys are older than I am. We catch a cab and go to the address on the paper. When we get there, we pay the cab driver and go up to the house. One of the guys knocks and a woman comes to the door and invites us in.

We walk into the living room and on the table are some bottles of bourbon, several bottles of mix and some snacks. Not the turkey dinner I had imagined. She says "I thought you boys might like this better than a dinner." There are two other women standing in the room. They are in their middle 30's, about twice my age. I can tell they are disappointed when they see that I am just a little kid, but they do not want to hurt my feelings. The other two guys are delighted at the prospects.

They start mixing drinks, but I decline and take a Coke. They put on some records and start to dance. And of course, I don't know how to dance either and the combat boots do not make for being light on my feet. One woman tries to dance with me, but it is not very successful. I end up going to the kitchen and staying there, drinking my Coke and eating snacks.

The woman that was supposed to be my date, gets drunk and then sick. The others seem to be having a good time. They are drinking and dancing. I stay in the kitchen and do not know if anything else is going on or not. I want to leave, but don't want to hurt their feelings. They do not want me, but they do not say anything either. In the evening, one of the guys calls a cab and we go back to the USO. They say that they had a great time. I walk to the train station and catch the train back to Fort Meade.

CHAPTER XXXIX

I am one of the first ones back from leave, but it is not long before the others start filtering back in, each one telling what they did while they were gone. I just say that I went to Baltimore and Washington. I do not elaborate much on what I did. A couple of the guys come in and say that they heard that we are sailing overseas on the Queen Mary. They say that some of the guys in another barracks told them. They said that they saw the Queen Mary tied up at the docks in New York City. Of course we hear so many rumors that we discount this one as well. We admit, it could be true, but not likely.

It is Tuesday and I do not have training today. I am going through what they call "deprocessing." This means that I am under orders to go to a Port of Embarkation. Mostly it means that they are going over my paperwork with me, to see that everything is taken care of. I make out a card addressed to my parents, which gives my address overseas. It will be mailed after I leave here. I have one letter catch up with me, but I still have not received any Christmas packages. If I do not receive them soon, it will be a long time before I get them. The letter says that they did not get any package from "Monkey Ward," that everything I ordered was not available. So much for my Christmas shopping.

I write a letter home, telling about my Christmas trip. I don't tell them about my "Christmas dinner." I enclose the receipt from Montgomery and Ward so they can get a refund. The day is rather boring. You get called to go to a certain building and when you are finished there, you go back and wait for the next thing.

Wednesday, is more of the same thing as yesterday. But today it is more serious. We are to go to the POE tomorrow morning. I gather up all of the things that I am not going to take with me and get a box to put them in. I pack everything I can into the box. The remainder, I throw on the pile of trash in the corner. When I get the box packed, I take it to the post office and mail it home.

I write a letter home. I let them know that I am feeling good, but do have a bad cold and a cough. This will be my last uncensored letter. From now on, everything I write will have to be read by someone else. I tell them about the address card they will receive later. Then I put it in the mailbox and go to bed. There are people all around me, but I feel so lonesome.

We fall out for reveille. They announce that we will be shipping out right after breakfast. We go to breakfast and most of us hurry through, because we are anxious to be on the way. I have all of my things packed and ready, and I sit on my bunk to wait for the call to go. The trucks arrive at the barracks and we go outside to load up. Then they take off for the train station.

The train is waiting at the station, so we get off of the trucks and walk right on to the train. There are a lot of others getting on this train. It is not long before we arrive at Fort Dix, New Jersey. Again, trucks are waiting and we ride to the barracks. They count off enough guys for a barracks full and send them to the first barracks, then the same number to the next barracks, until all have been assigned quarters. It really does not matter much, because we will not be here long enough to get much use of the barracks.

We no sooner get in the barracks, when a couple of corporals come in and tell us not to unpack any more than we have to, that we will get to do that later, and that the mess hall is about a block away and we can go for dinner when we are ready. Of course they told everyone else the same thing and the line is almost all the way from the barracks to the mess hall. The food is fair. After I eat, I go back to the barracks and wait until they tell me what to do next.

When all of us are back at the barracks, the same two corporals come back in to give us some instructions. First they tell us that we cannot call out and cannot send anything out, and that we will be going for a POE physical this afternoon or tomorrow morning. The only way we will not be going overseas, is if we do not pass it. Friday and Saturday is final inspection, to see that we have everything and are ready to go overseas. We need to remain in the area so they can contact us if necessary. The chaplain will be in his office for those that need to see him.

They come into the barracks and call several names, including mine and, tell us to follow them. We go a couple of blocks to a building and are ushered inside. Once inside, we take off our clothes and hang them on hooks on the wall. Then we walk into another room where we will get our POE physicals. There is a doctor sitting in a chair and we walk over and stand in front of him. He has us turn around and then he takes a big rubber stamp and stamps "APPROVED" on our papers. If you can walk in the room, you are fit to go overseas. He does not reject anyone that I can see in the whole bunch. We put our clothes back on and go back to the barracks to wait for what is next.

I get back from supper and am just sitting on my bunk when someone comes in the door and yells "MAIL CALL." That gets everyone's attention. We gather around, and I hope that my Christmas packages have caught up with me. No package, but I do have two letters from Mom. I go sit down on my bunk and open the oldest first. The first words in the letter proclaim trouble. My brother, Don, has been wounded in Germany. My folks have received a telegram saying he was wounded in action on December 2, 1944. That is all they know. They will let me know as soon as they hear more.

I open the second letter which was written a few days later and in it she says that they got a letter from Don. It was written by a Red Cross worker, because he is not able to write. He said that his right foot was badly smashed, and that he has shrapnel in both legs and his right arm, but that he is going to be okay. I so want to call my folks or even write that I have received their letters, but I can't. One of the guys on the next bunk asks me what is wrong. I guess he can tell by my expression that it is not good news. I tell him that my older brother, who is a first lieutenant in the infantry, has been wounded. He tries to comfort me and I appreciate his concern.

I go to bed but do not sleep well with all the different things going through my mind, worrying about Don and wondering what is in store for me. The night is a long one. I get up early and get dressed before the others. I am waiting when they call us to fall out for reveille. Breakfast is not my favorite. It is corned beef hash. I get some of that and grab a couple of boxes of cold cereal. The cereal will keep me going.

We get ready for inspection. We lay everything out on our bunks, so that they can see what we have. They show us again how to make a pack with a horse shoe roll around our musette bags. It will contain everything that we can get in it and the rest will go in our duffle bags.

Before we pack up our things, they hand each of us a Red Cross ditty bag. It is a khaki bag containing things we might need. Mine has a toothbrush, small tube of toothpaste, tube of shaving cream, a safety razor, a pencil, small note book, some envelopes and paper, a deck of cards, a sewing kit, a comb and two bars of soap, one regular and one for saltwater. After they go by each of us and check to see that we have everything, we pack our things back into our packs and duffle bags, putting the ditty bags into the top of our duffle bags. We are ready to go overseas. Saturday is another boring day. I go to bed early in the evening and it takes awhile to get to sleep, but I sleep sounder than I would have thought and I wake up to the sound of someone yelling to get up.

I look out and it is still very dark. They are telling us to hurry up and get breakfast, because we are moving out. We eat and then go back to the barracks to get ready for a trip. I have on my regular underwear, my GI longhandles, my wool pants and shirt, wool socks, combat boots, and new style field jacket. I put my overcoat on, throw my pack on my back and then buckle my pistol belt around my waist. I put my steel helmet on and shoulder my duffle bag. It must be hard to see me buried in all of that equipment. I have my wool cap folded and put inside of the webbing on my helmet and my wool gloves are in the pocket of my overcoat. They call us to fall out.

The trucks are waiting for us to load up. We have to help each other get in the back of the truck. With all the equipment, it is too hard to climb up by yourself. When we are all loaded, the trucks drive to the docks.

CHAPTER XL

I climb out of the truck and drag my bag out with me. I look and there is a boat at the dock. It does not look like what I thought the ship would look like. I ask if we are going overseas on that and several of the guys laugh. One then tells me that it is a ferry boat, and that we will ride it across the river. We march onto the boat and line up on the open deck.

One of the guys loses his nerve and approaches an officer. He tells the lieutenant that he is not eighteen, that he lied about his age and is only seventeen and wants to go home. The lieutenant takes him to some of the other officers and they talk to him. They take him off the boat and back on to the dock. We talk about it and some think that if he went with it this far, that they should just make him go on. But others think that if anything happened to him, that someone would be in real trouble.

They untie the lines holding the ferry boat and it starts moving across the river. As we go across the river, they pass out three K rations to each of us. This is supposed to last us until they get the mess going on the ship. We approach the other side and go up the river toward the city. As we get closer to some of the docks, I look and there she is, the Queen Mary. She is huge. She sticks up several sto-

214 ROBERT C. LOVELL

ries above the dock. We pull up to the dock and when they have the ferry tied off, we start moving to the exit. The line moves across the dock towards the gang plank on the Queen Mary. The gang plank goes up a ways, makes a turn and then goes up some more.

There is a soldier at the foot of the gang plank with a clipboard. When I get to him, he asks my name. I tell him "Lovell." He finds it on the list and then asks for my first name, middle initial and serial number. "Robert C. 38 711 637." He takes a piece of chalk and writes "683" on my steel helmet and tells me to go ahead and get on board. It is no easy chore carrying all of my things up the steep gang plank. I keep going up until I have gone several stories in the air. There is a guy there who guides me down the stairs to the next deck, and someone else shows me the way down another set of stairs and into a hallway. I go down the hallway and a guy shows me to a room. It is stateroom A-15.

I go into the room and other guys are coming in behind me. There are steel frames, with canvas, forming bunks. They almost fill the room and run from floor to ceiling. I take the lowest one in the corner. We put our duffle bags and packs under the bottom bunk and in the corners. There are eighteen bunks in the room. There is a small bathroom off to the side of the room, with just enough room for a toilet, lavatory and tub. They tell us to make room, because we will have thirty six in the room. We will each have to share a bunk with another guy, twelve hours each. Some of us go ahead and get into a bunk so that the others can find a place to put their things. The bunks are so close together that when you slide in, you can barely turn over. I am small and it is a tight fit for me.

One guy comes in and says he will share the bunk with me. He looks at it and then says there is no way he is going to get in there, that he has claustrophobia and can't stand to be even in the room, let alone in the bunk. He says for me to use it; he is going up on the deck. Some of us who have our things put away leave the room and go up the stairs and out on the open deck. They are loading supplies and men aboard the ship. There is a steady line of soldiers coming up the gang plank. They load all day long.

The deck has lifeboats and rafts all over it. On the end, there are the guns, but we are not allowed to get close to them. Some of the soldiers have been designated to man them in case of trouble. The sun deck up above is reserved for officers and nurses. The deck is crowded with soldiers milling around. I really feel lost with so many around me and not any that I know. Late in the afternoon, I go back to my room and dig in the duffle bag and get out one of the K rations marked dinner and take it and find a place where I can sit out of the way and open it up. It has a heavy paper wrapper on the outside and then a cardboard box covered with wax. Inside there are some crackers, a can of cheese with bacon, lemon juice powder, sugar cubes, a small candy bar, a stick of gum, four cigarettes, a book of matches and a key to open the can.

I brought my canteen and canteen cup with me when I came up here, so I take the lemon juice powder, put it in my canteen cup, add the sugar cubes and then pour water into the cup. I did not bring a spoon, so I just use my finger to stir it up. I am back in a corner, under a ladder leading to the main deck and out of the way of those walking around the promenade deck. I open the can of cheese and peel back the paper wrapper. I get out my pocket knife and cut open the package of crackers. I cut a piece of cheese and put it on a cracker to eat it. The cheese is really good. The crackers are not bad, but rather dry. I wash it down with a swallow of the lemon drink. The lemon drink will not win any honors, but does help the water from the canteen. When I have eaten all of the cheese and crackers and finished off the lemon drink, I eat the candy bar. It tastes good, but is rather small. I put the cigarettes, matches and stick of gum in my jacket pocket.

Later in the evening, I go up on the main deck and walk around. It is crowded with soldiers. It is New Year's eve and we can see people gathering for the celebration in downtown New York. I look over the side and the main deck is almost level with the dock, the ship is sitting so much lower in the water. They have put a lot troops and supplies on board.

I go back down to the room and someone comes in and gives us some information. The mess hall will only be open twice a day, in the morning and late afternoon, beginning tomorrow evening. We are not to throw anything overboard. The German subs can use that to track the ship. The PX is located forward on the promenade deck and is open from nine to ten each morning. We will have lifeboat drill every morning from nine to ten starting tomorrow morning. The chaplain's office is on this deck and down the hall. We can take turns using the bathroom to bathe, but the water is salt water and we will need to use the salt water soap. We are not to use the fresh water for anything except to drink.

I take most of my clothes off and put them on the end of my bunk and then slide in. There is not much room. I have the bunk above me right on top of me. The guy climbs into it and his butt makes a depression in the bunk and is sticking down into my space. I suppose the guy above him has the same problem. I am tightly pressed into the tight space. I go to sleep and do not wake up until I feel the ship move.

I get up, put my clothes on and head up to the main deck. The deck is crowded, but I am able to get to the rail and look out. We are sailing out of the harbor. I look over and there is the Statue of Liberty. I wave goodbye to her. The ship picks up speed and it is smooth sailing. I go back to the room and get the breakfast K ration, fill my canteen with water, dig my spoon out of my mess kit and head for my spot on the promenade deck.

I open up the boxes and take out my breakfast. There is a package of crackers, but these are more of a biscuit. The main course is a can of ham, eggs and potatoes. In addition, there is a fruit bar, four cigarettes, a book of matches, powdered coffee (Nescafe), sugar cubes, a stick of chewing gum and a key to open the can. I take the instant coffee and put it in my cup, with the sugar. I add water and stir it up with my spoon. I take a sip. It is terrible, but I guess I can drink it. Then I open my ham, eggs and potatoes. I taste it. It would be a lot better if it was hot. I open the package of biscuits and proceed to eat my breakfast. I wash it down with the cold coffee. I get the fruit bar out and eat it. It is a lot like a fig newton, only this one has apricots in it.

When I get below, I wash up my things and crawl back into my bunk and go to sleep again. A little after noon, I gather up my cup, canteen and spoon, pick up the supper K ration and head for my spot. The ship is moving around more now and the waves are hitting the ship and splashing high in the air. I sit back in my spot on the promenade deck and open my dinner. The main dish is a can of beef and pork loaf with carrots, a chocolate bar, bouillon powder, four cigarettes, a stick of chewing gum, a few sheets of toilet paper and a key to open the can.

I open the can of meat and it is ground meat with flakes of carrots in it. I open the biscuits and spread some of the meat on one. It is not bad tasting, a little like lunch meat. I go ahead and put the bouillon powder in the cup and pour water in, then stir it. By the time I finish, the ship is pitching more. I go put things away and crawl back into the bunk.

Someone comes into the room and says that it is our turn to go to chow. We all crawl out of our bunks and follow him out of the room and down the hall. We end up at the mess hall. Before the war, it was the swimming pool. They have a bunch of long tables set up with rims around them to keep the metal trays from sliding off, and they are needed tonight. The ship is pitching and rolling now. I go through the line and they are having greasy pork chops, boiled potatoes and peas. To drink, they have a mixture of coffee and tea. I get the food down, but it is not very good. I notice that several of the guys did not eat their food. They are starting to show signs of sickness.

By the time I get back to the room, the ship is really rolling. I slide into my bunk and it rocks me back and forth in the bunk. It keeps getting worse and several of the guys have gotten sick and left the room to go up on the deck. After awhile, I decide to go up on the deck and see what it is like. Out in the hall, guys have vomited and as I get closer to the stairs, it gets worse. I start up the stairs, holding on to the rail on the right side so that I will not slip. The white, thick, smelly vomit of seasick people is not quite up to the top of my combat boots, but is above the top buckle. It is over six inches deep. There are nearly eighteen thousand troops and two thousand crew on the ship. At least seventeen thousand of the troops are sick and probably some of the crew.

I go on up to the open deck. The ship is hitting huge waves and they are crashing over the top of the ship. The water is washing over the deck and cleaning it off. There are several sick soldiers huddled against the bulkheads and others are hanging over the rail. I feel queasy, but I am determined that I am not going to vomit. I stand at the rail and watch the waves crashing against the ship. The spray hits me, but it feels refreshing. Near me, a soldier is holding on to the rail and vomiting up everything he has ever eaten. A lieutenant walks up to him and tries to cheer him up. The lieutenant says "What's the matter soldier, weak stomach?"

The guy turns his head and says, "Weak hell, did you see how far I threw that last batch?"

I make my way back down through the vomit to the room. I go into the bathroom and sit on the side of the tub and run water over my boots and wash them off. It does not help too much, because the whole room has that sick smell to it. I take off my boots and slip into my bunk, and go to sleep.

I wake up in the morning and I still feel sick, but I am not going to vomit. I would probably feel better if I did. I go out and go up on the deck. They have washed down the stairs and the vomit is gone, but the smell remains. The sea has smoothed out some and the boat is not rolling so much. I go back down to the room and crawl back into the bunk. They come by and say it is time for us to go to breakfast, but most are not interested. I just stay in the bunk.

CHAPTER XLI

At nine o'clock, they sound the alarm and we have to all go up on deck for lifeboat drill. It is a sad looking bunch that shows up. We all have our life vests on, and stand in rows. They go over what to do, if we have to abandon ship. They also tell us that if anyone falls overboard, they will not stop. They can't endanger the whole ship for one person. You would not last long in the North Atlantic anyway. The Queen Mary does not travel in a convoy. It is too fast. It averages over twenty six knots per hour on the whole trip. It does however, take evasive maneuvers. Every seven minutes, it changes course. They do this because they say it takes a U-boat captain more than seven minutes to make a sighting and to fire a torpedo.

When the lifeboat drill is over, I rush to the PX, but it is already closed. I ask someone why they only have it open when we can't go to it and they say it is because anything that they do not sell on the trip over, they get to sell in Britain for a lot more money. I go back to the cabin and crawl into my bunk. I am almost hibernating.

There are crap games going on all over the ship. As some of the guys get tapped out, the winners move to a bigger game. I come out of my hole every once in awhile and go on deck to see what it is like. By evening, the sun is out and the sky is clear. I look around awhile, and then go back down to the room and crawl into the bunk. I do not have an appetite yet, so I skip going to the meals. I will do without food for awhile.

Wednesday, I go on deck when they sound the alarm for lifeboat drill. Later in the day, I get out my salt water soap, my towel and wash rag and wait until the bathroom is empty. Then I go in and run a hot bath. It looks so good. I climb in and start to notice the difference. It feels grainy. I lather up my washrag and try to wash. It feels like sandpaper. I rub the soap over my body and then rinse it off. I get out and dry off with the towel. I feel worse than when I got in the tub. My skin is sticky and gritty. I wish I had a way to rinse off. I spend some time on deck after that. We have reached warmer waters; they are smooth and we are sailing along, leaving the zigzag pattern behind us. It is so warm and sunny that several of the guys have their shirts off and are soaking up some sun. Then I go back to the bunk and spend the rest of the day there.

Thursday morning when they sound the alarm for the lifeboat drill, I stay huddled down into my bunk. When I am sure that they are not going to come looking for me and that everyone is on deck, I slip out and go to the PX. They seem surprised to see me, but they do agree to wait on me. I buy a box of twenty-four chocolate-covered marshmallow cookies. It is the closest thing they have to candy bars. I take them and go back to the room and crawl into the bunk. I open the box and get out one and slowly eat it. It is the first food I have had since the meal on Monday afternoon. It is not much as a candy bar, but does really taste good. I eat another and begin to feel better. After they come back from lifeboat drill, I get out of my bunk and spend some time up on the deck. A couple of the guys ask where I got the candy and I tell them what I did. They both resolve to try it tomorrow.

I spend more time out on the deck and live on my candy bars. We are leaving the warmer waters and it is starting to get cooler again. During the day, I notice the birds flying between the waves and wonder where they are going. After dark, I go up on the deck and look at the ocean. I never realized that you could see the phosphorescence glowing in the ocean at night. It is beautiful. I am feeling better and my spirits are much higher.

It is Friday and the crap game has moved to the main deck. There are only a half dozen guys left in it. They are the big winners of the many games that started down in the ship. I want to watch a little bit, but there is a crowd around the game and I can't get close. One of the guys who was near the game, says they are shooting for sixty-five-hundred dollars. That is about ten years' pay for most of us. That is big money. I go back down to the room and get in my bunk again. In a little bit, a couple of the guys come into the room and tell about what happened up on deck. It seems that one guy was caught cheating in the crap game. The other guys started fighting with him and were going to throw him overboard, but someone had gone and got the MPs when the fight started. They broke it up and saved the guy from being drowned. They took him off to the brig and locked him up.

I am still living on my chocolate-covered marshmallow cookies. I can't find my steel helmet. I look at every helmet that I see for one that has 683 on it. I start asking the guys if any of them have seen my helmet. None has, but they say they will keep a look out for it. I don't know how it would have gotten out of the room. I put it with my things when I got on board. I do not know what I will do when I have to march off of the ship without a helmet.

It is much colder again and I put on my overcoat when I go out on the deck.   We are all tired of being cooped up in the tight quarters. After dark, I crawl back into my bunk and go to sleep. In the night, I wake up and realize that the ship is not moving. At least, I can't feel the vibrations of the engines. After a few minutes, suddenly the ship moves and rocks. I am thrown against the bulkhead and then almost out of the bunk. This happens three times. The engines are really vibrating now. I can only assume that they stopped, then took off at full speed, while doing evasive maneuvers.

I wake up early on Sunday morning and go up on deck. We are moving very slow and I look to each side and there is a smaller ship moving away from us. Someone says that they are removing the anti-sub net. We proceed and it is light enough for me to see land off to the sides. As we pass, the two small ships move back toward each other. I go back down below and get my overcoat since it is damp and cold on the deck. When I get back on the main deck, I walk towards the bow of the ship. We are just pulling into a harbor. Suddenly something hits me. I look down at my overcoat and there is a big white streak going from my shoulder to past my waist. It seems that a seagull has just welcomed me to Scotland.

We ask where we are and they say the Firth of Forth in Scotland. The tug boats are moving the Queen Mary into position alongside of the docks. I am just glad to know that I made it across the ocean. I go back down to the room and wash the smelly mess off my overcoat and then have a breakfast of candy bars. While I am eating, one of the guys says that I should go see the chaplain about my helmet, that he thinks he saw it there. I know that he is kidding, because the most common expression in the army is to "tell it to the chaplain." But he insists that I check it out. I have nothing to lose, so I go along the hall until I find the chaplain's office. I go in and his assistant asks if they can help me with something. I ask if they might have a helmet in there with 683 on it? He says that there is an extra helmet there some place, but not sure what number. He looks around and finds it. It is mine. I still do not know how it got there from my room.

I go back and forth from the room to the deck to watch them unload the ship. They have not said when we will get off. But when evening gets there, it looks like we will not be getting off today. I am out of candy bars, so I decide to go to chow on the boat. I get in line and get my tray. They have a stew made from mutton, potatoes, onions, carrots and peas. With it they have bread, but it is kind of stale. They are still serving the same coffee, tea mix to drink. After supper, I go check to see that I have all of my things ready to get off of the ship. Then I slide into my bunk for one more night.

The next morning, they give us three meals of C rations, which is six cans, for the next leg of our trip. There are gulls flying all around, squawking loudly. Some of the guys take biscuits out of the C rations and throw them into the air to see the gulls scoop them out of the air.   While they are doing that, we get notice to get ready to disembark.

CHAPTER XLII

We help each other get our things on, in the crowded room. As each one gets their things, they go out of the room. We line up on the deck; I look at the helmets and take my place between 682 and 684. Then we start moving towards the gang plank. When I get to it, I start down the sloping ramp.

They have us fall in on the dock and call out the names to which we reply with rank and serial number. Then we turn and start marching away from the ship, carrying all of our things. I have on my regular underwear and over that my GI's, wool shirt and pants, field jacket and, combat boots on over wool socks. My overcoat is on over that, with my steel helmet on my head. On the outside of the overcoat, is my gas mask, harness for the musette bag, which is attached to the pistol belt, which has the entrenching shovel, canteen and cup and first aid pouch. My horse shoe blanket roll is wrapped around the musette bag and the rest of my things are in the duffle bag which is carried by a sling over my shoulder.

We march some distance to the train station. There we go along the side of the passenger train that is sitting there. The cars are compartment cars, with the doors opening to the outside. As we reach each compartment, four guys will drop off and enter the train.

I get into one of the compartments with three other guys and we start putting our things away. When we get our things put away, we sit down. It is really very comfortable, with padded seats and foot rests. Along the other side of the compartment is the door leading out into the hall, which takes you to the toilet in the end of the car.

We sit back and wait for the train to start. A conductor comes by to check to see that the outside doors are locked. Then the train whistles and we start to pull out of the station. The ride is very smooth. When we are on the way, I get up and get out my breakfast menu C ration to eat. When the others see me do that, they get theirs out too. Included with the C rations is a small can opener. It is like a small hinge, with one side that has part of it ground off, leaving a point. They call it a P38. I use it to open the can of ham, eggs and potatoes. Then I open one of the accessory cans. It has some round biscuits, just the size of the can. In with them are a few hard candies, a stick of gum, some cigarettes, instant coffee and sugar cubes. I do not have any hot water or any way to heat it, so I do not fix the coffee. I eat the ham, eggs and potatoes cold. It would be a whole lot better if it were hot. The biscuits are so hard that I can't bite them. I do break one and then put the pieces in my mouth and take a swallow of water from my canteen, so that they soak up enough to eat. I eat the sugar cubes and candy, but it takes some time to get through the hard candies. I ask if one of them wants my cigarettes and one of the guys says he will trade his candy for them and I quickly accept.

I am next to the outside window and door so I can see the countryside. We are passing by many small, but neat farms. We go through the small towns and people at the train station wave at us. A few even have small American flags that they wave. It makes me feel good. When we get to a city, we slow down and creep through the rail-yards, passing other trains on adjacent tracks. We see the flocks of sheep on the meadows and the farmers with their sheep-dogs herding them. We do not know when we leave Scotland and enter England. This is a lot nicer than being on the ship.

In the afternoon, I try another C ration. This one is beef stew. My accessory can is the same one I had with breakfast. My results are the same too. Cold stew goes down much like cold ham and eggs. I get it down and by soaking my biscuits in my mouth, I am able to eat them too. One of the other guys asks if I will trade my cigarettes for candy and we make a swap. We are getting further south and the country goes under a gradual change, with less pasture and more farmland.

As it gets towards evening, the conductor opens the inside door and says,"Lads, be sure that you close the blackout curtains before it gets dark and if ye go into the passage, to go to the loo, be sure to turn the light off, before you open the door." We thank him and say we will be careful. As he leaves, he says, "No need to give jerry a view of us." We are getting our first glimpse of what these people have been going through for years. We watch out the windows until it gets too dark to see, then we close all of the curtains tight and turn on the small lamps above the seats.   I dig out the last of my C rations. This one is pork and beans. I still get the same accessory can. Pork and beans taste better cold than about anything else. After I eat some of them, I break up my biscuits and put them in the juice in the beans. This helps the beans and the biscuits. We talk awhile and a couple of the guys smoke, but gradually we get quieter and I notice that the three of them are asleep.

This is such an adventure for me, I am awake all night. I kind of feel like I am guarding the others. When I can tell that it is getting light, I open the curtains and look out. We are going through an industrial area and here and there, I can see the remains of a building that has been bombed. We are in the war zone now. We are not going very fast as we move through the highly populated areas. The conductor comes along and says, "Get your things together, lads, we will be arriving shortly."

We get our things down and then try to get everything on, in the close space. We have to help each other with our packs. Of course, after we get our packs on, we can only sit on the edge of our seats. At last the train stops., and we wait for our instructions. Someone goes along side of the train and opens each outside door and tells us to fall out. It is not hard to line up, we are already strung out for the length of the train. We form a column of twos and start marching towards the front of the train. Then we cross the tracks and go toward the station. I figure we will load on trucks here, but instead, we keep marching.

We leave the train station and head towards the English Channel. We go out on some docks and there is a ship tied up at one of the docks. We are led aboard the ship. It is a landing ship tank or LST. We walk onto the main deck and are told that we can put our things down on the deck, because that is where we will be riding. I find a place in about the middle of the ship and pile my duffle bag down, lay my pack nest to it, put my gas mask against the pack. Then I curl up on top of the pile. I could not go to sleep on the comfortable train, but I go right to sleep on this mound of equipment. I must have slept for an hour or so, when someone wakes me up. I look up and it is a lieutenant. He tells me that they are serving chow down below. I tell him that I am not hungry. He says that I need to eat. I tell him again that I do not want anything, but he says that it may be real rough out in the channel and that I need to go eat. He says again that I need to go eat. I consider it a command this time and say, "Yes sir."

I walk across the deck and down the ladder and into the space below that they have set up for a mess hall. They are serving slices of spam with pineapple on it, mashed potatoes with gravy they made from the spam juice, green beans, bread and some apple sauce. They have coffee and it tastes like coffee. I have always heard that the navy feeds well, and in this case, they did very well with what they had. I am glad the lieutenant made me go eat.

I go back up to my spot and lay back down on my pile of stuff. I am out in the open, but it is not really cold. I guess the currents flowing through the channel keep it from getting very cold. I go to sleep again. I wake up when the ship starts to move. I go back to sleep and sleep most of the way across the channel.

I can tell we must be getting ready to dock, because the sailors are all moving around and taking up their positions. But then, suddenly the boat comes to a sharp halt and I slide off of my things. They have run it up onto the beach. Someone says for us to get our things together and that we will be getting off soon. They lower the bow of the ship down to the beach. If we were carrying tanks, this is when they would drive out and on to the beach. Instead, we shoulder the strap on our duffle bags and march down the ladder, through the ship and out on the ramp. I walk across the ramp and then step down about a foot to the beach. I am now standing on French soil.

I fall into line and we walk up the beach. It is D-Day plus one-hundred-and-ninety days. The beach is empty except for one lone, bare tree, which has a bathtub in the top of it. There is nothing but sand for at least two hundred yards in every direction. I have no idea how the bathtub got there. We walk off of the beach and on to the road. We start into the city of LaHarve, and cross the railroad tracks as we walk. We are loaded down with equipment and the streets have a layer of snow on them.

We walk several miles through LaHarve to a camp in some trees, which is called Camp Lucky Strike. It is not well named. There are a bunch of squad tents pitched among the trees, but they were pitched on the snow and we have to unroll our bed rolls onto the snow. It is really cold. I open my bedroll and spread the two blankets, with my shelter half acting as a ground cloth. It is almost dark by the time we get our bedrolls put down. They tell us that there is chow ready at the mess tent. I get in the line and when I get to the serving line, I find that they have stew and bread, and coffee. I get mine and then try to find a place to eat. They have some boards nailed between two trees, where you can set your mess kit, while you stand in the snow and eat. The coffee is so strong I can't handle it, but I get some canned milk and pour some in. The coffee is not as strong, but the canned milk has a funny taste to it.

After I eat, I wash my mess kit and crawl between my two blankets. I have trouble finding a place that does not have something poking me from the ground. Maybe if the snow were deeper, it would be smoother. I finally go to sleep, but do not sleep long, before I have to get up and piss. Fortunately, the slit trench and fly is just a short distance away and I did not take off my boots and overshoes, so it does not take long. I go back to sleep, but have to get up once more before morning.

In the morning, they have chow ready when I get up and I head for the mess tent. Well, we have corned beef hash and bread for breakfast. I drink a cup of coffee with canned milk again. Then I go gather up my things and get ready to move out.

CHAPTER XLIII

We walk all the way back through the city to the rail tracks. Too bad we could not camp by the rail tracks or on the beach. There is a train waiting there for us to board. The cars are wood and only have one set of wheels on each end. They are coupled together with a hook on the end of one car and a loop on the other that goes over the hook. There is an iron ball hanging down from the link to keep it from jumping out of the hook. The cars are kept from hitting each other by a couple of round spring bumpers on the end of each car. The cars are marked 40 hommes et 8 chevaux (40 men or 8 horses). They are pulled by a steam engine. They do not look very sturdy.

They start putting us in the cars. They are counting as the men get in, but someone can't count very well, because we end up with forty-four in the car I am in. We are all sitting around the car with our backs against the wall, except, there is not room for all of us and some of the guys are laying in the middle of the car. We have our things piled in the car.

After we are in, someone comes to the car and explains what we are to do. He says that we are to stay by the train at all times, and that it does not make very good time. The engineer may decide to stop for dinner or a drink or to visit a friend. They blow the whistle twice, when they are ready to go, but that the second whistle may be ten miles down the track. They have scheduled stops, where we will get a chance to eat. We are never to show a light at night, because it might cause the train to get strafed.

After he has gone, one of the guys says, "Do they really strafe these trains?" Another guy laying back, jerks his thumb towards the roof of the car and says, "What do you think made them holes, woodpeckers?" We all look toward the roof, which is riddled with splintered bullet holes. It is enough to make us think twice about showing a light. We close the doors to try to keep it warmer in the car. I am sitting with my back against the wall of the car. There is barely room to walk through the legs and bodies covering the floor of the car.

Sure enough, in a little while, we hear the train whistle sound two blasts and then the train jerks to a start. There is another jolt for every car behind us, as the slack is taken up in the train. We are not moving very fast, but the car sways, clatters and creaks as we travel. We go for about an hour and then the train stops. Someone opens the door and says that we are on a siding. Almost everyone climbs out of the car and stands in the snow. It is not long before there is a lot of yellow snow along side of the track. A train goes by on the other side and a little bit later, the whistle sounds twice. We all run and climb in the car. Both those inside and those outside aid everyone in getting loaded back up. We go about five minutes and stop again, this time to take on water and coal. We are there about a half an hour before the whistle sounds.

We stop a few more times, sometimes for only a few minutes and other times for up to a half an hour. Late in the afternoon, we stop at a siding and someone comes along side of the train and says to get off because they have chow set up for us. We all climb out of the car into the snow. My feet feel numb and I stumble as I walk. We walk away from the train a little ways and find the place where they have set up a portable kitchen. We each have our mess kits and get in line. It is beef and pork stew. We have some thick slices of white bread and coffee. We get our food and stand around in the snow eating. I learn an important lesson, be careful how you drink hot coffee from a stainless steel cup. The cup gets hot enough to burn you. Pour a little of the coffee over the lip of the cup to cool it before you take a sip. But it is too late for this time; I have a burn on my lip. The bread is fairly fresh, so they must have a bakery located someplace over here. I am hungry and eat every bit and drink all of my coffee. We wash our mess kits in the cans provided, and shake the excess water off of them. They feel a little greasy when we get through.

It is cold outside, so most of us have already got on board before the train whistle sounds. We move back onto the main track, passing over several other sets of tracks. They do not have the heavy switch levers for switching trains, that we are used to in the U.S., but instead are controlled from an elevated switch house by way of a series of wires attached to levers. I sure hope they pull the right one and do not get two trains on the same track. I sit back down in my space with my back against the wall.

It starts to get dark and we are still moving along. I am able to sleep for awhile. But then I wake up and wish that I had not drank that cup of coffee. I have to go. I get up and try to make my way to the door of the car. It is so dark that I can barely make out the outlines of the guys laying on the floor. I feel my way along. Fortunately I am not very far from the door. I would never make it if I were in the end of the car. I get to the door and pull it open.

But my troubles are just starting. I have to figure out how to get through all of the clothes I have on. I unbutton my overcoat and pull it aside and try to hold it back with my elbow. I take the bottom of my field jacket and tuck it up under itself. Then I unbutton all the buttons on the fly of my wool pants. I reach in and dig in through my GI long handles and my regular underwear to find my penis. The cold weather is not helping a bit. I finally have a hold of it and place my feet on the edge of the car door opening. Holding on to the door with one hand and my penis with my other hand and my overcoat with my elbow, I lean out into the cold night air.

There is another problem. Even with the slow speed of the train, there is still enough wind to blow back into the car. It is not long before I hear the guy next to the door cussing. I try to lean out further, but I know that if I slip, I am going to get hurt, if not killed. I finish and pull myself back into the car. Of course, about half runs down my leg. I apologize to the guy next to the door, button back up and feel my way back to my place. I remind myself not to drink coffee, until we get to where we are going.

I wake up in the morning when someone opens the car door and lets some light in. I look across the car and notice that every bolt head or metal fitting has frost sticking out from it, over an inch thick. Several guys are trying to stand up and shake the stiffness from their bodies. It has been a miserable night. Everyone needs to piss and a few can't wait and go to the door just as I did. The only advantage they have over me, is that it is light and they can see what they are doing. One of the guys asks the guy waiting behind him to grab his coat and keep him from falling out. This helps and soon that is the preferred method for going. It is a lot easier if you know you are not going to be chewed up by the train wheels.

A little while later, we pull on to a siding for the breakfast stop. We all bail out of the car. I fall when I hit the ground. My feet are so numb that I can't tell when I put them down. I have a long time to wait before I get to the serving line. They have thick pieces of bacon and eggs. These eggs have been dried into a powder and then mixed with water and cooked. Only if you are really hungry do they resemble real eggs. I take a half cup of coffee and pour some canned milk and sugar in it. I hope it is out of my system by night.

We climb out of the snow and back into the car. The rest of the day is just the same; sitting in the cold car, hardly able to move. Late in the afternoon, we stop again for a meal. It is corned beef hash and bread, this time. I pass on the coffee and only drink enough from my canteen to wash it down. Then it is back on the train.

The third day we get to stop for breakfast of canned ham, eggs and potatoes. Then we continue on. We stop in the afternoon but they do not have a kitchen set up. Instead, they have a bunch of K rations. Some get breakfast, some dinner and others get supper. We stand around in the snow and tear them open, getting at the things inside. I am not going to mix up lemon drink, so I go ahead and eat the sugar cubes. Then I eat the small chocolate bar. Then I open the can of cheese and the package of crackers. I gobble them down and drink enough water to wash it all down.

We keep traveling until sometime in the early morning, when we stop and they tell everyone to get out and bring everything with them. We have arrived, where ever it is. We climb out of the car and line up in a column of twos. I have trouble walking on my numb feet and carrying the heavy pack and duffle bag. We walk about a half a mile to several buildings. They look like they are some kind of warehouses. We are ushered into one that is full of wooden bunks and told to pick out one. They have a latrine outside, in back of the building. It is a trench with a board over it to sit on and a canvas fly encloses it. Of course, it is full of snow.

CHAPTER XLIV

We ask a guy in the building where we are. He says we are at a "repo depo," a replacement depot. He tells us that this is where they send guys, to decide what unit to assign them to, but that he was wounded and is now being sent back up. He said he may not wait, that he may go AWOL and go back to his old unit. Lots of guys do, because they want to be with their buddies and not some new outfit.

They tell us that they are serving mess in another of the buildings and we can go there and eat breakfast. I do not know what I was expecting, but when I reach the serving line, it is canned ham, eggs and potatoes with thick slices of bread and coffee, the same as we have had at the other meals. But I notice that they just put a small amount on my mess kit. I am really hungry, so I quickly lick it up.

When I have finished eating, I go back and take off my combat boots. I remove my socks and look at my feet. They look white and do not have any feeling in them. They appear to be frozen. I lay down and slide them down into my blankets hoping to get some warmth into them. I go to sleep.

I wake up after a couple of hours, sit up and start listening to the guys sitting around me.   One of the guys sitting on a bunk close by is showing us his arm. He got shot and the bullet went through his elbow and never chipped a bone. However, he has a scar about eight inches long, on the inside of his arm, where the doctors went in to clean out the wound. He laughs and says, "The Germans only made a little hole in my arm, and the American doctors did the rest." He has been released from the hospital for duty and has been sent here, to be assigned to some unit. He is trying to find someone that knows where his unit is now. He does not say so, but I bet as soon as he gets an idea where they are, he will disappear from here.

It is after noon now and I ask when they serve dinner. Several guys laugh and say they don't serve dinner, only breakfast and supper and not much at either of those meals. I ask if there is a PX around there, where we can get something. It seems there is no PX, but if you go to the end of the mess hall, there is a guy who will give you a few packs of cigarettes free. It does not help my hunger to not have anything to do, but just sit and think of it.

I check my feet and they are still numb. I take my thumb nail and press it into the top of my foot and it leaves a cut mark, but it does not hurt or bleed. I think my feet are in bad shape. I hope that I do not lose them. I put a clean pair of wool socks on and then my boots, so I can walk around. It is hard to walk, but I think it will help the circulation to my legs. Some of the guys are playing cards, but it does not seem to be for money. I doubt if most guys have much money. I turned in what money I had and will get it back in francs tomorrow.

Of course, we are interested in the stories of the guys that have been in combat, wanting to find out what it is like. I expect them to feed us a lot of bull, but most of them seem to be telling straight stuff. I guess when you are really there, you do not have to make up things. Later in the afternoon, they give the chow call. We all grab our mess kits and head for the mess hall.

I line up in the long line to eat. They have beef and pork stew again. But this time, we also get some green beans with it. Not a very big portion, but the slice of bread with it is very thick and they have some tropical butter to put on it. The problem is that the butter has something put in it so that it will not melt at 95 degrees in the tropics and with the temperature at about 35 degrees, you can't cut it with an ax. They also have coffee, but I decide to pass on it and drink some of the water in my canteen.

I go to one of the tall stand-up tables and find a space, where I can set my mess kit. I mix my stew with my green beans and eat it all at once. I eat every bit of it and mop up the mess kit with the last of my bread. I am still hungry.

I ask if there is any place to take a shower and they all say not here. I was hoping to get a chance to wash the salt off of me from the ship. The building is closed up for the night and blackout curtains have been pulled. To go out, you have to go through one curtain and then through another. I go out to the latrine. It is not too dark with the stars shining off of the snow. I follow the path tramped into the snow to the latrine and back. I take off my boots, but leave my heavy wool socks on. Maybe they will help my feet thaw out. Then I slide between my two blankets and get ready to go to sleep.

I get up in the morning and put my boots on and head out to the latrine. It is really cold out here this morning. I am glad that I do not have to sit on the board yet. I will worry about that after breakfast, when the mood hits me. I go back inside and pour some water into my steel helmet, get out my little bar of soap and wash my hands and face. Then I pour water from the canteen over my toothbrush, dig out my toothpaste and brush my teeth. It has been so long that they feel funny. Sure glad I do not have to shave with this cold water, like most of the guys.

I am one of the first in the chow line this morning. And they do not have canned ham, eggs and potatoes; instead they have canned corned beef hash. They make it seem like breakfast, because they have taken the bread and toasted it in the oven. The highlight though is that they have some grapefruit juice. I make my way to one of the stand-up tables, sit my mess kit down and start to eat the hash. They have some more of that tropical butter, but I haven't figured how to eat it yet. I look around and one of the older combat veterans takes his knife and breaks off a piece of the butter and then he puts it under his hash. In a little bit, some has melted enough to go into his hash, but there is some soft enough to put on his bread. Why didn't I think of that? I grab the container and dig out a chunk and poke it under what hash I have left. I wait a little bit and then dig out enough that is softened to put on my toast.

As I stand there eating, I am thinking about how this whole business is one of survival. I learn more and more every day about how to get by. Two of the things I have learned allow me to drink coffee without burning my lips and have butter on my bread, provided the food is hot, when we get to it. But even with the bread and butter, the small scoop of hash is not enough for my growing body. I wash my mess kit and when I finish with it, I am right in front of the table, where they give out the cigarettes. I walk up to the guy and ask what I have to do to get some cigarettes. He pulls out a carton of Chesterfields and hands me five packs. He says that this is my weekly ration, so go easy on them. I assure him I will and head back to the barracks building.

I get back, put my mess kit away and sit down on my bunk. There are not many around, since they have not come back from breakfast, so I decide this is a good time to learn. I put four packs away and open the other. There are three or four books of matches in the pocket of my field jacket. I get out a book and put a cigarette in my mouth and light a match. Well, I try to light a match. It takes three times before I get it lit. Then I hold it up to the end of the cigarette or at least where I think the end is and start sucking on the cigarette. At first nothing happens and then I feel the match burn my fingers. I drop it and step on it. I light another match and this time I get the fire to the cigarette. I feel the smoke come into my mouth and I blow it out. It is much milder than the grape vines, coffee and the old dried cigar that I have tried to smoke in the past.

I sit on the bunk smoking. It gives me something to do and I forget about being hungry for the time being. I don't try to inhale, I just suck it in and blow it right out. I try to remember how I have seen guys hold one. I need to learn to hold it down instead of up in the air. But I will work on it. When I finish, I go to the office and pick up the money I had exchanged into francs.

After a little while, I feel the urge to go to the latrine. I walk out through the snow. I have left my overcoat in the building and that is a help. I tuck the tail of my field jacket and my shirt tail up under and then take down my pants, GI's and shorts. When my butt hits the cold board over the slit trench, it almost changes my notion. One thing about it, you will not see anyone just sitting here reading. Everyone here is on a mission. The toilet paper is close by strung on the handle of an entrenching shovel, which is stuck in the ground.

I am glad when I get back inside. I celebrate by lighting another cigarette and sitting on my bunk smoking. I am learning how to handle one better. At least, it gives me something to do. While I am sitting there a guy walks in with some papers in his hand. He asks where a certain guy is. It is the guy with the bullet hole in his elbow. A guy says that he got his orders last night and shipped out. But the guy with the papers says, "Not likely, these are his orders and they just came." He turns around and walks away, mumbling something about another AWOL. I hope the wounded guy does not get in trouble and mention it to the other guys. One of them says, "What are they going to do to him? He is going back to the front lines as an infantryman and I don't know how they could punish him more than that."

While we are sitting around talking, another new guy comes into the building and we show him an empty bunk. He puts his stuff down and we ask him why he is here. He says that he is being sent back to the front after getting checked out from being a POW. That gets our attention. He tells us that he was in an infantry squad and they were over run when the Germans counter attacked. They were captured and started a march to the German rear. They did not give them anything to eat or drink and marched them all day.

At night, they would put them in a barn and lock them in. Some officers came and questioned them. He said he was so scared that he told them everything he knew and wished he knew more. They were sure that the Germans would probably get tired of guarding them and kill them. They were being marched down a road and came to a small village. A woman came out of the village with a basket of apples and gave each of them one. It was the only food he had.

After about two weeks, they were being held in a barn one night and when they woke in the morning, they looked through the cracks and could not see any Germans. They pried on the door and were able to get it open. They went out and they were all alone. They started back the way they came and ran into a U.S. armored column, that had broken through and got a ride back to the rear. They were sent to an army hospital for a checkup, spent a week eating and resting and now he is being sent back.

I get out my stationery to write a letter home. I tell them that I am somewhere in France and can't tell much more than that. I write mostly about my brother and how I hope that he is on the way home by now. And of course, I ask for mail, packages and letters. I finish the letter and go to get in the chow line. There is a box there to mail letters. They will all be censored before they are sent.

Chow is stew again. The cooks must get tired of opening cans, dumping the contents into pots to heat and then serving it. The same thing over and over. I take my stew and thick slice of bread. Then they also have some sliced peaches. We each get three slices. I pass on the coffee because I don't want to have to get up and go outside in the night. When I get to the tropical butter can, I dig out a big chunk and push it under my stew. I go over to the table and find a place to stand. I have my canteen cup and I fill it with water from the water bag, while my butter is getting melted. I take the softened butter and spread it on my bread. A large part of the butter melted in the stew and I mix it in. It will help the flavor.

After breakfast, they call out a bunch of names to report to the office. We all think that we are going to ship out, but instead, they send us to the supply building. They say we are to pick up a new sleeping bag. I can just picture one of those down bags like the troops had on bivouac. We get there and line up and as we go by the counter, they hand us one of the new wool bags and a cover. It is not a down bag, but is better than nothing.

Later in the day, they tell several of us to get up early the next day because we will be shipping out. I go to bed early, because I don't want to miss getting out of here.

CHAPTER XLV

I am up early in the morning and I am surprised to see that I am not first in line. I guess there are some other guys that want to get breakfast before they leave here. Same thing we had day before yesterday. Makes me think they only have two things to serve and they just alternate. I get my food and since it is so early, I drink a cup of coffee.

We are all sitting on the empty bunks with our bags and packs at our feet, just waiting to fall out. I put my pack back on my bunk and lay back, with it propping my back up. I may as well rest while I am waiting. I believe I will be sent to someplace where they have radios, but with the army, I can't be sure.

About noon, someone comes to the building and says for all of those on orders to fall out. When everyone is loaded on to the trucks, we move out. We go back to the rail-yard and get off of the trucks. They tell us to get on the train. It looks like the one we came in on, with the small wooden cars and a steam engine.

Most of the guys move toward the closest of the cars, but I move on down the train towards the end. It is a wise move, because the first cars have forty guys in each of them, but this car only has thirty-four. There is a lot more room to lay down. We pile our bags up out of the way and sit around the sides again. I open up my bedroll and take out my new sleeping bag and lay it on the floor and slide into it and zip it up. I am warmer right away. I have the top part of my body back against the wall, but there is room for me to slide down later if I wish.

We are going again, even though none of us know where. Later in the afternoon, it is obvious that it is going to be another cold trip. When we stop on a siding, we get off to move around and relieve ourselves. Some of the guys find an empty drum with a snap lid. They get it and pick up a few bricks and get back on the train. They take a bayonet and a hatchet and proceed to cut some slots in the base of the can and place the bricks loosely in the bottom.

A couple of other guys come back to the car carrying a piece of thin pipe about four inches in diameter. One guy climbs up on top of the car and in the middle, he uses a hatchet to chop a hole in the roof. They cut a hole the same size as the pipe, into the top of the can, beside the lid. The pipe is pushed up through the hole in the roof and then down into the hole in the can. Some other guys found a bucket and have filled it with coal from the train's tender. It is not long until the stove is hot and we can feel the warmth throughout the car.

The train moves out again and the guys are proud of their stove and how warm it is inside now. It is almost dark, when suddenly there is a crash and the car fills up with thick black smoke. You can hardly breathe. Someone yells to open the door. The door flies open and someone gives the stove a mighty kick out the door. Fire flies through the air as the stove hits the ground. Instead of getting stove pipe, the guys got a drain pipe off of a building. When the stove got hot, the solder melted and the pipe fell to pieces. We throw the pipe out and close the door.

It is not long before the car starts cooling off again. One of the guys says, that at the next stop, we are going to have to get a stove. So they start picking guys for the raiding party at the next stop. They get five guys. It is not long until we pull off on to a siding and stop. The raiding party takes off to get a stove. In a little while, the door is pulled open and the raiding party climbs in, minus a stove.

The leader says that he is going to have to have someone else in the party, that some of the guys chickened out and they did not get the stove. One of those that chickened out says that he just could not take that stove away from those little kids sitting around it.

About an hour later, we pull over again and stop. The new raiding party takes off. In about ten minutes, there is a banging on the door, someone pulls it open and they swing a stove, with a fire in it, into the car. Right behind them is a guy with the hot stove pipe in his hands. He sticks it through the roof and onto the stove. They throw in a little more coal and it keeps right on burning. In minutes we can hear someone yelling in French and pounding on the car next to us. Then he is pounding on our car. We stay quiet. Pretty soon, we hear both French and English shouts. Someone pounds on the door and yells "Open up. That is an order." I figure we are in real trouble, but about that time, the whistle blows twice and the car starts to move. The Frenchman is still pounding on the door and yelling, until we get up speed and leave him behind.

It gets warm in the car and I am thankful to the raiding party. I would have been one of the chickens, but I am enjoying the benefit of the others. Late in the afternoon, they have a stop for chow and everyone gets off.

After we eat, we all get back into the car. This time, I pull my sleeping bag out enough so that I can lay down. I use my pack for a pillow and in the warm dark car, I am soon asleep. I wake up in the morning and slide back up with my back against my pack. At the first stop, everyone climbs out and goes to piss. When we come back, they add a little coal to the stove and it warms up the car again.

In about another hour, they stop for breakfast. They have canned ham, eggs and potatoes, of course and some of the thick slabs of bread. I find the can with the tropical butter and chip out a piece to put under my meal to melt. Since it is morning, I go ahead and get a cup of coffee with canned milk and lots of sugar.

About noon, we stop on a siding and when I get out, I notice a wooden tank car sitting on another siding. It looks like the barrel that is used to make an AAA Root Beer stand. It is laying on its side on a flat car and steel bands hold it in place. It looks like it holds between a thousand and two thousand gallons. Several of the guys are standing around it. I go back and get into the car. In a little bit, a guy comes to the car door and yells to open the door. He hands in his canteen cup and it is full of wine. He climbs in and of course, those of us in the car ask where he got it and he says from that tank car.

Of course, we want to know then, how he got it. He said one of the guys was wondering if the tank was full or empty and another guy said to hit on the end and they could tell by the sound. Someone took a hatchet and smacked the end of the tank. When he did, the board split and wine started squirting out. Everyone began to get out their cups to catch it. Soon they were all full and they started filling their canteens. When they were all full, they used their steel helmets like buckets and caught what they could.

Sure enough, more of the guys are coming back and they are carrying their helmets and canteen cups full of wine. We have to help them in the car. About then, the train whistles twice and everyone makes a run for the train. The train starts moving and when we pass the tank car, I see the wine squirting out of the end, turning the snow around the end of the car purple.

It is a happy group in the car. Everyone who wants wine can have some. Some pass, including me. I would like to try some, but do not think this is the place. When we pull over later in the afternoon for chow, some of the guys do not get off of the car and some that do are not too steady on their feet. I get back to the car and then have to help some of the others climb in. Most of the wine drinkers are asleep by now.

In the morning, several have repented, and some have become drunk again, after drinking water to quench their thirst. It is a couple of hours before we stop for breakfast and by then, most everyone is hungry. We get off to eat and I take the opportunity to take care of some personal business. I look around and do not see a latrine, so I grab some paper and my entrenching shovel and go behind some cars. I dig a hole and like a cat, and cover it up when I am through. I go back and get my mess kit and go catch the end of the chow line. I do not want to miss out on the corned beef hash. I have it with my bread and butter and wash it down with coffee.

We spend some time here this morning and several trains go by, going the other way. Then we load up and head out on the main track again. We go until about noon before we stop again. This time we are in a very large train yard. There are many tracks and lots of trains switching. I look off in the distance and I can see the Eiffel Tower. I have reached Paris, something that I thought I would never see. Of course, I can't tell much about it, but at least I know where I am.

We go until early afternoon and stop for chow again. I am hungry and glad to see that they have pork and beans this time. I take my big slab of bread and wipe up every bit of it. We get back on the car and shut the door tight and then I realize that we may wish we had something else besides pork and beans to eat before the night is over.

We go until about ten o'clock and when the train stops this time, they tell us to get our things, because we are getting off here. They start at the front of the train and unload each car as they go back and have the men go climb on trucks. We are among the last to leave and as we do, we walk beside the cars and workers are going in the cars and cleaning them out. I climb on the truck, with the help of some of the other guys.

After about a half an hour, the trucks drive through a gate into a large compound. Someone opens the end gate on the truck and says, "Here you are." Someone says, "Where is that?" He answers "Fontainebleau."

CHAPTER XLVI

He said to them, "But now, let him who has a purse take it, and likewise a bag.
And let him that has no sword sell his mantle and buy one." Luke 22:36
And they said, "Look, Lord, here are two swords," And he said to
to them, "It is enough." Luke 22:38

Inside of the compound, we are directed to go to a lower roofed building. When we get inside, there are rows of double decked bunks. I pick out one and put my things on it. I ask where the latrine is and one of those already in the building says that I need to go back out the door, then around the building and it is on the back side. The truck ride in the cold has made the need to go important and so I head out to find it. This is not easy in the dark. I work my way around the end of the building and sure enough there is a building built up against the building we are in.

I push aside the blackout curtain and go inside. It is a long building and I am impressed. One wall is lined with what look like marble shower stalls. Instead, they are toilets. The stall is completely made of marble with a round hole in the center of the floor. Located in front and slightly to the sides of the hole are two raised, marble pieces the size and shape of a foot. They are slightly canted toward the front, so that if you stand on them, you will have to squat down to keep from losing your balance. This puts your butt in line with the hole in the floor. I only have to urinate, so the foot prints are not needed, but I can hardly wait until tomorrow, when I will try them out after breakfast.

I go back out into the night and back to the room where I am bunking. I tell several of the guys that they need to go see the latrine. "It is much better than a brick shit house, it is marble." Some take off right away to check it out and probably because they need it about as much as I did. I break out my bed roll and spread it onto the bunk and get ready to go to bed. It has been a long day and even with the heat, the train was still not the most comfortable place to be.

In the morning, I am awakened by someone hollering "chow time." I roll out, put on my boots and head back to the marble room. When I get back, I get out my mess kit and follow the others to the building they have set up for a mess hall. When I get to the serving line, I see that they are serving spam and eggs. They have some grapefruit juice and I down mine, while going through the line, and some fried potatoes. The portions are better that at the repo depo. I get a cup of coffee and go to find a place to eat. Again, they have high benches built, so that you can stand and set your mess kit on them while you eat. The eggs are made from powdered eggs, of course, but they are not as runny as those I have had before.

I go back to the barracks and straighten out my things. The urge hits me and I go to try out the marble stall. I get my pants and underwear down around my knees and then waddle into the stall and try to get my feet onto the foot pads. This is not as easy as it sounds. I get one foot on, but before I can get the other located, the first one slips off. I found that you have to squat before you try to get on the pads. It would be easier if my pants were not holding my knees together. After a bit of wrestling around, I get my butt in position, to do what I came here for.

When I get back to the barracks, there is a sergeant there telling us that we need to fall out in a half an hour for an orientation session. In about forty minutes, they call us out and we march over to another building. There are no chairs, so we stand in the building and the sergeant steps up on a small platform to talk to us.

He first tells us where we are. We are at Fontainebleau, France. It is a castle several hundred years old. The kings have used it for years as a summer palace and the woods nearby were used for hunting. Napoleon stayed here too. The building where we are bunked was the royal stable. The other buildings in back of us, including the latrine, were for the soldiers of the king's guard and hunting parties. I think it is kind of neat to be staying at a palace, even if I am only sleeping in the stable.

He goes on to tell us that while we are there, we will draw our weapons and get a chance to zero them in, that we will only be here a short time and then we will move on to some unit as a replacement. He tells us that we will not have any passes and that we are not to go outside of the compound, except when we are escorted to the firing range. He then says to go outside and line up as our names are called.

He calls my name and I go get in line with the others. When everyone is lined up, we march over to a supply building. The line starts in the building. When I get inside of the building, I see that there are a couple of guys issuing weapons. When I get in front of one of them, he asks my name and I tell him. He checks the list and reaches behind him and picks up an M1 carbine off of a stack. He then reaches into a box and hands me three magazine pouches, from another box, three more pouches of a different style. He then counts out thirteen carbine magazines to me. He hands me a string cleaning kit, sling and oiler and tells me to move on.

When we get back outside, we line up until everyone has their weapon. Most guys got carbines. Some got M1 rifles and a few got M3 submachine guns (grease guns). When everyone is back outside, they tell us that we are to go back to our barracks and clean our weapons. Cleaning supplies are there. This afternoon we will be going to the range to sight them in. They march us back and dismiss us at the barracks.

Inside of the barracks, it smells of rifle bore cleaner and oil. I clean my carbine, and each of the magazines. Then I fill my oiler and attach the sling to the carbine with the oiler in the slot in the stock. I put the magazine pouches on my pistol belt and fill them with the magazines. I have one left over to put in the carbine. I practice putting the magazine in the carbine and taking it out, as you would when reloading. I also practice putting the safety on and off to get the feel of it. I flip the rear sight up and down, so I can tell which position it is set on, by the feel.

We get to go eat dinner. This is the first place in France that we have had three meals a day and the portions are bigger too. It may be because this place is a headquarters for the army and they get first pick of the food. Today we have spaghetti with meat sauce, garlic bread and apple sauce. It is quite a treat. After dinner, we fall out with our weapons and load on to a truck for the trip to the range.

The range is located in the forest and it is not a long trip. Just outside of the compound, we see a Roman aqueduct. I had read about them in history class, but never thought any were still standing. It is a very impressive structure. We pass under it and travel on out to the woods. The range is not fancy; they just have some targets set up out in an open spot with a low mountain behind them. As we gather at the firing line, they hand each of us a box of ammunition. The ones with the carbines and grease guns each get fifty rounds and the ones with the rifles get a bandoleer containing forty-eight rounds.

They let the ones with the rifles go first, because they do not have to load any magazines. The rest of us take this time to load the fifty rounds into magazines. We are ready to go when they finish with the rifles. We sight them in at one hundred fifty yards. We shoot fifteen rounds and then go check our targets. Then we make our corrections and shoot the next fifteen. We check the targets and shoot fifteen and the final magazine of five rounds. We do not have any way to adjust the sights, so all we can do is to notice where our weapons are shooting and remember to correct for this.

They move up the targets to twenty-five yards for those with grease guns and they are to fire three round bursts. Some get a little carried away, but then they get yelled at. When everyone has shot, we load up and go back to the barracks to clean our weapons. By the time we have all cleaned them, it is time for supper. I go get in line for chow, even though it is cold outside. I am hungry and do not want to miss out.

I can't believe it when I get to the food line. They have pork chops, mashed potatoes and gravy, green beans and a peach cobbler for dessert, the best meal I have had for almost a month. I take my time eating it and savor every bite. When I finish, I wash my mess kit and go back to the barracks and put it away. I spend some time practicing loading my carbine, so that I can do it by feel. We sit around and talk about how our weapons shot and about where and when we think we will go next. I go to bed and go to sleep with a full stomach for a change.

We have to fall out in the morning. They tell us that after breakfast, we should get our things packed up because most of us will be shipping out. I go to breakfast and they have grapefruit juice to drink and I drink it while I am getting my food. They have some sausage patties and pancakes. The pancakes are not hot, but they have heated the syrup that you pour over them. There is nothing hot enough to melt the butter, so I leave it off. I get a cup of coffee and head over to the elevated benches to stand and eat. It really tastes good. I hate to leave this place, because they do feed well here.

We sit on our bunks with our things piled up beside the bunk, waiting for them to call us out. Time goes slow when you are just waiting. About the middle of the morning, a sergeant comes in and says, "The following men fall out." And he then proceeds to read off a list of names. When my name is read, I gather up all of my things and put my pack on, fasten the belt, shoulder my carbine and put the strap from my duffle bag over the other shoulder and struggle out of the door.

Outside, there are some trucks waiting. The drivers pass out a couple of C rations to each man and then help us get on the trucks.

This is unusual, because usually the drivers are not going to bother helping anyone. It makes me think that maybe they have something in mind for us. The truck fills up and then they start putting guys on the next truck. When everyone is loaded, the drivers load up and the convoy starts out. The MPs guarding the gate check the trucks and then open the gate and motion for them to proceed. We drive out into the French countryside. We can't see much through the small opening in the back of the truck. Of course, we have no idea where we are going.

We go for what seems like about an hour and then the trucks stop along side of the road. The back of the truck opens and the driver calls out, "Piss call." Everyone piles off of the truck and spread out along side of the road, relieving themselves. Cars are going by, but no one seems to care. "Welcome to France." We have about a ten minute break and then load up and continue our trip. It is cold and everything is covered with snow, so it is not too comfortable in the back of the truck. But certainly it is better than having to march across France.

We stop again about noon and they pull the trucks into an area just off the road. This time they announce that we will be there long enough for dinner. A couple of truck drivers gather up some wood laying beside of the road and pile it up on a bare spot. Another driver brings over a can of gas and pours some over the wood. They light a match and throw it into the gas. There is a slight explosion and then the wood catches fire. They wait as the gas burns off and the wood is going good and then after punching a hole in the top of their C ration can, they set it beside the fire to heat. They then invite the rest of us to put our rations there too.

Remembering the bean explosion from my scout days, I punch two holes in the top of my can of beef stew and set it next to the fire. I open the other can, and take out the biscuits, candy, cigarettes, toilet paper and sugar. I pour some water into my canteen cup and then hold it into the fire as best I can. Of course, it gets smoked up and I wonder how I am going to get it cleaned off. I do not need to worry; over here no one cares if your canteen cup has soot on it or not. When the water is hot, I empty the package of beef bouillon powder into it. I turn my can of stew and heat the other side. When it appears warm, I go ahead and open it up and eat my lunch. This is the first time I have ever had a chance to heat one of the rations. It tastes a lot better, even if it is not warmed all the way through.

We load up and they drive off again. We stop for a break in the middle of the afternoon and then late in the afternoon we pull into a small town and stop in front of the school house. We unload and they tell us to make ourselves comfortable, because we are going to spend the night there. We unload our things and put them in the school building. There is a wood burning stove in the room, so we go out and gather up what wood we can find and make a fire. Most of the wood comes from broken furniture from the school. Someone had hung some old quilts over the windows to make blackout curtains. We look around and find a couple of pieces of candles and when it gets dark we light them for some light.

We all spread out our bedrolls and lay on them. We still have one of our rations left, so I punch a couple of holes in the one can and place it on top of the wood stove. The other guys follow my example. I open the other can and get out the biscuits, candy bar, cigarettes, matches and coffee and sugar. I decide against drinking the coffee. I open up my can of corned beef hash and eat it with my biscuits and wash it down with water from my canteen. I go outside to look for the latrine, but the one at the school has been badly damaged and I decide to just go behind the remains. I go back inside and lay down on my bedroll. We talk for awhile and then I take off my boots and crawl inside of my sleeping bag and throw my overcoat over the top.

I wake up in the morning, put my boots on and go outside. It is still really cold and I can see my breath. My urine steams as it hits the cold snow. I go back inside and pack up my things. I assume that we will be moving on today. I no sooner get packed up when someone yells for us to get our things and fall out. I am ahead of the others and go outside with my things. The trucks are just arriving. We load up and they take off. I dig out a couple of the hard candies that I did not eat for lunch yesterday and suck on them. We go for a couple of hours and pull into another little town.

We unload and they send us to different buildings to stay. Some of the guys go across the street to a two-storied building, and the rest of us go to a bar and go in. I guess they would call it a bistro. It is not in service and there is nothing left to drink. The guys check that out right away. We move things around so that we can find a place to lay our bedrolls. We do not unroll them yet because we are not sure how long we will be here.

Someone comes in and says that they have food for us in a building across the street. We get our mess kits and go get in line. Of course, it is just the same thing we have been eating, but comes in bigger cans and they heat it in kettles. It has been a long time since the can of stuff last night, so I dig in. They also have a big water bag, where we can refill our canteens. When we finish we go back to the bar and wait for what is next. It is not long until we are called out to go to the supply. We are to take our magazine pouches with us.

I go to the building that they point out and go inside. A sergeant asks me how many magazines I have. I tell him thirteen. He says to give him one of the pouches and a couple of magazines. He says that is all I am supposed to have. He then hands me four boxes of carbine ammo and tells me to fill up my magazines. I fill every one, including the one in my carbine. He says to leave the rest of the ammo for the next guy. I put the safety on and insert the loaded magazine. I do not load the chamber, because I do not feel that we need to do that yet. I go back and put the pouches on my belt. Someone says that we might as well get comfortable, because we will not be leaving here until tomorrow.

Less than thirty minutes after they started issuing us ammo, we hear a bang. One of the guys goes out to see what it is. He comes back in a little while and says that one of the guys across the street started down the stairs, fell and shot himself in the leg. A few minutes later we hear the sound of a submachine gun. One of the guys was playing with his grease gun and let it go off, sending three or four rounds into the wall of the building. It is more dangerous here than in combat.

We go eat supper and then retire to the bar to get ready for bed. We do not have any curtains for the windows, so we will have to go to bed early. We also have to make note of where everyone is located, so if we get up in the night we can get out without stepping on anyone.

In the morning, we get up and go eat breakfast. They tell us to get our things ready because we will be moving out today. We sit around all morning, then go to dinner, and it is after dinner before the trucks arrive. They call out names and we load up on different trucks, depending on where we are going. They hand each of us one C ration as we board the trucks. We leave the town and go out on the rural roads. I can just tell that much by looking out of the back of the truck. They stop in the evening and we have a chance to eat our C rations. Then they drive on. It is after dark when we arrive at another small town.

As I get off of the truck, a sergeant says that the battery commander is waiting for me. He leads me down the street a ways, and we go in a door way and up a stairs. He opens a door for me and I enter. There is a captain seated behind a table. I come to attention, salute and say "Private Robert C. Lovell reporting for duty, Sir." I have arrived at my outfit.

CHAPTER XLVII

The captain says, "At ease, Lovell. Glad to have you with us.'
He then extends an open C ration can toward me, with some of the
hard candies in it. I take one and put it in my left hand and thank
him. He asks about my basic training and I tell him about what I
did at Fort Riley. He then asks me about operating the radios and
I tell him that I have had basic and some advanced training. There
are three other men in the room, but my attention is directed to the
captain. I am sure that this little kid is not what he thought he was
getting when they said he had a replacement coming in.

He turns to a sergeant in the room and says that he is going to
put me with Sergeant Kazaris, and asks him to show me to his quarters. I salute and he returns my salute and I follow the sergeant out
of the building. We go about a block down and on the other side of
the street. He leads me in an outside door into a hall. He closes the
outside door before opening the inside door to keep the light from
showing. This was probably the living room when civilians lived
here.

We walk into the room. There are six guys in the room. He
says, "Kazaris, here is a new replacement. He is a radio operator.
The captain said for you to put him up with your section." A stocky

built guy with sergeant's stripes on his tanker type jacket steps forward and reaches out and shakes my hand. He looks around the room, which is almost covered with bedrolls and says "You can put your bedroll together with Red's and sleep by him." I move over to where he motions and put my things down. Red reaches up from where he is sitting to shake my hand.

The sergeant who brought me over leaves and Kazaris introduces me to the rest of the men in the room. There is the sergeant, Red and four other guys. I make the seventh soldier in the one room. Red helps me take my bedroll apart and we fashion his and mine together, so that we both have room to sleep in our sleeping bags but on kind of a pad made of both of our blankets and shelter halves. I stow the rest of my things next to the wall. Some of the guys have mattresses, but everyone is sleeping on the floor.

The room is nearly empty of furnishings. There is a stove in the room. It is a beautiful stove, made of marble and ornate brass. I am sure that it is an antique. The room is lit by one electric bulb. It is connected to a six-volt battery outside of the house, with the wire running through the window. It is really a trouble light from one of the vehicles. The guys ask me where I am from and where I got my training. They also want to know about what songs are popular in the U.S. now and any other news from the States.

I ask what unit this is. They tell me that it is Headquarters Battery, Seventy-third Armored Field Artillery Battalion, Ninth Armored Division. They tell me that they were at the Battle of the Bulge and that they are some of the survivors. Most of the division was killed, wounded or captured. They are waiting for replacements of men and equipment so they can go back into battle.

We visit for awhile and then they say that some of them have guard duty tonight, so they need to get to sleep. I tell them it has been a long day for me too. I ask where the latrine is and they tell me it is about a half a block down the street and in the back. But if I only have to piss, to go piss against the building next door. A couple of the guys say they need to go too, and they will go with me. We walk next door and line up and wet down the front of the building.

Then we go back and get ready for bed. I crawl into my sleeping bag, put my overcoat over me and with the heat from the stove and the other six guys, I am warm enough. Then I fall asleep.

I wake up in the morning and it takes a moment to realize where I am. Some of the others are stirring around too. A couple of the guys are fully dressed, since they just came in from guard duty. I feel my feet as I put my boots on. Some of the numbness is going out of them and they are starting to sting. I get up and put my field jacket, steel helmet and pistol belt on and shoulder the sling on my carbine.

I go outside with a couple of other guys and we walk down the street towards the latrine. The street is one of the main roads and it goes through the middle of the town, running generally north and south. The old buildings face the street. The building we are stay- ing in has the numbers "1732" cut into the stone above the door. I am sure that is not the address. The little town is only about three blocks wide and less than a half mile long. I can see the top of the church steeple over on the next street. We walk nearly to the corner that makes up the center of the town, when they signal for me to turn and go between two buildings. We go out in back and there are two slit trench latrines, with canvas flies around them. One is marked "officers," and the other says "enlisted."

We walk into the opening to the enlisted and there is the slit trench with a board nailed over it. Of course, there is snow covering everything except the board, which someone has scraped off to make it warmer. The corner building, which is in front of the latrines, was the local bistro, and is now the mess hall. The back part is being used for the kitchen and meals are served in the main room.

We walk back out into the street and I notice that many of the buildings have sustained recent damage from fighting. The bistro has an unexploded 57 mm shell sticking out of the corner of the building. We walk back to the room and pick up our mess kits and go back to the mess hall for breakfast. They have spam and eggs, hash brown potatoes, grapefruit juice and coffee. I get my food and go with the other guys I know over to one of the tables to eat. When we are through, we go outside and scrape our mess kits, then use the cans with the heated water to wash them. I do not have to scrape mine much because I ate everything.

I notice that the guys with carbines are not wearing their pistol belts. They have taken one of the magazine pouches with a wide loop on the back, and slid it over the stock on the carbine so that they will have extra magazines with them. This gives them access to forty-five rounds. When I get back to the room, I take off my pistol belt and take one of the magazine pouches and put it on the stock of mine. Then I leave my belt in the room. One of the guys offers to show me around. We walk up to the north end of the town and he shows me where I will be standing guard. There is a tank parked there with its cannon pointed down the road. We walk back through the town to the south end and another tank is parked there. There is a tank parked on three sides of town. Other vehicles are parked on the side streets. There is quite a bit of traffic on the main road.

I go meet the sergeant in charge of communications and some of the other radio operators. As soon as they see me, the reception is cool. They, like most of the rest of the division, are expecting seasoned troops as replacements. They do not realize that there are not any available. They do take time to show me a couple of the radios in one of the half tracks. They are very similar to the ones we had in basic training. I hope that I am not assigned to one that takes code. I do not feel competent to receive messages on one of them. I thank them for taking time to show me and then go back to the room.

I am not at the room long before Kazaris comes in and says that I will be pulling guard tonight with one of the other guys. We will go on duty at midnight for two hours. I ask about getting up and he says that one of the guys that I will be relieving knows where I sleep and will wake me up. I decide I will check out the latrine. I walk down the street, between the buildings and then enter the opening in the fly and there is the board over the slit trench. I grit my teeth and then put my bare butt on the cold board. I am thankful for whoever brushed the snow off.

I go back to the room to wait for dinner. I ask one of the guys what they do about showers and he says that every once in awhile, they get to load in a truck and ride to some town that has showers available. I tell him that I would like to get one as soon as possible. I am feeling very gamey and I still have some of the salt water from the ship on me. He says that some of us should get to go get a shower in a few days. At noon, we go to the mess hall for dinner. The food is a mixture of canned rations and regular food. It is not great, but is much better than most I have had since I left Fort Riley and there is plenty to eat.

After dinner, I go back to the room. They have a large can that will just fit into the opening in the front of the little stove. There is no one else around, so I take the can and go the water bag by the mess hall and fill the can with water. I then put it into the opening in the stove and add a little more fuel to the fire. I write another letter home, while I wait for it to heat. By the time I get the letter written, the water is warm.

I take off my steel helmet and place it on a bare place on the floor and pour the warm water into it. I take off my clothes and get out a wash rag, towel and a bar of soap. I proceed to wash down my body as best I can with the soap and water. There is not any good way to rinse off, but I wring out the wash rag and dip it in the soapy water and then go over my body again. Not very good, but it will have to do. I find a clean pair of underwear, GI long handles and pants and shirt, and put them on. I feel better, but still wish I could get a real bath.

I take the two letters that I have written and go to the headquarters building and hand them to one of the officers there and ask if he will see that they are mailed. Some officer in the outfit has to censor the enlisted men's mail. I decide that I better make myself scarce, so I go back to the room and lay back on my blankets. It is not long until some of the guys start coming back in.

Sgt. Kazaris tells about some of the things that happened during the Battle of the Bulge. He said that when the Germans began their attack and the shells started coming in, the guys in his section dug a deep hole and covered it with rail road ties and then covered them with a deep layer of dirt. They put pine limbs in the bottom to line it and then put their bedrolls on top of them. They told about having to set up a road block to keep the Germans from getting through, but after they blocked the road with trees, the only thing they had to cover it with were some carbines, hardly enough to stop the huge German tanks that came. They told about the "screaming meemies," which were the German rockets, and how terrifying the sound was.

When it was time, we went to supper. Since most of us would have to get up during the night and go on guard, the light was turned out early and everyone except those on early guard went to bed. I went to sleep and finished my first day as a member of the 73rd.

CHAPTER XLVIII

I wake up when I feel someone shaking me and saying, "Lovell, time to go on guard." I twist around until I can find the zipper on my sleeping bag, slide it down and then climb out. I quietly put on my combat boots. I put on my field jacket, overcoat and steel helmet, sling my carbine over my shoulder and go outside. There are no lights to be seen, but the stars shining on the snow give enough light to see where I am going.

I walk to the north end of town where I will be standing guard. The another guy is waiting for me to arrive, so he can leave and go back to bed. I will be joined by another guard in a few minutes. I walk over behind the tank and stand in the snow. It is cold and the snow crunches as I walk. I can see my breath in the air. I can hear the footsteps of the other guard coming down the street and turn and see him walking next to the old buildings. We greet each other and get in position against the back of the tank, so that we can each see along a side of the tank. In the eastern sky, we can see almost continuous flashes like lightning in the distance. But this is not lightning, it is the flash from shells exploding.

We hear a noise and look up and an ambulance comes roaring down the road with no lights. I ask if we are supposed to stop it and he says, "Let it go. Those poor guys in there need to get back as soon as possible." I decide he is right and just hope that it is not Germans that have captured an ambulance. For a brief moment, I forget that I am cold. Our wool gloves with the leather palms, just do not keep our hands warm, so I stick them down in the overcoat pockets. It seems like forever before the church clock chimes one time. Our shift is half over.

The last building on the street is beside the tank, but it is just a shell. All the windows, doors and parts of the walls and the roof are missing. I walk over to it and step inside to piss. I have trouble getting through all of my clothes with my cold fingers, but at last manage to take care of it. It is not any warmer inside of the building than it is behind the tank. It is a good thing the wind is not blowing tonight. I stomp my feet to try to get circulation through them, but they are still numb and this cold is probably not helping them any. I was issued a flashlight today and have it in my field jacket pocket. I have it fixed for blackout by taking the lens out and putting a piece of carbon paper over it and then replacing it. This only allows a faint blue light to come through. It is supposed to not be visible from the air.

I take the flashlight out and shine it on my old watch and I can make out the time. We still have forty-five minutes to go. We move closer together so that we can talk in whispers. The time goes quicker as we visit and when he looks at his watch, he says it is time for him to go wake up our relief. With that, he leaves me alone to wait for my replacement. Now is when the time really goes slow. I keep looking for someone to get there to relieve me. The clock chimes two times.

It is nearly ten minutes before the first of the guards gets there to relieve me. I go back down the cold street, into the warm building and work my way over to my bed. My feet feel like a couple of blocks of ice. I slide down into my sleeping bag, zip it up and pull my over coat over me. I can hear all the other guys around me breathing.

I wake up in the morning and get ready to go to breakfast. They announce at breakfast that anyone not on detail will fall out at nine o'clock for a road march. Something to keep us in shape. They remind everyone to be sure that they are in proper uniform because of General Patton's orders. Anyone found out of uniform can be fined fifty dollars, which none of us have.

I go back to the room and straighten up my things and just before nine, I go fall out in the street. I leave my overcoat off, but of course have my steel helmet and carbine, which I have to have with me, anytime I am out of the house. We line up in a column of two with a lieutenant leading us and start marching out south of town. I notice that the new men are at the head of the column and the old timers are at the back. As we march along the road, there are yellow ribbons strung along the edge of the fields and every so often will be a sign reading "mines cleared to ditches." So it is not likely that we will be getting off of the road on our march.

We get out south of town and as we cross a bridge over a small stream, I look down and there is a rifle grenade lying in the water. It seems that there is danger all around us. We turn around and walk back to town and as we turn a corner, I look back and see that the last two men in the column have disappeared. The same thing happens every time we make a turn through the town. We get back and the lieutenant dismisses us and says nothing about those missing. I go back to the room and one of the guys is there putting some fuel in the stove. He says that we need to get some more and asks me to help him get some.

We borrow a couple of hatchets and move out into the hall and into one of the rooms. There is some broken furniture in there and we chop it up for firewood. I am sure that this was very fine furniture at one time and would be antiques in the right place. The hall goes on back to the back of the building, where there is a door. I ask what is back there and he says that it goes out into what is a field. I ask about going out there and he says, "We can't go out there because of the dead cow."

I say, "What dead cow?"

"The one that is laying against the back door."

I figure that he is kidding me, but I let it go and we take the wood back to the other room.

We come out in time for dinner and head for the mess hall. When we get there, I run into the first sergeant. He says that I need to go on guard early tonight, because I have KP tomorrow and will need to get up at four o'clock. It does not sound like I will have much sleep tonight. After dinner, I walk up the street to the empty building at the end and go through it to the back of the row of buildings. The guy was right, a field is in back of the houses. I walk close to the buildings, because I do not know if there are mines in the field. I get to the back of the house where we are staying and sure enough, there is a dead cow laying against the back door. She has a large hole in her side where a piece of shrapnel has hit her. I retrace my steps and go back to the room. No one is there, so I decide it is a good time to take a nap. I will need that sleep to make up for tonight.

A couple of the guys come into the room and I wake up. I ask them what is going on and they say that they have been working on some vehicles, getting them ready for when we move out. They also say that they took the battery from outside of the window and charged it up, so we will have light inside tonight. When it is time, we grab our mess kits and head down to the mess hall and get in line.

We go in and go through the line. The menu tonight is pork chops, mashed potatoes and gravy, green beans and they have made a sheet chocolate cake for dessert. They have some of the thick bread too, and some orange marmalade to spread on it. All in all, a very good supper. We eat in the mess hall and then wash our mess kits and head back to the room. It gets dark rather early and I will be going on guard at six. Just before six, I put on my overcoat, steel helmet and shoulder the sling on my carbine and set out for the guard post.

I am not at the guard post long before the other guard arrives. It is early enough in the night that we do not feel the need to whisper while we stand there, so we visit about things back home. The time passes faster this evening than it did last night. At eight, he goes to get the other guys to replace us. Someone will wake me about four, so I make a real effort to get to sleep, even though the guys still have the light on and are talking.

Four o'clock is sure early. I crawl out of my sleeping bag and get my boots on. I put on my field jacket and steel helmet and sling the carbine from my shoulder and head for the mess hall. When I get to the mess hall, the mess sergeant asks me if I know how to set up the cans for washing the mess kits. I tell him that I know how to set them up, but I do not know how to light the burners. He tells me to set them up and when they are ready, he will show me how to light them.

I get the two cans and set them in position and then carry water in a bucket from the well nearby. The water is not safe to drink, but it will be okay to wash the mess kits after it gets to boiling. It takes several buckets of water before both cans are filled to the proper level. Then I get a five-gallon can of gas and fill the tanks on the two gasoline heaters. I put them in place and then go get the mess sergeant to show me how to light them. He comes out and shows me how to do the first one and then I light the second one. It is just a matter of time before the water will be hot. I get the garbage can that the garbage is scraped into and set it at the head of the line.

When I have finished that, I go help set up the serving line to have it ready when the food is ready. When that is done, I go check the water to make sure it is getting hot. They are both getting really warm, so I get a bar of GI soap and cut pieces off of it into the first can. The GI soap looks just like the lye soap that my grandmother used to make. There is a paddle there made from a wooden board and I use it to stir the water and make it soapy. Everything is ready, so I go back inside and get ready to help serve breakfast. They have grapefruit juice in forty-six ounce cans and I get to serve it. I take a can punch and open the first can. They have been sitting in the storage room in back and it is just above freezing, so the juice is ready to serve.

The cooks have fixed cooked cereal today. It looks like Malt-O-Meal. They also have bacon with it. The bacon is real thick and not very lean, but the guys seem to like it. They have also fixed toast by putting the thick slices of bread in the oven. There is some more of the orange marmalade to go on it. Of course, there is coffee, lots of sugar, and canned milk, for their cereal and coffee, if they want it.

After the last one has been served, I get my mess kit and serve myself. I pour some of the grapefruit juice in my canteen cup and drink it, then put some of the cereal in my mess kit. It has started cooling off and is getting really thick. I get some of the bacon and since I am serving myself, I pick out some of the leanest pieces. I also get some of the last toast to come out of the oven. I put a little of the tropical butter on my cereal. I also doctor up my coffee with sugar and canned milk too. Some of the guys have finished and are leaving, so I find a spot to sit and eat. It is not the best food in the world, but I am hungry and really put it down.

After everyone has finished and washed their mess kits, I get to take care of the cans again. I turn off the fires in the two heaters and then get some hot pads to take the heaters out of the cans. I ask the mess sergeant if I can have someone help me to carry the cans and he sends another KP out. There is a big pit dug out back and we carry the cans out there and dump them in the pit. The garbage itself has to be covered and will be picked up by a truck that comes through. The mess sergeant actually says that I can take a break for about a half hour. This gives me a chance to visit the latrine and sit on the board again. After that, I go back to the room and write a letter home. It has been almost a month since I have heard from home. Surely a letter will catch up with me before long.

When my break is up, I go back and it is a repeat of the morning. I prepare the wash cans and then help serve dinner. After dinner, I clean them again and the mess sergeant gives me a break for awhile. This gives me a chance to rest. A couple of the guys are in the room working on some equipment and they promise to wake me in a half hour. The short nap really helps.

I go back to the mess hall and get ready for supper. We have corned beef hash for supper, and they have fixed some biscuits to go with it. They have canned sliced peaches for dessert. When we are cleaning up, there are still several peach slices left in the pan, along with a lot of juice. I ask if they are going to throw it out and they say yes. I ask if I can have what is left and they tell me to help myself. I pour off the juice and then pour the peaches into my canteen cup. It is completely full. A pint of peach slices. I eat the whole thing. We go ahead and finish up for the day and by the time I get through, it is after eight. I start back to the room, but before I get half way, everyone of those peaches comes back up. They were a lot better going down. I guess they were just too rich for my stomach. One good thing, I do not have guard tonight.

CHAPTER XLIX

At breakfast the next morning, they announce that anyone not on duty will again be required to go on a road march at nine o'clock. I fall out with the rest and we are greeted by a brand new second lieutenant who just arrived at the battalion the day before. Of course, he has been assigned the undesirable job of conducting the day's road march. We fall into a column of two's and follow him through the streets. This time we do not go very far out of town on the road, but instead march around through the streets. As before, the older guys are on the tail end and they start dropping off. Every time we turn a corner, someone else drops out. I am one of those at the head of the column, so I am one of the last to drop out. When the lieutenant gets back to the starting point, he calls for the column to halt and then turns around. There is no one there. He is furious and storms off to battalion headquarters.

When he reports what has happened, the other officers have a hard time not laughing, but the battalion commander hears of it and he does not think it is funny, since he was the one who ordered it in the first place. He schedules another road march for the next day and puts another officer on the tail end to see that it doesn't happen again. At least, we know that tomorrow morning we will be doing another road march.

They get in a couple of new half tracks and I am on the detail to help get them ready for combat. We will get rid of the extras on them and put on the things that we will need. My first job is to take off the .30 caliber machine gun mounts on the left side and the one on the back. There are other brackets here and there that have some special purpose and they are removed too. While I am doing that, the other guys are building a wooden box to go on the back of the halftrack to hold our personal things.

When we get through, they take metal bars and weld them to the side, to make racks to hold four additional five gallon gas cans on each side of the half track, right above the racks holding the six land mines. This will give us a lot more range. Then we strap a couple of machine gun ground mounts and a tent onto the front bumper. The weapons and ammo will be added later. Each one takes a lot of work to get it ready to go into combat.

The box goes across the back and has a hinged lid on top. The box will be used to hold our duffle bags and the things that we need to take with us, of a personal nature. It takes most of the day to get it completed. When we are through, I go back to the room and write another letter home. I still have not received any mail.

In the evening after supper, I feel the need to visit the latrine and make my way between the buildings and into the enlisted latrine and plant my butt on the cold board. It is already dark but you can make out shapes. It is not long before I am joined by someone else. He sits there too and asks who I am. I tell him and add that I am one of the new replacements. He asks what I do and I tell him I am a radio operator and he says that I am in his section. He asks me how I am getting along and I tell him just like it is, that the people there have not been very friendly. He says that things will get better in time, as they get used to it.

He finishes up just before me and I follow him out of the latrine and back into the street. As we walk out, there is enough light from the stars for me to see the gold oak leaves on his shoulders. Oh no, I have been talking to the battalion executive officer. Well, at least the brass knows how we replacements feel.   I go back to the room and get ready for guard duty; it is second shift, from eight to ten.

The next morning, they announce that there will be a road march at nine and that all personnel not on duty will attend and that all will finish the march. That is the bad news. The good news is that in the afternoon, trucks will be leaving for a nearby town, where they have showers set up and anyone who wishes may go and get a shower. I can hardly wait for afternoon and a chance to get clean again.

I finish eating my breakfast of bacon and pancakes and then start back to the room. When I get to the place to clean my mess kit, there is a French girl there about seven or eight years old. She is trying to get food out of the garbage can. I am embarrassed to see her digging in the can, but I do not know what to do. We are forbidden to give food to civilians, but I hate to see her hungry. The guy behind me takes care of it. He has her hold the can she has for food over the garbage can and then he scrapes the food out of his mess kit and it falls into her can. I notice that the pancakes and bacon he is throwing away have never been touched and I realize he has planned this all the time.

At nine, I fall out with the others for the road march. We take off following one lieutenant, while another follows the column. We march outside of town and then back around through the town again. Everyone is really in good spirits. We are marching along when one guy says, "I don't ever remember seeing this part of town before." Another says, "That is because you never finished a road march before." Everyone finishes this time.

After dinner, I gather up a set of clean clothes, a towel, washrag and bar of soap and wait for the trucks to arrive. The ground is still covered with snow and the air is cloudy and cold and looks like more snow. I bundle up in my overcoat. The trucks arrive and we climb aboard. They drive north on the main highway about twelve miles to a larger town, where the army has set up showers. It is cold riding in the back of the trucks. We get to the town and when they stop, we jump out, anxious for the hot shower. Then someone hollers, "Load back up." We climb back in and a sergeant comes to the back of the truck and says that the boiler for heating water has broken down and the showers are closed.

The trip back is longer and colder than the one going there. I feel a lot dirtier that I did before. When we get back, I put my things away and lay down on my bed to rest awhile. I will have guard duty again tonight. It will be from ten to midnight.

I admire the tattoo that Red has on his arm. He offers to make one for me, if I will get some ink. Fortunately, we do not have any ink for tattoos. But my fountain pen is dry too and I have had to switch to a pencil to write my letters home. The V-mail letters that are microfilmed and sent back to the states, where they are printed on paper and sent home, are supposed to be written in black ink for best reproduction, but I have to use a pencil for them too.

When I go out to go on guard, I find that the wind is blowing and it is snowing hard. Actually, it is warmer than before but it is not pleasant standing with the snow hitting you in the face. The other guard joins me and we both stand behind the tank trying to get out of the snow, but as big as the tank is, it does not seem to stop any of the wind or snow. My feet are starting to hurt more from the frostbite they received earlier and I am very uncomfortable. The time goes by very slowly and it seems like forever before I get to go back and crawl into my sleeping bag again.

When I wake up in the morning, my feet are really burning and stinging. I find that I can hardly stand to walk on them. On the way back from the mess hall after breakfast, I use my carbine as a cane to help me walk. I put my mess kit up and then go to the house where the medics are located. I tell them about my feet and ask if they can help. They look at them, but say that they do not know anything to do, that I will just have to bear with it. I hobble back to the room. It seems that they hurt more when I move them, but that is probably a good thing, since it shows circulation is returning to them.

I pick up a copy of yesterday's "Stars & Stripes" newspaper and read it. I am able to keep up with the news of the war better here than I did before. And of course, they often have one of Bill

Mauldin's cartoons in them, as well as the comic strip "Sad Sack." I find that the First and Third armies have linked back up, after being separated by the Battle of the Bulge. In the Pacific, the Burma Road has been reopened.

It has quit snowing but the wind is blowing and it is getting much colder. Some of the snow is beginning to blow up into drifts. I go back to the room where it is warm and get some rest to make up for the sleep I will lose tonight on guard. Before I lay down, I go to the back room and chop up some more furniture for fuel for the stove. It is not long before the other guys start coming back in too. No one wants to be outside on a day like this. We will wait in here until time for supper. Maybe they will have something warm and filling tonight.

When we are sure they mess hall will be open, we make a dash down the street and into the building. We get there just in time to get served. They are having beef stew tonight. They have also baked some biscuits. They even have some strawberry jam for them. I get some tropical butter and put it on top of my stew to get soft and then spread what I can on my biscuits before I add the jam. It really tastes good and it is warm and filling. I write a letter home before going to bed. I have guard duty from two to four, one of the worst shifts.

The guard wakes me up to go on guard duty and I feel around in the dark for my things. I get my things on and head out into the street. The wind is blowing and it is bitter cold. It goes through my gloves and I stick my hands into my overcoat pockets. When I get to the guard post, I do not see anyone, but when I move in closer, the guard I am replacing comes out of the ruins of the old building. He says it is too cold to stand out there behind the tank in the snow drift. I wait behind the tank until the other guard arrives. It only takes a few minutes before we have had all we want. We decide to go inside of the building. I get in the corner at the front and he goes on back into the building. It is not warm, but we are out of the wind.

We have been there for about an hour, when suddenly I hear a voice right at the front of the building. It is the officer of the day. A new second lieutenant, who else would be out wandering around at three in the morning, checking on the guards? He says, "If I were the enemy, I could have got you before you ever heard me here in this building." At that time, from further back in the building, comes the sound of a carbine bolt closing and chambering a cartridge and a voice says, "I don't think so." The lieutenant kind of gasps and says, "Carry on then." He turns and walks back out in the street. I figure we were lucky that we were spread out and not right here in one place. At least, it makes the shift go faster and it does not seem so long before we get to go back to bed.

CHAPTER L

Today at breakfast, the first sergeant catches me and says that he is putting me on a detail today. As soon as they get the mess hall cleaned out from breakfast, they are going to clean a shipment of .50 caliber machine guns in the mess hall and I am to be here and help. After I eat, I clean my mess kit and then take it back to the room. Then I go back to the mess hall to help clean the machine guns.

I am surprised when I get to the mess hall and see twelve wooden boxes sitting on the floor. Six are about eight inches by eight inches by three feet and six are about two inches by two inches by four feet. We pry the lid off of the first box and look in. It looks like a solid block of roofing tar. The guns are packed in cosmoline and it is so cold that it is solid. We take a knife and whittle shavings off of it. The task looks hopeless. Someone says that they used to clean them by using gasoline to cut the cosmoline. A couple of guys leave and come back carrying a five gallon can of gasoline and some paint brushes. We pour some gas into a gallon can and take the brushes and brush it onto the block of cosmoline. It just runs right off. I wonder about the safety of using gasoline in the room with a pot belly stove burning in the middle, but it does not seem to bother the others.

We see that it is going to take forever to get them clean, unless we figure out something. The guy who suggested using gasoline, says that when they used it before, the cosmoline came right off, but it was warm weather then. Someone suggests that if the gas was warmer, that maybe it would do better. Someone else goes out and gets a galvanized wash tub and brings it into the room. They pour the rest of the five gallons of gas into it and then set it on the stove. In just seconds, the gas is boiling. They take a C ration can and dip up some of the boiling gas and pour it on to the machine gun and the cosmoline just runs off of the gun, leaving it stripped clean, ready to be oiled and put in service.

I open one of the long boxes that contain the barrels and take out a long narrow block of cosmoline with the barrel embedded in it. I stand the barrel in the wooden box, dip up a can of boiling gas and pour it over the top of the barrel. The gas and cosmoline run off of the bottom of the barrel into the box. The outside is completely clean. I take a screw driver and dig a small hole into the bore of the barrel and pour a can of gas into it and a .50 caliber worm of cosmoline comes out of the bottom. One barrel down and five to go.

We are about half through cleaning and everything is going fast, when a lieutenant comes in to see what we are doing. He stands there watching for a little bit and then asks, "What is in the tub?" Someone says in a low voice, "Gas."

The lieutenant says "What?"

The guy repeats "Gas......gasoline."

The lieutenant screams "GET THAT OFF OF THERE." and runs out the door. A couple of guys set it off onto the floor and we keep on working, but within three or four minutes, the gas is too cold to work and the cosmoline will not come off. Finally, one guy says, "The war will be over before we get these clean, if we do not heat that gas." So two guys lift the tub back up onto the stove and we continue cleaning the guns until they are all cleaned.

We take the rest of the gas out, clean up our mess and we have six of the cleanest .50 caliber machine guns in all of Europe. I guess if the gas had exploded, the 57 mm shell in the corner would have probably gone off too.

After dinner, I go with three other guys to deliver the machine guns we cleaned. We load them one at a time in a jeep and then drive to where the half tracks are parked. We mount the gun in the ring mount at the front of the vehicle and then screw in the barrel. We screw it all the way in and then back it out the required number of clicks, to set the head space. We put the covers on and then go get another, until we have installed all six.

There are four of us in the room, when Sgt. Kazaris and the other two guys come in. Sgt. Kazaris is limping and someone asks what is wrong. One of the two guys with him, says, "He got shot." That gets everyone's attention and someone says "How?" Then Kazaris goes on to explain what happened. He had a .25 caliber automatic pistol tucked into his waistband. He found a German hand grenade and decided to explode it. He pulled the cord in the handle and threw it as far as he could. When he did, the small pistol fell out of his waistband, hit the ground and fired. The bullet hit him in the back of the left thigh and traveled forward and upward and lodged just under the skin on the front of his thigh. He went to the medics, they cut the bullet out, bandaged both holes and gave him some sulfa tablets to take. We ask if he applied for a Purple Heart medal and he says that he was afraid to push his luck any further.

We are issued shoe dubbing, which is a mixture of lard and paraffin, to rub on our boots to make them water proof. I have never cared for the stuff, because it bleeds through the leather and greases your socks. Besides it collects dirt and does not really keep your feet dry either. When we were getting fitted with gas masks, we were also issued some shoe treatment to keep poison gas from getting on our feet. The instructions were to put it on your boots and rub it in and let it dry. I think that they mean to do this in event of a gas attack, but it seems to me that would be a little late. I decide to do it now. It is a smelly black paste. I take an old rag and rub it all over my boots, making sure that it goes into the seams. Then I rub the excess off and place my boots close to the stove so that the stuff will melt and go into the leather.

After a little while, it has all melted and soaked up in the boots. The boots are too hot to put on, so I set them outside for a little bit. When they have cooled, I put one pair back on. They are hard as a board. But they are shaped like my feet, so I can get them on. They look black instead of brown like the rest of the boots. I hope I do not get in trouble.

After supper, I write another letter home and then read Life Magazine. It is five weeks old, but most of what is in it is new to us. Almost everyone is getting ready for bed and those on guard duty first, are going out to their positions. I have the four to six shift, so I will get to sleep some before I have to go on duty. That is the last shift of the night now, since it is starting to get light earlier.

I go on guard duty and it is still cold and snowy. My boots feel funny, they are so stiff. I hope they will break in or I may have to go see if I can get the supply sergeant to give me new ones. My feet are still hurting anyway and the cold does not help them. I tell the other guy about what happened on guard last night, when the lieutenant came out checking on us. We decide to move into positions so that we can cover anyone that might come from any direction, not just from outside of town.

After breakfast, I go back to the room and one of the guys is working on the stove. It does not seem to want to burn. The old furniture and things we have burned in it have seemed to clog up the flu and it does not want to draft well. There are four of us besides the guy working on the stove in the room. We are doing different things. I look up just in time to see him throw a C ration can of gas into the stove. It starts to steaming in the hot stove and I holler, "OH NO!," as he lights a match. The four of us go through the door at the same time, with the stove right behind us. The instigator was back of the stove and just got his eye brows singed and his jacket scorched a little.

Anyway, the beautiful little stove is ruined. The marble is broken and the fire box spread out. And when the soot finally settles, it coats everything in the room. We have to carry out bedding and shake it out to try to get some of the soot off. Sgt. Kazaris was one of us in the room, and he told the guy that since he blew up the stove, he has to go find another one.

About a half an hour later, they return with another stove. It is a small potbelly, designed to burn wood or coal, not as nice as the first one, but it will do. They also found a small bucket of coal some place and we have that to use after we get a fire going in it. About this time, the first sergeant comes to the room and says that anyone not on duty is to fall out for road march, by order of the colonel. It is his pet project and he is still mad about the other day. A couple of us go fall out and get in line for the march. Sgt. Kazaris says that he and the others have duty. He has to do something; his leg is too sore to make a march. But he made good time getting out of the room when the stove blew up.

Another road march and we take off in a different direction today. We follow the road out north of town where we can see the Moselle river to the west. We get out of town about three quarters of a mile, and then turn around and come back towards town. When we get close to town, we turn and go along a road to the east. It leads us to the northeast corner of the town. There is a bare field there leading towards a forest. A single barbwire fence runs along the outside of the field with signs hanging from it about every hundred feet. The signs say

"Achtung Minen." We all know enough German to know that the field is mined and that we will not be going out into it.

The march is hard on my feet, but I am able to make it all the way through. I think the walking helps my feet, but not without a lot of pain. When we get back from the march, I decide that I should get one set of my clothes washed, so if I ever get to go get a shower, I will have a clean set to put on. The guys have already told me that they get a Frenchwoman to do their laundry, so I ask what I need to do. They tell me that you take your dirty clothes, a bar of soap and a pack of cigarettes to a certain house. Just knock on the door and when someone opens it, just hand the package to them; no need to try to speak French, they will know what to do. They will hunt you up when the clothes are ready. I hope this is not a joke.

I do as they say and go to the house and knock. A woman comes to the door and I hand the clothes, soap and cigarettes to her. She smiles and says, "Merci." I go back to the room and get ready to go to dinner. In the afternoon, I help get some more of the vehicles ready. It is not hard work and I feel like that I am doing something constructive. I wonder how long it will be before we are ready to go into combat.

CHAPTER LI

Today the skies have cleared and the sun is shining. I think this is the first time I have seen the sun since I was on the Queen Mary. I just can't help but be in better spirits. I wash my underwear and socks and hang them outside to dry. It gets warm enough so that some of the snow is melting and puddles of water are standing in the street. I work in the afternoon putting first aid kits in each of the vehicles. We are gradually getting them equipped for combat. The day goes fast and it is time for me to go on guard duty.

We are standing guard behind the tank and the water is standing there too. It has a film of ice on top, but I break through when I step on it. The water is up over the toes of my boots, but they do not leak. The treatment I gave them has made them completely waterproof. My feet are cold, but at least they are dry.

It is February first, and we have two new additions to the unit. We have received a generator mounted on a trailer and a movie projector. I help move the trailer in position in front of one of the vacant buildings. We go inside and clean out the building. There are several chairs and we set them up in rows and then go scrounge the other buildings for other chairs and benches. We do not have any sheets, but we find a mattress cover and cut the threads so we can unfold it. Then, we nail it to the wall for a screen. This is one time I am glad that I have late guard, because I will get to see the movie tonight.

After supper, several of us go to the building where we have set up the theater. We get set and they start the movie. It is "The Arizona Kid," starring Roy Rogers. It is a corny movie, but we all really enjoy it. Of course, the movie has to stop at the end of each reel, so that they can rewind the film and put on the next reel. That just gives us time to discuss the movie. It does not take much to entertain us. After the movie, I go back to the room and wait until time for me to go on guard.

After breakfast, I get put on another detail. I am to help prepare the vehicles for abandonment. We go to each vehicle with a steering wheel and tape a thermite grenade to the steering column, below the steering wheel, where it will not be in the way of any of the controls. That way, if the vehicle has to be abandoned, all they have to do is to pull the grenade pin as they leave. It will burn the steering column so it can't be driven, and probably will set the vehicle on fire and burn the whole vehicle.

In the evening, I am back at the movie to watch Bud Abbott and Lou Costello. This movie should make all of us feel better. After the movie, I start back to the room and find that it has clouded up and is starting to rain. When it is time to go on guard duty, I dig out my raincoat and put it on. It is warmer with the rain and the remaining snow is starting to melt. Again, I am standing in a pool of water.

When I get up in the morning, it is still drizzling rain. We wait until we are sure the mess hall is open before we leave the room. At least, we have a dry place to eat. It is later in the morning when I make my trip to the latrine, that I get to really hate the rain. I try to keep my rain coat around me and at the same time, lower my pants and underwear, so I can sit on the wet board. I get it over with as fast as I can. Fortunately, someone put a gallon can over the roll of toilet paper, and it is only a little wet. I pull out enough to wipe and then some more, to dry my wet butt. I get my clothes back on without getting them in the mud beside the slit trench.

Someone comes up with the idea that we ought to do another road march. This does not go over very well and most of the guys are able to find some way to get out of going. But I can't think of anything that I'm supposed to do, so I fall in with the others who couldn't think of anything. They have a lieutenant leading the march and another following up so that we don't slip away like we did before. Of course we still can't get off of the road except just to the ditch because of the land mines. It is not raining as hard now but is still drizzling and it is hard to keep dry. I am glad that I have my boots treated, so that at least my feet are not wet.

After dinner, I go back to the room and write some letters home. I still have not heard from home, but I should be getting a letter before long. Then I lay back on my bed and rest awhile. I will appreciate this tonight while I am on guard duty. After awhile some of the other guys come in. They tell me about getting the Dodge command car.

It seems that some of the guys went to London while they were in England and saw the command car parked there. It had the red flag with the white star of a general mounted on it. None of the vehicles in the Army had keys. The customary way to keep someone from stealing them was to take out the rotor. But most of the guys carried a rotor with them. When they saw the command car, they took one of their rotors and stuck it in the distributor and started up the vehicle. When they got back to their base, they repainted all of the numbers on the vehicle, took off the flag and then brought it with them when they crossed the English Channel. The battalion commander now uses it.

After breakfast today, I am put on another detail. This time, I am to help distribute .30 caliber machine gun ammunition to the different vehicles. We load it into the back of a three-quarter ton truck and then drive to each of the vehicles that are equipped with a .30 caliber machine gun. Then one of us gets in the back of the three-quarter-ton and hands the cans of ammunition to the other guy in the other vehicle and he stores it away. It is not real hard work, but does take time. The hardest part is lifting the cans up and over the side of the vehicle.

We work until noon, take a break for dinner and then go back to work in the afternoon. In the evening, we quit in time to rest up before supper. After supper, most of us are in the room either waiting to go to bed or to go on guard duty. Sgt. Kazaris and another guy come into the room. Kazaris says that he has stopped them from sending messages. We ask who and what messages. He says that the French have been using the clock chimes to send secret messages to the Germans. But that he climbed up the tower and smashed the clock, so they will not be able to do it anymore. I know that many in this part of France have German sympathies, but I don't think they have been using the clock to send messages. I have never heard anything from it other than the time being chimed.

When I go on guard duty later in the night, we have to rely on my old watch to tell when to change shifts. I miss the old clock already. The guy on guard with me asks why the clock is still and I tell him the story. He says that Kazaris is crazy, but not to tell anyone he said so.

The next morning, when I am finishing breakfast, the first sergeant calls to me. I am sure that it is another detail, but instead he says that some of the guys are going on pass to Metz and wants to know if I want to go with them. It does not take long for me to say yes. He tells me to get ready and report to the orderly room at nine o'clock for my pass and that the truck will pick us up there. This sounds wonderful to me. There is not much to do to get ready. We have to carry about everything with us that we carry around here. I only have a few francs, so I will not be buying much.

By nine, it has clouded up and is raining. I put my raincoat on and go to the orderly room and get my pass. The truck is only about fifteen minutes late. We climb on the truck and head out the road south to Metz. It is only about ten or fifteen miles. The truck pulls up in front of a bunch of buildings that are being used for division headquarters. We climb out of the truck and about the only thing I can see are GI's. The difference between Metz and Ay, is that Metz has about one thousand times more GI's than Ay.

I walk around looking at the old buildings for a little while, as it continues to rain. I can't see anything to do here. I stop another GI and ask if he knows anyplace I can go to get out of the rain. He directs me to the Red Cross building about four blocks down the street. I walk down the street and there is a building with portable cookers parked in front and a large Red Cross sign. I go inside and it is crowded with other GI's trying to get out of the rain. I find a place to sit down and there is a Life Magazine that I have not seen, so I start looking at it. It also gives me a chance to watch what is going on.

After awhile, someone announces that they have a fresh pot of coffee and a new batch of doughnuts coming out. I get up and go get a couple of hot doughnuts and a cup of coffee before I head back to my chair. The doughnuts taste good and the coffee is not bad. I relax and just enjoy being there. I look out every once in awhile, to see if it is still raining and see that it has not stopped. It ends up that I spend the whole day in there eating doughnuts and drinking coffee. I leave in time to catch the truck back to Ay at four-thirty.

We had another casualty today. One of the sergeants took hold of the barrel on his carbine and pulled it out of a jeep. It went off and shot him through the hand. The medics bandaged it and took him to the aid station. They cleaned it up, replaced the bandage and marked him for duty. I don't know if he thought he would get sent back or not, but if he did, it didn't work.

After supper, I am back at the room when Kazaris comes in and tells me that I have early guard and need to get ready to go on duty. I do not care about that, because then I can get uninterrupted sleep after that. But he continues and says that the early guard is because I have KP tomorrow. I should have known there was a catch to getting to go on pass. Guard from eight to ten tonight and then get up at four for KP.

I get my usual jobs on KP. I have been on enough that they just let me do what I think needs doing, not any easier, but not someone after me all the time. The day is long, but the mess sergeant does let me take a half an hour break after we get through with each meal, and I do not have to pull guard duty tonight. I get off KP about eight-thirty in the evening and it does not take long for me to get into bed.

The next morning at breakfast, Sgt. Kazaris says that I am to report to the orderly room as soon as I finish breakfast. I am sure it is more duty and I will be paying for that pass forever. I walk into the building that is used for the orderly room and the first sergeant hands me a sheet of paper and says for me to read it. I start reading it and break into a smile. I can't believe it, I have been promoted to technician fifth grade. I am a T/5 and will be getting a corporal's pay. I thank him and head back to the room.

I tell the guys about my good luck and of course, they all congratulate me. A couple of the T/5's dig in their things and find some stripes for me to put on. I get out my Red Cross sewing kit and sew them on the sleeves of my shirt and my field jacket. Then, I write home and tell my folks to change my address from Pvt. to T/5. This is a better day than yesterday.

CHAPTER LII

This morning after breakfast, we all meet in the mess hall for a class on land mines. The man teaching it is from an engineering battalion and has had a lot of experience. He tells us about different kinds of mines that the Germans have and how they place them. He tells about how they booby-trap the mines and some of the things to look for. He is an interesting instructor and everyone seems to be paying attention. Just before dinner he asks for one man to volunteer to go with him at noon, to go get some land mines. One of the guys agrees to accompany him. The rest of us go get our mess kits and come back to the mess hall to eat dinner.

After dinner I return to the mess hall for the afternoon session. The guy has returned and brought with him four different examples of land mines that he found around the town during the hour's time that we were eating dinner. It is hard to believe that there are that many land mines in this area. We spend the rest of the afternoon studying the different mines. It doesn't seem to bother anyone that we are dealing with live explosives. The whole day has been interesting, much better lesson than you usually get in a classroom.

After the classes I go back to the room and write another letter home before time for supper. After supper I'm in the room with most of the other guys, when one of the guys comes in carrying a couple bottles. One of the other guys asks him what he has and he says he's got some beet juice schnapps. It is obvious that he has already sampled it, but he asks who wants some? One of the guys reaches out and gets one of the bottles. He pulls the cork out of the bottle and smells of the bottle. When he does he starts to gag and almost vomits. The guy who brought the bottles in tells him that you don't want to smell it, that you have to learn how to drink it. He says that you need to stick your finger in the neck of the bottle and then stick the bottle in your mouth, pull your finger out, take a swig, put your finger back in the bottle and take it out of your mouth so that you don't smell it.

This time instead of smelling it and getting sick, the guy does as he says and gets a swig of it. After he takes a swig and gets the bottle out of his mouth without smelling of it, he shakes his head and says "Damn, that is foul stuff." One of the other guys says he wants to try it. He sticks his finger in the bottle, puts the neck, finger and all into his mouth, takes a big swig, puts his finger back in and takes it all out of his mouth and says "Damn, you are right, that tastes like shit." This should have ended it right there, but another guy says that he wants to try it too. It ends up that they all have a go at it. Someone turns to me and asks if I want to try it? Well, I figure that I am just as tough as they are. I didn't smell it, but it tastes like moldy beets. They are right, it is bad.

The stuff is made of fermented sugar beets. I am glad I can't see how it is made. The guy traded some cigarettes for it. He takes the remainder and goes out of the room, probably to see if he can find someone else to drink with him, since we all told him that we had all we wanted. He comes in later, sick as a dog. I think he has had all he wanted too.

Today I am on detail again. This time we are delivering .50 caliber machine gun ammunition to the vehicles that have .50 caliber machine guns on them. It is about the same as before, except that there are more .50's than there were .30's and the ammunition cans are about twice as heavy. We take our time and spend the whole day on the job.

Today we have a class on the bazooka and rifle grenades. They go back over what we learned in basic in the morning and in the afternoon we go out west of town to a field between the town and the river. There is an old pill box located there. It must have been built in World War I, but looks older. They take the bazooka first and select a couple of guys to fire it. They aim at the pill box, but the rocket falls short and hits in the soft mud in the field and does not explode. The second round hits the lower left hand corner of the pill box and blows out a chunk of concrete.

Then it is time to fire the rifle grenades. I have been picked for that. I put the grenade launcher on the end of my carbine and put in a blank cartridge. The grenade launcher, has three marks on it marked from one to three, with three being the closest to the end. This is backwards to me, because the further you put the grenade on the launcher, the further it should go. I put the anti-tank grenade on the launcher and push it all the way down, so I can get maximum range from it. I get ready to shoot, but before I can pull the safety pin, the sergeant conducting the class stops me and makes me pull the grenade back up to the three mark, telling me that is three hundred yards. I know he is wrong, but he is watching me and I don't dare contradict him.

I pull the safety pin, release the safety on my carbine, hold the stock tight against my shoulder and pull the trigger. I am rocked back on my heels and my eyes are jarred shut. I open my eyes and see the grenade hit in the mud about half way to the pill box. I look down at my hands and I am holding the carbine stock in them, the barrel and action are hanging down from the sling and the fore stock is about ten feet away. So much for shooting a grenade from a carbine.

After we get through shooting, there are four dud rockets and grenades in the soft ground between us and the pill box that have to be disposed of. They have some captured German TNT available. It is in small blocks of about three or four ounces each. The blocks have a threaded insert in each one and we also have some detonating caps and trigger mechanisms. The Germans used these for booby traps. They would put a detonating cap in the hole in the TNT, screw one of the triggering mechanisms in on top of it and tie a string to the pin in the mechanism and then pull out the safety pin. Any pull on the string would set off the TNT. We rigged them up and placed one under each of the duds, ran the string out for some distance, laid down and pulled the string. The charge would set off the dud too. We blew all four in this manner.

Today we are going on a little practice road trip. We get about a half dozen vehicles and make a small convoy to let the new drivers get a chance to practice driving in convoys. We drive a few miles and then stop for a break at a very interesting place. It is one of the bunkers that is a part of the Maginot Line. It is a dome that sticks up about fifteen feet above the ground and is about twenty-five feet in diameter. It is made of thick concrete and has a thick steel door to enter. The side facing east has an opening for a large gun. The gun has been removed. There are many of these spread out all along the east side of France. These bunkers are connected by a series of tunnels. I want to go inside and see what they are like, but we know that the Germans occupied them and they may be mined and booby trapped. There are a lot of empty GI ration cans about, which indicates that American forces have been there, but nothing to show that the inside has ever been cleared. I can't take the risk of going inside. I have read about the Maginot Line in school. The French built it after World War I to keep the Germans from invading again. The cost back then was about a million dollars a mile. It was very formidable, but the Germans just went around and came in from behind.

We make the road trip without incident and get back in time for supper. In the evening, I go to the movie. I go every night that I do not have early guard. It helps keep me from being so homesick. I still have not received any mail from home and I keep wondering how my brother Don is and where he is now. I do not have much to complain about. My feet are not hurting much, only a tingle sometimes, the food is pretty good and there is plenty of it, I am not working very hard, I get to read "Stars & Stripes" everyday and Life magazine every week, that is only a month or so old, plenty of cigarettes and I get to go to a movie almost every night. I am sending money home, since there is nothing to buy here. I have a warm dry place to sleep, so I am really very well off.

After the movie, I go to bed. I have to get up and go on guard duty at two. The guard wakes me up to go on duty at two o'clock and I make my way to the post at the north end of town. The days have been warm, much like early spring lately, but the air is damp and chilly out on guard duty. The other guard and I stand where we can talk and still see both in and out of town. I learned my lesson about that before. Tonight, I am the one who watches outside of town.

About three-thirty in the morning, I am looking to the northwest and I think I see a flashing light. I watch closely and then I do see a light flash in the trees on the other side of the river. I quietly call to the other guard and have him look. He sees it too. There are lights flashing every so often in the woods. Our first thoughts are that German paratroopers have landed and are signaling to join up. I stay and watch and send him to notify the sergeant of the guard. I put a cartridge in the chamber of my carbine and get down low beside the tank.

In just a few minutes, the other guard comes back with the sergeant right behind him and behind him is the officer of the day, one of the new lieutenants. I point out to them where to look and they see the lights too. They send the other guard back to alert everyone. It is not long until all of the brass in the outfit is there looking. The battalion commander gives the order for the tank crews to start up their tanks and get ready in case we have to go into action. All of the men are out and moving around, getting their weapons ready in case we are attacked.

The crew for the north tank arrives and tries to start their tank. The tank has a diesel engine and has not been started for several weeks. No way is it going to start tonight. One of the officers sends me to check on the other tanks. He really does not need to send me, because if one of them was running, we would hear it. They keep working on the tanks and finally a little after daylight, they get the first one started. They then use it to pull the others and get them started.

Now that it is light, we can see no German forces in the woods, and I slip off and go back to the room and go to bed. I do not want to be around when they start to look for someone to blame for getting everyone out. But at least, they found out that they are not ready for an attack. About noon, they get a report on what the lights were. It seems that last night for the first time, they let every fifth vehicle in a convoy turn on its lights. But they neglected to notify all units of this. What we saw were the lights of those trucks, going by the woods, so that it looked like the lights were flashing.

CHAPTER LIII

The weather has warmed up considerably the last few days. Someone mentions that the dead cow at the back door needs to be moved away. We all agree that we are going to have to move her before long. I notice that no one volunteers to move her. We all leave the room and head for the mess hall. After breakfast, we all have duty to go to. I get to pass out small arms ammunition today. We have cans and boxes of .30 caliber carbine and .45 caliber submachine gun and pistol cartridges to put in the different vehicles. There is a compartment under the floor of the half tracks for ammunition, and we store it there. We do not deliver any to the tanks. They are to be replaced with gasoline powered tanks, later today. We will deliver to the new tanks when they get here. The .50 and .30 caliber machine gun ammunition that we put in the tanks, will be transferred to the new ones.

I still have not received any mail from home. I keep wondering about my brother Don and how he is doing. I write another letter home and enclose a money order for $75. I tell my mother to use it if she needs it, and if not, to put it in the bank for me. There is not much to spend money on here. We get our cigarettes, soap and what

candy we get at no charge. Only thing we have that requires pay-
ment is our laundry, and we use soap and cigarettes for that.

We are sitting around after supper and someone again mentions
that we are going to have to get rid of the dead cow. We all agree
and decide to do it tomorrow. We will get a jeep and hook on to her
and drag her across the field and down by the river. After we make
that decision, a few of us, assigned to later guard duty, go down the
street to the movie building and watch the show. After the show, I
wait up until it is time for me to go on guard duty at ten.

Today is February 16th and at breakfast, they announce those
not on duty and who want to, can go to Metz and get a bath. After
breakfast, I take my musette bag and put clean clothes, soap, wash
rag and towel in it and get ready to go. The ride to Metz is not too
long and it is not really cold today. We get to Metz and they pull up
in front of this big bath house.

They have lockers for us to put our clothes. We all strip and
head for the showers. The steam is so thick that it is hard to see
where you are going. I find an unused shower and turn it on. The
hot water feels so good on my body. This is first shower I have had
since December 31st at Camp Kilmer, New Jersey. Other than the
bath I had in saltwater on the Queen Mary, the only bathing I have
done is out of my steel helmet. I get wet, soap up good and then
wash it off. Then I start all over again. I wash myself three times.

In the other part of the building, is an indoor swimming pool.
I leave the showers and then go dive into the pool. I swim around
for awhile and then go back and take another shower, before putting
on clean clothes and getting ready for the trip back to Ay. I feel so
good. I do not think I could have stood being dirty much longer. I
relax on the way back. The new tanks came this morning and we
have to transfer the machine gun ammunition to the new tanks. We
also have to help load 75 mm cannon shells into each of the tanks.

After supper, we are sitting in the room and I ask if they got the
dead cow moved today. No one says anything, so I say, "I didn't
think so." Someone says we will get it done tomorrow, for sure.

Someone else says "We sure need to, she is getting real ripe." No movie for me tonight, I have to go on guard at eight.

Today after breakfast, we go on another road march. This is just to keep us in shape for what is to come. In the afternoon, they send me to the motor pool to help service the vehicles to make sure they are ready for travel. All I do is check fluids on them. When I finish that, the first sergeant tells me to go clean out the theater. I do not mind that, because I enjoy the movies so much.

After supper, we are in the room and someone mentions that we still have not moved the dead cow. We agree that we need to do that tomorrow. When it is time, some of us go to the movie. The movie is "Abroad with Two Yanks ," starring William Bendix and Dennis O'Keefe. It is about two soldiers in Australia falling in love with the same girl. After the movie, I go back and go to bed. I have the two to four guard duty tonight.

Today's duty is passing out hand grenades. We open the wooden crates and inside are the black tubes with a grenade sealed in each one. We take the tubes and put some in each of the vehicles. I take a grenade out of the tube and put it in the pocket of my field jacket. The guy helping me takes one out of the tube and hangs it under the dash of one of the jeeps.

In the evening, one of the lieutenants yells at the guy, who was passing out grenades, with me. The lieutenant says that he was in the jeep and the pin fell out of the grenade, but he caught it before the lever could come off and kept it from exploding. I doubt the story. If that pin came out, he is not fast enough to catch the lever. But just to make sure, I spread the end of the pin a little more on the one in my pocket.

Today I am on KP again. Except for the long hours, I do not mind it. But getting up at four and not getting off until about eight at night makes a very long day. I am glad the mess sergeant lets me take a little break after each meal. But of course, I have been on enough times that I know what needs to be done, so I make good help. I hope the guys moved the dead cow today, but I bet they didn't.

The guys said they could not get a jeep yesterday to move the dead cow. I do not know why they did not get some other vehicle and pull it away. I would do it myself, but I am not authorized to get a vehicle and no one else seems interested. If they ask, I will help them. That is after I get back from the road march. At least my feet are not hurting as much and the marches give me something to do. This afternoon, I go along on a road trip. There are six vehicles, and the drivers are practicing driving in convoy and also it is kind of a shake down for the vehicles. After supper, I go to the movie and see "Arizona Trail," starring Tex Ritter. Another corny movie, but I still enjoy getting to see it.

Today I get to help unload and store supplies. Most of them we put in vehicles and the rest are stored so that they can be loaded up quickly. I have the feeling we will be moving out before long. This evening I am writing a V-mail letter home. It is February 21st and I tell them that I have not had any mail yet. I get about two thirds of the way down the page when the clerk comes in with the mail. I have a letter from my mother, one from my dad, one from the mother of one of my friends and one from the minister of our church. I am so glad to get mail at last.

I open the letter from my mother first and I am devastated. My brother Don died from his wounds on December 13th. She tells me all they know about it which is not much. I was so close to Don and can't stand the thought of him being gone. The other letters try to comfort me, but I feel so suddenly lost. I really do not know what to do. The other guys in the room know something is wrong when they see me crying so. They tell me that I need to feel bad, but to not let it overcome me because where we are going, I need to have my mind on what I am doing or I will be in more danger.

I finish the V-mail letter and then write a longer one to my dad and then one to my mother. I get them finished and one of the guys offers to take them to the orderly room to be censored and mailed. I lay down but it takes me a long time to go to sleep. When they wake me at two for guard duty, I feel like I have been dreaming. At least I hope I have, but after a few minutes, I know that it was not a dream.

The other guard is good enough to let me ramble on about Don. It does me good to be able to talk to someone about him. Also, it makes guard duty go by much faster. At four o'clock, I go back and crawl into my sleeping bag and curl up. I remember how I used to curl up against Don's back, when we were kids in bed. I have tears running down my cheeks, but I finally go back to sleep.

I am rather numb this morning and go to breakfast after most of the guys have eaten. Word must have gotten out about me losing my brother, because several of the guys look at me and kind of nod with an understanding look. I appreciate them and it is good to be with people. After breakfast, I go gather up one set of my clothes and take them to the French woman to be washed. I should get them back tomorrow or the next day. Then I go help organize the supplies.

The rest of the day goes on, but I do not really feel a part of it. In the evening, the little French girl finds me and gives me my clean clothes. I am surprised because they usually take a day or two to do them. As she hands them to me, she says, "You leave." I do not understand what she is talking about. The guys start coming into the room and one of them sniffs the air and says "We have to move that cow tomorrow no matter what else we do." We all agree that tomorrow, the cow gets moved. After supper, I go to the movie and then go back to the room and go to bed. I have the four to six guard duty, so I will get some sleep tonight.

I am wakened for guard and go stand behind the tank with the other guard. He is watching away from town tonight and I am watching back. Just before five, I look and someone is coming towards us from town. When he gets close, I see that it is the first sergeant. He tells us to go wake everyone right now. We are pulling out this morning. Then I realize what the little French girl was trying to tell me.

CHAPTER LIV

I go down the west side of the street and the other guard goes down the other side, going to each building that has guys staying in it, and wake them all up. I tell them to get up, get their things together, that we are moving out. There will be early breakfast before we go. Then I go back to my own room and start to get my things together. Red and I take our bed roll apart and make up a couple of individual bed rolls. I roll mine up and tie it with a piece of rope. I pack the rest of my things in my musette bag and duffle bag and get my pistol belt ready to wear. Then I go to breakfast.

When we leave breakfast, they hand each of us a C ration to take with us for dinner. I go back to the room and then get my things and carry them to the battalion executive officer's halftrack, where I will be riding. I put my duffle bag in the box on the back of the halftrack and my musette bag, gas mask and pistol belt in the back of the half-track. They have rolled the cover on the halftrack back a little ways in front, so that the major can stand up and see what is going on. I am back under the top and can't see much.

We are under radio silence, but the major tells me to turn on the radios and listen to see if I hear anything. Since the communications sergeant has not given me any frequencies to use, this is wasted effort, but I do not argue with the major. In a little while, we start to move out. There is a jeep in front of us and we are the second vehicle. We head out of town going north. I feel like I am boxed in. We move forward and then stop, move and stop. It is easy to see that an armored division does not move very smoothly.

When we stop a little longer than usual, I ask if I can open up some more of the top, so that I can see out. The major agrees and the driver and I roll the top back about half way. This allows me to stand up behind the major and watch where we are going. This is a lot better than being cooped up down inside of the halftrack. We have not gone far before we have to stop for some time. The units stationed in the town to the north of us are pulling out onto the road and we have to wait until all of their vehicles get on the road, before we can continue. Now that I am standing up, I look back and as far as I can see, there is a line of vehicles. The 9th Armored Division is on the move.

While we are just sitting in the road waiting for the other unit, I suddenly start laughing. The major asks me what is so funny and I tell him that I just remembered that we left Ay and that the dead cow is still laying against the back door. He does not know about the dead cow and I tell him the story and he laughs too. I wonder who will have to move her.

I do not know what unit is ahead of us, but finally they get on the road and we move up to follow them. The road is asphalt, so there is not much dust, but there are a lot of fumes. The road is one of the main roads in France, so it is of better construction than some, but not many roads can handle the traffic of an armored division.

We move about a quarter of a mile, then stop again. We sit there for about five minutes and then start up again. This time we go about one hundred yards before we stop. Occasionally, there will be other vehicles passing, going the other way. Empty trucks returning from taking supplies to the front and unfortunately, every so often, an ambulance heading back with wounded. We are not moving very fast, but after the boring time we have been having, it is great to at least be doing something.

About noon, we are stalled on the road, so four or five of us, from the closest vehicles, gather some sticks, pour a little gasoline on them and make a fire. We punch holes in our C ration cans and set them beside the fire to heat. The fire no sooner gets to going, when the column starts to move again. We take out gloves, grab our cans and jump back into our vehicles and take off again. We go about two hundred yards and stop again. We get out again and gather some more sticks and make another fire. We look back and there are several guys gathered around the fire we made before. This time, we have time to get our meal hot and eaten, before we have to move again.

We spend the afternoon slowly moving across France and by evening, we have entered Luxemburg. We keep moving and it gets dark. The drivers turn on their blackout lights. We pull off of the main road and go down a narrow road towards a school. One of the halftrack drivers fails to see the turnoff and hits the rock wall bordering the road. It bends the front suspension on the halftrack and he is stopped. The maintenance men from Service Battery come up and are able to get a jack under there and push the suspension out enough so that they can move the vehicle, but it does not steer very well.

We park the vehicles in the school yard and set up camp for the night. The mess crew sets up and starts to fix the evening meal. I take my bedroll and go find a place in one of the school rooms to unroll it. Then I go back out to the halftrack and take cans of gas from the outside racks. I use the filler spout on each can and refill the gas tanks in the halftrack. I take the empty cans and throw them along side of the road. They will pick them up later and take them back to be refilled.

A little while later, a two-and-a-half-ton truck drives up, full of cans of gas. As the driver moves along, someone climbs up on the truck and hands down cans of gas. I get three of them to replace the ones we used. Of course the tank drivers have to have a lot of cans, since they only get about a half a mile to the gallon. I admire the guys that drive these supply trucks. It takes guts to drive a truck at night with no lights and with a load of gasoline or ammunition.

The driver and I lower the armored plate that covers the windshield, so that we can cover up the halftrack. We do not realize that you are supposed to remove the windshields before you lower it and the bolt on the back of it cracks one half of the windshield. Then we roll the cover back over the half track and fasten it down.

It is not long until they say chow is ready. We get our mess kits and go get in line. We have corned beef hash for supper, along with some peas. The corned beef hash is the same thing as is in C rations, only it comes in gallon cans. They also have some of those thick slices of bread to go with it, and they have some apple sauce for dessert. Of course, there is coffee, but I pass on it, because I want to be able to sleep as much as I can tonight. After supper, I check and find that I have guard from ten until midnight, out on the other side of the school.

I go back inside the school room and take off my pistol belt and steel helmet and lay them and my carbine beside my bedroll. My field jacket I lay over my bedroll and I sit down and take off my boots before I slide into my sleeping bag. It does not take long before I am asleep, but ten o'clock comes quick and I have to put everything back on and go out by the road and stand guard for a couple of hours.

The next morning, I get up and roll my bedroll up, put my equipment back on and go see if I can find breakfast. This morning, they are having spam and powdered eggs. They have more bread and some orange marmalade and of course coffee. I eat all they give me and drink coffee this morning too. I go back to get my bedroll loaded and in the school room I see a bottle of ink. I take it and put it in with my things. I really need it to write home. I hope that the people of Luxemburg will forgive me.

We roll back the top on the half track, load up our bedrolls and then put up the armored plate that covers the windshield.

I walk around the other side of the halftrack and pass the back of the three-quarter-ton truck that is used for supplies. I glance in back and there are all kinds of things piled in there, but sitting on top of the pile at an angle is a wooden case of TNT. About one half of the top of the case has been removed and laying on top of the TNT are five electric blasting caps. Anything hitting one of those caps would set off the whole twenty-five pounds of TNT and would blow the truck and anything around it to bits.

I see the lieutenant, that is the supply officer, across the way and go over to him. I say, "Lieutenant, did you ride in the supply truck, yesterday?"

"Yes, why?"

"Come here I want to show you something." We walk over to the back of the truck and he pulls the flap aside and looks in. He turns white as a sheet and yells for the supply sergeant. I do not want to get in trouble with the supply sergeant, so I get out of there before they get back.

They are passing out C rations for dinner and I go to pick up mine. They have given out all the dinner rations and are down to the breakfast rations. I get my can of ham, eggs and potatoes and the accessory can to go with it. I find the communications sergeant and tell him that I do not have the frequencies for the radio. He says that he has not given any out because of the radio silence, and that I should just keep the radio off, until we get orders later on. I tell him about Major Jones having me listen to the radio yesterday and he laughs.

Everyone is loading up now. Major Jones decides to ride in the jeep today and the lieutenant will be in the halftrack where I am. Again we will be the second vehicle in our unit. I do not know what our position is in relation to the whole division. We find a break in the column and start to fall in. It is like it was yesterday, move up and stop, move a little ways and stop.

We move out of Luxemburg and into Belgium. We reach a city and as we move through the city, many of the people wave at us. We pass one older man standing on the curb. He is holding the hand of a small boy with one hand and waving with the other, all the time pissing into the street. I turn to the lieutenant and say "Lieutenant,

I think he is trying to tell you something." The lieutenant laughs and says that he got the message. No doubt about it, Europe is different.

Close to noon, we stop and after we are there for a few minutes, we decide to eat our dinner. Several of us gather sticks and with a little gasoline, we soon have a roaring fire. I set my can of ham, eggs and potatoes beside the fire. The fire is really too big. It is not long before I decide that my can should be hot. I open the can and start to eat. One side got too hot and has scorched the contents. It tastes terrible. I eat what I can from the other side, but the taste is still there. I throw the rest away, and make do with what is in the accessory can. Not much dinner for a growing boy.

We travel the rest of the afternoon and in the evening pull into the yard of a large Catholic Church and school. Some of the Sisters show us where to put our bedrolls in some of the classrooms. After I put my bedroll down, I go back to the halftrack to get it ready for the night. We go ahead and fill the gas tanks from the cans on the sides, before we put the top on. This time, we remember to take out the glass, before we lower the armor plate in front. The mess truck pulls in and starts setting up for supper. The fuel truck arrives and we get cans of gas to replace those we used to fill the tanks.

Some of the men come in and are looking for the medics. They were riding in vehicles in back of some tanks that were diesel and the fumes from the exhaust burned their faces. The medics put some kind of cream on their faces and it seems to help. Since I did not have much dinner, I am first in line for supper. I am not surprised to see that it is meat and vegetable stew. In fact, I would have been surprised if it wasn't. Stew, green beans, bread, peanut butter and canned pears for dessert.

After supper I go to the school room where I have my bed. They have blackout curtains up and have a few candles in there, so I go back out to the halftrack and get my stationery. I write a letter to my folks and put at the top "Somewhere in Belgium." This will let them know that we are on the move. I give it to one of the officers and then go back and crawl into my sleeping bag. I have guard duty from midnight until two o'clock.

CHAPTER LV

It looks like we may be going to stay here in Belgium for awhile. They seem to be settling in more. There is an auditorium here at the school and we set up the picture show there. I help get it set up. They have electricity in this part of the school, but it is European voltage, so we still have to use the generator. We can, however, use the lights in the building, which makes it nice. The cooks get the ovens set up and they can now use them. This morning we had SOS for breakfast and they used the ovens to toast the bread for the shingles.

This is a very interesting place, but we are not supposed to go very far from our location. If we could, I am sure there are a lot of things to see and the people seem very friendly. We are going over some of the things we did on the way here, to try to make the traveling go smoother. Also we are checking the vehicles to see if they need anything done to them. We are supposed to get all of our equipment ready, because we are having an inspection tomorrow.

After dinner, which is a repeat of the corned beef hash from the other day, I get busy on my equipment. I take my carbine apart and clean it completely, even the magazines for it. Then I reload the magazines. I make sure that my canteen is clean and shiny but I will

305

wait until after breakfast in the morning to clean my mess kit and canteen cup. I clean all my web gear and make sure that my musette bag is clean and properly packed. Then I take some rags and clean off my boots. That is about all I can do with them since I put that gas proof treatment on them.

I go out and help the halftrack driver to straighten up the vehicle. Not much we can do. But we stack things neatly, clean off the lights and wash the windshield. He goes around and takes a rag and wipes all the grease zerks and then gives each one a light shot of grease so that everything is freshly greased. I take some rags and wipe off both of the machine guns and then run an oily rag over them to protect them. Each gun has ammunition with it, but the guns are not loaded yet. When we get closer to combat, we will pull the charging handle twice on each one so that they are ready to fire.

When we finish, I go back to the school room and write a letter home. The post offices in the states will not allow people to send packages overseas unless the serviceman has asked for what they are sending. So in every letter I request candy and cookies or some-thing to eat. I feel like a bum and my letters sound like it, but if my mother decides to send me something, she has that request. And they stamp the letter so that she can't use the same one twice. Of course, I am still writing about my brother Don dying. Probably my letters will get cut up by the censor.

I finish my letter just in time to go to supper. I am glad they have the stoves going because tonight they serve pork chops, mashed po-tatoes, gravy, green beans and for dessert, peach cobbler. All of the guys are excited about chow tonight. I get my food and go back to the school room to eat. There are some tables and chairs there and even though they are a little small for me, I sit down and eat.

Everything is ready for the movie and the corporal who runs it, gets it started. We have a much bigger crowd than usual, but it is probably because it is in a better building, more like a theater. Tonight's movie is "Bathing Beauty," staring Red Skelton and Esther Williams. Most of the guys like it. Red is funny and Esther is beautiful. After the movie, I go back and go to bed. I do not have guard until four in the morning.

This morning at breakfast they let us know that we will be having the inspection about ten o'clock this morning. I am glad that I got my things ready, or at least I think I have except for my mess kit and canteen cup. After I wash my mess kit, I get a little GI soap and a wash rag and scrub down my utensils.

I decide that it may be a long time before I have another chance to get any clothes washed, so I gather up all the dirty ones I have, get a bar of soap and a pack of cigarettes and go looking for someone to wash them. I go to a house that I think is the one that they said would do wash, and knock on the door. The woman comes to the door, and I try to tell her what I want. I am not having much luck. Finally, I start using sign language and she indicates that she understands and takes the clothes.

At ten, we fall out and line up beside the school. The officers go by and inspect all of our equipment. I am doing fine until they tell me that they want to look at my gas mask. When I pull it out, my extra T/5 stripes fall out on the ground. I had forgotten that I had put them there. We are not supposed to have anything in our gasmask carrier. After they inspect us, they go check all the vehicles. When they get to our halftrack, they ask what happened to the windshield. We tell them just how it happened. Instead of raising hell with us for breaking it, the major who is inspecting, tells the supply sergeant to see if he can get a replacement.

After the inspection, they come around and pass out the PX rations. We get our cigarettes and more candy than we have ever had before. In addition, we each get two Cokes, first Cokes that I have had in over two months and the first some of these guys have had in over six months. I have more cigarettes now than I can use, but the candy and Cokes will not last long. Now that we are in the First Army instead of the Third Army, the PX rations are sure a lot better.

They bring the mail up with the PX rations and I get a couple of letters. They are always welcome. After I read them I go back to the room and write a couple of letters, one to my mother and another to one of my friends. The ink I got is not very good, but it works in my fountain pen. The rest of the day goes fast and in the evening after supper, I go to the movie. I do not have much time after the movie before I have to go on guard duty at eight.

I get to go to bed about ten and sleep until morning. After breakfast, we have mail call again and I get several letters, some new and some old that have just caught up with me, but they are okay too. I love getting mail. I still read the "Stars & Stripes" paper every day to stay up with the news, but there is nothing like a letter from home. I am taking it easy today and it seems that about everyone else is too. The food we are getting now is the best that I have had since I left Ft. Riley and the championship mess hall, and it is plentiful too. I guess they are fattening us up for what is to come.

After dinner, they call several of us to go help unload supplies. It looks like a lot of stuff, but it takes a lot to run a unit this big. There are regular supplies for the kitchen, but in addition, there are many cases of C rations, K rations and 10-in-1 rations, an indication that we may not always have the mess available.

When we get through with the supply detail, I go write another letter home. I just get through writing my letter when one of the guys asks me if I have some laundry being done. He says he thinks that the girl outside is looking for me. I go out and a little girl is there with laundry in her arms. I go check and they are my things. She hands them to me and says, "Here. You go." I thank her and take them back in and pack them in my duffle bag. Right now, all of my clothes are relatively clean.

I go with the rest and stand in line for supper. It is a treat tonight. We have meatballs and spaghetti, along with some garlic toast and apple cobbler for dessert. After supper, I go to the movie. Tonight it is John Wayne in the "Fighting Seebees," a good exciting movie. I stay up after the movie until time to go on guard duty at ten. I get off at midnight and go to sleep.

At five o'clock, the guard comes to the room and yells for us to get up and get our things together. Breakfast will be at five-thirty and we will be moving out right after that. I get my things on and roll up my bedroll. I now realize what the little girl was trying to tell me last night. They knew then that we were going to leave today. I go out to the halftrack and the driver is there. We raise the armor plate from the front windshield and then roll back the top. With our things loaded, we take our mess kits and head for the chow line.

After breakfast, the first sergeant comes by and tells us to help get the kitchen taken down and loaded up. They move fast when they are putting things away. Some of the burners are still hot, so they have to watch where they pack them. With the kitchen loaded, we go back to the halftrack, load up and wait for the signal to move out.

CHAPTER LVI

How do you get to the war? You go to Belgium and turn right.
We follow the executive officer's jeep out of the school yard and
on to the narrow road until we are back ready to turn onto the main
road. Even the main road is barely wide enough for a tank and a
truck to pass. Right now, the main road is packed with vehicles
moving forward, with an occasional supply vehicle going the other
way. There is an MP at the corner directing traffic. Evidently he
knows what units are to go where, because after a little while, he
stops the traffic on the main road and motions us to come on. We
turn onto the road and join the procession. It seems that everywhere
you look there are vehicles moving.

As we move along, we see a lot more damage from the war
than was evident the night we got here. As we approach the area
where the Battle of the Bulge took place, the remains of the war are
everywhere. Wrecked and burned vehicles have been pushed off of
the road. The huge beautiful trees that were cut down to block the
roads have been pushed to the side and the ragged stumps remain as

a border to the road. A few of the trees still have the explosives tied to them that were to be used to cause the trees to fall across the road. In the forests, the trees have been chopped to pieces by the artillery fire, leaving the stubs of the trunks sticking up. Once in awhile, we see the fox holes dug in the dirt along side of the road. The narrow slit trenches and round fox holes of the Americans and the "V" shaped trenches of the Germans. The countryside is littered with ammunition crates, empty gas cans and ration boxes, along with discarded equipment from both sides.

I hate it about the trees, some of which are hundreds of years old. Here and there are dead cows and horses, more of the casualties of war. They make a bigger impression on me than the military equipment, which is made to destroy or be destroyed. The battles went on for some time in this area, going back and forth and this accounts for the magnitude of the destruction.

We seem to be moving more smoothly today than before, but of course, we still have enough stops to cause more than one GI to say, "Hurry up and wait, hurry up and wait." Each time we stop, there are always those of us who have to piss and stand lining road, oblivious to the civilians nearby. And at nearly every stop, at least one GI will be seen moving away from the column with his entrenching shovel and a roll of toilet paper in his hands. Often, the column will start up again and he will have to hurry back to the vehicle. If he is not quick enough, he will have to hitch a ride on one of those following and then get back to his own vehicle at the next stop, which may only be a hundred yards down the road.

We move out of Belgium and into Germany, but I do not know when we cross the actual border. There are no signs saying "Welcome to Germany," to let us know, but the damage is tremendous. The towns and cities have been nearly leveled. We have seen pictures in the magazines and the newsreels of the damage, but they do not have the impact of seeing it in person. It is hard to think that not long ago, people lived here. We seldom see a civilian anywhere.

About noon, we start looking for a chance to build a fire and heat our C rations. The more efficient the column is in moving, the less time we have for cooking. We gripe when the column stops all the time and we gripe when it doesn't. We get a stop and only build a small fire, but it is enough to get four or five cans around it. It is cloudy today and damp. We could not have gotten the fire going without the addition of gasoline. We do get them heated some, before we have to move on again. I eat mine while we are moving, but the driver just sets his beside him and every so often digs out a spoonful.

As we go into Germany, we get closer to the city of Aachen. They say that before the war, you could stand on a hill and look all the way across the city. Now you do not have to stand on a hill. As it gets close to evening, the sky is dark and the air has turned cold. They halt the column and we are sitting in a small town which is on the outskirts of Aachen. We leave the half track parked in the street as well as the rest of the vehicles. There is not one roof in the whole town. In fact, most of the walls are not more than six feet high, and the part that is left is riddled with holes. There are no people here, because there is nothing here for anyone. Anything of value has been stripped from the ruins.

We get the halftrack ready for night and when we have finished, a couple of guys come back from over in the damaged buildings and say that there is a dead German there. Several of us go back with them to see him. He is lying in the corner of one of the wrecked buildings and he is a young soldier. He has an entrenching shovel sticking out of his head. I do not know if that is what killed him or if someone hit him after he was dead. This is the first dead person that I have ever seen and I am sure that some of the other young guys have never seen one either. It is kind of bad leaving him lying like that, but he is the enemy. Someone will bury him before long.

They set up the mess and get ready to serve us supper. Not enough time to cook anything, but they dump some big cans of stew into the pots and heat it up and we eat it along with some of the bread. We are still under radio silence, so I do not have to pull a shift on the radio, but I do have to pull a shift of guard duty. I take my bedroll and unroll it beside the halftrack. They will wake me up at two for guard duty.

I go to sleep almost at once, even though this is the first time I have slept without anything overhead. At two they wake me and I go out a ways and stand guard. When my shift is over, I go back and get in my bed. I wake up in the morning and my bedroll has a layer of snow on it. It is not flakes, but little pellets like soft sleet.

I go get in line for breakfast. The cooks have had time to cook so we are having bacon and powdered eggs, grapefruit juice and they have toasted some of the bread. There is even some grape jelly to go on the toast and of course, there is coffee to wash it down. They tell us to pick up a C ration for dinner after we finish breakfast. The breakfast tastes good. The cooks do a better job of fixing powdered eggs than most places.

After I eat, I wash my mess kit and go by the box of C rations and pick out one. I find a can of pork and beans and a dinner accessory can. We get the halftrack ready to move and then help the cooks get packed up. It is not easy to serve a meal and then have to pack everything up and move out in such a short time. The communications sergeant finds me and gives me the frequencies for the radio and says to turn on the radio and listen, but not to transmit until I receive the word.

People are loading up and we can hear vehicles from the other units running as they move into their positions. The major is still riding in the jeep and the lieutenant gets in our half track. We are getting close enough to the war now, that I go to each of the machine guns and pull the operating handle back two times. Both guns are now fully loaded. All you have to do is to press the triggers and they will fire. I then turn on both radios and tune the CW radio to the correct frequency. The other radio is FM and is preset for our frequency. I get out a couple of sections of antenna and screw it into the base. This will give me enough signal to reach anyone near us, but will not stick up so high as to hit anything. When we stop and set up, I will put on extra sections to get a stronger signal.

We follow the jeep out of the town and onto the main highway again. We are getting closer to Aachen now and the devastation is worse than before, if that is possible. The city appears to have been bombed and shelled until nothing living remained. We have seen war damage before, but nothing to equal this. We keep moving east across Germany heading for the front lines. About noon, we build a fire again and actually have time to get our rations heated and eaten before we have to move out again.   My pork and beans taste good and I take the lemon juice powder and sugar and mix some lemon drink in my canteen cup to wash it down.

We slowly make our way across country. In the evening, we pull in next to a farmstead, and park next to some of the buildings. Out in front of us is an open field and along this side of the field is a battery of 155 mm, "long tom" cannons. They have partially dug them into the ground. Leaving the dirt piled up around the front of the cannons. It is evident that they have been firing by the remains of the ammunition laying around. We get the halftrack ready for the night and then I go dig me a hole. I figure that if these guns can reach the Germans, the German guns can reach us.

The mess sergeant gets the kitchen set up and once again, they heat up a batch of corned beef hash for supper. And of course, they have the ever plentiful bread. We are eating supper when suddenly the ground shakes and we are hit with a tremendous boom. One of the long toms has fired. In a little bit, another one fires and another until they have all fired one round. I do not know if they had a specific target or if they are just firing a harassing fire. After that, it is quiet. We finish eating and get our radio assignments. I decide that I am not going to be out in the weather again, so I go into one of the barns and find a place on some hay to lay my bed roll. I sleep soundly until they wake me to go on the radio and after my shift, I head back to the barn.

The cooks have fixed breakfast and we are having pancakes and sausage. First time we have had sausage in a long time. It seems to me that we are getting much better supplies since we came to the First Army. After breakfast, I go to pick up a ration for dinner, but today, they have K rations. We get packed up and get ready to move out again.

Today, the major decides to ride in the halftrack and that puts the lieutenant in the lead jeep. Both radios are on, but I will not be transmitting until I get the word. Again, we move out to the main road and they have an MP there to direct traffic.

We pull out onto the main road and fall in behind the other unit. We have to stay as far to the right of the road as we can so that the supply trucks can get by going the other way. We have to keep an eye out on the sky, because we are in range of German airplanes and they would love to strafe this column.

CHAPTER LVII

We are traveling along the road when the major decides that we are going past where we should be going. He tells me to get on the radio and tell them to stop. I tell him that I have not received orders to break radio silence yet and he tells me to hand him the microphone. I do as he says and he presses the microphone button and says "This is Les from Missouri. Halt the column." Well, we stop and of course all of the vehicles behind us stop too. The ones in front stop up the road a ways. I do not know if it is because they got his message or just one of the usual stops. We find a place and get the vehicles pulled off of the road into fields and on to smaller roads. The ground is very muddy and hopefully not many of the vehicles will get stuck.

The major goes back along the column to talk to the colonel and go over the maps. After awhile he comes back, we move out again and go down the road a couple of miles, before we turn off on a side road and go out to a farm. We pull in beside one of the barns and the firing batteries move out in a line along the edge of the field. The headquarters sets up in the farm house and the mess truck pulls into the courtyard and sets up in front of one of the barns. There are numerous farm buildings surrounding the courtyard with the big entry gate. Some of the out buildings have lofts overhead that project out, forming a porch for the ground below. The whole courtyard is cobblestone, except in the very middle, there is a wall about sixteen inches high and eighteen feet in diameter, forming kind of a shallow well. In the middle of the well is a big pile of manure. The place looks like the home of a well-to-do farmer.

The radio comes to life and I finally get the message to break radio silence. I get a couple more sections of antennae and put them up so I can get better reception. The CW radio starts in and I answer. They send a message and I write it down. It is in code, so I have no idea what it says. As soon as it is completed, I rush it over to the headquarters and hand it to them and then go back to the halftrack. They will have to have the code operator run it through the decoder and see what it says. Anyway, it is not long until the FM radio comes to life and I can hear them telling the firing batteries to get ready for a fire mission. We have now been committed to battle.

Soon I can hear the commands coming through for a fire mission. They give the coordinates and tell them to have one gun fire a smoke round and the rest of the battery to adjust. Although only one gun will fire, the other five will be sighted on the same place. In a couple of minutes, I hear the boom of a 105 mm cannon and over the radio I hear, "On the way." Then over the radio I hear, "Right two hundred, down three hundred." Another pause and again "On the way." A couple of minutes later, "Battery, two rounds HE, fire for effect." The ground shakes and the sound bounces off of the wall behind me as they fire. In the matter of two or three minutes, twelve rounds of high explosive shells will be landing on the same place. They did not say what the target was, but I suspect it was a concentration of enemy troops to require that much fire power in the same place.

The wire crews have moved out and are stringing telephone lines between the different batteries. When they have completed that, they will use the telephones instead of the radios for much of the communications. It is more reliable than the radios and the Germans are not listening in on their conversations, yet. The forward observers are still using the radios to call back the target information. Every so often, the radio will come alive and they will give a fire mission and the firing batteries will respond.

At noon, I dig out my K ration and open it up. The mess crew is working to set up, but will not be ready to serve food until evening.

The radio continues to have traffic and the halftrack shakes when the cannons send a volley out. It is especially loud, bouncing off of the building behind me. The CW radio sounds and I pick up my sending key and answer. They tell me to stand by for a message. As the dots and dashes start coming in, I write the letters on a message pad. When the message is finished, I acknowledge that I received it and sign off. I take the message to headquarters and hand it to the code clerk. One of the other new radio operators offers to go stand by the radio for awhile to give me a break. I take him up on it and we head back to the halftrack.

I get my bedroll from the halftrack and go back into the court-yard and find one of the buildings that is not being used. I find a bunk type bed with straw on it for a mattress. Over that is a feather tick. I lay my bed roll down on top and unroll it. I am ready for bed when the time comes. Then I go back to the halftrack and relieve the other operator. We will be taking shifts on the radio tonight, not much different than regular guard duty.

The guns are quieter now. I assume that our troops are in position now and that the enemy has been pushed back. If they counterat-tack, then the firing will really pick up. And of course, the radio is quiet now too. There is not much to do and I stand in the ring mount holding the .50 caliber machine gun and smoke a cigarette. I hear something and I look up at the sky to see if I can see any planes. Way high, I can see the vapor trails of bombers returning from a mission over probably Berlin or some other city. Of course, I am also look-ing lower, in case a German fighter comes flying in to attack.

In the evening, I holler for someone to come and relieve me so I can go get chow. They are all eating, but one promises to come, when they get finished. I am really hungry, because that K ration did not fill me up at noon. Of course, I am always hungry. At last one of the other operators comes and I go over where the mess is set up. At least there is no line. I can have extra if I want it, since almost everyone has eaten. They have hamburger patties, with fried onions and also fried potatoes, green beans, green salad and apple cobbler. I get two hamburger patties, lots of potatoes and a couple of servings of dessert. I go back to the halftrack and stand beside it to eat.

When I am finished eating, I go wash my mess kit. I check with the other operator on my radios and he wants the early shift. Of course, everyone wants the early shift, but I agree and tell him where to find me when his shift is up and then head off to bed. I leave everything on except my field jacket and steel helmet. I lay them next to me on the bed and place my carbine on top. This is the best bed I have had in a long time, and I go to sleep right away.

The other operator shakes me awake and tells me it is time for me to go on the radio. I slide out of bed and head out to the half-track. When I get inside and close the door, I turn on the trouble light, so that I have light to see what I am doing. I forgot to ask the other operator how long it has been since he ran the engine to charge the battery, so I go ahead and start it up. It seems to make a lot of noise in the night.

Time goes slowly just sitting by myself and I reach into my left breast pocket and take out the small New Testament that the Gideons gave to me when I left for the service. I read until I figure that the battery is charged and then go up to the front and shut off the engine. I have three old letters from home in my pocket. We are not allowed to keep a diary and are told to not keep any names or addresses on us, in case we are captured. The letters I have, have had the names and addresses removed.

It is good to read the old letters again. It inspires me and I dig out some V-mail paper and my fountain pen and write a letter home. The V-mail is much faster than regular mail and both of them are free, but the fastest is airmail and it costs six cents. I would send airmail, but I do not have any stamps. I have my order in for some airmail stamped envelopes, but have not received them yet. When

I finish the letter, I put it in my pocket and will hand it to one of the officers in the morning to censor and mail.

I straighten up things in the halftrack and put things where they will not be in the way when we are moving about. My pistol belt with canteen and my gas mask are hanging on the back of the ring mount. They are out of the way, but easy to reach if I need them. I turn off the light and open the door and climb out of the halftrack. It takes awhile for my eyes to get used to the dark. It is cloudy and no stars tonight, but after several minutes, I can make out shapes of buildings and vehicles. I go to the side of the building and piss, then go back inside, make sure I have shut things tight and turn on the light.

I start up the halftrack again to charge the battery and let it run until time for my shift to end. I shut off the engine and the light before going out and finding the guy who will relieve me. I have to shake him a couple of times before he is alert enough to get up. I tell him that I have charged the battery and send him on his way. I find my bed and crawl back in. I can sleep until early morning and then I will have to go back on the radio.

This morning, I am back on the radio. Things have been quiet all night. I holler for someone to take over for me so I can get some breakfast. I get my food and move out to the center of the courtyard to eat. One of the guys comes by and says, "Lovell, how long have you been over here?"

"Almost two months, why?"

"I just wondered how long it takes."

"What do you mean?"

"Well, look where you are standing."

I am standing with one foot propped up on the wall around the huge pile of manure and eating my breakfast. I tell him that I guess that I have been here long enough. We both laugh. We are all getting conditioned.

After breakfast, I go and roll up my sleeping roll and carry it out and put it in the halftrack. The driver shows up and we roll the top back and get ready to hit the road again. We are waiting beside the halftrack for orders and the battalion armorer shows up. He hands me a small box and says don't lose this or you will have to pay for it. I open it up and inside is a GI watch. The new watch has hands and numbers that glow in the dark and seems to be a very nice watch.

CHAPTER LVIII

We load up and pull out of the farm and on to the road. We are advancing every day, pushing the Germans further back into their own country. Many are surrendering and we pass groups of weary soldiers, who are glad that the war is over for them. We pass one group of German soldiers with one man in the lead carrying a white flag. They seem to be unarmed and there is no one guarding them. They are marching toward the west to give themselves up. It seems that the war can't last too much longer.

We push on east and the skies are dreary and it starts to mist. Later in the day, we arrive at a small town and they decide to hold up there for the rest of the day. The road runs along side of a hill, with higher ground to the south and a rock wall along the north side of the road forming a terrace. My halftrack is parked out in the open on the road, not the safest place to be. I have the top up on the halftrack and have it ready for night. I have to stay in there on the radio, so I decide to write some letters. I write three V-mail letters to friends and put them in my pocket.

I have no sooner finished the letters when an artillery shell whistles over the halftrack and slams into the side of the hill on the south side. I jerk open the north door on the halftrack and bail out and fall about four feet to the ground below the rock terrace. I hug the ground and two more shells hit on the far side. It does not take long for me to figure out that shooting is more fun than being shot at. I lay there awhile and decide the shooting is over for now. I climb up on the road and get the shovel off of the half track and dig a slit trench at the bottom of the terrace.

I get back in the half track and pull out the letters that I have just written and they are wet and the ink has run, so that you can't read them. I will have to do them over, another time. It is chilly in the halftrack now and I cup a cigarette so that I can light it, thinking that maybe it will make me feel better. I take my bedroll and put it in the first house behind me. The house has a floor that is level with the street and a basement that is level with the lower ground. It also has an upper story. I take my bedroll up there and lay it out on the floor. I go back down and they have set up kind of a headquarters in the basement. I ask if they will be fixing supper and they direct me to a case of K rations by the door. I know what that means and I grab one and head back out to the halftrack. The radios are quiet, so I assume that no one has been looking for me.

It is pitch black now and I do not have a light on in the half track. My new watch glows bright. I plug in the trouble light and turn it on and it is very bright. I hope that I have covered all the cracks so that no light shows outside. I open my K ration to see what is on the menu for supper. It has a can of beef and pork loaf with carrots, together with the usual hard biscuits. I get my canteen out of my pistol belt and will drink water with my meal. I will need to fill my canteen in the morning. I take the little wooden spoon and dig out the meat and eat it together with the biscuits. I wash it down with a swig of water.

I light another cigarette. I have found that when I am hungry, a cigarette seems to help. Maybe that is why they furnish them. I am sitting in the dark smoking when down the road to the east, a shell comes in and hits on the hill to the south. I start to get out and get in my hole, but change my mind and lay down on the floor of the halftrack.

I stay on the radios until ten when someone comes to relieve me. I go back to the house and before I go to bed, I go down to the basement to see what is going on. They tell me that the last shell that came in wounded one of the captains. It seems that he was up on the hill and lit a cigarette and shortly after, the shell came in and hit nearby. He got shrapnel in his left side. They bandaged him up and evacuated him. I go up to the top floor and crawl into my sleeping bag.

Sometime later I wake up when I hear a shell come in and hit the hill beyond the halftrack. A little bit later, I hear another shell hit a little east of the last one and five minutes later, one comes in on this side of the first one. Then another shell a little further east followed by one to the west. They know we are here, but not exactly where. They started in the middle and are going back and forth, out a little further each time. They are getting closer to the house where I am every other shot. I am laying in my sleeping bag listening to the shells. I start praying that they will not hit the house. Then I ask God what I should do? Something tells me that I should get out of there. They are almost to the house and that shell will go clear through the upper story.

There is another guy laying near me and I shake him and tell him that we need to get out of there. We go down stairs and I decide that I should go get in my slit trench. I take off running across the yard when suddenly I go flying through the air and there is a loud bang. I am laying face down on the ground, my carbine that was on my back is now underneath me and my steel helmet is off my head. I heard shrapnel hit the ground when I went flying and I start to check to see that I am okay. I feel around for my steel helmet and get it on. I decide the basement is better than here.

That was the last shell of the night, and it gets quiet again. I go out and relieve the other operator. He is glad to see me, because like me, he has been laying on the floor of the halftrack. I spend the rest of the night on the radios. When daylight comes, I leave the halftrack and go back to the house. I look out in the yard and I see what happened. When I was running toward my slit trench, I hit a clothesline with my neck and it flipped me through the air just as the shell exploded. That clothesline may have saved my life. I walk out into the yard and look at my slit trench and it is completely full of water. It would not have been any good anyway.

I go back up stairs to get my bedroll. When I pick it up to roll it, pieces of glass and shrapnel fall out. The window in the room has been blown out. I shake it out and roll it up. As I go past the other guy who was up there, I tell him to be sure to clean out his bedroll. He thanks me for getting him out of the room before the shell hit. I go back down to the basement and grab a K ration out of the box and take it with me to the halftrack.

I eat it and again wash it down with cold water. My canteen is about empty, so I go out to the water can on the front of the halftrack and pour water into my canteen and fill it back up. The water can is almost empty. There is a well in back of the house down the road, so I take the can back there and pump enough water to fill it. I get a bottle of halazone tablets to purify the water. It takes two tablets for a quart of water. The five gallon can has twenty quarts, so I need forty tablets. The bottle has fifty tablets, so I pour out ten tablets, throw them away and dump the rest in the can. By the time we drive a few miles the tablets will be well mixed and the water will be aerated and fit to drink.

The firing batteries fire a few missions and I hope that they get the gun that was harassing us last night. It is a good thing they were shooting high. If they had been a little lower, they would have knocked out several vehicles, lined up on the road. I thought we would move out early this morning, but we are still here. I still think that we will move on today.

A corporal, one of the jeep drivers from another battery, is here sporting a .45 automatic pistol. The captain that he drives for gave it to him. He says that a bullet went through the holster, the slide and then through the captain's leg. They bandaged him up and sent him back to the aid station to be evacuated. He could not take the pistol with him, so he gave it to his driver. The driver took it to division ordinance and they put a new slide on it. That makes two captains that got wounded yesterday.

My old buddy, Gene, is radio operator in another unit of the Ninth Armored. I am talking to some guys about the two captains getting wounded, and one of them asks me if I know Gene in the other unit. I tell him that I do and ask why. He says that Gene got shot a couple of days ago. He was holding a German pistol, when it went off and shot his ring finger off. They bandaged it up and he stayed with the unit. Gene was always a little reckless, so I am not surprised.

About noon, they announce that we will be moving out in a few minutes. I take off towards the mess supply truck and tell one of the guys that I would like to have some food. He reaches into an open K ration box and grabs four rations and throws them to me. I hurry back to the halftrack and tell the driver that we have dinner. It has quit raining and I pull the top back most of the way and get ready to move out. The lieutenant is riding with us today and the major is in the jeep.

We move forward the rest of the afternoon and in the early evening we stop in a rural area. We pull the vehicles off of the road and spread them out. My halftrack is just off of the north side of the road in an apple orchard. It is cloudy and dreary and the ground is muddy. The mess is set up on the south side of the road by some farm buildings. We are on the west side of a rural village. Since we have not had a hot meal since night before last, they decide that they better cook one for us. I shared the four K rations at noon, but I ended up with most of two of them. Nevertheless, I am still hungry.

I know why we have steel helmets. Every time I go in or out of the door on the halftrack, I hit my head. This evening, I start to climb in, hit my head and my muddy boot slips on the step and I fall back out, skinning my shin as I fall. I stay on the radio until some of the other guys have eaten supper and then one of them relieves me, so I can go eat. I am not surprised to find that we are having beef stew for supper, the kind out of a can. But they have opened some peas too and they have some of the GI bread to go with it.

Fog starts drifting in and by the time I get through eating and cleaning my mess kit, it is so foggy that you can hardly see anything. I start back to the halftrack, and with the fog and darkness, I just hope that I am going the right direction. I run into the halftrack before I see it. I go back on the radio and stay until two o'clock when I am relieved. I do not have to go back on until morning, so I decide to get some good sleep. I take off my field jacket and tonight, since my boots are muddy, I take them off before I slide into bed. I sleep like a baby until after daylight.

CHAPTER LIX

I get up and roll up my bedroll. One of the guys comes into the room where I am and says "Boy that was close last night."

"What?"

He proceeds to tell me about the battle last night. It seems that the Germans counter attacked and were only halted at the railroad about a quarter of a mile east of us. They had a big battle and I slept through the whole thing. He says "Didn't you hear all the shooting?"

"After I went to bed, I didn't hear anything until a little bit ago when I woke up."

"You must have been tired."

I start thinking about what if they had broken through. There I was without any boots on and sound asleep in my sleeping bag.

I get my mess kit and head for the chow line. We are having thick slices of bacon and some cream of wheat. It does not look very good, when it is plopped into my mess kit. I load it up with sugar, put a little iron cow on it and eat it anyway. I drink coffee today. It sounds better than the cereal looks. After breakfast, I go back to the halftrack and get back on the radio. It is still damp, so I only roll the top back about a third of the way.

The vehicles are starting to load up and then move into position. One of the other half tracks is stuck out in the orchard. The driver pulls ours out onto the road and then turns it around and points it toward the other halftrack. They loosen the winch on the other half-track and start to stretch the cable toward my halftrack. It is way short, so they start to play out the winch on my halftrack. Both winches are all the way out and still do not reach. Only thing to do is for my halftrack to move toward the other one. They can't get it too far into the orchard or it will be stuck too. When the two winch cables are hooked together, both halftracks start to winch them in. The other halftrack slides out of the orchard, leaving deep ruts through it. An apple tree is in the way and the halftrack goes right over the top of it. With both winches going at the same time, the halftrack moves out quickly.

We get turned around and ready to fall into line on the road. We are back a ways and have to wait. I look over where the mess was and there is about a half a case of K rations setting there that they forgot to load. I holler to hold up, I jump out of the halftrack and run to get the K rations. I am glad to have the K rations. My breakfast was a little meager. I am back just in time for them to pull out into the line of traffic.

We move slowly forward, with the usual stop and start, hurry up and wait method. The lieutenant is with us today. The major is okay, but it seems that things just go more smoothly with the lieutenant in here. Maybe I am just more at ease with him. I pull out a K ration and ask if he would like to have it. He takes it and seems to be glad to get it. He probably did not like breakfast any more than I did. I ask the driver if I can open up one for him. He says that he would appreciate it. I cut the box open, spread it out to lay the food on. The next time we stop, he will be able to open the packages and set the food so he can get to it while he drives. With the others fed, I peel open a carton for myself.

It is one of the breakfast K rations and although the ham and eggs are not my favorite, it will have to do. I kind of spread it on my thick crackers and eat it that way. I wash it down with water. When

I finish with that, I open the fruit bar. It is like a fig newton, except it is made from apricots. It is the best thing in the box.

We have been advised to watch for German planes strafing the column. The lieutenant is standing in the ring mount with the .50 caliber machine gun and I am back of him, standing and holding to the back of the ring mount. The radio is quiet for now. We are moving along. Not fast by some standards, but very fast considering that we are advancing through enemy territory. The road straightens out some and I can see both ahead and back and realize how many vehicles there are. It is a massive force as it advances.

There are a lot of motorcycles over here. In fact, it seems that one out of every ten army vehicles has a motorcycle tied on it some-place. They are on the bumpers, hood, top of the cab, on the sides and even underneath. I hope they are not all planning on taking them home with them.

There is a lot of abandoned equipment along the road. At one stop I am able to get a German rifle and bayonet. They will make good souvenirs. I also find a German flashlight. It is fixed so that you can have different colored lens by sliding buttons on the front. It is made so that you can hang it on a button on your coat and it will light the way, without having to hold it in your hand. The battery is dead in it and that is probably why it was discarded. We have to watch picking up things like this because the Germans booby trap them.

We slowly advance the rest of the day and when evening comes, we pull into another farmyard and set up beside the buildings. After we park, I take time to find a place to sleep for the night. Not that I will get much, but I want to enjoy what I get. This looks like it might have been for several hired hands, because there are a half dozen bunk type beds in the one room. They are the usual with the straw laid on wooden frames with a feather tic on top. I unroll my bedroll out on one to stake claim to it for the night and then go back to the halftrack.

I gas up the halftrack from the spare cans and then unroll the top cover and lower the armor plate covering the windshield. I make sure to remove the windshield first. By the time I get it properly covered for the night and string out the trouble light, the gas truck has arrived and is slowly moving along, passing out cans of gas. I get enough to replace what I used to fill the tank and put them in the rack on the side. I stay close to the halftrack so I can take any messages that might come in. The radio is quiet except for occasional talk coming in on the FM radio from the forward observers.

From where my halftrack is sitting, I can watch the mess crew set up. They will be in a hurry this evening trying to get some kind of hot meal ready for us to eat before it gets too dark.   They are setting up the stoves and getting out the big pots to heat up cans of either stew or hash. They do not have enough time to fix much more than that. They already have the water in the garbage cans heating to wash the mess kits. I have to stay close to the halftrack, but I decide to get a jump on supper. I have some bullion powder, so I build a small fire a little way from the half track and take a canteen cup of water and set it beside the fire to heat.

When I can see the water steaming in my canteen cup, I pour in the package of bullion and stir it up. My canteen cup is black, of course, from the fire. I can see the guys lining up for chow, but I will have to wait until someone comes to relieve me before I can go get in line. I doubt if anyone will come until after they have eaten. This is one of the disadvantages of being a radio operator, you have to stay with the radio until someone is willing to help you.

By the time someone comes to relieve me, I have already drunk my bullion, so I set another cup of water in the fire to heat while I go get my food. I get in line and since most have eaten, I can have as big a serving as I want. They ladle out a big batch of stew into my mess kit, and they have some green beans with it and I just add them to the stew in the one compartment. For dessert, they have opened some fruit cocktail. This is a rare treat. I have them put it in the other side of my mess kit. I get a couple of thick slices of army bread and put it on my stew. I go back to the halftrack to eat it. I stir up another cup of bullion and sit in the doorway of the halftrack to eat. It tastes better than I thought it would.

I stay at the halftrack and when it starts to get dark, I go inside and start up the engine to keep the battery charged and also to help take the chill off. I will have to stay a couple of more hours before I can have any relief. I never get enough sleep for a growing boy.

While I am just sitting here, I take the CW radio and start scanning through the frequencies to see if I can pick up anything. I pick up a station that is broadcasting in English and listen in. It is from England and they are sending messages to either the underground or undercover agents. They first read a list of agents that they have messages for tonight and then tell which agents they do not have messages for. The voice is very British and he speaks slowly and distinctly. Tonight there is a message for Frankenstein. I wish I knew who that is. Then he starts giving the message in phonetic alphabet, saying each letter very slowly. Of course I can't understand the message since it is in code, so I leave the station and get the radio back on to the frequency for my own messages.

Nothing has come in yet, and I shut off the halftrack and settle down to wait. I have to be careful to not go to sleep. It is hard to stay awake. I get out a K ration box, open it and read the labels on each item. It is something from home and that is important. Then I get out my New Testament and read from it for awhile. The time goes very slowly, but finally it is time for me to go wake up my relief. I go to the building and using the low light from my flashlight, I locate where he is sleeping.

When my relief gets here, I take off to where I left my bedroll and this time, I only take off my field jacket and steel helmet, as I slide into my sleeping bag. I am asleep almost immediately. Of course, it is only for four hours and then someone wakes me up to go back on the radio for the rest of the night. It is quiet tonight and lonesome, so I will be glad when daylight comes. I can hear noises from where the cooks are getting breakfast ready. At last it gets light enough to see.

I get out of the halftrack and walk around. I am close enough so that I can hear if either of the radios sounds off. I take my canteen cup and make a quick trip over to where the mess is set up to see if

I can get some coffee before breakfast. There is no one else around except the mess crew and when I ask for some coffee, the mess sergeant says sure. That does not sound like him, but I am glad. They are cooking pancakes for breakfast and he asks me if I want a pancake to go with my coffee. I can hardly believe it, but of course, I say that I do and thank him. The pancake is hot and I juggle it in my hands for a bit until it has cooled enough so I can hold it. I eat my pancake and drink my coffee beside the halftrack. It is hard to believe, but the halftrack seems something like a home and I like to be close to it. I guess it is because it represents a relative degree of comfort and security.

CHAPTER LX

I am glad that I got the cup of coffee and the pancake, it tides me over until someone comes to relieve me on the radio. I get a stack of pancakes, pour some of the formerly hot syrup over them. They have cooked some spam and I put a couple of slices of that on top of the pancakes. They have grapefruit juice to drink and since I am the last one in line, they hand me the can, so I can have what is left. I get another cup of coffee and find a place to sit down to eat. The can of juice is about a third full and I drink most of it before I start on the pancakes and spam.

I go back to the halftrack and start getting ready to move out. When I get the top pulled back, I go pick up my bedroll and throw it over the side of the halftrack. I check the water can and it still has enough water to last through the day. I have been up so long, that it seems like it is a lot later than it is. I am ready to go, and just waiting on everyone else. The lieutenant joins us again today and we move out on the road. It seems that we cover more territory and advance further every day. We continue to send large numbers of prisoners back.

We go through many small towns and farm areas. We are moving so fast that most of them suffer little damage. Only those where the Germans make a stand are hit hard. However, some of the small towns have narrow streets and the large tanks have trouble making the corners. Sometimes, they knock the corner out of a building, when they make the turn. Before long, the column is going through the building. At one corner, we drive right through the living room of a house, with the second floor above us.

Later in the afternoon, we stop alongside of the road and the officers go for a meeting. I assume it is to decide how far to try to go, before we stop for the night. Three of us are standing beside the halftrack, when a GI approaches from somewhere off to the side. He has an M1 slung over his shoulder, so I figure that he is an infantryman. What catches my attention, is that he is carrying his helmet in his hands. He gets closer and he holds out his helmet and says, "Look at this." There is a nice round bullet hole in the side of his helmet. He turns it around and on the other side, straight across from the first hole is a very jagged hole. He could not have had the helmet on and the bullet not gone through his head, but he did. We examine the inside of the helmet and we can see the path the bullet took. It went in one side, hit the helmet liner and turned and followed around the helmet between the liner and the steel, until it got to the other side where it came out.

While he is there, some other guys see us gathered around him and they come over to see what is happening. One guy asks if he is okay and he says he has a headache. Someone else says "Not as much as you would, if it had not been for that helmet." I notice that he is not real responsive and I am afraid he might be going into shock. I tell him to come with me and I will take him back to the medics and get him something for his headache. We walk back about a half dozen vehicles to the medic jeep and I tell them what he told me. They say they will send him back to the aid station, so they can watch him. I tell him to hang on to that helmet because it is his lucky piece.

The officers return and we move out again. We go two or three more miles and then we pull off of the main road and go toward another farm manor. We move in and they set up around the outside of the farmstead. Not as many buildings at this one and I find a place in a stable for my bedroll. It has been a while since they had many horses here. I manage to avoid the stalls where horses have been recently. None are here now, they have either been taken away by the army or have been hidden some place by the owner. One of the firing batteries is set up in the field south of the farm. We will probably have noise soon.

As soon as I get back to the halftrack, messages start coming in on the CW radio. I copy them and run them over to the code clerk. Something big is going on. It is not long until the FM radio starts sounding off. There are fire missions for all of the batteries. Suddenly, the guns start firing. They continue to fire, one fire mission after another. Ammunition trucks are coming in bringing in more cannon shells for the 105's. The lieutenant comes out to the halftrack to get his map case and I ask him what is going on. He says that Combat Command B has captured a bridge across the Rhine and troops are pouring over it to the other side. We are shelling the other side to keep the Germans from coming down the banks of the Rhine and pushing them back.

I stay on the radio and run messages back and forth to the headquarters that has been set up in the farmhouse. One of the guys comes out and says that if I want to go get supper, he will man the radio.

The cooks have made spaghetti tonight with canned sauce. They also have some canned pears to go with it and of course, some of the GI bread. I load up my mess kit and go back to the halftrack to eat. I thank the other guy for watching the radios for me and eat my supper. When I get through, I make a quick trip over to the wash cans, to wash my mess kit. It comes out greasy again. I hate that. I will be lucky if I do not get the GI shits.

When I get back, it is late enough, that I put the cover back on the halftrack. I have already filled the gas tanks from the cans. I will replace the cans when the truck gets here. I turn on the light and check outside for light leaks. Then I go inside and listen to the radio. Sometimes they list the target on the fire missions, but other times, I do not know what they are firing at. There are probably plenty of targets on both sides of the river, since we were pushing Germans back and they are now blocked by the river.

I stay on the radio until ten and then go to find my relief operator. When I go outside, I can see flashes almost continuously to the east as shells are exploding. I find my replacement and he is still awake, so he goes right out and I go find my bedroll in the stable. I slide in and go to sleep. Someone will wake me at two o'clock to go back on the radio and it will be a short sleep.

When I go back on the radio, the flashes are not as intense. They may not have targets in sight or they may have run low on ammunition. But I am sure that the firing will increase again when it gets light. I dig out the chocolate bar from a K ration and use my knife to scrape pieces off of it to eat. I am afraid I will break a tooth if I try to bite off a piece. It tastes okay and I am glad to have something to eat since it makes the time pass quicker. The radios have quieted down and it is hard to stay awake. I start up the halftrack to charge the battery and then sit back and read some more out of my New Testament. I am glad that I have it; it is a comfort.

I am on the radio the rest of the night. No messages coming in now, so it is quiet and lonesome and I am sleepy. I go outside every once in a while to move around and exercise to keep awake. The sky has cleared off and I can see the stars. There are still some flashes in the east. I can hear trucks running over on the road hauling supplies. I admire those truck drivers, it is hard and dangerous work. They drive mile after mile in blackout, only seeing small dots of light on the vehicle ahead of them. Most of the drivers are Negro soldiers and they call the supply line the "Red Ball Express." I see that they have already dropped off cans of gas while I was asleep and the other operator put them in the racks on the side of the halftrack.

I hear the cooks working, getting breakfast ready. When I think they have had enough time to make coffee, I slip away for a few minutes and go ask if I can have a cup. They seem glad to pour me one and the mess sergeant asks if I want a biscuit. They have just come out of the oven. I do not know what has come over him, he is usually not this generous. I take a glove out of my pocket and grab the biscuit, the cup of coffee, and head back to the halftrack. I get back in and the radios are still quiet, so I was not missed.

The rest of the night goes faster now and it is not long before the whole place is active. The news of the breakthrough at the Rhine has increased the pace. I see one of the other operators and holler at him to come and watch the radio, while I go get breakfast. He comes over and agrees to watch it, while I go get my chow, but he wants me to come back here to eat it. I agree and go get in the line. The line is longer this morning and it takes a bit to get served. Besides the biscuits, they have cooked up some thick bacon and some of the corned beef hash. I load up my mess kit, get another cup of coffee and head back to the halftrack to eat.

It looks like we will be moving out early today, so I go get my bedroll and load it, as soon as I get the top rolled back. It is not long before everyone is loaded up and we get ready to try to get out on the road. The road is solid vehicles, all heading in the direction of the bridge across the Rhine. Some are going to cross the bridge, others are going there to provide support and others are bring up supplies. They make a break in the traffic so that we can pull out on the road. We do not go far before we turn north and as we do, we get closer to the river, as well as closer to the bridge.

When we get to the road that runs east and west to the river and which is about a mile south of the road leading to the bridge, we turn west into a cluster of farm buildings. The road is cobblestone and goes as far as the field west of the farm buildings. We pull our vehicles into the farm area and park. The driver turns the halftrack around and backs it up on the cobblestone road so that it is between a large barn, on the right side and a stable on the left side. From where we are sitting, we can see towards the Rhine River and the wide valley along the west side. We can also watch the traffic heading toward the bridge to the northeast. The bridge is about three miles northeast from where we are.

CHAPTER LXI

I can stand in the back of the halftrack next to the radios and still see a large area along the river. They are moving artillery and antiaircraft guns into the valley by the hundreds. Almost as soon as the artillery pieces are in position, they start shelling across the Rhine. And every so often, the antiaircraft guns will start firing as a German plane tries to get in and drop a bomb on the bridge. I can see American fighter planes flying back and forth above the river. They too are lying in wait for any German plane that may make a try for the bridge.

I am standing at the very back of the halftrack when there is an explosion right behind the halftrack. I get out and go behind it and find a small hole blown into one of the cobblestones. It looks like the work of a 20mm shell. I assume that it was fired by one of the aircraft or one of the antiaircraft guns up into the sky and fell back to earth, where it exploded. It did not miss me by more than two feet. If it had hit my helmet, it would have blown my head apart. Just another reminder, that even back here, there is still danger.

The mess truck gets here and they want to set up the mess in the stable on the north side of the road. They ask us to move the halftrack, so they can park the mess truck there. The driver pulls it forward a little ways and then backs it in beside the big barn. There is just barely room to walk between the side of the half track and the barn. It's just a little back from the road, so if I stand in the front of the halftrack, I can still see much of the scene down below. This whole thing is unbelievable. Thousands of vehicles, guns and other equipment moving up to either go across the bridge or to spread out in the large valley in front of us.

We can hear the constant rumble of the cannons and can see the layer of smoke settling over the whole valley. Some of the smoke is from the cannons and some is from smoke generators placed along the river to try to hide the bridge and the troops around it. We watch as the P-38 fighter planes patrol back and forth and then to our shock and horror, two of them collide and spin toward the river. We do not see any parachutes. Another reminder that this is for real.

They have taken the main house for headquarters and that leaves a smaller house, where I find a place to put my bedroll. I do not think we will leave this location before tomorrow. The FM radio is busy, but I am not getting as many messages on the CW radio as I did yesterday. The FM radio, seldom has any traffic for me, but is used more by the forward observers. They are interesting to listen to. They often get excited, with good reason, because they are usually right up with the front line troops.

About noon, it looks like the cooks may have thrown together some dinner, so several of us go across the street and line up along the side of the stable, under the overhang above. While we are in the line, we are visiting and talking about what all we have been seeing, when suddenly the guy in front of me, grabs his carbine, points it straight up and yells "Kommen ze aus!" I step back and look up as a German soldier slowly pushes the hay off and stands up with his hands on his head. They have him climb down, they search him and have him sit over in an open spot, where he can be watched, until someone can take him back to a PW camp.

We asked the guy how he knew that the German was up above us? He said he just happened to look up through a crack and saw the blue-gray of his uniform and it did not match what he was seeing through the other cracks. Anyway, the German had been there for several hours, just a foot above our heads. He was not armed, and probably was just waiting until he had a chance to get away from there, or to turn himself in.

We go through the chow line and get fed. Not anything exciting, but it is edible. After everyone has eaten, one of the guys gets an empty can from the cooks, puts some food in it and takes it over and hands it to the German. He will have to eat with his fingers, but I am sure he will not mind that, because he probably has not had anything to eat for some time. The Germans are still trying to bomb the bridge and shell it. The airplanes they are sending in are suicide missions, because very few of them get back out. Every time one comes in, the antiaircraft guns open up and shoot them down or the American fighters hovering high above dive down and get them.

We are watching when two funny looking planes fly across the sky over the bridge. They look something like bumblebees. As they fly, four P-38's dive towards them. We can see the tracers streaking down behind the two planes but suddenly the two shoot across the sky and away, leaving the American P-38's far behind. We start asking each other what was that? With all of the cannons firing, only seldom do we hear the boom of bombs or shells coming into the bridge area, so we do not know if they dropped bombs or not. I start back to the halftrack and another 20mm shell explodes on the asphalt road, less than three feet from me.

Back in the halftrack, I stand and watch as there is a solid line of traffic moving down the road toward Remagen. I know that they can't get that many across the bridge. They must be piling up on the west side of the river. Some units wait to cross the bridge and others set up in the valley to provide support for those across. We have an ideal vantage point to watch what is going on and still be out of the way and not in as much danger as we would be if we were closer.

Later in the afternoon, they bring by copies of "Stars & Stripes" and the story is the headline on the paper. There is also a picture of the bridge from the west end, with a sign saying "Cross the Rhine with dry feet, courtesy of the 9th Armd. Div." I am sure that this story will be printed in the states too and I am glad that I told my folks to watch the news for stories about the Ninth Armored Division. That of course is the main story, but there are also other stories of other advances and it sounds like the war may end before too long. The "Stars & Stripes" is really wonderful to keep us informed and entertained, with the cartoons and stories. I am amazed that they can get it printed and delivered under these conditions.

After supper, I stay on the halftrack, but there are no messages coming in, so there is not much to do, but watch what is happening down toward the river. I go ahead and fill up the gas tanks, but it does not take much gas to fill them, since we have not traveled far today. As it starts to get dark, I put the top up on the halftrack and check for light leaks before it gets really dark.

I crawl back in the halftrack and sit and listen to the noise outside. The time goes very slowly now that it is dark. There is still some firing from the valley, but it is not as heavy as it was when it was light enough to see the targets. I reread the "Stars & Stripes" and then get out my stationery and write a letter home. I wish I could tell them what I am experiencing, but I am not allowed to. They will just have to get it from the newspapers. At least, they have an idea where I am now, by the stories mentioning the Ninth Armored Division.

When it is time for my relief, I go find him and wake him to come out and I head for the house where I have my bedroll. I am not feeling real well. My stomach is acting funny, but I am able to get to sleep as soon as I get in the sleeping bag. I sleep soundly for the four hours that I have, until I have to go back on the radios.

He wakes me up to go back out and I have a hard time getting my eyes open. I have sure not had enough sleep for tonight. I will have trouble staying awake until morning. I get in the halftrack and sit down, but I do not feel good. My stomach is rumbling and churning. I do not have any kind of medicine for it, so I drink some water. I start the engine to charge the batteries and sit in the driver's seat while the engine runs, so I have a cushion to sit on and a back rest. When the engine has run the required time, I shut it off and go back by the radios.

I peek out and see that it is starting to get light. About that time, a serious cramp hits my stomach and I know something is going to happen. I bail out of the halftrack door, run as hard as I can for the barn, pulling down my pants and underwear as I run. I get in the barn, spin around and as I bend over, there is an explosion from my guts and I squirt shit across the barn. I let out a loud sigh of relief, knowing that I made it without messing my pants and I hear "GAAWD DAMN!"

I turn around and there are soldiers laying on the hay in the barn. I have just sprayed the hay between two of them with a most foul substance. I immediately start to apologize and figure I will be lucky to get out of this alive. I tell them I am sorry and that I did not know anyone was in there. One of the soldiers, probably the squad leader, says that it is okay because they have all had the same thing. I apologize again and get out of there before they change their minds.

It was a squad of infantry and they had come in last night while I was asleep and bedded down in the hay in the barn. I notice that they do not stay in the barn long and move out and head down the road towards Remagen. I almost single handed, or should I say single butted, wiped out a squad of infantry. You can bet that I make sure that my mess kit does not have a bunch of grease on it after this. I will find some way to get it clean so that it does not give me the GI's again.

When the other radio operator comes back out, I ask him why he did not tell me that the infantry were in the barn and he says that he never thought of it and asks me why. I tell him what happened and he breaks out laughing. He is laughing so hard, that some of the others want to know what is going on and he tells them and they are all laughing too. It was not funny when it happened, but now even I am laughing. I am not sure about the infantrymen, but I doubt if they are laughing yet.

The word has got around and everywhere I go, guys are asking me about how I about got the infantry squad. The only break I get in the teasing is when we get the order to move up by the river. Everyone forgets about me for the time being and starts to gather their things and load up. We know it will only be a couple of miles at the most at this time, because the firing batteries are still here on the west side of the river. Of course, we are going to be moving into the target area of the bridge.

CHAPTER LXII

We start to move out and go closer to the river. We have to cross the main road leading to the bridge, but traffic is moving so slow on the road, that we are able to pass between the vehicles and go straight down toward the river. This road goes all the way to the river. I believe that in the past, there was a ferry boat at the end of the road. When we get close to the river, there are several houses lining the road. The houses on the south side of the road are level with the road, but those on the north side are about twenty feet above the road and the bank leading down to the road is covered with concrete. It runs from the intersection about a quarter of a mile west of the river, down to the river. In a couple of places, there are concrete steps leading from the road up to the houses above.

Most of the vehicles go down and park among the houses on the south side, but my halftrack turns north at the intersection and then goes through the field so that it is north of the upper houses. In fact, we are parked right next to a chicken pen in back of one of the houses and we are pointed to the east. One of the firing batteries is lined up, facing east and located a hundred yards north of the halftrack. As soon as everyone is in position, the wire crews start stringing wire from each battery to the headquarters located in one of the houses down below. Once they get them connected, I will be able to shut down the radios and I will have more freedom to move around.

I can look to the north about a half a mile and see the bridge sticking up above the river. There is a high cliff along the east side of the river. The cliff made it hard for the soldiers crossing the bridge to move on. It was so steep that they had to climb it by hanging on to roots sticking out. The Germans dropped rocks down on them to knock they off and some fell to their death. Everyone else that crossed the bridge had to follow the road along the east side of the river. It was a mixture of Americans and Germans and both sides were shelling the road. There was a lot of confusion.

The battery located to our north, is made up of six self propelled 105mm howitzers. They have also captured a German artillery piece and several rounds of ammunition for it. They pull it behind a halftrack. When they get their regular guns set up, they unhook the German gun too. When they get a fire mission, they adjust the gun along with the others. When they start firing a barrage, they fire the German gun at the same place. This has to be demoralizing to the Germans, because it seems to them that they are getting shelled not only by the Americans, but by their own troops as well.

This is really a beautiful spot, but now it is covered with all the material of war. Looking back to the west, and both north and south along the valley, it is covered with artillery pieces and antiaircraft guns. There are hundreds of them dug in. There is almost constant firing by different ones. The number of German planes coming in has decreased, since many have been shot down, but still there is an occasional plane that comes in and the antiaircraft guns open up and we can see the tracers flying through the air.

On down the river to the north, the British forces have put up a bunch of barrage balloons. They are held in position along the river and cables hang down from them to engage any airplane that might try to fly low along the river to bomb the bridge or any of the troops amassed along the river. Most of the German planes come in flying low over the cliff at the east and try to bomb the bridge by flying along its length to give them more of a target.

One of the infantrymen stands in the ring mount with his .50 caliber machine gun pointed at the top of the cliff in line with the bridge. He stands there hour after hour intensely watching and slowly smoking a cigarette. If a German plane tries to come in at that point, he is already on target and only has to press his thumbs on the trigger to fire a burst of shells at the target. He has already shot down two German planes and has said he wants to become an "ace." He will have to shoot fast or the many antiaircraft guns will cheat him from his prize.

Someone finally comes to relieve me on the radio and I go to find a place to put my bedroll for the night. I walk around the chicken pen and back to the front of the house where there are steps leading down to the street. I cross the street and go into the house there. I walk into the living room and three guys are sitting on a divan. I glance at the wall across from them and see what I think is a mirror with their reflections in it. Then I give a second look. It is not a mirror, it is a hole in the wall and what I see is not a reflection, but three guys sitting on a divan in the other room. The house is a duplex and the rooms are exact opposite. The long hole in the wall was caused by the vibrations from all the guns firing over the house, shaking the plaster out of the walls.

I go upstairs and find a bedroom and since someone beat me to the bed, I unroll my bedroll on the floor. It does not occur to me that by being on the second floor, I am that much closer to the path of the artillery shells going over the top of the house, or that the blast from the guns will be shaking the house that much. Every time one of them fires, small pieces of plaster fall from the walls and ceiling. I look around and the mess is being set up in back of the house where I will be sleeping.

It appears that they will not have time to get chow ready for dinner today, so I go out and get a couple of K rations from them and then head back to where the halftrack is parked to eat. My stomach has settled down some and I have cleaned my mess kit really well but I will use the K rations and maybe it will help. The ones I grabbed are for dinner and I made sure of that. Maybe the cheese in it will tighten up my system again.

I cut slices of the cheese and put them between two of the crackers for a small sandwich. I have the lemon drink to wash it down with. I take the chocolate bar, go to the front of the halftrack, raise the hood and place the bar on top of the motor. Then I start it up to charge the battery. By the time I finish my other food, the chocolate bar is really soft and I use my knife to remove it from the engine. I carefully open the wrapper and I can actually eat it without breaking a tooth. It tastes much more like a regular Hershey. I think I have learned something today.

Sitting up here on the halftrack, the war is all around me, but right here seems like a little safe pocket. No one seems to be particularly interested in this area right now. Of course there are always those shells that fall out of the sky or fail to hit their intended target and land here. I have some time and the weather is so nice, that I decide to sit out here and write some letters. I wish I could tell them what I am seeing, but I have to limit my letters to generalities. I ask that they hold up on sending me packages for awhile. We recently over ran a German warehouse and captured large quantities of candy, cookies, cheese and jam.

Most of the candy is small semi-hard candies like we used to get inside of glass candy canes, etc. It is not real sweet and does not have a strong flavor, more bland. The cookies are more like ginger snaps. I have eaten some of the cheese too, but it is a cream cheese and not just to my tastes. The jam they took and have it set out at the mess to put on our bread. It came in about five gallon cans, so it is not what you would carry around with you.

The driver comes out to the halftrack and sees the chicken house inside the pen next to us. He climbs over the fence and goes into the chicken house and comes out with a couple of eggs. He is able to climb back out by grabbing onto the side of the halftrack. He asks me if I want one of the eggs, but I am not into eating raw eggs. He proceeds to suck each egg out of the shell. I go back in the back of the halftrack and dig around and find some cookie crumbs from the last box that my mother sent me. They are really not very good after their long hard trip to me, but they are from home and that is worth a lot.

It is so peaceful and then suddenly, a battery of big guns west of us start firing. The ground shakes and the shock wave from the blast moves over us. I have finished my letters, so I put my stationery away and put the letters in my pocket to be mailed. I am having to use V-mail, because I still do not have any airmail stamps. We have to order them in advance and then they bring them up with the mail when it comes.

I have a chance to watch the gunners on the firing battery north of me. Some are throwing a softball back and forth and a few others are passing a sorry looking football around. They try to keep busy doing something while they wait on their next fire mission. When they get the call, they run back to the guns and while one sights the gun, another will be selecting the shell and setting the fuse. It does not take long before the shell is on its way over the Rhine.

The bridge is far enough away that we can't make out what is going on there. The sides of the bridge block the view of what is going across. All you can see is that there is movement. Suddenly one of those strange planes streaks across the sky and all hell breaks loose. Antiaircraft guns start firing, but it is to no avail. By the time they see it and swing the guns, it is long gone. One of the guys says that it is a jet airplane. They got the word on them from headquarters. It is powered by a turbine mounted in the airplane and is very fast. In fact, it is the only kind of German airplane to get in, attack the bridge and get out. We do not have anything that is fast enough to catch it.

It is getting late enough in the evening to be close to supper. It is awhile, but finally a guy comes to take over for me. I get out my nice clean mess kit and head down to the chow line. Once again, there is no line by the time I get there. They have cooked spam slices with pineapple, canned sweet potatoes, apple sauce and GI bread with some of the captured jam to go on it. I get my food and sit on a stone wall with some of the other guys to eat. I decide that I am entitled to take a break to eat and should not have to go back on the radio until I get through.

I go back up to the half track and go ahead and top off the gas tanks, even though we did not use much gas today. Used more keeping the battery charged than we did in getting here. When I get done with that, I go ahead and pull the top back over and get it ready for night. I will not have to be on the radio unless the wire goes out, but I want it ready. I will still have to pull guard around the area, but it is only two hours on and then four off, so I will get more sleep than I have been getting.

CHAPTER LXIII

My last shift on guard ends while the cooks are getting breakfast ready. I go over and beg a cup of coffee again. They do not have any pancakes or biscuits today, but they give me a couple of pieces of toast and put a gob of captured jelly between them. I thank them and head out with my pre-breakfast snack. It is too late to go back to bed, so I head up to where the halftrack is and after my toast and coffee, I go ahead and roll the top back to be ready for the day. The guns are quiet right now and I can hear the vehicles on the road west, heading for the bridge. It is a beautiful morning in March. The fruit trees are starting to bud out and spring will be here before long.

I wait until I think breakfast is ready to be served and get my mess kit and head for the chow line. I make sure that my mess kit is clean. I have been taking special care of it since I got the GI's. I get powdered eggs, thick bacon, more toast with jelly and another cup of coffee. I go back to the stone wall, sit down and eat my breakfast with some of the other guys.

There are lots of interesting things to discuss. The war is all around us. We try to find out more about jet planes, about how the bridge is holding up and about how long we will be here, before we cross the river. Some of us, by the nature of our jobs, do not have as much to do as usual. As soon as the brass realizes that some of us are not doing much, they will find something for us to do. The best thing is to stay out of sight, or act busy.

Taking my own advice, when I finish my breakfast, I head back up to the halftrack. Here I am out of sight of the headquarters and they are not likely to make the trip up here on the chance that I will be available for a detail. I unroll the top back over the halftrack about half way, crawl back under it and then pull the center down so that I am out of sight. I get a bag to lay my head on and go to sleep. I get in about a half hour nap before I wake up and crawl out.

Some of the guys take off and explore around the area. They tell of a leather factory back up the road to the north. One of the guys has a billfold that is cut out of one piece of leather and formed by folding and tucking in tabs to use for a pattern. Three of us decide to go to the leather factory and get some leather for ourselves.

I cut out one and have it to use to make others. I will put my things in one of them to use and make others to send home. Soon almost everyone in the outfit is working on a new billfold. At least it will keep us out of trouble for awhile.

I am doing my leather work up at the halftrack and the driver comes up. He climbs in the halftrack and then jumps down in the chicken pen and goes into the hen house. No eggs this time, the owner must have beat him to them. In a little while, we hear a chicken cackling and so he goes to the hen house and comes back with a fresh egg. The owner comes out but he realizes he is too late.

It is noon and time for dinner. I have been busy and the morning has passed really fast. I go down and get in the chow line and get my chow and then take it back up the hill to eat it. Up here, I can hear when a German plane comes over, by listening to the antiaircraft guns. I think that the Germans have been pushed back far enough by now, that they can no longer reach the bridge with their cannons.

When it gets closer to time for supper, I move back down to the lower level and go in the house and sit down and visit with some of the guys. We have not moved much in the last four days and supplies are catching up with us. They received some ground beef, so tonight we are having meatloaf, mashed potatoes made from powder, gravy, peas and carrots, an apple cobbler for dessert and, of course, some more of the thick bread with more of the jelly. This is the best meal we have had for some time.

Most of us have finished eating when we hear the sound of "mail call." Of course, that brings everyone running. I get three letters and a package from home. I go sit down and read my letters. They also brought the day's "Stars & Stripes," so everyone has something to read. My mother goes around town and talks to everyone so that she will have lots of information to pass on. Since she writes to thirty-two different service men, she needs lots of things to fill the many letters.

When I get through reading the letters, I open the package. It has four Hershey bars, a package of candy corn and some homemade cookies, that are still in good condition. She has packed it with copies of the Hennessey Clipper, the local newspaper, and the comics from the Oklahoman. I enjoy all of these. I pass out a cookie to all the guys around me and tell them I will let them read the comics as soon as I finish with them.

I go check to see what guard detail I am on tonight and get the passwords. I do not have to go on guard until midnight tonight, and when my detail is over, I will get to go back to bed until morning. I will get almost twice as much sleep tonight as I usually do.

I make another trip back up on the hill to the halftrack to make it ready for night. And also to take my package up there and hide it in the halftrack. I do not mind sharing, but if I leave it out, the whole thing will disappear. Things from home are so treasured that you just do not want to use them all at once, but spread them out and savor them.

I go back down to the house and sit and visit for awhile before I go to bed. Midnight comes fast and I crawl out to go on guard duty. The air is cold this early in March, even though the sunshine has made the days very pleasant. I stand guard on the post, but there is no one around and nothing happens, so the shift goes slowly. Not that we should not be on guard, because there are still many German soldiers in the area, hiding out. They were pushed back here and when they could not get across the river, they went into hiding.

I get up and go line up for breakfast. They have received some sausage and they make pancakes. We have syrup and there is also some of the jelly left as well as some peanut butter. This is a popular breakfast with most of the men. We have plenty of coffee to wash it down and I enjoy it. While we are eating, we get to talking about how we are going to get our clothes washed. We can't just take them to a German woman and get them washed. We are not allowed to fraternize with them. The fine for getting caught is fifty dollars, which is much more than most of us have.

I suggest that we fix up something and wash them ourselves. Another guy agrees to go in with me on washing. We find a wash tub and carry it up on the hill to the field just north of the halftrack. We dig a little trench in the ground, put some wood in it and start a fire. We pour water in the tub, cut up some GI soap in it and then add our clothes. The water boils and we stir it with a stick swishing the clothes back and forth. As the water boils, a green scum forms on top of the water. It looks terrible. When we think they have boiled enough to kill all of the germs, we take out the clothes, throw the dirty water away and then fill the tub with fresh water and rinse the clothes.

We take our clothes and hang them on the chicken yard fence to dry. We are proud of our effort until we look closer at our clothes. They are mostly wool and seem quite a bit smaller than before we started. I think boiling them has shrunk them. We will just have to wear them anyway. When they are dry, I put my underwear in my duffle bag and take my shirt and pants and fold them and slip them into one of the seat covers, so they will have some kind of press to them.

One of the common things over here is for one soldier to approach another and say "Look at that uniform, soldier. It looks like you slept in it, " knowing full well he has slept in it for many nights.

I am hoping that when I take my uniform out of the seat cover, it will not look like I slept in it.

While we are washing clothes, one of the hens cackles and the halftrack driver jumps over the fence and runs in and gets the fresh egg. The German comes out in time to see him going back over the fence. They seem to be in a contest to see who can get the eggs. Of course, they are the German's eggs in the first place.

CHAPTER LXIV

While we are washing clothes, some of the guys decide that we should fix up a ball diamond, so we can play softball. They pick out the flat field east of where the halftrack is parked. It has been worked, so the ground is rather soft. There are some shell holes in it and out just beyond center field is a huge bomb crater. They decide that the soft dirt will be ok for the outfield, but the infield needs to be firmer. They go get one of the tanks and bring it up here. Under the guidance of one of the sergeants, they move it forward and back across the area, as they cover the entire infield. It is now packed firm.

They get a couple of boards and make home plate. The bases are sacks with some sand in them. The chicken house and the fence will make a back stop. Some of the guys are already practicing ball while we finish up the laundry. After we get through, we go join them. All we have are two bats, three balls and one mitt. The catcher gets the mitt. One of the guys is hitting practice balls to us out in the field and we are throwing them back in. We are not very organized, but it is fun, helps keep us in shape and out of trouble.

When we quit, we go back over by the halftrack and one of the other radio operators goes to get his carbine where he left it. It is not there. He should not have left it where he could not see it and losing your weapon is a serious offence. He knows right where he left it, so someone had to have taken it. He decides not to report it and see what happens.

While we have been doing this, some of the guys found three old motorcycles in a building in back of where the mess is set up. They have been working on them all afternoon. It is not easy, because everything on the motorcycles is metric and they only have standard tools. They get one of them running, but either they do not know how to operate it or the clutch is out, because it has to be started in gear.

In the evening, everyone seems to head to the other side of the road where the mess is located. Then we all go over and line up to eat. At least while we are here, we are getting better meals and three a day. Tonight, they have pork chops, mashed potatoes and gravy, green beans, the usual bread and apple sauce. The pork chops are a little strong, but we all eat them.

We sit on the stone wall, like a bunch of birds on a wire and eat our supper. We just get started when a jeep drives in, a corporal climbs out and yells "mail call." We set our mess kits on the wall and gather around him. He starts calling out names. I get two more letters, one from my dad and one from Emma. I put them in my pocket, grab a copy of "Stars & Stripes" from the jeep and go back to my supper.

After supper, the first sergeant comes in and gives us our guard assignments and the passwords. We light a couple of candles and a lamp and read our mail. It is so good to hear from home. After I finish reading the letters, I read the "Stars & Stripes." It says that they have built up a sizeable bridgehead along the east side of the Rhine. Since most of the artillery and antiaircraft are still on this side, I wonder how long it will be before we cross to the other side.

I have early guard tonight, and when it is time to go on guard, I go out to the post and settle in. I find a place back against a building, where I can see anything out in the open. Nothing is very light. I never thought you could see at night without a moon, but with the stars you can see very well, after your eyes get used to it. The two hours go slowly and I am glad when they are over and I can go get into my bed.

Four hours is not very long to sleep and when I get out of the warm bed and go outside, I feel the chill. I go back to my place beside the building and spend what seems to be an even longer two hours. I sleep late and am awakened by a guy coming into the room where we sleep. He says that the room smells like a boar's nest. I had not really noticed until he said that, but it does stink in here. With the unwashed bodies sleeping in there, it is bad enough, but that cowhide over the window sure adds to the odor.

Almost everyone has eaten by the time I get to the chow line. I get my food and join some of the guys on the stone wall. A couple of the others from my room upstairs are there too and I mention about the room smelling. I tell them that as soon as we get done eating, we need to go up there and take down the cowhide and take it outside. We can then open the window and let it air out today. We need to find something else for a blackout curtain and leave that cowhide out.

After we finish breakfast, we go remove the cowhide and open the window to the room. We find an old quilt in one of the other buildings that we can use for a curtain this evening. It is dusty, but smells much better than the cowhide and probably better than we do.

While some of us are standing there, the guys that worked on the motorcycle ask us if we will help them. They were able to get the bike to run, but never got the clutch to work. They have to put it up on the stand to start it in gear. They say that they want us to help them ride it. We agree to help.

They go get the bike and push it up the driveway just past where the mess is set up. The driveway goes north and enters out onto the road going down to the Rhine on the east and back west the way we came in. They have decided that two of them will get on the bike and have three of us pick up the back end and hold it off of the ground, while they start it. When it is running, we can let it down and they will ride out to the road.

The two riders get on and the three of us pick up the back end of the motorcycle. They kick the starter and the engine takes off. The back wheel is spinning good and they holler for us to let it down. The three of us drop the back wheel. There is the scream of the tire, gravel flying and the smoke of burning rubber as the motorcycle shoots down the driveway. By the time it gets to the road, it is going like a bat out of hell. We run down the driveway as fast as we can trying to see what happens when they hit the road. We can see them headed straight for the concrete wall on the other side of the road. They hit the shallow trough at the bottom of the wall and fly into the air. They have the wheel turned and when they hit the concrete wall, they shoot back to the west, riding on the side of the concrete wall, about ten feet above the road, just like a barrel rider in a carnival. They are doing fine until they get to the intersection about a block west and they run out of wall. They sail out into the intersection, the two guys fly off of the bike and slide along the road. The bike continues and slams into the wall on the north-south road and pieces fly in the air.

We run down there and help them up. They are scratched and bruised, but no serious injuries. The bike is a total wreck. They leave it in the shallow ditch there at the base of the wall. They will remember this ride for a long time. Of course, as soon as we see that they are not seriously hurt, we all burst out laughing. It was quite a show, even though it did not last very long. Someone says that it was not a very long ride and one of the riders says it was a long ride where he was sitting and he had time for his whole life to pass before his eyes.

Someone says that we should all meet at the ball field after dinner and we will get a game of softball going. The halftrack driver and I, together with the other radio operator, go up to where the halftrack is. We look around some more for his carbine, but do not really expect to find it now. While we are looking, one of the hens cackles in the chicken house. The driver starts that way to see if he can get the egg. The German runs out of the house and into the chicken pen. He comes out of the hen house with an egg in his hand. He holds it up, looks at the driver and says "Ah ha!" It looks like he won this time. We all laugh, including the German.

After dinner we go to the ball field, choose sides and I play center field. We have played three innings and I am standing out in center field when we hear a terrible noise. It sounds like a boxcar flying through the air. The guys all hit the dirt and I make a dive for the huge bomb crater and end up about half way down in it. I lay there for awhile and do not hear anything, so I crawl out. Everyone is asking "What was that?" No one seems to know. We go ahead and finish our game, but we keep listening for the sound again.

After the game the driver and I go back to the halftrack and straighten it up and replace some of the things, that have shifted around during our travels. When we have finished, we go back across the road and go in the house to wait until supper is ready.

Someone comes in and says that they just got word at headquarters, that what we heard was the shell from one of the giant railway guns going over. The Germans had over shot and the shell landed some distance back from the river and was a dud. I am sure glad they were not on target. As big as those shells are, if it had exploded anywhere near it would have killed us all.

One of the sergeants comes in and says that he is supposed to go around and tell everyone that by order of the Battalion Commander: "No one is to ride a motorcycle." When he leaves, we all start laughing. In a little while, I go crawl in my bed.

CHAPTER LXV

Someone is shaking me. "Lovell, get up."

"What is it?"

"Go get on your radio and turn it on, but do not transmit until you receive word. They think that the Germans are going to drop paratroopers and we will need the radio, if they cut the wire."

I pull on my field jacket, sling my carbine on, hurry outside, across the road, up the stairs and find my way around the chicken pen to the halftrack. There is enough light from the stars so that I do not have to use my blue flashlight. I sure do not want to show light if they are planning an attack. I get in the halftrack and turn on the radios. They only make a little light and it does not show outside.

I go outside of the halftrack and stand against it, where I will not be seen. I am close to the back side of the radios, so I can hear if they send any messages. I listen to see if I can hear any planes. The whole area back to my west is filled with antiaircraft guns and I am sure that they will start firing if they sense any planes.

Suddenly, every antiaircraft gun in the valley fires. The noise is tremendous. The sky looks like it is afire. There are 90 mm guns firing, 40 mm, quad .50 machine guns, dual .50 machine guns with 37 mm between them. Anything that can fire into the sky is shooting.

This is the largest concentration of antiaircraft guns ever assembled. They are on preset patterns so that the entire sky is covered and no plane or paratrooper could get through the fire. The tracers cover the sky like a sheet of red light and of course for every tracer, there are four other bullets. They are throwing tons of steel, copper, lead and explosives into the air. I stand there looking up with my mouth open in wonder. There has never been anything like this before and probably never will be again.

It lasts several minutes, but is probably not as long as it seems and then the guns all stop firing. There is an old saying: "What goes up, must come down." It is like a giant hail storm as the spent shells and shrapnel start falling back to earth. I hit the ground and roll under the halftrack. It seems that the storm lasts longer than the firing, but I suppose they were approximately the same length of time. I wait under the halftrack until I feel that everything has already arrived and then I get up and look around.

It seems real quiet now. I stay hidden as best I can, in case some Germans did get through. I stay there about an hour before I hear the radio. I climb in the halftrack and answer the call. They tell me to secure the station and close down. I can now go back to bed. I go back across the road and up to my bed, but for once, I have trouble going to sleep. I can still see and hear all of those guns firing, the tracers lighting the sky and then hear them falling back to earth. At least, I do not have guard tonight and may get to sleep until morning, unless they get another alert.

I get up and go get in line for breakfast. Everyone is talking about what happened last night. Up on the hill, I had probably the best view of it. After breakfast, I go back up to the halftrack to check things out. I look toward the bridge and it is still there, but there are no barrage balloons flying over the river. All thirteen of them have been shot down. I look at the ground and unlike other hail storms, these stones have not melted. The ground is covered with bullets and shrapnel, mostly .50 caliber bullets. I take the toe of my boot and soon have a pile six inches high raked up. I wonder how much money was spent in those few minutes last night.

I visit with other guys and, as near as I can tell, no German planes were shot down and no paratroopers killed. It must have been a false alarm. But it should have discouraged the Germans from attempting it. They have tried so many things to destroy the bridge. In addition to the explosives on the bridge, the airplanes and artillery, they also sent underwater swimmers down the river with explosives to try to take it out. They floated mines down the river and even sent explosive-laden barges down to try to destroy it. It has received a lot of damage from different sources, but is still standing. If they blow it up now, it will not make much difference, because we now have four pontoon bridges across. But this bridge made a lot of difference, since it allowed them to establish a bridge-head, clear the other side of the river and allow them to put across the pontoon bridges with less interference.

We spend the rest of the day doing very little. I do write some letters. I also go to the place they are using for an orderly room and take care of some business and I pick up my airmail envelopes that I had ordered.

When I finish taking care of business, I go back up to the ball field and we practice softball. Most of us are not doing much now and we are getting bored. The front has moved so far east that our 105 mm howitzers are of little use. We will probably be crossing the river before long. Some of the artillery has already moved out of the valley. I go back to the house in the evening and get my guard assignment for the night.

I do not have early guard, so I will get to get some sleep before I have to go on duty. Even though my sleep was interrupted last night by getting called out, I still got more than usual. Tonight will be about average. The mail jeep is late today and it is after dark before we have mail call. I get a letter from home and I pick up a copy of "Stars & Stripes." We have enough light in the room that I can read them. I am glad to get them. I hunger for something to read.

They wake me to go on guard and I go pull my shift. It is quiet tonight and the time goes slowly. I am more than glad to go get my relief and head back to bed. I sleep soundly until morning. When I get up, almost everyone has already had breakfast. I hurry and get in on the tail end of the line I go out and sit on the wall again with some of the other guys.

They send several of us to one of the firing batteries to help them unload ammunition from trucks and then take it out of the crates and put it in the racks in the self propelled howitzers. It is not easy work, but it does not take long and then we hang out with the gunners until time to go back to Headquarters Battery for dinner.

We gather at the ball field and choose up sides. As usual, I am playing center field. I get a hit the first time at bat, but get left on second base. It is the last half of the second inning and we are taking the field. I start to run out to center field when I suddenly stop and yell "IT IS GONE!" I repeat it and they want to know what is gone. "The bridge. The bridge is gone." They join me and look down the river to the north and the bridge is no longer standing. We can see the towers, but the span has disappeared into the river and the view of it is blocked by the trees. It is sad to think that it has finally given up. But it served its purpose and allowed us to get across the Rhine, shorten the war and save hundreds if not thousands of lives.

We go ahead and finish our ball game and then go back across the road to get ready for supper. Someone brings the word from headquarters. They were working on the bridge to try to strengthen it when it collapsed into the river. Several lives were lost when the bridge fell. Now that we can no longer cross there, the Germans will quit using it for a target and the antiaircraft guns can be pulled out.

I have company at the guard post tonight and we talk about the bridge. We have given it a personality. I go get my relief and crawl into my sleeping bag. The other guys are already asleep in the room. I remind myself to air out the room tomorrow, and wonder how much longer it will be before we find a place to get a shower.

I am called out to finish up with the last guard session of the night. I am really sore. It has been a long time since I have played much softball and my muscles are protesting. When it gets a little light, I go to the mess and beg a cup of coffee. They have a special treat for me this morning. They received a shipment of flour to make doughnuts and they decided to make some for breakfast. I will not want to miss breakfast this morning.

I am not first in line, but I do get in third place. We have powdered eggs, some of the thick bacon and each man gets two doughnuts. Of course, we have coffee to wash it down. I did not hear a single guy gripe about powdered eggs. It is amazing what a couple of doughnuts can do. While we are eating, the first sergeant comes by and tells us to get our things together and make sure that our vehicles are ready to travel. We are told to get everything stocked up, because when we leave here we may not have a chance for supplies for awhile. I ask him when we are going to leave and he says they have not received marching orders yet, but they think it will be before long.

I go with the driver to the halftrack to check it out. We top off the gas tanks to replace what gas we used in keeping the batteries charged and then get a part of a can of gas from the firing battery to refill all of our cans. I go fill the water can and put the halazone tablets in it. The driver checks the oil and greases all the zerks. All we have to do now is to put our bedrolls in and we are ready to go. The driver says that he would like to have one more egg before he has to leave and he sits up on top of the halftrack waiting for a hen to cackle.

I go down to the mess truck and the cooks are all busy loading up their stoves and things. There is a case of K rations, that is almost half full, sitting in the back of the truck, so I put it under my arm and walk back up to the halftrack. I doubt if anyone even saw me.

When I get there, the driver is climbing up the fence and back into the halftrack. He has an egg in one hand. I show him the box of K rations and tell him that we will be able to get by for awhile. I store it under the cover in the back of the halftrack. We still have not received any orders and it is getting close to noon. I can see the firing battery and they have packed up their things and are pulled into position to move out. We go back down and get our bedrolls and load them up, so we are ready to roll if we get the word.

At noon, the lieutenant comes up and tells us to start up the half-track and go down to the north-south road but do not pull out yet. We start up and turn around and head back the way we came in. We get to the road and stop and wait. No one is moving yet, so we shut off the engine. I have the radios turned on, but am maintaining silence. While we are waiting, I go back and pull out three K rations and pass them out. The lieutenant says that he knew that I would have food, that he never worries about eating when he is with me.

While we are eating and waiting, I get to thinking about this place, wondering what the Germans will do with a softball field. I bet it is plowed up before long. I think about being part of the first army to advance across the Rhine in hundreds of years...about how important the bridge was to the advance. I also think about witnessing the largest concentration of antiaircraft guns in the world firing, and seeing the largest number of artillery ever assembled. I got to see the first jet aircraft ever in combat. I also got to be on the receiving end of one of the huge railway guns, and didn't get hit.

CHAPTER LXVI

We wait to get the word to move out. It may be awhile because they may have traffic backed up at the pontoon bridge. Everywhere we look, there are vehicles waiting to go. We will probably follow the executive officer's jeep, since the lieutenant is here with us. No one seems to know anything yet. I notice that the gunners from the firing battery are out moving around. They are throwing a softball back and forth and some others are passing a football. That seems better than just sitting around. We get out and walk around and I can go a little way from the halftrack, as long as it is not too far to hear the radios.

The time drags on. It is getting later in the day. Finally, a jeep drives up to where we are, turns around and signals us to follow them. We rush to get on board, the driver starts up the engine and we move out. Other vehicles are starting their engines and following behind us. We move out to the road, the way we came in. We turn and follow the road back south for a few miles, until we get to the place where they have gone across country toward the river.

We can only move a short distance and then we have to stop. This is really stop and go. Somewhere up ahead, the line of vehicles is slowly moving on to the pontoon bridge. It is getting later and I am getting hungry. I go get three of the dinners out of the K ration box and open them up. I take the three tropical Hershey bars out and place them on the transmission. I then pass out the rest of the rations to the other two. For the driver, I open up his so he can eat as we slowly move along.

We eat our meat and biscuits and wash it down with water from our canteens. When we finish with that part of the rations, I go back and dig out the last package I received from home and get out three cookies. I open the floor panel and take out the three candy bars and they are now soft enough to eat. I pass a cookie and candy bar to each of the others and sit back to enjoy my own. The lieutenant says that he did not realize that I would be serving dessert too.

It is very dark now. It is cloudy and there are no lights. The driver follows the tiny blackout lights on the vehicle in front of us. There is a self propelled 105 behind us and I hope the driver can see our little lights, so he does not run into us. We are getting closer to the pontoon bridge now. I have the top pulled about halfway back and stand between it and the ring mount on the halftrack. I decide that there is nothing I can do and I can't see anything so, I lay down on the floor and go to sleep. I just hope that they do not run off of the bridge into the river.

I wake as the halftrack lurches down the bank leading onto the bridge. I get up on my knees where I can see out the windshield. The engineers have little lights that they use to guide the drivers onto the bridge. After that it is up to the driver to stay on the tread that is laid across the row of pontoons. I lay back down and go back to sleep. One of the great moments of my life, crossing the Rhine on a pontoon bridge and I sleep through it.

When I wake up, we are pulling into a staging area somewhere on the other side of the river. It is a small town and the driver parks the halftrack next to one of the houses. I will have to man the radios since they will not be trying to string wire here. The firing battery behind us has moved on through this town and is parked somewhere out east of the town. I will get someone to relieve me about midnight and then I can sleep until four in the morning.

I check to see where my relief will be sleeping and carry my bedroll into the house and put it on the floor just inside of the door. I let them know where I will be when they need to wake me at four o'clock, then I rush back out to the radios. I go ahead and pull the top back up and close the windshield off so I can have some light inside. One of the guys had a "Stars & Stripes" and he passed it on to me, so now I have something to read. Some way, they seem to always get these papers to us.

I fill my canteen cup with water from the can on the fender and take it back inside. I find one of the lemon juice drink packages and some sugar from the rations and mix me up something to drink. I open up another of the K rations with meat and eat it spread on the biscuits. I wash it down with the lemon drink. I feel like I am in my own little place back here in the halftrack. I have enough light to read and I have food and drink and I just as well enjoy it.

At midnight I put away all of my things and go get my relief to take over. Then I get in my sleeping bag. It seems that I just laid down when they wake me to go back on duty. I struggle to wake up and make my way back to the halftrack. The radios are silent, but someone needs to man them in case they want to send messages through to us. I get out the "Stars & Stripes" again and starting at the back this time, re-read the entire thing, word for word. Then I read the wording on the K rations boxes. When I have read all of them, I pull out my New Testament and start reading it. I hope that the Lord does not mind being last on the list of reading materials. The print is not very big and in what light I have, it is hard to read.

When it gets light, I go outside and look around. I could not tell much last night when we pulled in here in the dark. The cooks are across the street about one hundred and fifty feet away. I watch them and when it looks like they have had time to make coffee, I make a quick dash over and beg a cup. They apologize for not having anything to go with it, but I am glad to get even a cup of coffee. I sip on my coffee and watch the camp come to life. I have a feeling that we will be moving out of there before long.

I watch the men line up for breakfast and I wait for someone to finish their breakfast so they can relieve me while I eat. At last one of the other radio operators comes over with his breakfast so I can go get mine. They have grapefruit juice, wheat cereal that looks like Malt-o-meal and some of the bread toasted and orange marmalade. I get that and another cup of coffee and head back to the halftrack. I put sugar on the cereal, but all we have is canned milk and it sure does not taste like the Malt-o-meal that we had at home. But I am hungry and eat it while I listen for the radios to sound off.

 I am so sure that we will be moving on, that I slip away and get my bedroll and load it up. I put the top all the way back so that I can gas up easier. I reach over the side and pull up a five gallon can of gas and pour it into the gas tank. I throw the empty can out beside of the road and then get another can from the other side and finish filling the gas tank. We did not go far yesterday, but we idled so much that we used ten gallons of gas. I do not know when we will get a new supply of gas, now that we have crossed the river. The halftrack gets about two miles to the gallon, but the tanks and self propelled howitzers only get about one-half mile to the gallon.

The mail has caught up with us and at the sound of mail call, everyone comes running. I get several letters and papers. I certainly do enjoy them. Anything from home is welcome. My folks ask questions about where I am and what I am doing and, of course, I can't tell them. They probably know about as much about where I am as I do. They read the papers and it shows the progress of the different units.

I was right about staying here. As soon as the cooks get through serving breakfast, they start loading up. At least, they must have got the word. I have not heard anything. Then the driver comes and says that we will be moving out soon. The lieutenant comes out and gets in and tells the driver to pull out on the road as soon as there is a clear place. We will be leading Headquarters Battery. We get on the road and the other vehicles fall in behind us. We pass by where the firing batteries are spread out and move on southeast. We make good time for a little ways and then traffic starts to back up. We go back to start and stop again.

Often we are stopped long enough to make a fire and heat up something for dinner, but we do not have any C rations to heat up. I only have a couple of K rations left and they are better eaten cold. I ask the lieutenant if he will listen to the radio while I am gone for a little bit. He wants to know where I am going and I tell him I am going to go shoot something for dinner. He laughs and says to go ahead. I jump out of the halftrack and start back toward the mess supply truck.

I no sooner leave the halftrack when the column starts to moving again. I just stop and wait until the mess truck get even with me and then I grab hold and swing up on the step beside the cab. The driver wants to know what I am doing and I tell him that the lieutenant sent me back there to get some C rations. He wants to know how I am going to get them back up to the lieutenant? I will just have to wait until the next time we stop and run back up there with them.

I do not have to wait long, and when the truck stops I jump off and run around to the back. I lower the tailgate and climb up in. I find a case of C rations, slide them to the rear of the truck, jump out and grab them. The driver has come back and he closes the tailgate as I trot off towards the front of the column. When I get back to the halftrack, they are already moving forward again. I shove the case of C rations over the side of the halftrack and run alongside. The lieutenant opens the door and reaches out to take my hand and swing me into the halftrack.

Someone up ahead has built a fire and we stop not far from it. I grab three cans of beef stew and put them beside the fire to heat. Some of the other guys around us are asking for rations too, so I pass out the rest of the case, except for three that I put away in the back. I always want to know where the next meal is coming from. We start to move again so, I use my gloves to grab the three cans and set them on the front of the halftrack.

We go on a little way and then stop. The guys in the vehicle ahead of us start to build a fire, so I ask if I can put our cans in it too.

The fire is really too hot and the cans get black. I open one of them and take a spoon and stir the contents. It was burned on the outside, cold in the middle, but by stirring it up, it is warm all through. It is not very good, but it will have to do.

Early in the evening, we stop in a little town, which looks a lot like the one we left this morning. We pull in beside a house and watch as the firing batteries pass by on their way to the outside of town, where they can set up. Headquarters sets up in one of the houses and some of the guys check out the house next to us. We are close enough to the house that I can hear the radios if they call, so I take my bedroll in and stake claim to a spot. I go back out and stay with the radios. When we are moving, there is not much radio traffic, but now that we are stopped, both radios have come to life. I screw a couple of more sections of antennae on so I can receive better and settle in beside them.

I get a message on the CW radio and take it into the headquarters house and give it to the major. He will have the code clerk decipher it. I have to get back to the radios. The FM radio is busy as the firing batteries get into position and start getting fire missions. I know that we have now caught up with the front again.

CHAPTER LXVII

A few of us are standing beside my halftrack when a two and a half ton truck pulls up and just off of the other side of the road. The driver gets out and opens the tailgate and calls out a name. A tall kid climbs out of the truck and drags out his duffle bag and his pack. The driver closes the tailgate, climbs back in the truck and drives off. The kid stands there for a little bit looking confused. It is obvious that he is a new replacement. He is probably about my age. His uniform gives him away. It does not look like it has been slept in very long. He just does not have the look of someone that has been here for awhile. A sergeant comes up to him and tells him that he is being assigned to a scouting party and that they are just about ready to go out. The sergeant tells him to put his things inside of the house and go get in the jeep, as the others are already ready to go.

The jeep takes off with the corporal they call "Dog" driving, the sergeant sitting beside him and the new kid next to the lieutenant, in the back. I wait around the radio for any messages that come in. The cooks are trying to get set up so that they can serve a hot meal for supper. The driver comes out and says he will check the halftrack over and asks if I will fill up the gas tanks. I pull another can from the side rack and pour it into the gas tank. It is not enough to fill it, so I get another from the other side and finish filling the tank. We are now down to two cans on each side.

The driver just finishes greasing the halftrack when a truck arrives hauling gasoline. I get down and get four cans and they slowly move along. I put them in the empty spaces in the racks. We are now fully stocked with fuel and the halftrack is ready to go. I notice that some of the guys are already lined up over at the mess. I am hungry, but will have to wait until someone comes to relieve me before I can eat.

I get another operator to stay with the radio so I can eat. I get my food and come back to the halftrack . I can eat and listen to the radios at the same time. It does not give much time for looking around like some of the others, but it has its advantages too. There is a stir across the way by the house where headquarters is located. The scouting party has not returned. They get one of the halftracks and follow the route that they took, looking for them.

It is about a half an hour before the halftrack returns. The scout jeep was ambushed. Two are dead, one seriously wounded and one with a slight wound. Dog is alive and he goes into headquarters and gives a report. When he comes out, we call him over and ask him what happened. He says they were driving along the road when suddenly, a German machine gun opened fire from up ahead on the right. The first shots hit the lieutenant and the sergeant, killing the lieutenant. The sergeant rolls out of the jeep and into the ditch on the right hand side. Dog rolls out on the other side and into the ditch. The new kid stands up and is dead before he hits the ground.

The Germans keep firing at them, keeping them pinned down. The sergeant is able to reach up into the jeep and get a Browning Automatic Rifle (BAR) and return fire on the Germans. Dog only has an old revolver that he has been carrying, so it is not of any use in the battle. He rolls out of the ditch and down the hill, until he is out of sight of the machine gun. He crawls along until he gets in the basement of a house. He looks up and there is a German soldier in the basement too. He covers the German with the pistol and waits.

When he thinks that the Germans are going to advance and take him prisoner, he turns the revolver over to the German and becomes the prisoner. However, the sergeant has been able to keep fire on the machine gun with the BAR and the Germans pull out when they hear a halftrack coming. Now that it looks like the Americans will be the ones to come, the German gives back the pistol and becomes the prisoner again.

The guys in the halftrack pickup the sergeant and Dog comes out and gets in too. They mark the spot for graves registration so they can come and get the lieutenant and the new guy. We ask Dog what happened to the German and he says that he shot him. I hate it that he did, after the guy surrendered, but in war the right thing is not always done. The new guy had not been in the outfit fifteen minutes and he is dead. None of us even know his name. I suppose they have it on the copy of orders he brought with him, but at least none of us had a chance to get close to him. I would hate to be the one to have to write to his parents.

The main thing that guys look for is pistols. They prefer to find a Luger or P-38, but will take about anything. A Luger or P-38 will bring a hundred and twenty dollars, which is a great sum of money, when most are only getting five or ten dollars a month. Of course, if you capture a German with a pistol, that is even better, but most of the enemy have disposed of their weapons before being captured. One important thing about a pistol is to be able to have a supply of ammunition for it.

The pistol that Dog has is not very desirable because it is a .32 caliber revolver and there is little, if any, ammunition for them here. However, Dog found that a carbine cartridge would fit in an empty chamber, but the cylinder would not turn, because it was too long. He took some carbine shells and put them in a vise and took a hacksaw and cut off enough of the bullet so that it would fit the chamber. He then had ammunition so that he could fire it. This is extremely dangerous since the carbine cartridge is much more powerful than a .32 caliber shell and could blow the gun up when fired.

Dog fired several of these shells in the gun with no adverse effects, but decided it was too much trouble to saw the end off of the bullets, so he just pushed the bullets into the shell case, until they were short enough to fit in the cylinder. This is even more dangerous because it greatly increases the pressure when fired. However, he shot many of these without any of the expected effects.

I get relieved on the radio and get to go into the house and crawl into my sleeping bag. It will only be for four hours and then I will have to go back out there and sit with the radios again. I start thinking about the boy that was killed this evening and the next thing I know, someone is shaking me and telling me it is time to go back on the radios. I go out and get in the halftrack and start up the engine to charge up the battery. I dig out my bag that has some goodies stored in it. I have a few cookies left and I get one of them and a few pieces of candy corn that my mother sent to me. I nibble real slowly on them so that they last a long time.

I spend the two hours on duty, eating my treats and reading everything I can find. When the time is up, I go wake my replacement and crawl back into my sleeping bag. I will get to sleep until morning now. When I wake up, they are already serving breakfast. I go get mine and take it to the halftrack and relieve the other operator, so he can go get his breakfast. I go ahead and roll back the top on the halftrack and get ready to move out.

Today is just about like yesterday. We slowly move along the road but we are gaining territory all the time and pushing the Germans further back into Germany. We are getting K rations for dinner and the cooks are fixing breakfast and supper. All in all, it is not bad. And I have learned something, Most of the guys do not like the chocolate bars in the K rations. I have more cigarettes than I can smoke, so I trade the little pack of cigarettes in the K ration for one of the tropical Hershey bars. Then I take it and put it under the floor panel of the halftrack, on the transmission. In an hour or so, it will be soft enough to eat.

In the evening, we pull into another of the small towns along the road. They all resemble each other and it is hard to tell the difference. Again we park next to one of the houses and we put our bedrolls inside of the house. Like usual, I have to stay on the radio for awhile when we stop. Several of the guys have been looking around the town and one comes back to where I am and tells me that there is a house full of guns, different guns from different countries, that the Germans have captured. I get one of the other operators to take over for me and then go find the operator that lost his carbine.

I tell him about the guns and that there might be a carbine there he can get. He and another guy go with me to find the house. When we find it, it is late in the evening and starting to get dark. We go in and the floor is covered with guns about a foot deep. The guns are from probably every country that Germany has been fighting with. There are guns in every room. It does not take long for him to find a carbine, but I am looking for a pistol. I do not see any, but do find a Thompson submachine gun. I have wanted one of these and pick it up. The magazine is jammed in the gun. I can probably fix it, but maybe there is another that is not damaged. It is really too dark to see much, so I decide to wait until it is light in the morning and come back and get a Thompson and to see if there are any pistols.

The other operator is really thankful for the carbine. He has gone for several days without a weapon and it was only a matter of time before someone would notice that he was not armed.

The cooks have set up the kitchen and heated food for supper. I watch as the guys line up for chow. The CW radio starts up and I get my mind off of eating while I take down a message. As soon as I get it copied, I cross over the street to the house where headquarters is located and hand the clerk the message. I would like to know what it says, but if I asked, they would probably tell me it was none of my business. By the time I get back to the halftrack, the guy that found the carbine is here to take over for me.

I have a couple of shifts in the middle of the night, so there will be someone else on the radio in the morning and when it is light enough, I will go back to the house and see what I can find. At least I should get a Thompson and with any luck, there are some pistols down under all of those rifles.

CHAPTER LXVIII

I am on the radios and it is a little after midnight. I realize that today is March 27, 1945, my birthday. I am nineteen years old today. I am a long way from home and in a war zone. What a way to spend a birthday. I dig out some of my letters from home and reread them, my way of celebrating my birthday. Yes, I believe I am a little homesick right now.

A little after one o'clock, one of the sergeants comes to the half-track and calls me to come out side. He tells me to go wake up everyone and to tell them that breakfast will be served at one-thirty and we will be pulling out at two. I go into the house and yell for everyone to wake up and then tell them the news. I gather up my bedroll and take it back out to the halftrack. I will not need it anymore tonight. I roll the top back so I can put the bedroll in and so that it will be ready when we leave.

Everyone is stirring around now. I find one of the other radio operators and ask him if he will come and man the radios, as soon as he gets his breakfast, while I go get mine. Breakfast is a little slim today. They have some cream of wheat, some toast with orange marmalade and coffee. I figure I better get what I can, while I can. I take it back to the halftrack and eat it there while listening to the radios. Listening is hardly the word, because nothing has come over either of them all night.

I am ready to go but most are still loading up. I take a chance and make a quick trip over to the mess supply truck while they are loading up. I ask if I can have some K rations for dinner. One of the cook's helpers says to take what I want. I open a case and take out all the boxes I can carry. I go back to the halftrack and store them under some of the things in the back. I always like to have plenty of K rations; you never know when you will need them.

The driver gets in and starts up the engine. We are just waiting on one of the officers to tell us to pull out. The lieutenant climbs in and tells the driver to move out to the road and see if he can find the jeep that we are to follow. This is very tricky in the blackout conditions. There is traffic moving on the road. We will have to get in the flow. We slowly pull up close to the road and can just make out the little blackout lights of the jeep. The jeep starts moving and we follow it. We are out on the road now. I am back in the halftrack and can see nothing. I only hope that the driver and the other drivers can see.

We are slowly moving along the right side of the road. Supply vehicles are passing us on the left. I hope that we do not meet anyone going the other way. It is still stop and go as we move forward. For all I know, there may be Germans all around us and probably are. It seems that we have gone many miles, but probably not near as far as it seems, because of the stop and go and that we are not going over twenty miles per hour when we are moving.

We have been traveling for over four hours and it is just starting to get light. I look back and there is a mixture of vehicles as far as I can see behind us, and the same thing in front of us. There are no supply vehicles passing us on the left now, all the vehicles on the left are going the other way. We watch overhead for German planes. They would love to find a column spread out like this. They could start at one end and strafe the whole thing. Fortunately, our planes are keeping them away.

We pull over for awhile and surprisingly, a three quarter ton truck pulls up and they have a sack of mail for us. The clerk gets the bag and starts going around and passing out the mail. Everyone is passing the letters on to the addressee. I get two letters and then down in the bottom of the sack is a package. I have received a birthday present. I can't wait to open it. I open it up and it has several candy bars, some homemade candy wrapped in waxed paper and some more candy packed in a can. The packing in the box is funny papers and the school papers from home. I pass out candy bars to those guys near me and put the letters and the papers away to read later. We pull out onto the road again and keep slowly moving.

Suddenly, the halftrack picks up speed. We have reached the famous Autobahn highway. It is four lanes wide and allows us to speed up and we do not have the start and stop of the narrow roads we have been on before.

About eleven in the morning, we reach the city of Limburg. Here we have to stop. The Germans have blown the bridge across the Lahn River. We pull off of the Autobahn and into a large field, northwest of the city. We go into the field and circle back so that we are close to the opening into the field and where we can see down into the city. The other vehicles follow us into the field. Soon there are hundreds of vehicles filling the huge field. From the hill, we can see the large church which looks over the city. This is a beautiful scene, but I know that there are enemy troops within the city and beyond.

Trucks come up carrying pontoons to make a bridge. They pull off of the Autobahn and down into the city to where the Lahn passes through. The engineers are working to get the bridge across so we can continue. Evidently someone fires on them, because they scatter and then one of them gets a bazooka and fires it towards the church. The Germans are known to use church steeples for observation posts and for snipers.

Guys are moving around through the vehicles. The lieutenant has gone to check with the other officers, to see what we are to do next. The radio operator that lost his carbine comes over to my halftrack and asks if I have any food. I dig out a K ration for him and get one out for myself and the driver. I also give him one of my candy bars that I just got. We sit around eating and wondering what we are going to be doing next. About this time, a jeep drives up and the lieutenant riding in it says for us to move out, that we are blocking the other vehicles and we need to move. The driver starts forward, following the jeep.

We move out of the field, back across the Autobahn and down towards the river. I get in the ring mount and man the .50 caliber machine gun. I look back and there are several self propelled 105's following us and behind them are all the other vehicles. The other operator is back by the radios. We follow the jeep down the bank of the river and up to the pontoon bridge. The engineers motion the jeep forward and it slowly starts across the bridge. When it is over, we move on to the bridge. The halftrack sways around as we cross, but we make it safely across.

We follow the jeep as it goes through the town. We go through the streets and work our way back to the Autobahn, on the east side of the river. When we reach the Autobahn, we turn on to it and start moving again. We go out east of Limburg. We are on a high rise, following it along, with a higher bank on the north side of the road. The south side of the road has a berm shielding us from the wide valley leading down to the river. We are moving along at a good pace when we get to a place where there is a break in the berm. A shell goes right across the hood of the halftrack and crashes into the bank on the north side of the road. It passes close enough that I could have reached out and touched it. I look back and the other operator is laying on the floor, trying to dig deeper with his fingers.

We continue on across the opening until we are back behind the berm again. The self propelled 105 behind us is hit in the side, just back of the front. The one behind it is hit right in the middle and the one behind it is hit in the side, right at the back. The next shell goes behind the next 105. The rest of the vehicles hold up where they are protected. In just a matter of minutes, we have lost three of our cannons and I do not know how many men. The last 105 shot at, goes across the median and around the vehicles that are knocked out and joins us behind the berm.

I jump out of the halftrack and run over to the side of the road and look over the bank. I see a German tank moving away from us and going southeast. It is probably the one that shot at us. To the southwest is another German tank. I see two German soldiers going across the field. They are several hundred yards away, well out of the effective range of my carbine, but I aim over them and fire four rounds at them. It must have been close, because they start running and make a dive for something piled in the field. I do not know if it is a pile of sugar beets, a hay stack or a hidden pill box.

I go back to the halftrack and get the .30 caliber machine gun and go back to the bank. I put the gun on the bank and start firing at the remaining tank. I know that I can't do any damage to it with this gun, but I can keep those inside buttoned up until we can get the big guns turned on it. I can only shoot a few rounds at a time because with the gun on the ground, the empties pile up and block its operation. While I am firing at the tank, they get the other two 105's around to where they can put direct fire on the tank. It is not long before they knock out the tank and set it on fire.

The lieutenant in the jeep yells for us to come on and get out of there. I carry the machine gun back and stick it in the mount on the side of the halftrack and get in to the ring mount holding the .50 caliber machine gun. The other radio operator has gone back to his own halftrack, I guess. Our lieutenant has not shown up, so it is just the driver and me now. The jeep takes off down the Autobahn and we follow with the self propelled 105 right behind us. I look back and do not see anyone else, but I guess they will come as soon as they get around the knocked out vehicles.

We are really moving now and when we hit the next open space in the berm, the drivers open up the engines all the way. The oval tracks on the halftrack are almost round now from the speed they are turning. We keep going east and when we reach one place where the road is at its highest point, there is no bank on the north side and we see a battery of German horse drawn artillery going along the side of a forest. The lieutenant has the 105 come up there and get in position to fire on them.

The lieutenant hollers for us to set up a machine gun to protect their rear. I get the .30 caliber machine gun and the driver gets the tripod for it to set on and we go to the side of the road. There are woods to the south, but a wide opening right in back of the 105. He puts the tripod down there and I start to put the machine gun on the tripod and my field jacket swings out and the trigger on the machine gun catches in the button hole in the coat. It fires and when it does, that causes it to fire again and again. It is firing and I can't do anything about it. I wonder how long I can hold that gun with it getting hotter by the second. After what seems forever, the belt twists and the gun stops firing. I finish mounting it on the tripod and am ready in case the Germans try to come up between the trees. The lieutenant asks if someone is coming up from the rear and I tell him "Not now." I am embarrassed about what happened. It could have happened to anybody, but I am not just anybody; I am me. I know how to handle weapons better than that.

In the meantime, the 105 is firing round after round into the German artillery. When they have destroyed the guns, the lieutenant tells us to load up again and get ready to go on. I am glad I did not have to watch the shells hitting those horses. I can see them laying in the field. Some are still kicking. I do not see any German soldiers, but I am sure that there are a lot of them dead too. The cannons are wrecked among the horses

CHAPTER LXIX

We start back down the road. I have my fingers on the triggers of the .50 caliber machine gun and am looking in every direction, turning the gun on the ring mount as I do. We are way behind the German lines and may be attacked at any time. We just keep rolling down the road toward the southeast. When evening comes and it starts to get dark, we pull off of the Autobahn into a small village, only about a dozen houses. No white flags here, they did not have time to put them up. But we do not see any people. Something has alerted them to our arrival.

We pull the halftrack up against the side of the first house. On the adjacent side, they park the jeep. The self propelled 105 is parked against the side of the last house in the group. This way, we have a machine gun covering each end. The lieutenant decides to make the first house our headquarters. It has been a long day and we are all hungry. The guys in the 105 have a few K rations and I have several, so I pass them around so that everyone has one. We gas up the halftrack and the jeep from the cans on the side of the halftrack. Then we carry the rest of the cans over to the 105 and pour it into their gas tank. We have enough to operate for at least another day. We will not be getting supplied here soon.

I am sure that the lieutenant wonders what we have gotten ourselves into. As commander of this group, he is responsible to make the decisions about what to do. We are out of range of the FM radios and I can't send anything on the CW radio that is not encoded and we do not have any way to do that. It appears that no one is coming behind us tonight and we certainly can't go back tonight. We will have to make the best of it. There are eight of us and we are over fifteen miles behind the German front lines.

We have the two .50 caliber machine guns covering the ends of the village and the one .30 caliber directed back towards the Autobahn. The 105 is pointed out to the open area to the north. We have five carbines and three submachine guns (grease guns). We have lots of ammunition, except for the 105, which only has about half of their rounds left. But we really have no way to dig in to defend this position, since the Germans could come from any direction. We decide to have two guys stand guard at a time, one at each end. The others will try to get some rest.

I take the first tour of guard. I find a place where I can stand back against a building and use what light is available to look three different directions. The lieutenant and the two drivers go into the house across the street and the gunners put one man on guard and the other three are in the house next to the 105. I have only been on guard for a little bit when I hear the sound of incoming artillery. Usually I would fall flat on the ground, but I decide to press tight against the building. A piece of shrapnel slams into the wall beside my left leg as the shell explodes. Then I hear the pieces of shrapnel rattling off of the tile roofs of the houses.

A few minutes later, another round comes in and explodes as it hits the roof of one of the other houses. Another few minutes and another round comes in and explodes as it hits another house. So far they have not hit the two houses where our guys are. I figure that we are safe from attack as long as they are shelling us, but if they stop, it may be the sign that a counter attack has started. I strain my eyes trying to see if I can see any movement. There are no more rounds, just those three. But it is a sign that they definitely know that we are here. I do not know why they do not attack. There have to be more of them than there are of us.

I stay on guard until two in the morning and then go into the house where the lieutenant and the two drivers are. I enter through the basement door. I use my flash light and see that there is a keg in the basement. I open the spigot and using my finger, I lick it and I can tell it is white wine. I see a couple of glasses and fill them with the wine. I taste it, and it seems to be good wine. I carry them up the stairs to the room, where the other three guys are. One guy is asleep, but the lieutenant and the other driver are still awake. I hand them the wine and tell them where I found it. The driver goes out to take over my guard post and I go into a bedroom and lie down on the bed. It is after two o'clock in the morning and I have been awake over twenty-seven hours. I think, "what a way to spend a birthday," and with that, I am asleep.

I wake up and it is just getting light outside. I get up and see that the halftrack driver is in the room. He says that the lieutenant and his driver have gone over to the other house where the 105 crew is staying. I have a hard time believing that the Germans did not attack last night, and I do not know what we would have done if they had. I go outside and look around. Three of the houses have been hit by the fire last night and there are shrapnel and pieces of roof tile littering the street. I climb into the halftrack and dig out a couple of breakfast K rations. I tear open one and open the can of ham, eggs and potatoes and a package of the biscuits. I dump the can out onto one of the cracker like biscuits and put another biscuit over the top and make a breakfast sandwich. I open my mouth wide and bite off a chunk. It is not very good, but it nourishment and right now, I need that. I drink enough water from my canteen to wash it down and then go back in the house.

I give the other breakfast K ration to the driver and then we walk outside of the house. We look out at the field and two Germans are walking across the field toward us. They are carrying a white flag. We both jerk the carbines off of our shoulders and point them toward the Germans. As they get closer, we can tell that one of the men is an officer and the other is an enlisted man. We wait for them to approach and when they get close, the enlisted man says "Take us to your leader." I motion toward the house where the lieutenant is and we follow in behind them.

We walk into the house and the first room is empty, so I tell them to sit down there. They sit in a couple of the chairs and I go into the next room to get the lieutenant. I walk into the room and the lieutenant and a couple of the gunners are looking at a map, trying to figure just where we are. I say "Lieutenant, there are a couple of Germans here that want to talk to you." He says, "Tell them I will be there in a little bit." I go back in the room and tell the Germans that our commander will be with them in a minute. I don't want them to know that the highest ranking officer we have is a lieutenant and I sure do not want them to know that there are only eight of us. But they probably already know that, if they know we are here.

While we are waiting for the lieutenant, the driver is standing there with his carbine in one hand and the breakfast K ration in the other. For some reason, he hands the K ration to the German officer. He shows it to the enlisted man, who reads what it says and says something in German. I assume he is telling the officer what it is. When he says that, the officer turns to us and says, "Danke." I know enough German to know that means thank you. About that time, the lieutenant comes out and asks them what they want. I thought that since they came under a white flag, they might want us to surrender. But the enlisted man says, "He wants to surrender."

The lieutenant replies "OK, you are surrendered."

The enlisted man says again, "He wants to surrender."

The lieutenant says "You have surrendered."

The enlisted man says, "You do not understand. He wants to surrender his battalion!"

We stand there for a little bit with our mouths hanging open. Then the lieutenant asks where the battalion is? And he says they are located in the woods across the field. We talk some more and it appears from what they say, that the colonel told his men that he would go turn himself in and if everything was okay, he would come back and get them, so they could surrender too. I guess when the driver handed them the K ration, they decided that the Americans would treat them well and that it was safe enough for the rest of the troops to surrender.

We make plans to carry this out. The lieutenant has them turn the 105 so that it is aimed at the woods on the other side of the field. If anything happens, they are to shell the woods and anyone coming out of them. Then the jeep driver and the German enlisted man get in the front of the jeep and the colonel and the lieutenant get in the back. We follow in the halftrack. The lieutenant says "Lovell, you make sure you cover us with that .50." That I intend to do. I realize our chances of being killed or captured are very good. I have a German rifle and bayonet in the halftrack that I picked up earlier and I throw them away. The driver has a German belt and he hides it under the seat of the halftrack. If we are captured, we do not want them to have an excuse to kill us.

We move slowly out across the field with the German enlisted man holding up the white flag. When we are about two hundred yards from the woods, we stop. We are sitting out in the middle of a bare field knowing that there are Germans all around. We are a perfect target for a mortar shell or a machine gun attack, or for that matter, about anything that they might want to send; we are in range. The colonel gets out and takes the white flag and starts toward the woods. We keep the enlisted man as hostage, but a lot of good that would do, if they decide to open fire on us. It is a nervous time. I have my thumbs on the triggers of the .50 and am aiming at the woods, where the colonel went in.

It seems like ages, just sitting out here in the open, but really is not very long before the colonel comes out of the trees, carrying the white flag and behind him are the German soldiers with their hands on their heads. There are two or three hundred soldiers coming across the field. They turn the jeep around to lead them back to the village and we stay in position covering them, until they pass and then we follow behind them.

When we get back to the village, the first sergeant is there and with him are two truckloads of infantrymen. The first sergeant is driving our battalion commander's command car. He was sent to bring us back. It seems that we were supposed to have turned off of the Autobahn several miles back and gone north. By going ahead on the Autobahn, we are getting into Third Army territory and they are not happy about it. General Patton does not like for someone to get ahead of him.

We turn the prisoners over to the infantry and they start marching them back on the Autobahn toward the rear. We get our vehicles out and start back. The first sergeant takes the lieutenant's jeep and leads off. The lieutenant and his driver get in the Dodge command car, in second place, we follow them in the halftrack and the self propelled 105 brings up the rear.

There will be no medals for breaking through the German lines and advancing over fifteen miles, destroying an artillery battery and capturing a German battalion, instead, we catch hell for invading another army's territory. Such is war.

CHAPTER LXX

We pull on to the Autobahn and start back west, heading back to where we were supposed to have turned off, if we had of known. We soon catch up with the prisoners being taken back to go into a POW camp. We have not gone very far past the prisoners when suddenly the jeep goes flying into the air and rolls over into the ditch. The first sergeant is thrown from the jeep and hits the ground on his feet. He runs back down the bank and out on the road just as the command car is coming up. They slow down and the lieutenant reaches out to take the first sergeant's hand and swings him up and into the back seat of the command car.

As soon as they have him aboard, the driver gives the command car the gas and they race down the Autobahn as fast as it will go. We take off as fast as we can and the self propelled 105 is coming as fast as they can too. I never saw the gun that fired on the jeep, but it was probably one of the tanks that shot us up yesterday.

The German SS troops are known for shooting their own men if they surrender. Those prisoners may be in for a rough time, before they get back to Limburg.

We slow down just a little, so that the 105 can keep up with us and keep moving west. I am watching everywhere I can for danger and I keep my thumbs on the triggers of the .50. We get back just a little way east of Limburg and the first sergeant shows us where we were supposed to turn off of the Autobahn. We go two or three miles north of the Autobahn and run into some of our battalion. They are sitting on a hill outside of a town that is down in a valley. They are waiting for a special tank to come up. It is equipped with loud-speakers so they can send a message to the town.

When the tank arrives, they point the large speakers toward the town and then have one of the guys, who can speak German, get on the microphone and tell all the German soldiers in the town to come out or we will start shelling. It is not long after they make the announcement that one older man comes out carrying a white flag. He says that he is the burgermeister, or mayor of the town. He says that the town was full of German troops, but they all pulled out last night and left the area.

The commander sends a couple of tanks into the town and they signal that they have not found any troops, so we all move down into the town. Several of the units move on through the town and our firing batteries set up on the far side of the town. Headquarters takes over a house in the center of the town. The driver pulls our halftrack up next to a house. When we get set, several of the guys come over and want to know what we did yesterday. We tell them, but I don't think they believe us. I guess that the lieutenant is having to explain to the brass why we did what we did. I keep thinking they will call one of us enlisted men in to verify what he has said. But I guess that now that they have us back where we belong, they want everyone to forget it.

I am glad to see that the cooks are setting up the kitchen across the road from us. I passed out the last of the K rations about noon. I am glad that I still have some of the candy that my mother sent to me. That wrapped in waxed paper was one lump, but I could break off pieces to eat. I even have time now to read the comics and other papers she used to pack the box. With what candy I have eaten, I am not quite so hungry, but I am still sleepy. I have not had much sleep the last two or three nights. Maybe I can get some tonight.

I have some time, so I write a letter home. I tell them that I got the package on my birthday and that I have been in battle and came out okay. I don't know how much the censors will cut out. I get the letter written and hand it off to be mailed. The gas supply truck has moved up to where we are and I get enough cans of gas to refill the gas tanks and also fill the outside racks. While I am doing that, one of the sergeants comes out of headquarters and says that they have received information that the garrison at Limburg had been reinforced by a German SS Panzer Division. That is what we went through yesterday. He says that the Germans were low on fuel for their tanks and that is probably why the one tank was not moving and got destroyed.

I notice that the cooks are about ready to serve supper, so I ask one of the operators if he will man the radios while I go get my supper. Good news, they have received some hamburger meat and we are having hamburger steak with onions, some real potatoes fried, some peas, and apple sauce. Of course, there is the GI bread that has caught up with us. This is the best we have had for several days.

As evening gets closer, we get our assignments for the night. I will be on the radios early and then will be off until tomorrow morning. That is great news because I can get more sleep than usual and I really need it. I get the halftrack ready for night and settle in by the radios. The CW radio sounds off and I take down the message and take it to the headquarters. The FM radio is not very active, but they do have a couple of fire missions while I am on.

Things seem to be quiet and since the Germans have left here, I decide to do something different. I take off my field jacket and lay it on the floor beside my bed roll. I put my carbine on it and then take off my boots, socks, pants and shirt and lay them on the pile. I am down to my GI long handles, first time I have had my clothes off for several days. I slide into the sleeping bag and at first it feels funny not to have all of my clothes on. Then I go to sleep and sleep like a log until morning.

I get up in the morning in time to get in line for breakfast. We have sausage and eggs, tomato juice, toast with some grape jelly and coffee. The eggs are powdered, but they have done a good job of fixing them. After breakfast, I go to the halftrack and clean both machine guns. The .50 has not been fired, so I just wipe the dust off of it and run a patch through the barrel. The .30 caliber takes more work. I field strip it and clean the carbon off, lightly oil it and put a new belt of ammo on it.

I get the halftrack opened up for travel, while the driver checks the water and oil and greases the suspension. The trip yesterday and the day before gave it a workout. We get the word that we are moving out again. The lieutenant joins us and the major takes his position in the jeep in front of us. There is not much traffic on this road, so we move on out. As we go out the north side of the town, we start seeing piles of abandoned materials. Mostly German equipment, several rifles, machine guns and the round magazines for the machine guns. I am not sure what happened here, whether they left it when they retreated or they dropped it to surrender.

We are moving mostly north and a little east now. We are making good time. It gets close to noon and I realize that I forgot to get something for dinner. I am not the only one that notices. The lieutenant asks me what is on the menu for dinner? I confess that I have fallen down on the job and do not have anything. We luck out. Passing us on the left is a three-quarter-ton truck. I look in the back of the truck and there are several cases of C rations. The three-quarter-ton is only moving a little faster than we are, so while they are along side, I climb over the side of the halftrack and jump into the back of the three-quarter-ton.

I grab one of the cases of C rations and motion for the lieutenant to move to the back of the halftrack. I throw the case to him and then reach out and grab the side of the halftrack and climb back in. The two guys in the three quarter ton never knew a thing about it. The lieutenant laughs and says that he never ceases to be amazed at me.

The two guys in the jeep behind us saw what I did and they start motioning me to give them one. I grab the four cans and stand in the back of the halftrack and pitch them to the guy riding in the jeep.

He stands up and leans out over the hood to catch them. Then I get to eat mine. It is ham and lima beans.

We are making about the best time today that we have made since we started. That is, except for when we went racing down the Autobahn. But we did not have a bunch of other vehicles slowing us up there. At the rate we are going, will cover thirty or forty miles today.

Late in the afternoon, we stop in a town and this time we park beside a small hotel, or large gasthaus, which is a place where they serve meals and have a few rooms to rent out to travelers. I go in, pick out a room, and get one with a bed this time. Not much of a bed, but I unroll my bedroll on it to stake my claim and then I go back outside to stay with the halftrack.

The fuel truck comes and I get enough gas to replace what we have used. When I have refueled, I put the top up to get ready for night. I notice we are low on water in the can, so I find a place to get water. They still have running water in this town, but probably not for long, because the light plant has shut down.

I notice a jeep pull up in front of the building that headquarters is using and a guy gets out with a duffle bag, bedroll and pack. He must be a replacement, but unlike the others we have received, this one has staff sergeant stripes. The sergeant goes into headquarters and in a little bit, he comes out with the first sergeant and they walk over to my halftrack. The first sergeant introduces him as Sergeant Solow and says that he will be assigned to the battalion executive officer, so he will be with us in the halftrack. I welcome him and help him stow his duffle bag in the box on the back of the halftrack and help him hang his pack in the halftrack. Then I tell him to take his bed roll and stake a claim in one of the rooms in the building.

He comes back in a little bit and says that he even found an empty bed too. He says his name is Herb Solow and he is from Brooklyn, New York. He seems very friendly and I am glad to have him join us. His job will be mostly paperwork, but he will be riding in the halftrack during the day.

While we are standing around the halftrack talking, one of the tanks drives up. They had been guarding the rear and have caught up with us. The sergeant, who is the tank commander, climbs out of the tank and walks over to us. He wants to show us his combat boot. It seems that his grease gun went off in the tank. The bullet went down along the side of his boot and cut through the shoe part. The boot is just held on by the top. He sits down and takes the boot off and removes his sock. He has a red mark down the side of his foot where the bullet traveled. He says that the bullet may still be ricocheting around inside of the tank.

CHAPTER LXXI

I have a later shift tonight. I hate to get up in the middle of the night to go on the radio, but by doing that, I get to sleep more. I just have to do the one shift. I go get in my bed as soon as I get relieved on the radios. I sleep soundly until someone wakes me to go on duty. I wander out in the cold night air and when I get in the halftrack, it feels even colder. I wonder if they have run the engine to keep the batteries charged. I go to the front and sit in the driver's seat, turn on the switch and press the starter button. It gives a low moan, and that is it. They have not kept the batteries charged and now I can't start the halftrack.

I go back and shut off the radios so they will not draw any more juice from the battery. Then I go over to one of the other halftracks and ask the operator if he will move the halftrack up beside of mine, so I can jump start the engine. He has to shut down his radios too, to make sure that it does not damage them and then he pulls it up beside of mine. I dig in one of the tool boxes and find a set of jumper cables. I hook them up to the two halftracks and then try again to start it. This time, it catches and the engine fires and it is running again. I remove the cables and the other operator moves the his halftrack back to its position.

Now that mine is running, I go back in and turn on the radios again. They come on and I call on the FM radio to make sure that there have not been any messages for me. After going to all of that trouble, I go dig around in my things until I find a tropical Hershey bar and put it down on the transmission. As long as I have to run the engine for awhile, I just as well use it to make a chocolate bar edible. Tomorrow, I will give a lecture to everyone operating the radios and remind them to be sure they do not go too long without charging the batteries. I know what happened. The operator before me tonight is used to only having the FM radio. He does not realize how much current the CW radio uses, in addition to the FM.

I dig out my chocolate bar. It could have used a little more heat, but it is not too bad. I eat it and check the time and I have used up over half of my shift. I dig out some of the papers I got in my package and read them again. It seems that there is always something that I miss, even though I read them from front to back and back to front. Anything from home is so welcome.

I go wake up my relief and tell him to make sure that he keeps the batteries charged, then I go crawl back into my sleeping bag. I get to sleep until morning. I wake up in time to go get in line for breakfast. When I have finished eating, I go relieve the operator on the radios and then get the halftrack ready to go again. The driver comes out and checks the vehicle and Sgt. Solow comes out bringing his things. We three are ready and waiting to get on the road.

The lieutenant comes out and we all load up and the driver starts the engine. The jeep is in front of us, just waiting for the major. When he comes, we move out onto the road and move forward. We are going more east now than north. We move through the German army on the roads, leaving the main forces to the side. The infantry divisions behind us will have to gather them up. We have cut off many of the German forces and they are surrendering by the thousands. We take those we capture and send them back with a couple of guards and turn them over to the infantry, to move them into the POW camps.

Sgt. Kazaris is often detailed to take the prisoners back to the rear. One of the guys that went with him, comes back and tells us that Kazaris shot some of the prisoners. He said he made them run and if any fell down, he shot them. I guess word of this got back to headquarters, because now anyone taking prisoners back has to get a receipt for them, showing how many were delivered. Kazaris is Polish and he does have any love for the Germans.

The lieutenant is standing in the ring mount, Solow is sitting behind him and I am on back, in front of the radios. When it gets time for dinner, I move some of the things in the back and uncover the rest of the C rations that I stole yesterday. We do not have any way to heat them while we are moving, so we all eat them cold. Not the best, but they are filling and nutritious. Not many of the others have anything to eat. The lieutenant tells Solow that he is lucky to get with me, because I always find something to eat.

We have turned back more north now and are still making good time. We have probably gone another forty miles today. By evening, we have reached the Eder River and pull into a town on the river bank and prepare to spend the night. They have picked one of the buildings for headquarters and the lieutenant and Sgt. Solow go there to work. The driver and I service the halftrack. I fill the gas tank and put the top up. The driver checks the oil and water and greases the suspension.

The cooks have set up the kitchen and are preparing the evening meal. While we are waiting on supper, the fuel truck arrives and we get enough cans to replace those that I used earlier. The fuel truck leaves and a three-quarter-ton truck arrives with mail. They set up right in front of my halftrack and start passing out the mail. I get a letter and two packages. These were mailed a long time ago, but just now caught up with me.

I take my mail and retire to the inside of the halftrack. I would like to see what I have without opening the packages in front of everyone. I will get more for myself this way. I open the oldest package first. The box is really beat up and it is a wonder it has held together. I open the box and then pull out the packing. It is made up of the comics and the school papers again. I lay them aside and see what else is wrapped inside. I have two Hershey bars, two Mars bars and two Snickers bars. There is a package of homemade candy too, and a sack of roasted in the shell peanuts. Down in the bottom is a sack of cookie crumbs. I taste them and they are peanut butter.

I cut the string holding the other package and open it up. It has not been traveling as long as the other one and is in better shape. I have more comics and papers and some clippings from different papers. This time Mom sent some chocolate chip cookies with pecans in them, half dozen Hershey bars and some salted peanuts. I am truly grateful for these packages. I hold them close to me and think about where they came from. My mother had to sacrifice to be able to send all of this to me.

Before I can read my letter, I hear someone calling out that chow is ready. I go outside and wait until one of the operators is coming with his food and ask him to stay beside the halftrack and listen to the radios while I get mine. There is not much of a line by the time I get there and I am able to get my food without much trouble. They have fixed spam with pineapple, green beans, mashed potatoes and gravy, canned pears and some GI bread with grape jelly. I fill my mess kit and go back to the halftrack to eat.

After I get through eating, I catch another operator and get him to stand by until I can wash my mess kit and take my bed roll into the house. When I get back out, the communications sergeant comes by and gives out the night's assignments. I will be working the first and last shifts. That means I have to work late and get up early.

The good thing about being on duty here is that I have a light, a place to sit and I can read the letter and the papers that my mother sent, in peace and quiet. I get out one of the candy bars and very slowly eat it and savor it, as I read her letter. She is able to put more information in a single letter than anyone I know.

When it is time for my shift to be over, I take all of my things and put them away in my musette bag out of sight. I do not mind sharing what I get, but I want to be the one to do it. I go wake my relief and then crawl in my sleeping bag for a few hours sleep.

Someone shakes me awake and I crawl back out of my sleeping bag and go back out to the halftrack. I start the halftrack and charge the battery while I re-read the letter and the papers from home. I can't resist, I get out another of the candy bars and eat it. I try to save them and spread out eating them, but my willpower is weak.

I spend the rest of my shift reading the papers over and over. I can hear the cooks working and decide it must be getting close to daylight. I take a chance and rush over to the mess and beg a cup of coffee. They never seem to mind giving me a cup early in the morning. I guess it is because they think anyone that is up before they are should be entitled to a little luxury. I know where there are some cookie crumbs that will need some coffee to wash them down.

Sgt. Solow is up early and comes out to the halftrack and brings his bedroll to put away. I call him Solow and he asks me to call him Herb. That is fine with me. He goes and gets a cup of coffee too and I share some cookie crumbs with him. We visit and he tells me that he thinks that I should know that he can't be taken prisoner. He says that when they see that "H" on his dog tags that they will kill him. I say, "H?" And he says, "Hebrew. I am Jewish." I tell him that I understand. I tell him that I do not have any desire to be a POW either and that if it gets to that point, we will just fight it out. He thanks me.

One of the operators comes out of the house and I tell him to stick by the radios while Herb and I go get our breakfast. I am surprised, but he does not question me, just tells me to hurry back. We get our breakfast and Herb and I sit at the halftrack and eat. We come from totally different ways of life, but I like him and think we will be friends.

While we are eating, one of the sergeants comes out of headquarters and says that they just received word about a battle behind us. That just after we left the town, just north of the Autobahn, German SS troops moved in and took it over. They dug in and the army moved an infantry division up there to try to get them out. They are still fighting. I remember taking my clothes off the night we stayed there because it was such a quiet place and there were no

German troops around. Boy, was I wrong. It seems every time I think things are safe, I find out differently.

CHAPTER LXXII

We take off in the morning heading mostly north, toward the city of Warburg. Traffic is heavy and we slowly move along. Sometimes we are passing vehicles and sometimes vehicles are passing us, but the road is full of traffic moving forward. When it gets about noon, I open up the case of K rations and pass them out. It was a good thing I thought about it before we left this morning. I waited until just before we left and went over to where the cook's helpers were loading the mess supply truck. I asked one of the helpers for some K rations for the men at noon and he grabbed a case and threw them to me. I carried them back to the halftrack and put them in the back.

We are in the outskirts of the city now and the highway follows along side of the railroad, which is about a block away. We can see people all along the railroad tracks and realize that they are looting the train cars parked there. There is no one to stop them. The German army has fled out of the city and almost every house has a white flag hanging out of the upstairs window to welcome us.

We are moving along, slowly passing another column, when Herb calls to me to come to where he is the back of the ring mount. He points over the side of the halftrack and says "Look at that." I look where he is pointing and it is the back of a three-quarter-ton truck. But this time, instead of rations, it is carrying three cases of champagne. One case has been broken open and you can see the bottles laying there. I have had experience in this kind of thing, so I climb over the side of the half track and into the back of the truck. I take out a bottle of champagne and pitch it to Herb who sets it down in the halftrack. I keep throwing bottles until I have seven and we are almost past the truck and then I grab the side at the back of the halftrack and climb back inside. The two guys in the truck have no idea that anything is going on. We stow the champagne in the back and keep going down the road.

We have gone a few more miles when Herb yells "There is a German soldier." He jumps out of the halftrack and takes off after him. I follow him out of the halftrack, but the lieutenant stops me. He tells me to come back, saying "Lovell, I don't want to have to go out and round you up." We watch as Herb runs down the street and turns into an alley. In a little while, he comes back and says that he captured the German soldier, but he was a real old guy and was not armed. He said he was sorry that he went after him. He turned him over to some other troops that were there.

While we are stopped beside the road, I find some K98 Mauser rifles that have been thrown down. I keep one and the rest, I pull out the bolts, stick the barrels into the bumper on the halftrack and bend them in a "U" shape. Some of the German helmets we find, we line up under the tread of the halftrack and run over them, smashing them. We try to destroy as much of the German equipment as we can.

We stop in the outskirts of Warburg and take over what buildings that we need for our use. The headquarters sets up on the east side of the street and we park the halftrack next to a building on the west side. The building that we picked was a laundry on the ground floor and had living quarters upstairs. I carry my bedroll upstairs to one of the rooms. I go back outside and stay with the radios. I will get some relief later on. In the meantime, I watch all of the vehicles pouring into the city.

When another operator takes over for me, I go inside and look around. I find a bunch of wax they use in the laundry to iron the clothes. The wax is in round blocks with a square hole in the center. We have been using candles that we made by scraping the wax from K ration boxes, for some time. They are small and do not put out much light. I decide that I should make some candles from these wax blocks. I stack five blocks on top of each other, stick a piece of tent rope down the center for a wick and then using a can, I melt enough wax to fill the holes around the rope. I make a half dozen candles this way.

In the evening, we light four of the candles in the room and we have plenty of light to read or write letters. These are the best candles we have had. We let them burn all evening. I do my shift on the radios in the night and then get to go back to the room and go to bed.

I wake up to someone yelling "I am going to kill him." I realize his tirade is directed at me. I ask what is the matter? He says look at me. It takes a little bit for me to get my eyes open, but when I do, I see that his face looks like a black face minstrel player. I look at the others and they all look the same. He says, "You and your damned candles."

I say "I am sorry, but you are the ones that lit them. I did not know they would put out black soot." It seems that the candles put soot into the air and during the night, it settled on everything in the room. The only part of us that was showing out of the sleeping bags was our heads and they are covered in soot.

We go get cans of water and start washing our heads and faces in our steel helmets. It is a mess, but we get as clean as we can. I ask them if they think I should throw the candles away and that brings on a burst of profanity. I have started to think it is funny, but they have not gotten to that point yet. We take our bedrolls outside and try to brush off the soot, but a lot of it remains embedded in the shelter half covering the bedroll.

It looks like we will be staying here for awhile longer. Some of the guys have been out scouting around and they say that there is a big railroad roundhouse not far up the road. When I get a break from the radios, I talk another guy into going with me to the roundhouse to see if we can find some lanterns that they use with the trains. I want to get some to make up for the candles.

We walk up the road until we come to the roundhouse and then go along the side until we find an entrance. This is a huge building. It has numerous tracks in it, all going to a center pivot where the engines can be turned around and put on outgoing tracks. There are several locomotives in the building. We look around for some lanterns and can't find any. We notice that every locomotive we can see has bullet holes in it, attesting to the effectiveness of the Air Corp. There are open windows every so often in the wall around the building, but they are about ten feet above the floor.

We keep going, trying to find where they keep their supplies, but the building is so huge that we never get there. Suddenly, the antiaircraft guns open up all over the city. We can hear a plane swooping in. I run to where I can see out of a window but all I can see is sky and then a plane crosses the sky and tracers are flying at it. We do not have any way to get out of the building, other than the way we came in. We start running back toward the entrance and by the time we reach it, the firing has stopped.

We walk back to the troops and ask what happened. They say that it was an American P-51, but that it had German markings on it. It was trying to bomb the railroad roundhouse, but that the anti-aircraft fire drove it off. I look at the other guy and he looks at me. There we were right in the middle of the target. I am glad they drove the plane off.

I still have some time before I have to go back on the radios, so I do some more exploring, but closer this time and not out in the middle of a target. I go through a couple of the buildings nearby. They have shops on the ground floor, but living quarters upstairs like the one where we are staying. I am upstairs in one of them and near the window, I find a German Nazi flag. It appears that they brought it in and put out the white flag. If we had pulled back out, they would have put the Nazi flag back out. I take it back to the halftrack and put it in the bottom of my duffle bag. I will send it home when I get a chance.

I have used up my time and go get on the radios again. I will have to stay here until later tonight when my relief will come on. The radios are relatively quiet this evening. No orders coming in and few fire missions. Once in awhile, some forward observer will see something and call for fire on it, but there are no organized positions near here, so there are not many rounds fired.

It is supper time, but from where I am, I can't see the mess. But I think they are getting ready to serve, because I see people moving in that direction. As one of the operators passes by, he says that he will relieve me soon. That is not something that we really want to do, but we each have to depend on someone to cover for us. He comes back in a few minutes carrying his food. He will stand by the halftrack and eat while I get my food.

I take my mess kit and go get in line. They have chicken and noodles tonight, not my favorite dish, but I am hungry and get a big spoonful. They have some peas and carrots, the GI bread and some pears. All but the bread was canned and then heated before serving. I carry it back to the halftrack. I start eating it and it does not do anything for me. I reach in the back of the halftrack and dig out a K ration and open it. I get out the canned meat and put it on the bread. I eat it and then take some of the cookie crumbs from my package and mix them with the pears and eat that.

I roll the top back up on the halftrack, put the shield down and get it ready for night. I have one thing here that they do not have in the room; I have a light to read by. I get out my letters and papers and reread them. Anything to pass the time. Before the night is over I break down and get out something from my packages to eat.

When it is time for my shift to end, I go wake up my relief and then go to the room and crawl into my sleeping bag for a few hours. It does not seem very long before someone wakes me and says it is time to go back out. It is harder now to go out of that warm place into the cold. The halftrack does not seem too cold and I know that they have kept the battery charged tonight. I have some time before I need to start the engine again. I have read everything in the halftrack, including today's "Stars & Stripes." I get out my New Testament and read some more of it. The print is so small and the light is so weak, that it is hard to see and I can only read for a short time. I get through the rest of my shift, go get the next operator and then crawl back into my sleeping bag until morning.

CHAPTER LXXIII

We get notice that we will be moving this morning. We load up our things and get ready to move out. It is not too difficult to get on the road now, since the bigger units have moved on up and most of the traffic is just supply vehicles. We move slowly through the city. This is different from most of the places we have seen. The German forces pulled out of the city and other than previous bombings, the part we are in is relatively unharmed. Many of the civilians are trying to get back to their regular life. Merchants are opening stores and people are trying to buy from the limited stock of supplies.

I thought we would go a long way today, but we only go a few miles and are still in the city. We stop and set up headquarters on the other side of the road and we go across too. We have just switched sides. I really can't see why we moved at all, but the army doesn't need a reason. We find a place to sleep in back of the buildings fronting the road. I watch as the mess goes around the corner to find a place to set up. It is not too far away, but I can't see it, so I will have to watch others to see when they are serving.

It does not appear that they will be serving anything for dinner, so I dig out a K ration from my stock and open it. It is a dinner ration and I do like the cheese with bacon bits in it. I just get started eating it when Herb and the lieutenant come out to the halftrack. They see me with the K ration and the lieutenant says that he knew that I would have some food, if anybody did. Then he asks if I have anymore. I go to the back and pull out a couple more dinner rations and hand them over. They find a place to sit and we eat our rations together.

When we finish our K rations, I tell them to hold on a minute and I go back to where I have my packages stowed and get out three candy bars. I pass them out and tell them that I even serve dessert at my mess hall. Herb says it has been a long time since he had a Milky Way and it really tastes good. The lieutenant gets one of the Snickers and he says it is the best thing he has had in months. I tell them they need to thank my mother because I am sure she went to a lot of trouble to get them. I take the other Snickers and slowly nibble on it, savoring each tiny bite. I am careful to not drop any crumbs.

I stay right there until supper time and then get a short break to go get my supper. I bring it back to the halftrack to eat it. I get my schedule for the night. I will be on early, get a break and then have to come back on in the middle of the night. I leave the top down so that I can watch what is going on until it gets dark. Then I put the top up, check it for light and crawl back inside. I turn on the light and read the "Stars & Stripes" that came a little bit ago. It shows massive gains by troops all along the front. But I notice that there is really no one out in front of us, even though we have not moved much the last few days.

My relief comes and I get to go back to the house where I will be sleeping and get some rest. I unroll my bedroll and slide into my sleeping bag. I am glad to be able to get some rest and go right to sleep. I wake up when they come to get me to go back on the radio. I drag my weary body back out to the halftrack and inside. I decide to run the engine and charge the battery just in case they have not done it. While it is running, I am really thirsty and get out my canteen. It only has a swallow of water left in it. I drink that and I am still thirsty. I decide to fill my canteen and go out to get the water can off of the fender.

When I get outside, I find that the water can is missing. I look around and I can't find it or any other water can anywhere close. I get back in the halftrack and I am very unhappy with who ever took the water can and did not bring it back. Now that I know I don't have any water, I get all the more thirsty. I don't have anything to drink. Then I remember the champagne hidden in the back. I crawl back and pull out a bottle and open it. I take a drink and it goes down really well. I put the cork back in it and set it back.

In a few minutes, I am thirsty again and get the bottle out again. This time I just leave it out. It seems the more I drink, the thirstier I get. I keep taking sips of the champagne. About this time, the CW radio comes on and I answer. They have a message. I tell them to send it. I copy it and then they tell me they have another message. And I take it down too. Then I take the two messages to the headquarters and hand them to the sergeant in charge. I hurry back to the halftrack just in time to receive another message. I take it down and deliver it too.

When I get back to the half track, I am thirsty again, so I drink some more champagne. Then the CW radio comes on again and they have another message. I have never had this many messages in one night before. I take it down and deliver it. I go back to the halftrack and drink some more champagne. After awhile, I look at the time and see that I have not only done my shift but the next guy's too. So I go wake up the guy that is to take over after him and then go get back in my sleeping bag.

I wake up in the morning and look over at my helmet. There is no way that helmet is going to go over my huge head. I have a headache like nothing before. I am really hung over. It is not enough that I feel so bad, but one of the sergeants from headquarters comes looking for me. He tells me that the messages that I took last night were all screwed up and headquarters is really mad. He says they know that I got drunk on duty and he is not sure what is going to happen.

I will be lucky if I only get busted back to private. I may get a court marshal. The least I will get is battery punishment. I go find the water can and pour myself a canteen cup full and drink it. It felt good, but I am having trouble walking now. I am drunk all over again. I go find a place in one of the buildings where I can hide out for awhile and lay down and go back to sleep. I sleep a couple of hours and wake up feeling only slightly better than the first time.

I go out to the halftrack and the operator there tells me that they are ready to have my hide, that they had him call back and have them send the messages again that I took last night, and he got them and delivered them to headquarters. He says that he does not know what they will do to me, but it will probably not be good. He leaves and I sit down and wonder what will happen.

Herb comes out and says that they were ready to really unload on me, but then they found out that it was not my fault. The code clerk got drunk too and he messed up the decoding. Well, they only have one code clerk and they have to have him, so they can't very well do anything to me, unless they punish him too. I know how to operate the code machine, but I don't want them to know it. When they got the messages again they found that I had only missed three letters in four messages, which is way above average performance. I have a feeling though that they will not let me off easy.

I keep a low profile the rest of the day. I go get my meals and take them back to the halftrack to eat. I stick by the radios and am relieved that there are not any CW messages coming in. Evening comes and the communications sergeant comes around and gives me my assignment. He asks me if I think I can stay sober tonight. I tell him I am sorry, that I did not intend to have that happen, and I will not let it happen again.

I pull my shifts on the radios and get what sleep I can. The shifts I have, do not leave me much time for rest. But I do get to sleep the last part of the night and only get up when I think that breakfast is about over.

About the middle of the morning, the first sergeant comes out and tells me I am being assigned to a different job. I am not sur-

prised, but I wonder just what dirty job they have in mind for me.
He says that I will be assigned to the liaison section, that I need to
get my things gathered up and moved to another halftrack. He tells
me that one of the lieutenants is the liaison officer and that Sgt.
Solow will be going too, and that one of the drivers has been assigned also. He never mentions what happened last night. I guess
they figure this will get rid of me.

Another operator comes out to take over for me. I start to find
Herb and meet him coming toward the halftrack. I ask if he knows
which halftrack we will be using and he says that the driver has gone
to get it and will bring it there, so that we can transfer our things. I
start getting my things together and after all of this time in the same
halftrack, I have things all over it.

We get all of our things moved over. I ask Herb if I should
transfer the champagne too and he says, "Hell yes, you have already got in trouble over it, might just as well keep it." I pitch the
bottles to him and he stows them away. We get all of our things
located and stowed away. Then we go to one of the three-quarter-
ton trucks to get the lieutenant's things. The driver has his things
already on board. The lieutenant comes out and hands us his things
to put away. When he finishes, he asks if we are ready to go and we
tell him that we are.

I ask where we are going and he says we are going to go to CCR
(Combat Command Reserve) headquarters. That we will be liaison
between them and our unit. We start off and when we get to where
the mess is set up, I ask the lieutenant if we can stop for just a minute. He says okay, if you need to.

I go to the mess sergeant and tell him that I have been assigned
to the liaison section and we will be away from the unit and not able
to eat at a mess. I ask if he can furnish us with some 10-in-1 rations
for while we are gone. He wants to know how long we will be out
and I tell him at least three or four days. He tells one of the cooks
helpers to help me load four cases of 10 in 1 rations. We put them
in the back of the halftrack and I climb in and tell the lieutenant I am
ready to go now. Herb says to the lieutenant "I told you he would

take care of us." Herb does not say anything about it, but I have a feeling that I am here because of him. We head out on the road to find CCR headquarters.

CHAPTER LXXIV

This halftrack is the one that ran into the wall in Belgium and can't make a tight turn. It would be the one that they would give to a new unit, but we will take it. I am really glad to be assigned to this unit and be away from headquarters for awhile. I am also pleased that I do not have a CW radio to mess with. The FM radio is just fine with me. I am in contact with headquarters and will be passing messages back and forth from CCR headquarters to battalion headquarters.

We continue on the main road to the northeast side of Warburg. I am still within radio range. We find CCR headquarters and locate a place to park the halftrack beside a building. The lieutenant and Herb go meet with the commander to find out what is expected of us. The driver goes to find a place where we can sleep. He comes back and says that he found a good place, just inside of the building where we are parked. He takes our bedrolls in and then comes back to service the halftrack.

I tell the driver to listen for the radio while I go see if I can find some gas to replace what we used. I go to where I see some gas cans stacked up and there is a sergeant who seems to be in charge. I ask him if I can get some gas to replace what we have used and he says to help myself. I need three cans and there is a jeep sitting there, so I ask if he would mind hauling me and the gas to the halftrack. I fully expect him to refuse, but he says that he would be glad to help and grabs one of the cans, while I get the other two.

We load them in the back of the jeep and he drives over to the halftrack and helps me put them in the rack on the side. I tell him to wait a minute. I climb into the back of the halftrack and get a candy bar out of my box from home and hand it to him. He is really surprised and keeps thanking me. I tell him to thank my mother, because she is the one that sacrificed to send it to me. I bet if I need any gas in the future, he will see that I get it.

Now that I am back, the driver takes off to see what he can find. Since there is only the four of us, we will have to take turns on the radio. The lieutenant will not pull a shift at night, but the driver and Herb will spell me. During the day, I will have to man it most of the time, with them taking over once in awhile to relieve me. It is getting to be evening and the K rations we had at noon are wearing thin. I wonder how we are going to cook our 10-in-1 rations.

I am still thinking about supper when the driver comes back and says that he came to get his mess kit, because CCR headquarters and some of the other units have set up a combined mess. He tells me as soon as he gets his food, he will come back and relieve me so I can go get mine. This sounds better than having to cook tonight. While I am waiting for him to come back, Herb and the lieutenant return. The lieutenant is going to sleep with some of the other officers in another building and Herb says he will bunk with the driver and me. I tell him that he will have to wait for the driver to get back because I do not know yet where we are going to sleep. I tell them that they might as well go get their supper and they can find their sleeping spots later.

The driver gets back and I grab my mess kit and hurry to catch up with Herb. We get in line and get our chow. They have some minute steaks, mashed potatoes and gravy, green beans, a mixed salad, GI bread with jelly and peanut butter. They have a sheet cake for dessert. With all the brass around headquarters, they get the choice rations.

We take our supper and go back to the halftrack to eat. We find a place to sit by the driver, where we can hear the radio if it calls and eat our supper. We all three agree that this may be a good deal for us.

I go ahead and start getting the halftrack ready for night. Before I get done, Herb and the driver get back to help me. This helps, because one guy can check the outside for light, while the other turns it on inside. It is all ready to go. Herb asks how I want to do the shifts and I tell him he is in charge and should make the assignments. He says he will take the first shift, Ralph, the driver, the second and I can finish out the night. I tell him that is fine with me. I do not mind taking a longer shift than the others, as long as they remember to relieve me some during the day.

Herb has been around radios enough that he knows how to operate them, at least the FM ones. Ralph has not had much experience, so I give him a short course on what is expected. He seems to understand what I am saying and I do not think he will have much trouble. The hardest part will be staying awake because we probably will not have much traffic tonight.

Ralph and I go to where the bedrolls are and find a good place to unroll them. It is dark enough in the building that we have to use our flashlights to get around. We take Herb's bedroll and roll it out for him. He knows which building we are in and should have no problem finding Ralph.

I wake up when Herb comes to get Ralph and then I go back to sleep as soon as Herb gets in his sleeping bag. I sleep sound until Ralph shakes me awake. I gather up my things and go out to the halftrack. I forgot to ask Ralph if he has run the engine to charge the battery, so I go ahead and start it up. As usual I am hungry, but this time I have food. I get out my knife and cut open one of the boxes of 10-in-1 rations. Inside I find, among other things, a can of cherry preserves. I take them, dig out some of the biscuits and spread the cherries on them. It is really sweet and I love it.

I have a long shift to do, but I take my time eating and it goes much faster. I go through the items in the ration box and try to figure out how I would cook the ones that need cooking. I would really need more equipment than I have to do a good job. I will have to make a raid on a house someplace and stock up.

When it gets close to daylight, I turn off the light and go outside. I get my canteen cup out and make a quick trip over to the mess and beg a cup of coffee. They gladly give me one. Here at headquarters, they are used to some of the brass coming by and wanting a cup, so it is no problem to give me one. Unlike the cooks at the 73rd, they do not offer me anything to go with it. But I still have a little of the cherry preserves left and some of the biscuits.

I am sitting comfortably when the halftrack door opens. It is Herb and he asks me if I know that it is light outside. He tells me that he will stay here while I go get my breakfast. I get my mess kit and go get in line. I get my food and then go back so that Herb can get his. We have finished eating before Ralph comes out. He goes and gets his breakfast and comes back here to eat.

While Ralph is close by, I decide to take off on a scouting trip. I go into the house where we slept last night and make my way to the kitchen. I look around and find a couple of heavy skillets stuck in the oven. I liberate them, together with a large fork, a spatula and a couple of big spoons. I find a cloth bag or pillow case and put them in it and wrap them up so that they do not clatter. I return to the halftrack and store them in one of the lockers under the seat. Now if we have to, we have the equipment to cook our meals.

Herb comes out and says that he is sure that we will be moving up this morning and that we might as well load up. We are all packed and waiting. I go back into the house and in one room I see a typewriter. That would really make it easier for me to write letters home, especially V-mail letters. I pick it up and take it out to the halftrack and stow it away.

The lieutenant comes out and looks at us and says he can't believe that we are all packed and ready to go. Herb tells him that we do not want to hold up the war. He says that we might as well move out, because he knows which way to go and we will be out of the way when the headquarters moves. We go north a short distance to a main road and then turn east.

The FM radio sounds off and I answer. They want to know if we are in range of the radios and when I answered the radio, I answered their question. They do not say anything over the radio, but that leads me to think that they are on the move too. They are somewhere behind us. The lieutenant keeps checking the map to see where we are located. We are moving at a rather brisk pace today, because we are ahead of most of the units. We are still behind the front units though. We can see the abandoned and destroyed equipment along the road.

About noon, the lieutenant has Ralph pull the halftrack off the road and into some kind of loading area, where we can park without getting stuck. He asks me to contact 73rd headquarters to see if we are still in range. I try four times, but do not get an answer. He says he was afraid of that. We are traveling a lot faster than they are and have outrun the radios. He says we might as well wait there for awhile, for them to get closer. Then he asks what we are going to have for dinner.

Since we do not know how long we will be there, I get out four of the K rations I had stowed away and pass them out. We will have the 10-in-1 rations later. Every little bit, I try to call on the radio. We are there almost an hour before I get an answer to my calls. While we are waiting, we see some of the CCR headquarters go past. We wait a little longer and then fall into the column going down the road.

Late in the afternoon, we get to the place where CCR headquarters is going to set up and find us a place beside of one of the buildings in this small town. Herb and Ralph go check out the house to find a place for us to sleep. In a little bit, they come back and have me throw down our bedrolls so they can take them in to the house. They leave the lieutenant's things, but he comes back in a little bit and says for them to put his things in there too. While they are doing that, I get the halftrack ready for night.

CHAPTER LXXV

The next morning, we load up and move out again. We are moving deeper into Germany. About noon, we pull into another small town. We pull off of the south side of the street and park. On the north side of the street, are the remains of a small German rocket launcher vehicle. It is not one of the multiple tube launchers, but has a large, single tube in the middle. The vehicle looks like a cross between a motorcycle and a German jeep. Someone has scored a direct hit on it not very long ago.

I cross the street to look at it and I step on something squishy under my right boot. I scrape my boot across one of the pieces of metal laying in the street and what comes off looks like a piece of stew meat. I look around on the street and it looks like someone spilled a package of stew meat. There are little cubes of meat scattered around. It is then that I realize that it is not stew meat, but the remains of the German, who was manning the rocket launcher. I feel sick and I don't know if I will ever be able to eat stew again.

I go back to the halftrack and get ready to pull out again. The lieutenant comes back from the headquarters and says that we have finished here and are going back to the 73rd. Ralph and Herb have not returned, so we will have to wait until they get back. While we are waiting, I see an M1 rifle laying next to a building just ahead of us. There is no one around, so I get out and go pick it up. I suppose some infantryman got wounded and they left his rifle here. I open the bolt and take out the clip. It has five rounds left in it. I go to the end of the belt on the .30 caliber machine gun and take out three rounds, fill the clip and replace it in the rifle.

Ralph and Herb return and the lieutenant tells them that we are going back to the unit. He tells me to get on the radio and call the 73rd to tell them we are returning. He gives me coordinates to send telling them where we will meet them. With that, we move out on the road heading east. We get a few miles down the road and then we turn south to go towards our meeting place.

We catch up with the 73rd and fall in to the column. We are moving really fast now. There is not much resistance. We have driven so far in such a short time that the equipment is beginning show it. We are going along and look up ahead and there is a very high bridge spanning a stream far below. When we get about to the start of the bridge, a tank ahead of us suddenly turns to the right and hits the guard rail. The tank goes through the rail and hangs half off of the bridge, teetering back and forth. We stop and get out and run up to where they are.

The occupants of the tank climb out of the hatches and are making their way back over the tank and on to the bridge. They are standing there shaking at their close call. The right track broke and when it did, it spun the tank into the rail. A few inches further and they would have gone crashing into the canyon far below.

One of the officers comes up and the sergeant, who is the tank commander, tells him that he is not going any farther until they get new tracks on the tank. The officer says that they will get someone to come up and repair the track. The sergeant says, "I guess you did not hear what I said. I said, I am not going any farther until we get NEW tracks on the tank."

The officer says, "okay, new tracks it is."

We keep moving until night and then stop in another small town. We find a place to park and a building to stay in. Since we are back with the unit, there is no need for me to have the radio on, so I shut it off. This gives me a chance to move around some. I go look through the town and find that they have just had a battle here. Many of the buildings show scars from the fighting. I move along a wall and see where some unit has taken cover. The ground is covered with empty cartridge cases and there are several empty M1 clips. I gather the clips up and take them back with me.

I go to the halftrack and load the empty clips with cartridges from the machine gun belt. I notice that they have set up the mess and guys are starting to get in line. I get my mess kit and go join them. I get my food and find a place on a stone wall to sit and eat. A couple of the guys join me and they want to know what we did at CCR headquarters. I don't think they believe me when I tell them, that we really did not do anything. I just get to the halftrack when I meet the first sergeant.

The first sergeant says that he has been looking for me, and that since I am not on the radio tonight, he has a detail for me. I start to wonder what kind of dirty detail I have come back to, but he says that they are sending some dispatches to one of the other units and he wants me to go ride shotgun for the jeep driver. He tells me to come along, because he is ready to leave. I follow him over to the building they are using for a headquarters. The jeep is sitting there and the driver is just coming out with a pouch.

We get in the jeep and head out of the town. I assume the driver knows where we are going, but I have no idea. We have not gone very far before it gets dark. We are traveling blackout, so we have no lights. I can tell we are going into the mountains by the sound of the engine and when I can glimpse the pine trees against the sky. We go up one mountain and over and down the other side until we reach the destination. I stay in the jeep and the driver goes in to deliver the pouch.

It takes about twenty minutes before the driver comes back out with the pouch and starts up the jeep. We go back the way we came. We have gone up the mountain and just started down the other side, when a bullet cracks right above our heads. It has come from some place on the right, but I can see nothing but darkness. As soon as the driver hears the bullet, he pushes his foot all the way down on the accelerator. We are going down that winding mountain road in the dark as fast as that jeep will go. I can see the glow of the hand and dots on the speedometer. The speedometer goes up to sixty. I watch as the hand goes past sixty and up to ten. We are going seventy miles an hour. I can't see a thing outside. I hope the driver can see the road.

The Germans often run a cable across a road at an angle so that when a vehicle hits it, it forces the vehicle off of a cliff. Or they run a piece of piano wire across just under head high, so that it will cut the heads off of anyone in a jeep or on a motorcycle. I can only hope that they have not done their work on this road. When we get to the bottom of the mountain, the driver slows up and we follow the road back to headquarters without any further problems.

The next morning, we hold up while and they send out scouting parties. One of the parties is in a M37 armored car. It is armed with a .30 caliber machine gun, a .50 caliber machine gun and a 37 mm cannon. When the armored car comes back, the sergeant in charge goes to headquarters to make his report and I go to talk to the other two guys on the team. They tell me about their mission.

They say that they were moving forward and got behind a barn. They pull up so they can see and there is a German tank out in the field firing its cannon. They turn the turret around and aim the 37 mm cannon at the tank and fire an armor piercing shell at it. The shell hits the tank and bounces off. They quickly pull back behind the barn and reload. Then they pull up again and fire the second shot at the tank and again it bounces off. They move back and reload and then move out for the third time and fire and hit the tank. It too just bounces off. He says when you hit a tank, three times with the heaviest weapon you have and they do not even pay attention to you, you better get out of there.

About noon, they give the signal to move out. We fall into the column and travel with the main body of vehicles. I have the radio on and the firing batteries are busy. I can hear the forward observers call in their fire missions. They have the observer in the Piper Cub aircraft up in the air today too. We must have pushed into the Germans, because it seem that they are firing in almost every direction.

Later in the afternoon, the observer in the air calls in and asks if they can get a message to the lead tank on the left. He says that there is a German tank right in front of him. He says to tell the tank to just fire his cannon, he is aimed right at the German. Evidently they are not in position to see the German tank. They try to get through to the American tank but do not seem to be able to. When this fails, the aircraft calls for them fire on the German tank with artillery. He better be right, because they will have to fire right over our own tanks. They fire and they are close enough that the German tank starts to move. That may be his mistake, because then the American tanks see him and open fire. The pilot reports that the tank is on fire.

It seems that all of the forward observers have targets in sight and the firing batteries are busy firing. I have a great opportunity to hear what is going on with the calls back and forth between the observers and the firing batteries. Then I hear one that is really interesting. The aircraft reports a troop train moving east. It has tanks and guns on some of the open cars and probably other military equipment and or men in the enclosed cars. Since the train is moving, it is hard to give a location for the target. Then he sees a highway overpass over the railroad ahead of the train. He tells the gun crews to look on their map and locate the overpass and to aim their guns just ahead of it. When they have it located and the guns are aimed, let him know and he will give them the signal to fire.

The firing battery tells him that they are ready and he tells them to stand by to fire. He watches how fast the train is moving and figures out about what time it will reach the overpass and gives that to the firing battery as the time on target. They calculate how long it will take the shells to get there and at the right time, they fire all guns. I hear them say, "On the way." I anxiously wait to see what happens.

Then the pilot comes on and says, "Right on target. You got the engine." Then he tells them to drop twenty-five and to fire for effect. He has them adjust their aim until the entire train is either blown up or on fire. Then he comes back on and says, "Congratulations, you just destroyed a running train." I am not sure, but I doubt if very many other artillery units can claim credit for blowing up a moving train.

It is evening and they announce that we are going to move up. We will be moving forward under cover of darkness. This is extremely dangerous with all of these vehicles moving down the road with just those little cat eyes, blackout lights showing. However, it does lessen the chance of being attacked by a German plane.

Our lieutenant and the medical officer are good friends, so the lieutenant asks if I will trade places with the medical officer for the trip tonight. Of course, I say yes. It means that I will be riding in an unarmed jeep, instead of an armored halftrack. I don't know if it is within Geneva Convention or not, but I am not going to leave my carbine; I am going to have it with me. The medical officer says he will operate the radio for me. I show him what to do. With the FM radio, once you know the call signs, it is not much of a problem.

I go climb into the medic jeep. They have the inside and bottom covered with small sand bags, to offer some protection from a mortar shell or a mine. I'm not sure how much good it would do, but it makes you feel safer. Of course, the part of you sticking out above the side of the jeep is the main part of your body and subject to much more danger.

The column moves out and we are blocked off from getting to where we are supposed to be, which is right behind my halftrack. We have to wait some time before we can get into the column. After we are able to move along with the column, the driver decides that we should pass the other vehicles until we are where we are supposed to be. He pulls out and we move forward on the other side of the road. No one is moving very fast and we slowly make our way alongside of the column. It is so dark, that we can only make out the other vehicles as shadowy figures beside us.

I feel the jeep going down and I look toward the sky and I can see the tracks of a tank above us. I hope it does not come down on us. I only have a short time with my heart stuck in my throat, before we start up again and we are alongside the tank. We had driven down into a bomb crater.

CHAPTER LXXVI

We stop for a little bit just as it is getting light and the medic officer comes back to the jeep and says that I can go back to the halftrack now. In a few minutes, we are moving forward again. We are advancing against the Germans and have covered many miles. At this rate, the war can't last too much longer.

We stop next to a farm on the edge of a small village. I take this chance to refill the water can. I go over to the farm house, where there is a pump beside the building. While I pump water into the can, I notice that unlike earlier, here there are animals in the barns and the people are still in the house. After I get the can filled, I put in the halazone tablets, set the can back on the fender and fasten the strap that holds it in place.

For some reason, we pull off of the road and head across country. We are driving over fields and the dust is so thick that we can't see the vehicle in front of us. I have some cheaply made German goggles that I get out and put on. They are made of a kind of oil cloth with a form of plastic lens sewed into them. They are crude, but do protect my eyes some from the dust. I have to keep wiping them so that I can see out.

I look down and see the remains of several bicycles buried in the soft dirt. Evidently, they were left by some German troops that were riding them. They probably got caught in the open and were shot up. As I am looking down, I see a hand sticking up out of the dirt as if reaching up for help. The wheels and tracks of our vehicles pass beside it, while the rest of the body has been pressed beneath the surface.

We travel for a few miles across country and then move back on to the road. After a few more miles on the road, we find a place to pull off and stop for awhile. When we do, we all gather around the water can and pour water into our steel helmets. We stick our faces into the water in the helmets and try to wash off some of the dust. I take my handkerchief out and use it for a wash rag. It is too slick to do much in the way of cleaning, but does help get some of the dirt out of the corners of my eyes and out of my ears.

We travel on until early in the afternoon, when we pull off the road and go towards a farmstead. It is the home of a wealthy farmer, as shown by the well-kept buildings and the fields surrounding them. We park in the courtyard and pick out one of the buildings to sleep in. I pick out a place on the second floor to put my bed roll and then go back outside to the halftrack. A couple of the guys come walking up from out in the field and say that there is a dead soldier out in the field. Four of us walk out in the field to a haystack and on the other side is a dead American soldier. He has a Ninth Armored patch on his jacket, so he likely was one of the infantrymen in the division.

He is lying at the foot of the haystack and there is an empty bazooka laying beside him. He has a bullet hole in his forehead, just above his nose. It is a small hole and even the exit hole is not much bigger. It appears that he was looking over the top of the haystack, when someone in the very room that we picked to stay in, shot him. It is one thing seeing the dead Germans, because they are the enemy, but someone from your own division is a different story. We console ourselves in that he probably never knew what hit him, since death would have been instantaneous. One of the guys checks his dog tags and says who he is. It is better that we do not even know. We are not allowed to tell anyone back home about it and his commander will be the one to write his parents about what happened. Their first notification will be by the graves registration people in the form of a telegraph. My folks know about that.

We leave him and go back to the buildings. I get back on the radio and stay with the halftrack until supper time. We left the battery today and are back on liaison again. They have a kitchen set up and will be serving a meal. This group is not as good as the ones at CCR headquarters or our own 73rd. They have heated some canned corned beef hash and they have some of the GI bread and some canned peaches. Not the best, but enough to get by. If we stay with them long, I will start cooking for us.

We take shifts on the radio tonight and of course, I take the long last shift, but I am ready to go in the morning that way. I go over to the mess and ask for a cup of coffee about daylight and the mess sergeant says that I will have to wait, that they are not serving anyone yet. This bunch is not very friendly.

Herb comes out and asks if I have had coffee yet and I tell him what happened. About that time the lieutenant comes out and Herb tells him. The lieutenant says for me to give him my cup and he and Herb take off. They are back in a couple of minutes with three cups of coffee. Herb says that they were more than glad to give him and the lieutenant coffee. I say, "Rank has its privilege," and laugh.

In a little bit, I see guys going for breakfast so I take off and go get in line. They have spam and dried eggs and they have dried some bread in the oven. It is probably supposed to be toast, but it did not get brown. This lacks a lot of being the quality we have been used to. After I eat, I go back to wash my mess kit and one of the cooks helpers is there and I tell him that we are liaison and will not be able to get to the mess all the time and ask if I can have some rations to cover us until we can get back to the mess. I really do not expect anything, but he goes over and gets a case of K rations and hands them to me.

I take the rations back, load them and then open up the top of the halftrack before I go get my bedroll and load it. I am ready to move out. We have been traveling about fifty miles each day now, driving deeper into Germany. We will be in Berlin before long, at this rate. The lieutenant comes out and says that we are going to go to another unit today. He says that he knows that I will not be sad to leave this bunch.

I contact the 73rd and tell them that we are moving out and that I may lose contact if we get too far away from them. I ask the lieutenant where we are going and he says that we are going to "Divarty," Division artillery. We get on the road and fall into line with the other vehicles on the road. We are moving much faster than usual. We travel some distance before we make contact with Divarty.

The lieutenant and Herb meet with the officers and noncoms at Divarty and Ralph and I stay with the halftrack. Herb brings me a message to send to the 73rd and I read it to them. It has already been encoded, so I do not know what I am sending. In some ways I feel foolish sending an encoded message by voice. When we stopped, I put up a couple more sections of antennae, so I am able to reach the 73rd without any trouble.

I find that we will not be staying here long, so I send a message to the 73rd and tell them that I am going to lower my antennae, so if they can't reach me they will know why.   By evening, we have caught up with our own unit so that we are all in close proximity to one another.

Since we are so close, we do not need the radio very much and it gives me some time to look around. I am walking around when I see the guys with the armored car parked in back of a building. They are looking at a shed. I walk over and ask what is going on and they tell me to look at the padlock on the building. It is a huge iron padlock. One of them says there must be something important in that building with a lock that big on it.

He walks over to the building, pulls out his .45 pistol and says that he will open it. He fires at the lock and it just swings back and forth. He fires again. Same thing. He empties his pistol and the lock is still just swinging back and forth. He reaches into the armored car and pulls out an M1 rifle and aims it at the lock and fires.

The lock just swings back and forth. He empties the rifle at the lock and it is still hanging there, swinging back and forth. He is really mad by this time.

He climbs into the armored car and starts to turn the turret around and lower the cannon. The rest of us run behind the armored car and hold our ears. There is a loud explosion as the cannon fires and the shell hits the lock. We look around the armored car and see a big cloud of smoke and dust. When the cloud clears, we see that the right side of the shed, the door and half of the front of the shed and the back side are all missing. Hanging on the remaining half of the front is the iron padlock, swinging back and forth. All that for an empty shed.

I go back to the halftrack and find Herb and Ralph. I tell them I have an idea to make things easier. I will stand watch on the radio tonight by myself. I will turn off the transmitter, that pulls most of the current and only have the receiver on. I will turn the volume up high and I will sleep with my ear beside the receiver. I will tell the other operators that if they call me, to wait a couple of minutes for an answer, since I will have to wait for the transmitter to warm up. Of course, Ralph and Herb are in favor of that, because they will not have to man the radio and can get a night's sleep.

I would not dare do this if we were still with the battalion, but technically we are with Divarty right now, so I doubt if anyone will even notice, except for the other operators and I doubt if they will care. I unroll my bedroll on the floor of the halftrack so that my head will be next to the radio receiver. There is not much room down on the floor of the halftrack, but I am so skinny that I have room to lie. It would not be very comfortable for most guys. I get on the radio and tell the other stations of my plan and they agree to go along with it.

I get the top closed tight, place the trouble light where I can reach it easily and settle down in my nest. I have access to some snacks and I have a supply of rations if I need anything. I took a cardboard box and put it in beside the radio and put the things I got from home in it, like cookies and candy. Herb got a package from home and he put the things he got in there too. This way we can share. I got cookies and candy and Herb got things like canned pickled herring. I guess there is a difference between Christians and Jews after all.

Since the units are so bunched up, I doubt if we will have many messages tonight. I lay down and go to sleep. I wake up every so often to listen if they are calling me, but nothing is happening. After awhile I am able to relax and sleep the rest of the night.

CHAPTER LXXVII

We are still assigned to CCR headquarters, but we seem to be traveling along with different groups. We are moving so fast that units have a tendency to get mixed up. In the afternoon, we stop in a small city and it looks like we will be staying for awhile. We park and there is a fine house located nearby. We go inside and the entryway has a marble floor. Near the entrance is an umbrella stand with several umbrellas and walking canes in it. There are four of us and we each take out either a cane or an umbrella and start prancing around.

About this time the military government officer, a first lieutenant, comes into the house. It is his job to help restore law and order, after we conquer the area. He looks at us with the canes and umbrellas and he is not a bit happy. He tells us to put them back where we got them. He says that we are not here to loot. We put them back in the stand and with sheepish looks on our faces, we leave the house. When we are outside, one of the guys whispers, "If we were really looting, we would not be taking a damn umbrella." We all grin and nod in agreement.

We find out that we are not staying here and we go get in the column again and push on down the road. About supper time, we get word that we will not be stopping tonight, but will keep moving while we can. One of the guys notes that it is April 12th and that tomorrow is Friday the 13th. He says that Friday the 13th is bad luck. I say that maybe it is bad luck for the Germans instead of us.

Ralph, Herb and I are in the halftrack, and the lieutenant is riding in one of the CCR headquarters vehicles. Since we are moving along, I dig out three K rations for us to have for supper. As usual, I open the one for Ralph and fix it so he can reach it as he drives. Herb is standing in the ring mount and I am sitting back by the radio. It is really dark again and I am glad that I am not the one to have to try to drive. I lay back against the bedrolls and doze off. I wake up every little bit and then go back to sleep.

I get up and stand up to try to see where we are, but things are mostly just shadows that I can see against the skyline, either trees or buildings. Later in the night, I trade places with Herb and he gets to take a nap while I man the .50 caliber machine gun and try to help watch the road for Ralph. I know Ralph must be getting tired but he keeps driving. He tries to keep those little blackout lights in his sight and not get too close to them or too far behind.

At last, I can see it getting light in the east. As it gets lighter, I can see that we are passing buildings on our right and that the military government officer is in the jeep in front of us. We are entering a town and ahead on the left is a burning telephone pole on the corner. Since it is light now, they widen the gap between vehicles. The jeep is ahead of us and I do not see any other vehicles ahead of it. They turn left at the intersection where the pole is burning. Just as we start to turn the corner, a bullet whizzes right behind my back. I swing the machine gun around to the right, but I am afraid to shoot since we do not know where our troops are.

The halftrack is pointing north in the intersection when the jeep ahead of us explodes. It has received a direct hit from a German 88 mm gun. The driver and the lieutenant are killed instantly. Ralph pulls as hard as he can on the steering wheel and pushes down on the accelerator. This is the halftrack that does not turn short, so we make a wide turn and drive up across the sidewalk and into a yard, as he tries to get us going back in the direction that we came from. There is a picket fence and the halftrack bumper is stripping the pickets off and they are flying through the air like something out of a cartoon movie. We are going down the sidewalk now and right in front of us is a fire plug. We hit it dead center and it flies through the air and as it does, it slowly spins, before hitting the ground. We drive right over it. I do not know if water came out or not, I do not look back, as I am too anxious to get out of there.

We go on back west, the way we came and can hear explosions back to the east. When we get back a ways, we see an open area on the north side of the road and Ralph turns the halftrack around and parks there. He and Herb leave and go across the road to the south side where there are some buildings. CCR headquarters is located there now. They are going to report what happened when we went into the town. I stay in the halftrack and listen to the radio. I am standing with the .50 caliber machine gun, but do not see any targets. I would like to fire on the area where the shot came towards me, but I still do not know if we have troops there.

I am standing up in the halftrack and there is an explosion beside me. I dive out of the halftrack and hug the ground. The Germans have fired an 88 mm cannon at me. While I am laying there, three more shells come in. The 88 shell travels faster than the speed of sound, so if you hear it, it did not get you. I am laying as flat to the ground as I can get, waiting for them to stop shelling.

I hear someone yelling and look up and it is Herb coming across the field. I turn to face him and he yells at me to get up and get out of there. I jump up and follow him across the road and into the buildings. He acts mad at me, but he thought I had been hit and was coming to help me. I have to admire him though, because he risked his life, when he thought I had been hit. It is always nice to know someone cares enough to do that.

While we are there, we find out why we got into the town. There was supposed to be a soldier at a corner further back to tell us to turn and go north so that we could bypass the town. He left his post and there was no one to tell us to turn. As a result of his actions, two men are dead and there could have been more casualties, including me.

Now that we know where we should have gone, the lieutenant joins us and we four go get into the halftrack and go back to the right road and go north. We go north a mile or so and run into more of the division. We are still not out of danger though because the Germans are still shelling. Every little while, one round will come in followed shortly by three or four more.

I am outside of the halftrack, and the others are off trying to find out where we should go next, when a round comes in. Of course, I do not hear it until it explodes, but I make a dive for a ditch and land in the bottom. A moment later someone else dives into the same place. We lie there waiting for the next rounds to hit. They explode nearby and we decide that this batch is finished and start to stand up. Our arms and legs are tangled together. As we unwind, I look and see gold oak leaves on the other guy's shoulders. I say, "Sorry Major, but I do believe I was there first." He laughs and says, not by much."

Every little while, shells come flying in and we have to dive for cover. They have not hit anything important since they got the jeep this morning, but they keep shooting four or five shells in a bunch at us. Finally, the firing stops and sometime later some infantrymen come to where we are and they are marching some young boys. They are ten to fifteen years old. They were captured manning the 88's. The infantrymen ask the major what they should do with them. The major says that we probably ought to spank them and send them home to their mothers. But they line them up to send them back to the POW camp. We will let them decide what to do with them.

Actually, some of them do not look much younger than I do. It seems from what they tell us that some German SS officers rounded them up and showed them how to fire the 88's. They took the anti-aircraft guns, that provided the defense around Leipzig, turned them down and used them to fire on us. They had about five guns and they would direct the boys how to load them, then tell them how to aim and that is why we got hit with groups of four or five shells. It also explained the lack of accuracy. If those had been regular gun crews, they would have inflicted a lot of damage on us. The regular gunners probably fled when they heard we were coming.

Things are more peaceful now with the guns knocked out. We are kind of milling around waiting on the word to advance. There are a group of us standing by a jeep that has a .50 caliber machine gun mounted on a post, in the center of the jeep. Suddenly we hear the antiaircraft guns open up. One of the guys jumps in the jeep and grabs the machine gun. A German plane flies over with streaks of tracers following him. The guy in the jeep presses the thumb triggers and it fires. The jeep seems to jump up in the air. It only fires one round. He has to work the charging lever and then he fires another round. The clip that allows it to fire fully automatic has not been engaged. Anyway, he got two shots off. As far as I know, the plane was never hit.

We are standing there talking about the air raid, when we look up and see some men coming towards us. They are just walking skeletons, dressed in rags. They stare with blank eyes. They are near death. With our attack, their German guards fled leaving them unguarded and they escaped from a slave labor camp.

I go over to the halftrack and get out all of the rations that I have and start handing them out. I give each one a K ration as long as they last and then I start in on the 10-in-1 rations. I open the cans and try to divide up the contents. They can't eat the biscuits because they do not have enough teeth. I show them how to break them and I pour water into the empty ration cans so they can drink it and soak up the biscuits in their mouths. The ones that got meat take their hands and stuff it in their mouths. They start moving toward the west, as soon as they get something to eat.

I give out all the rations I have. I know it is against army regulations to give food to civilians, but these people are about starved to death. They smell so bad, like a dead body already. I am afraid to touch them, because I do not know what kind of disease they might be carrying. I just hold out what I have and they take it. After I run out of food, the ones that did not get any just keep moving on by, with the same blank look. I guess freedom is more important than food. I hope there is some place back behind us, that is set up to help these poor people.

Herb and Ralph come out to the halftrack and say that the lieutenant will be there shortly. We are going to move up. We are to keep moving and we will be going around Leipzig, now that we have penetrated the outer defense. The lieutenant comes and we pull out onto the road and find a place in the line of vehicles.

When it is almost dark, we pull into another small town. We will not be traveling any more tonight. Ralph pulls the halftrack up next to a small hotel and we get ready for night. I fill the gas tanks from the cans. We used a lot of gas the last twenty-four hours. We will need to watch for the gas trucks. We still have enough to go a lot of miles, but we do not know how long the supplies can keep up with us, as fast as we are moving. I put the top up on the halftrack and put up a couple of more sections of antennae before I check in with the 73rd. They are not that far away from us and I am able to communicate with them. I remind them that I will have the transmitter off and for them to give me time to warm it up before I have to answer, if they call me in the night.

The lieutenant comes out and asks if I have any food. I tell him that I am out. I do not tell him why. I don't think he would want to hear that. I just tell him that if one of them will watch the radio, I will go see what I can do. I go back a ways and find the CCR mess truck. The mess sergeant, who would not give me coffee the other day is there. I ask him what we are going to have to eat and he says that they do not have time to cook anything. That we will have to eat rations. With that, he kicks a box of K rations off of the truck and it lands in front of me. I pick it up and leave, before he can tell me not to.

In the evening, I decide to write some V-mail letters. I have some blanks and I get out my pilfered typewriter. I roll one of the blanks into the machine and start to type. What comes out is not what I thought I put in. I look and it does not have a standard key-

board. It has special German keys. I take the typewriter and throw
it out beside the road.

CHAPTER LXXVIII

The next morning, they have the mess set up and fix breakfast. They fry some of that thick army bacon and some powdered eggs. They have even made some biscuits and there is grapefruit juice and coffee to drink, not the greatest, but better than what they have been putting out. When I go back to wash out my mess kit, the cook's helper is back by the truck and I go ask him if I can get some 10-in-1 rations. He is a lot more friendly than the mess sergeant and asks me if there is one kind I like better than another. I tell him to make sure that it has canned bacon in it. I will need the grease if I cook anything. He pulls out a case and tells me to go around the other way, so that the mess sergeant will not see me.

When I get back to the halftrack, I store the 10-in-1 rations in the back and start to get things ready to travel. I do not know what we may run into, so I get the cleaning things out and clean the .50 caliber machine gun. While I am cleaning it, one of the guys comes by and takes my picture. I get down and ask him where he got the film. He said that he found some film and development supplies in a shop. The film is not bad, but the printing paper is not very good. The camera he has is an old box camera and he had to cut the film and roll it onto the spools. Before he leaves, he takes another picture of me standing at the back of the halftrack. He says that when he gets them developed, he will give them to me.

The other guys bring their bedrolls out and load them up. We are ready to go. The lieutenant says that he wants to get further back in the column today. He does not want to run into something like we did yesterday. We wait until some of the self-propelled 105's go by and then fall in behind them. We are moving along at a good pace today. We only stop for short periods of time, so dinner today is K rations again.

We pull into an area and stop for awhile. Some of the armored infantry guys are parked there. We are sitting there when one of the infantrymen comes over to the halftrack and asks me if I am not the man that was looking for a BAR. I told him that I was wanting one. He said he had an extra that I could have. I went with him and he had it in their halftrack. He said that someone had abandoned it and he picked it up. It only had one clip with it and it was empty. I thanked him and took it back with me.

I had told a bunch of infantry guys that I would like to get one. I did not remember the guy that had it and I am surprised that he remembered me. I dug out the remains of a belt of .30 caliber machine gun ammunition and pulled out twenty cartridges and loaded the clip. This meant that every fifth bullet was a tracer and the rest were armor piercing. I now had in addition to the two machine guns and my carbine, a M1 rifle, a German K98 rifle and a BAR. The lieutenant asks what I am going to do with all of those guns and I tell him that I am a boy scout and our motto is to "Be Prepared." He laughs and shakes his head.

In the evening, we stop in a small town and pull up beside a building. It is much like other places in the small towns. There is a business in the lower part of the building and living quarters above. Apparently, the owner repairs clocks and watches. When I see that we will be staying here, I open the box of 10 in 1 rations and get out some canned goods. I take a can of orange marmalade, a can of spam and one of beef stew and tell Ralph to listen for the radio.

I go around the building and head out towards the edge of the town. There are some houses there with chicken houses in the back. I go to one and the woman comes out to meet me. I know the words for eggs and potatoes. I use signs as best I can and try to make her understand that I want to trade the canned goods for some eggs and potatoes. It takes awhile, but I finally get through to her and she brings me seven potatoes and four eggs. I think it is a good trade for both of us. The canned goods are worth more to her than the eggs and potatoes and we would rather have fresh eggs and some potatoes than what is in those cans. I put the potatoes inside of my field jacket and carefully carry the eggs in my wool cap that I brought with me. I hope no one saw me talking to her. I do not have $50 to pay a fine and I do not know what the penalty is for trading off rations.

I get back and ask Ralph if we have had any messages and he says it was all quiet, but that the gas truck came by; he filled the tanks and replaced the empties on the side. I ask him if he will stay there for a little longer and I will go get supper started. I go through the lower part of the building and see a bottle of fluid there that looks like it is some kind of cleaning fluid. I pick it up to use to start a fire. I go upstairs to the kitchen and there are a few sticks of firewood beside the cast iron cooking stove. I put some of the wood in the stove and then take the bottle of fluid and sprinkle some over the wood.

When I am ready to light the fire, I stand back, light a match and throw it into the empty hole, where I removed the iron lid. It goes WHOOM! and the other three cast iron lids fly up and hit the ceiling, leaving three nice round, black circles on the plaster. I do not know what was in that cleaner, but it was sure potent. Any way, it gets the wood to burning and I retrieve the lids and replace them on the stove.

I go back down to the halftrack and Ralph wants to know what happened. I tell him I was just getting a fire started. I get out my cooking equipment and the rest of the things I need from the 10-in-1 rations to cook supper. I take them back up to the kitchen and get ready to fix supper. I put one of the skillets on the stove to get hot. Then I get out a can of bacon. The bacon comes in a long slender can. I take my little can opener and open both ends of the bacon can. I carefully push the contents out onto the other skillet. The bacon comes rolled up in waxed paper and the rest of the can is pumped full of lard. The lard is more important than the bacon. It is the main thing needed for me to cook.

I scrape all of the lard off and save it. I lay slices of bacon in the hot skillet so it can be cooking and then I start to peel the potatoes. I keep removing cooked bacon and adding more to the skillet as I get the potatoes ready. When I have the potatoes sliced, I leave some of the grease in the skillet and put it on the stove. When it is hot, I add the sliced potatoes. When all of the bacon has fried, I pour off and save most of the bacon grease but leave some for flavor. There is a large can of pork and beans and I pour it in to the skillet so that the bacon grease can flavor them. I go to the window and holler down to Ralph to tell Herb and the lieutenant to bring their mess kits, because supper is almost ready.

When the potatoes are almost done, I take the four eggs, crack them and pour them over the potatoes. I use the salt and pepper from the 10-in-1 ration to season them. The kettle of water that was sitting on the stove has heated too, so I get out the instant coffee so that there will be coffee to drink with the meal. The lieutenant comes up first and then Ralph. He says that Herb sent him up to get his food and that he will go back so that Herb can come.

I start dishing out the food. We have potatoes and eggs, bacon and pork and beans, some of the ration biscuits and coffee to wash it down. I have enough cookies from home so that we can each have one for dessert. The guys start raving over the food. Ralph says, "Lovell, I may want to marry you, if you can cook like this all the time." It is not all that great but is different than what we are used to and does have a good flavor. Ralph goes back down so that Herb can eat. After they all get their food, I get my mess kit and eat too. I tell them that I waited to see if any of them got sick, before I tried any of it.

We eat every bit of the food and when we finish, I find a large pan in the kitchen, pour some of the hot water in it and wash up the pans. I dry them off and pack them up so that they are ready for travel. Herb wants to know what time breakfast will be served. I tell him that it is any time he wants it. To just grab one of the K rations and start in. The lieutenant says that he knew this was too good to last. Then he says, "Where did you get the eggs and potatoes?"

And I say, "What eggs and potatoes? I don't see any eggs and potatoes. Do you see any eggs and potatoes?"

He laughs and walks out of the room.

I put the things back in the halftrack and get it ready for night. As usual, I will sleep in the halftrack with just the receiver on and the others can get a night's sleep without having to stand watch on the radio. The radio is mostly quiet tonight and I get a better than usual night's sleep. In the morning, Herb wakes me and says that he is going to provide breakfast this morning. I wonder how he is going to do that, but he says that one of the firing batteries is a short distance away and they have a mess set up. He will go get his food and then come back so I can go. This will give me time to get my things put away and the halftrack ready to go again.

While he is gone, the lieutenant comes and says that we will be joining our own battery today. I have mixed emotions about that. Things are usually more pleasant when we are away from headquarters, but I probably have mail waiting for me when I get back with them. Herb comes back with his breakfast. I holler at Ralph and he joins the lieutenant and I as we walk over to the firing battery to get food. There is no officer's mess here, so we all line up together. When we have our food, we go back to the halftrack to eat it.

The lieutenant says that as soon as we are ready, we can leave. The 73rd is a few miles south of us and we can join them before they get too far. I knew they were not too far away, because I have been in radio contact with them on the FM radio. We have to get back on the main road before we can get to a place where we can turn south. We move up to the road and wait until we can find a place to get into the column. The traffic is not really heavy because most units have not moved out yet.

We go a couple of miles on east and then turn south and go about three miles before we find the 73rd. We find a place to park next to a building and the lieutenant and Herb go to report in. I really do not have much to do right now, because I got to shut off the radio as soon as we got back. It is nice not to be tied to the radio. I walk over to the headquarters and ask if I have any mail. I have four letters and two packages. I get my mail and go back to open it. I read the letters first. I have one from my minister, who was also my scout-master, and he says that he renewed my membership in the scouts. That way, I will continue to get the Scouting magazine.

Another letter comes from a friend of my mother. She has questions for me about what I am doing. Most of her questions I can't answer, but one question she asks is, who censors our mail? I will tell my mother to tell her that it is the officers in our unit. My uncle has sent me a letter and of course, I get one from my mother. Then I open the packages. They have Hershey candy bars in them. In one box, they are fine, but in the other box, they are broken, stale and have absorbed odors. It is all I can do to eat them, but I don't want to waste them. There are also cookies in each box. They have crumbled some, but still taste good. The boxes are packed with papers, including the school paper and the comics.

I read the comics and then pass them around to the other guys. They all like to see them. When we have all looked at them, we pass them on to other units. I suppose they keep getting passed around until there is not enough left of them to be read.

CHAPTER LXXIX

Two guys come by the halftrack, just as I am coming out. They say they are going to look at a factory and want to know if I want to go with them. I join them and we walk about four blocks to where the factory is located. It seems to be a place where they make machine parts. We go into the office and look around. It looks like we advanced so fast that the workers just ran off and left the place. There is a large box, filled with small manila envelopes, sitting on the desk. Each envelope has a name on it. I open one of the envelopes and it has money in it. It looks like today was payday and everyone ran off and left their wages. There is a slip in the envelope, I can't read German, but it appears to be the pay record.

There are both currency and coins in the envelopes. German money is of no use to us, because we are only allowed to use American printed script, sometimes called invasion money. I take the money and throw it up in the air. The other guys follow my action and soon we are outside throwing the money into the air. One of the guys asks if we shouldn't be saving the money. I tell him that it is worthless because there is no government to back it up. Then I tell him that I remember reading that after World War I, in Germany, it took a wheelbarrow full of money just to buy a loaf of bread, that even if there was a government, it would be practically worthless.

A couple of the other guys had done better than we did. They found a store full of cigars. They filled the jeep and now were passing them out to the rest of the guys. I got a couple of boxes of them. Of course, we had to see how they tasted. I lit one and it was not too strong, but I doubt if it had much tobacco in it, because it tasted more like how burning elm leaves, smell.

After dinner, some of the guys say they heard that there is a warehouse full of tools some place and they want to check it out. I tell them I want to go if they find out where it is. About a half an hour later, three guys come by in a three-quarter-ton truck and say that they found out where the warehouse is located. I climb into the truck and we drive out of the town and go back northwest to a place out in the country.

It is a large building made of tile blocks. It is about two hundred feet long and fifty feet wide. It is two stories high. The doors are unlocked and it appears that everyone just ran away and left it. Lined up on the floor are metal lathes, from small ones to very large. There are drill presses, milling machines, and all kinds of machine tools. Some are used, but most appear to be new. There are hundreds of tool boxes and all kinds of tools. There are some boxes that contain complete sets of mechanic's tools of the highest quality.

The second floor has miles of electrical wire, boxes, fittings, switches and lights. It is hard to believe all of this is just sitting out here in the middle of this field. But the thing that really catches our attention is that there are portable electric generator plants mounted on shock frames. They came in two sizes, big ones with about ten horse power gas engines and small ones with about five horse power engines. There are about twenty-five of the big ones and thirty of the small ones, stacked up.

We load up two of the small ones and one of the large generators and gather up three of the tool boxes full of mechanics tools and go back to where the battery is located. When we get back, we go find the motor sergeant and give him the three boxes of tools. He looks at them and says, "this is just what I wanted," and then he turns one of the tool boxes upside down and dumps the tools out into the dirt. Then he says, "the tool box is great, but those tools are not worth a damn; they are all metric." Well, so much for our good intentions.

We take the generators back to the supply sergeant and then is when we find out that they are all two hundred twenty volt generators. But they do not have to be thrown away because the power in all of the houses is the same and we can use them by hooking them to the house wiring. Our foraging was not as successful as we thought, but it was still something to see all of those things.

The lieutenant comes out of headquarters and says we need to get ready to move. We are going to move up a ways, so we are closer to the firing batteries. I go tell Ralph and Herb and we get ready to pull out. We move out to the road, but we do not get on the road yet. We wait until several of the other vehicles are moving along the road before we get on. Our experience in the town with the burning telephone pole taught us to let some of the others lead out.

We go a few miles to the southeast and stop in a very small village. It is hard to say if it is a farm or a village. They set up a guard post on the road to guard our headquarters. Since I am not on the radio, I will have to do guard duty again. They are manning this post twenty four hours a day, so we will have several shifts. I look in the building in back of the house where we are parked and I find an old bicycle. The tires are still inflated, but it does not have a coaster brake. The chain runs from the crank sprocket to the sprocket on the rear wheel. Your feet have to move all the time. If you want to stop, you just hold back with your feet. I guess if you were good enough, you could ride it backwards as well as forward.

When it is time for me to go on guard duty, I get the bicycle and start riding down the road toward the guard post. I am doing just fine, peddling away, when I look up and here comes the Dodge command car with the colonel riding in the back seat. I remember what I was told at Fort Riley, about what to do when riding a bicycle, so I sit up straight and when the car gets close, I raise my hand and salute, until the car is past. Out of the corner of my eye I see the colonel frowning. I don't know why he would; he is an old horse cavalry man.

I get to the guard post and relieve one of the other guards. When I finish my shift, I ride my bike back to where we are parked and park my bike. It is not long before one of the sergeants from headquarters comes by. I watch him going from building to building and I figure he is handing down some kind of orders.

When he gets to where I am, he says, "The colonel has sent me out to tell everyone that no one is to ride any bicycles. Some dumb shit was riding a bicycle and the colonel saw him." I tell him I will sure keep that in mind. He turns around and walks away and never sees the bicycle leaning against the front of the halftrack. As soon as he is out of sight, I grab the bike and push it back out to the shed.

I have another shift of guard in the night. But you can be sure that I do not ride to my post. I get there and the two guards are huddled around a small fire. I am pretty sure that we are not supposed to have a fire here, but in a little bit, it quits blazing and becomes just some faintly glowing coals. They found some charcoal bricks someplace and lit them.

The next morning after breakfast, we start moving again. We know that we are following the Germans because of the abandoned equipment laying all over. When we stop, we pickup German rifles and destroy them. I don't think it is necessary, but we have been trained to kill and destroy, so if we are not killing, at least we are destroying.

We are moving along when we meet a jeep going the other way. There is an enlisted man driving, and the captain is standing up in the jeep waving at each vehicle. When he reaches us, I can finally hear what he is saying. He is telling us to get our gas masks ready because we may run into poison gas down the road. It is no problem for me; my gas mask is hanging on the ring mount support. In fact, all four of us have our masks there. We each get our mask and strap it on, so we can get it on our faces quickly if we need to.

Other guys are out on the road running along the column, asking if anyone has an extra gas mask. We reach some officers standing beside the road and ask them about the danger. They say that there is an ammo dump at the next town and it also has a stockpile of poison gas. We shelled it before we knew what it contained and some of the gas may have been released. This is something that really brings fear to us.

They reroute us around the town so that we will not be in as much danger. I keep my mask ready in case I need it. At one time, when we are passing the town, I think I get a whiff of something that smells like garlic and suspect it is gas and start to pull out my mask, but I do not smell it anymore. We get by the town and things settle down more. We, like all of the others, would like to be the first troops to reach Berlin. We are not meeting much resistance now and we can move forward at will.

We move on further east today and then we get orders to bypass the next town. Some Catholic nuns came out and met the first troops. They said that the town is a hospital town and is full of wounded German soldiers, and that there are no active German troops in the town. They ask that our officers declare the town a noncombat zone and not to fire on it. The officers agree and we get the order to go around it.

By late afternoon, we arrive in a small town southeast of the City of Leipzig. Ralph pulls our halftrack into a courtyard just off of the main street. There is a Catholic church, across the street from the gate, leading into the courtyard. We back up next to a chicken house and park there. The Germans are standing back in the houses looking out at us, wondering what is going to happen next.

CHAPTER LXXX

The lieutenant goes into one of the houses on the south side of the courtyard and tells the people they will have to go stay with friends for awhile because we were taking over their quarters. The people living on the west side get to stay for the present time. I dig out a few cans of food from the 10-in-1 rations and go over to the people living on the west side and try to make them understand that I want to trade for eggs and potatoes. It takes a lot of sign language, the few words of German that I know and what little English they know, before I am able to make my trade. I do better this time, getting a dozen potatoes and ten eggs.

I go into the house that we have taken over, and there is already a fire in the kitchen stove. I find some pans and dishes there too. I have a little grease that I saved from before, but I would like to have bacon anyway, so I dig out a can and open it up. I had good luck before when I cooked, so I decide to do the same thing again. I use the one skillet that I have to fry the bacon and the other to cook the potatoes and then I add the eggs in with them. One of the 10-in-1 rations has some dehydrated baked beans, so I take one of the pans in the kitchen and put the beans in it, add water, then set it on the stove to cook. I hope that by the time the water gets to boiling, the beans will be ready to eat.

I tell Ralph to go round up the other guys, that I have plenty to eat tonight. Herb comes in shortly and I ask him if he will get some of the plates and silverware out so we can eat in style. When the lieutenant comes, he brings another lieutenant with him. We make room at the table for an extra. The other lieutenant has brought a bottle of wine with him. I have them hand me their plates and I dish up the food and hand it out to them. They wait until I have my food before they start to eat, but first Herb offers a toast. We all toast what they call a banquet and then toast to a quick end to the war, followed by a toast that we all make it safely home.

I get lots of praise during the meal for my cooking, but they are so hungry for something that is not out of a can, that anything would taste great to them. I turn to the officers and say "You do know that we enlisted men eat like this all the time, don't you?" They laugh and say that they would have been eating with us a lot sooner if they had known we ate like this. It has been a fun thing and I am glad to have been able to provide it. I also noticed that no one asked where I got the eggs and potatoes.

While we are visiting, I say that I wonder how long it will be before we get to Berlin. The other lieutenant says that we will not be going to Berlin. I ask why and he says that Roosevelt has made a deal with the Russians and they get to take Berlin. In fact, we are as far east as we are going. We have been ordered to hold here until the Russians meet us. None of us like that, but it is what we will have to live with.

We put our dishes in a pan on the cabinet. If we stay here for awhile, we will have to wash them, but if we move out soon, we will leave them for the Germans to wash. No one has said anything about pulling guard, so I am going to be quiet about it. The first sergeant has probably forgotten that we are back with headquarters and has not put my name back on the list for details. I am sure he will remember before long, but for now, I am going to try to get a full night's sleep.

Herb got up early and reports that the battalion mess is in operation, so I will not have to rustle up breakfast. We go get in line to eat and while we are waiting in line one of the guys asks me if I would like to have a bipod for my BAR? I tell him that I would like to get one and he says that he saw a bipod in the alley about two blocks west and he thinks it is for a BAR.

After we eat, I go looking for the bipod. I go down the street a block, then go back to the alley and follow it back of some small stores. Sure enough, laying next to a building is a bipod. I take it back and mount it on my BAR.

There is a nice stream just in back of the house where we are staying, but to get to it, you have to go out into the street and go back west about a half of a block to the street that leads to a bridge across the water. Somehow, the battalion has acquired a weasel, a light tracked vehicle, like they used to bring me out of the snow in Kansas. A couple of the guys are driving it around. They get to talking about how the weasel can go through water, so they decide to see if it can.

They drive the weasel around to where there is a sloping bank down to the stream and drive down into the water. Immediately, the weasel starts to fill with water. Someone did not put the plugs back in the bottom. It fills with water so fast, that they can't get it back up the bank and it settles down on the bottom of the stream. The two guys climb up over the end and we reach out and help them climb out of the water.

They bring a halftrack around and unwind the winch. Fortunately the weasel has a tow ring on the front and they hook the winch to it. They start winching it out of the water and up the bank, with water streaming out of the holes in the bottom. They let it set for about a half an hour, then the two guys get in it and drive it off. At least they know now not to try to cross a river with it.

Later in the morning, a guy says that the Germans have been ordered to turn in their guns and they are supposed to do it at a house on the west edge of town. Three of us take off in a jeep to go see what has been turned in. We get to the house and I am the first one in the door. I ask the woman in the house where the guns are and she points to an enclosed porch on the side of the house. I go out on the porch and there is a long box sitting on the floor with a lot of packing papers in it. I reach in and feel a gun and pull it out. It is a shotgun, but it does not have a barrel. I drop it back into the box, reach in again and come out with what I think is a fine sporting rifle.

By now the other guys are there and one reaches in and pulls out a long flat wooden case. The other guy pickups up the gun without a barrel, that I previously grabbed. He reaches back in and comes up with the barrel. That is all that is in the box. Now it is time to see what we have. The guy that got the gun with the barrel off, puts the barrel on and screws the cap on that holds the fore stock in place and he has a Browning Sweet Sixteen shotgun. The other guy opens the wooden case and laying in the plush felt is a kit to turn a K 98 Mauser into a .22 caliber training rifle.

I examine the rifle that I got and find it is not a firearm, but is an air rifle. It is a beautiful rifle that looks like a Mauser sporter but it shoots round lead BB's. I dig in the papers in the bottom of the box and find a box of BB's for it. All of the guns look brand new. We are all pleased with what we got out of the box. We go back and I start shooting the BB gun. It is powerful and will shoot through both sides of a C ration can.

After we shoot it at cans for a little bit, I start looking for better targets. I move the sight up and take aim at the bell in the church steeple across the street. It is no problem to hit the bell and hear the ding as the BB bounces off. I take the gun and go across the stream to the open field south of the town. I shoot the blooms off of wildflowers, insects and then I see some grapevines on trellises and among the vines are many large snails. They make great targets and I figure that I am helping whoever owns the vineyard. I sit down and shoot dozens of snails. After I have shot until I am bored, I get to thinking that some people in Europe eat snails and I wonder if these are some that they keep for that purpose. Maybe I was not helping as much as I thought.

Some of the nuns from the hospital town contact our headquarters asking for some supplies. While they are there, one of the officers asks if they have a place where some of our troops could take a bath. They say that they have room for a few of us at a time. They tell us to come to the hospital and they will be glad to exchange baths for supplies. They say they will expect some of us to come tomorrow. The word is passed around that tomorrow those who want to take a bath need to report to Headquarters.

When I get back from my shooting trip, the lieutenant asks me to go with him to check out some weapons. We get in a jeep and go about a mile southwest of the town. There laying in a field are a bunch of "Panzerfausts." (German antitank rockets.) They look like a bunch of metal toilet plungers. They have a big round head mounted on a slender pipe shaft. They are deadly on a tank or pill box, but even the German soldiers are afraid to shoot them. There are also about a dozen German "potato masher" hand grenades.

The lieutenant marks the location on the map and will give it to a demolition squad so they can destroy the rockets. We take the hand grenades to dispose of ourselves. We go back to the stream and start to throw the grenades into the water. They have a wooden handle with a container on the end holding the explosive. There is a screw cap on the wooden handle that you take off and a wooden ball on a string falls out. To explode the grenade, you pull on the little ball and it is supposed to go off in five seconds. Just as we get ready to pull the cord, I tell the lieutenant to hold up.

I had read about how sometimes the slave laborers sabotaged these, by taking out the five second delay cap and inserting a regular blasting cap, so that when you pull the cord, it goes off instantly. We do not know that these were not altered the same way, either in manufacturing or by the Germans as a booby trap. We do not want to take the chance, so we just unscrew the cap on each one let the ball come out and then throw them into the stream. We hope that the water will get inside and kill the explosive.

When we get back to where we are staying, there are some guys there and they are drinking out of glass bottles. I ask what they are drinking and they say it is soda water. I ask where they got it and they say there are several bottles in the back of the small store down the street. I tell them I want to get some too, so one of the guys offers to go with me. We find several cases of bottles in the back of the store. We each take two bottles and go back to the house where we are staying.

I open a bottle and take a drink. It tastes just like the carbonated water we used to drink when I worked in the drugstore. It is okay, but not anything great. I remember how we used to use it to make fountain drinks by adding a flavored syrup. I go get a K ration, take out the lemon drink package and the sugar packet. I pour the sugar and the drink powder in the bottle, close the stopper and gently shake it. It is the closest thing to a bottle of lemon soda I have had in a long time.

CHAPTER LXXXI

While I am in line for breakfast, I tell the first sergeant that I would like to get to go take a bath. He tells me to come over to the headquarters about nine and they will have someone going so that I can get a ride. My other set of clothes are clean, so I get them, a towel, washrag and a bar of soap. I pack them in my musette bag and I am ready to get the first bath I have had in weeks.

A little after nine, a jeep pulls up in front of the building they are using for headquarters. There is a corporal driving and a staff sergeant from headquarters. I go climb into the back of the jeep and they tell me that we will go as soon as the other guy gets here. It is not long before the other guy shows up and climbs into the back beside me. He is a private from the wire section.

The other town is five or six miles west of where we are located. We are traveling along and when we have gone about three miles, we get to an "S"curve in the road. When the jeep comes out of the "S" curve and turns back west, the driver yells, "OH, SHIT!", and slams on the brakes. Sitting in the middle of the road about one hundred yards ahead of us, is a massive German tank, with the cannon pointing right at us. We sit there and every one of us is holding his breath.

After what seems like a long time, but is probably less than a minute, the sergeant says, "If there were anyone in it, we would be dead by now." I let out a cautious sigh of relief and the driver starts slowly forward. He drives out around the tank and we look up at the huge bulk towering over us. As we go around the tank, I look at the back of the tank and see that the engine has burned. It probably got hit in the rear by fire from an airplane. Our division has advanced so fast, that we have left pockets of German soldiers all around and of course, there are also those Germans that are fleeing back west from the Russian advance. I am just glad that this tank has been knocked out.

We travel on until we get to the hospital town. We drive into the town and there are wounded German soldiers everywhere. They line the sidewalks and stare at us as we drive down the street. Most of them are crippled and have lost one or more limbs. Their glares are not friendly and of course, they have reason not to be. We do not see any weapons any place. The four carbines we have would not be much protection for us if they did bring out their weapons. It may be that all weapons were put away to ensure that this town was not attacked.

We have no trouble recognizing the hospital when we see it. It is well marked and the signs are visible, both from the ground and the air. We park the jeep and before we get to the door, one of the nuns comes out to meet us. She speaks English very well and tells us to follow her. We go through the front of the hospital and then back to another part that I believe would be the therapy section. There are several rooms and she has us each go into a room and then she shows us how to turn on the water before she leaves.

The tub in the room I am in is about seven feet long, three feet wide and a foot and a half deep. The water comes into the tub in a big stream and is steaming hot. I turn on enough cold water to get it to a temperature that will not burn me and carefully lower myself into the tub. My dirty clothes are laying on the floor, my carbine hanging on the hook with my towel over it. I have the washrag and soap with me. I sit down in the hot water and then slide down so that I am laying flat in the tub, just soaking in the hot water. When I have soaked for awhile, I start scrubbing off the layers of dirt. Then I soak some more. It feels so good, that I lay back and close my eyes and doze off.

I wake when the door is opened and I hear the nun say, "Here he is."

The sergeant comes in and says, "Come on Lovell, get out of there. We are waiting on you." I climb out, dry off and dress as fast as I can. I stuff my dirty clothes in the musette bag, grab my carbine and hurry outside. They are waiting in the jeep and I climb in and they take off. They say that they got part way back and realized that they had forgotten me, so they had to come back and get me. They said they thought about just leaving me there. I guess for a little bit, I was the only American in a town with ten thousand German soldiers.

It is a beautiful spring day and I feel so good from my bath that they can kid me all they want and it will not bother me. When we get back to Headquarters, the first sergeant is waiting for us. Or more particularly, for me. He says he has a new title for me: assistant in charge of special services. Sounds impressive, but I wonder what he really means; I do not have to wonder long. He says that I did such a good job setting up the theater back at Ay, that he wants me to set up one here. He tells me to pick out one of the buildings that would make a good theater and get it set up, so that they can show movies tonight.

I look over the buildings as I go back to put my dirty clothes away and see one of the stores that looks like it might do. I put my things away and then go back to the store building. I can look through the glass and see that it is nearly empty. The front door is locked, but I take my knife and push through and trip the catch on the inside. The building has some counters in the front part and then there is a divider towards the back.

I push the counters over to the side and stack them up so that most of the front is open. There is one small table there and I push it to the center to set the projector on. I find a broom in the rear of the store and use it to sweep out the building. Then I go find the special service sergeant and have him pull the trailer with the generator on it up by the front of the building. We hang the screen on the divider, put the projector on the table and line it up. We put the speakers below the front of the screen and run the cords back to the projector.

We crank up the generator and get the projector focused. Then I start going from building to building, gathering up all of the chairs and benches I can find and arranging them in the building to sit on. We are now ready for a movie. I ask what we will see and the sergeant says that we have received the movie, "Adventure," starring Clark Gable and Greer Garson.

When it is time for the movie, most of the guys that are not on duty head for the building. The sergeant starts the projector and everything works fine. The guys all enjoy the movie, but it would not make much difference what it was, as long as it is from home.

They announce the next morning that anyone not on a detail is to fall out for physical training at nine. Since I have the job of taking care of the theater, I go there at nine and start sweeping out the building. This job has a lot more benefits that I first thought.

We just get settled in here, when we get orders to move. We are to pull back west a ways, then turn south, before turning back to the southeast. We will be making kind of circular movement to get down toward Czechoslovakia, to trap the Germans still fighting in that area. We load up our things and get the column going back against the normal flow of traffic, for a ways and then we turn and head south. While we are traveling, I notice that the German rifle I have has gotten rusty, so I destroy it and throw it away. I will pick up another as soon as we get down the road to the next town.

We get back close enough to the front lines that we have some more fire missions. One fire mission is at an airfield and they shoot to try to stop any planes from taking off. Later in the day, we go past the airfield and there is a German ME109 airplane standing on its nose at the end of the runway. I guess the shells stopped him from taking off. The forward observer in the Piper Cub keeps spotting for targets for the firing batteries, but there are not many opportunities to fire on viable targets.

The forward observer lands his plane close to where we are parked. I go help him gas up and he asks if I want to go with him on a mission and of course I do. But we pull out before I get a chance to fly. I was hoping that I could go and act as a spotter for him.

We stop in a small town to spend the night. We are moving into more dangerous territory, so we will be pulling more guard. We set up guard posts all around the town and man them at all times. This means more shifts on guard duty. The next day, we move further south. The only Germans we see now are marching down the roads carrying white flags. I keep wondering where they have dropped their weapons so I can pick up another rifle, but I can't find one. After destroying so many, I can't find even one for myself.

We stop in a larger town and set up on the corner of the town in some of the houses there.   We post guards, but they are only to be on from dark to daylight. We do not have to pull as many shifts. The "Stars & Stripes" says that the war will end soon. Hitler has committed suicide, the German troops in Italy have surrendered and the Russians have taken Berlin. They are trying to get a surrender signed for the rest of the German troops.

This morning, they announce that the Germans have surrendered, the war is over, it is VE day, May 8, 1945. I am sad to see it end in some ways, because my chance to be a real hero is gone. I also feel that we are not very important anymore; we have done our job. A couple of us are standing beside the halftrack when we hear a roar. We look up and two German jet planes fly over head, going toward the southwest. I wonder who had enough pull to get a jet and leave Germany before they were captured.

Ralph and I decide to walk around. We are walking down the street when we see a crowd of people in the street in front of us. They are milling around and when we get closer, we see that they are throwing things at something. As we walk up, they lower their heads and start walking away. We see that we are at the entrance to a slave labor camp. Lying on the ground, just outside of the gate, is a body. The last few people are kicking it. They look at us and then walk back inside of the camp with the others. The body on the ground is that of a German soldier. We assume that he was one of the guards and the workers have stoned him to death. We figure that he probably had it coming, so we keep walking on down the street.

CHAPTER LXXXII

Ralph and I get back to where the battalion is located and the first sergeant meets us. He says that he has been looking for us, that they want us to follow their jeep with the halftrack and give them cover, because there is a riot going on in town and we need to go control it. I say, "Sergeant, I think......"

He says, "You are not paid to think. Get in that halftrack and lets go."

We follow them down the street and they stop when they see the body lying in the street. There are no live people to be seen; everyone has disappeared into their barracks.

The first sergeant goes over to look at the dead German soldier and then he comes back and says that it looks like he was beaten to death. Then he tells us to follow them. We drive through the town and everything is quiet. Finally he says, "We might as well go back, there is nothing going on here." I know better than say anything, but I wanted to tell him that I tried to tell him that. We would just get in trouble for being here when they were stoning the guard.

When we get back, they set up the guard schedule for the night. He wants extra guards and it is probably a good idea, because those people are going to be out trying to find food and the Germans do not have much to take. Taking care of all of those people is going to be a job. I guess the military government people will come in and try to work things out. We will be on our way tomorrow and unless some unit comes in, there may well be a riot as those workers try to find food.

Since the war has ended, we are not in as big of a hurry to get down to where we have been assigned. But we move out and head mostly south until we reach the city of Naila. The 73rd will have their headquarters here. We find a place just south of the railroad tracks on the east side of the city. The headquarters will be in a former Mercedes dealership. The mess will take over a gasthaus across the street. It has a large meeting room, bar and dining room. There are rooms above where some of us can stay. The others will be in buildings close by.

The headquarters has enough room for their operations and there is a building for the doctors to set up an infirmary. Out in back where they used to repair cars, the motor pool will be located. There is a hayfield in back of the gasthaus that will make a great ball field and parade ground. I get with the special services sergeant and we fix up a theater in the gasthaus. It is not hard; all we have to do is to hang the screen on one wall of the meeting room. The chairs are already there, and we pull the generator up beside the building and run the wires through the window.

After we get our things located, four of us decide to go explore this small city. The city is located south of a flat top mountain. The city begins at the base of the mountain and spreads out along the base and up the slope leading to more high ground to the south. There have been no battles here and the city was not a target for bombers, so there is no damage. We walk west from where we have located, into the heart of the city. No white flags here; people for the most part seem to be going about their daily business. Most of the people seem friendly and some young women lean out of windows in one apartment building and greet us. We hold out sticks of gum to them and they come down to get them.

We are not supposed to be talking to them and I am afraid that we will get arrested if we get caught. A couple of the guys exchange the stick of gum for a kiss and I decide that this town may be a great place after all. The girls call it "kaugummi," but when they say it, it sounds like "cowgummi" to me. I guess the kau means chew and gummi means gum. I wish I had guts enough to grab one of the girls and kiss her, but I am afraid to push my luck. I walk on down the street. One of the guys goes with me and the other two soon follow. I am not sure, but I think they made a date for later. That is, if they could speak enough of the language.

The next day after we arrive, I get a change in my duties. I am assigned to a five-man team that will be doing outpost guard. We will be out at one of the surrounding towns for four days and then we will be back at the battery for three days. When I am at the battery, I will have my job in special services.

I meet with the other members of the team to get ready to go. Rich, a sergeant, is the leader, and Slick another sergeant is the assistant leader. Robbie, a corporal, is the jeep driver and Old Jack, a PFC, is the halftrack driver. I am the fifth member. I guess they have heard about me, because they send me to pick up what rations we will need for the four days. We load our bedrolls and musette bags in the halftrack. We will leave our duffle bags here at the battery. We take off with the jeep leading with Robbie driving, Rich and Slick riding. We follow with Old Jack driving the halftrack and I ride, as usual, in the ring mount.

We go north out of the city, going through the underpass, under the railroad and out into the farm land. It is a beautiful drive through the country, first climbing the gentle slope to higher ground and then dropping back down to the little town of Neuhaus. The town consists of a gasthaus that is not in operation and a dozen farm houses. We will be staying at the gasthaus. There is a family living in one end and we will occupy what looks like a small auditorium. This would have been where the people in the community came for entertainment before the war.

The family consists of a middle aged woman, her mother and a young boy. We send word that we want to see the burgermeister or mayor of the village and an elderly man soon reports to the building. Rich tells him that we need five beds before night, and that we will need someone to cook our meals for us and asks if the woman living there can do it. The burgermeister says that he will get us some beds by evening and he will talk to the woman and see if she can do the cooking. He goes to talk to the woman and then he comes back and says that she will do the cooking, but she may need help with the English to know what she is cooking. Then he leaves to go find some beds.

We take food out of the 10-in-1 rations and pick out what we would like to eat and what we think she can cook and give it to the woman. Hopefully we will have supper sometime this evening. A little while later, the burgermeister arrives with an even older man driving a horse that looks even older and pulling a cart. On the cart are five wooden frame beds. In addition, they have brought some hay to put on the beds. They carry them inside of the building and line them up before putting a layer of hay on each bed to make kind of a mattress. It looks better than many of the places we have slept in the last few weeks.

The German woman comes into the room and says something in German and motions for us to come that way. She has set five places at a table and brings the food to the table for us. She has done a good job. It tastes better than what I expected. We sit and eat most of the food, but are careful to make sure there is something left for the two women and the boy.

After supper, we go out and look around the small town. I am sure that the people are looking at us at the same time. The town seems to be mostly old women, a few real old men and a few young children. There are no stores. I am sure that they raise most of their food. We walk back to the gasthaus and I decide to write a letter home before it gets dark. After I get through writing, I unroll my bedroll on one of the beds, take off my boots and slide into my sleeping bag. I go to sleep with the other guys still talking.

We get up and the woman has breakfast ready. She cooked the bacon and made patties out of the corned beef hash and fried them. She took some of the instant coffee and brewed up some of it. It turned out kind of strong, but that is okay. After breakfast, we take a small table and chair, load them on the jeep and drive out southeast to the corner of the town, where there is a "T" intersection and set up the table for a checkpoint. We will check the papers of anyone going by the checkpoint. I do not expect that business will be very busy, because both of the roads are back roads. But we might catch someone trying to bypass the main checkpoints.

Robbie agrees to take the first shift. We go back and leave him sitting at the table waiting for someone to come by. When we get back, I walk around the building and go down across a meadow towards a forest. Along the edge of the forest, on the green grass, are several large rabbits. I take aim at one and shoot it with my carbine. I know I hit it, but I watch as it runs off into the forest. I aim at another and shoot it, but before it can run away, I shoot it again. It is still trying to get away, so I have to shoot it a third time. It seems that the carbine bullets are just going right through them. I go get the one rabbit that I shot and it is really heavy. I start back and see another rabbit. This time, I aim at his head and it only takes one shot to get him.

I take the two rabbits back to the gasthaus and get Slick to help me dress them out. We then take them in to the woman to cook. She seems pleased to have them. I am sure that with the things in the 10-in-1, she will be able to cook us a nice dinner. He says that he wants to go get some supplies and wants Slick to go with him. He gathers up some of the cans from the 10-in-1 rations and they set out to do some trading. I go down to relieve Robbie.

I sit at the table and wait for something to happen. After awhile, a small German car comes around the curve and I signal them to stop. It has three well dressed men in the car. I ask for their papers and they each present me with something written in German, but it has signatures and seals on it, so I figure it must be okay. I waive them on. We do not have any guidelines for who to detain. They may have been high ranking Nazis and I would not know it.

When it gets to be noon, I walk up to the gasthaus to see if dinner is ready. Rich and Slick are back and have traded for potatoes and eggs. We are not having rabbit for dinner; it takes too long to cook. She will have the rabbit cooked, with some of the potatoes, for supper.

After dinner, Rich tells Jack to go down and man the checkpoint. Jack says that he can't read or write. Rich says that is all right, everything will be written in German and none of us can read it either. So Jack goes down to man the checkpoint. There is really not much use of us being here, but it does get us out of the battery for awhile.

CHAPTER LXXXIII

When evening comes, the woman calls us to come in and eat. I am not much for rabbit, but this is delicious. She has done very well with the food from the 10-in-1 rations too. We are sitting down at a table and eating off of plates, not out of a mess kit. I am sure that the family will enjoy their part too. But these people probably endured the war as well as anyone in Germany. They were able to raise food and never had to deal with starvation.

I find that Jack was serious about not being able to read or write. He brings out a letter from his folks and asks me to read it to him. I read the letter and then ask him if he would like to answer it. He says that he would really like to let them know that he is okay. I get out my stationery and start writing. I tell them that he is glad the war is over and he is alive and doing very well. He has plenty to eat and a good bed to sleep on. He gets to see a movie every few days. He has enough money, his PX items are free and he hopes that the money they are receiving from his allotment is enough so that they are getting by okay. I finish off by asking if they are all well.

I get the address off of the envelope that his letter came in and get it ready to mail when we get back to the battery. He is very grateful to me for writing the letter for him. He is from the south and although he has not said so, I think that he probably lived out in the backwoods. As soon as he gets out of the army, I am sure he will head back there. Slick is from the south too. Robbie is from Pennsylvania and Rich is from Illinois.

It is after dark when Rich and Slick come back. They have a couple dozen eggs, about ten pounds of potatoes, some carrots and some onions. They take the food in to the cook and then tell us that they did not have any trouble trading. The people were just as anxious to get the canned goods as we are the local produce.

I do not know where the power comes from, probably Naila, but we have electric lights here. I take off my clothes down to my underwear before I slip into the sleeping bag. It is a real luxury to be out of all of those clothes. Rich and Slick are still talking and Robbie has not come back when I go to sleep.

This morning, we have bacon, eggs, some of the thick canned crackers and coffee for breakfast. Slick showed the woman how to make the coffee, using the instant coffee in the rations. This is living really well. Even the duty manning the check station is easy, just a little boring with no one coming by. But if you get tired, you just go up to the gasthaus for awhile. No one really cares.

We finally get some action. Six German soldiers come towards the town. One is out ahead on a bicycle. We stop them and ask to see their papers. They each have a piece of paper issued from an infantry division, saying that they were taken prisoner and that they are being sent back for processing. Any unit that is able to process them should detain them until they have been discharged from the German Army. We have them sit down beside the building in the shade until they can be taken on back.

We go through their things to see that they do not have weapons and then they are lined up to be marched to Naila. The one protests about having to leave his bicycle, but it is likely that it is not really his anyway. Rich and Slick get in the halftrack with Jack driving and follow them down the road to Naila. They drop off the prisoners, pickup our mail and start back. They are going by the forest and see some deer on the grass next to the trees. They take the .30

caliber machine gun and open fire. They get one small doe and bring her back.

They dress out the deer and give it to the cook. They used to have a butcher shop in part of the gasthaus, and she has had a lot of butchering experience. She knows what to do with the deer. We will have meat for supper again today. They hand out our mail. We all have mail except Jack. I invite him to come and sit beside me, while I read my two letters from home. My mother writes interesting letters, so he gets to enjoy them too.

Each day goes slowly, but the four days seem to pass very quickly and it is time to go back to the battery and let one of the other teams come out here.

When we get to Naila, we find that today is PX ration day. They have more things available than usual, but the problem is, that whereas last week our PX rations were free, we now have to pay for them. Cigarettes are only a nickel a pack, but many of us only get a few dollars a month and do not have even enough money to buy what we are allowed. We take up a collection and those that have money put it in, so that everyone can get their PX allowance.

There have been some changes made since we left. The bar in the gasthaus has been opened up, so in addition to having movies in there, you can now get a drink. The catch is that the drinks are rationed. We have to go to the orderly room and get our drink ration cards. This is not as bad as it seems for those of us who have been on outpost. The ration card is good for three drinks a day. We have been gone for four days, so that is twelve drinks we have coming, plus the three for each day we are there which is another nine drinks. So we get an average of seven drinks a day.

If this is not enough, they contacted the owner of the local brewery and agreed to take his entire production of beer. So in addition to the hard liquor, you can have all the beer you want. They have a keg in the bar and the bartender will draw you one any time the bar is open. The rest of the time, you have to help yourself.

Out back in the field, they have POWs working to make a softball diamond. They cut trees from the forest to make poles for the back stop. They found some chicken wire to finish off the backstop. They have cut the grass and the POWs are scraping off the grass to make an infield. It will be ready to play on soon and they have scheduled a tournament for next month.

Since I am back on special services, I take a room upstairs over the bar. We even have an inside toilet. It is not a flush toilet, but waste goes down a chute and into a kind of cistern, where it is collected and then hauled to the fields to fertilize. They are not used to using toilet paper and the first time they haul out a load after we get there, they are not happy to see those bits of paper all over the field.

From what I hear, most of the guys here at Naila have found a willing girl and sex is the main evening entertainment. I do not seem to be able to find one that is interested in me. I finally ask one of the guys how you go about finding a girl that wants to have sex. He says that you just go across the railroad track and you will find a trail leading up the side of the flat topped mountain. Just walk along the trail and when you see a girl, ask her if she would like to go for a walk. The German word for going for a walk is"sparzierengehen." If she says yes, you go along the trail until you find a place where you can get off in a secluded location and make love to her. Most of the women on the trail are not there for the walk; they are there looking for the same thing you are.

This is the last night that we will be in Naila for awhile, because we will be going out to another outpost tomorrow. In the evening, I clean up and then head out down the road, under the underpass and sure enough, there is a well worn path going up the side of the mountain. I get on the path and slowly walk along. It is not long before I hear someone behind me and turn around and a nice looking girl is coming up the path. She is probably about twenty-one, medium build, light hair and blue eyes. As she gets close, I pull my nerve together and in my best German, ask her if she would like to go for a walk. She says "ja."

I fall in beside her and she slows her pace some so that we walk together. As we walk on the narrow path, I brush against her side.

My hormones are about to explode and my heart is pounding. We get to a narrower side path and she turns on it. Now, we are tight against each other as we walk along it. I put my arm around her waist and hold her against me as we walk. We reach a clump of trees and she turns to go into them. We are now out of sight unless someone is really looking for us.

She turns to face me and I put my arms around her and pull her toward me and lower my head and kiss her. It is a long hot kiss. By now, my heart is pounding, but it is not pumping any blood into my brain. It is all going the other direction. She says "Haben sie gummi?" I smile, reach into my pocket and pull out a stick of chewing gum and hand it to her. She looks at the stick of gum, looks at me, shakes her head, turns around and walks away, leaving me standing there with my mouth open.

I walk around the paths, but do not see another girl who is alone, so I go back to gasthaus and get there in time to see the last of the movie. Then I go climb into my bed and get to sleep, still wondering what I did wrong up on the mountain.

The next morning, we load up our rations and our same team heads out for another town. This time, we are going to Selbitz, which is east of Naila and is the capitol of that area. It is not quite as big as Naila, but of course, much larger than tiny Neuhaus. They have set up the checkpoint on the main road leading to the city of Hof. It is at the bottom of a hill on the northeast side of Selbitz. In fact, the table for the checkpoint is next to the road marker showing that it is thirteen kilometers to Hof.

We will be staying in what used to be the office at a rock quarry. The team before us had put five bunks in the building. There are double doors going in off of the road and a single door in the back leading to steps that take you down one floor to where it is even with the sloping ground. They have been doing their cooking down on the lower level and sleeping up above. I guess we will have to do the same thing. And it looks like we will have to do our own cooking this time, since there is no one around. We are about seven miles from Naila and only about six miles from Neuhaus.

When we arrive, Robbie takes over the checkpoint, Jack goes in to clean up, Rich goes to see what food he can trade for and Slick and I go exploring. We go up the road a ways and find a path leading into the trees. We follow it about a hundred yards and come to an old quarry that has water in it. The water is nice and clear. On one side, there is an opening in the quarry wall where you can get to the water. There is a pike swimming in the water and Slick shoots at it. It turns over and we go use a stick to get it out. We take it and go back.

Rich is back and has some fresh vegetables that he traded for. We save them for supper and will have them with the pike. For dinner, we will just heat up some of the canned goods. While we are waiting for dinner, Robbie comes in and takes his coat off. He is cleaning out the pockets and starts putting things on the table. He throws a condom on the table and as he does he says "Good old gummi." A light goes off in my head: she was not asking if I had gum, she was asking if I had a rubber.

CHAPTER LXXXIV

We are getting ready to eat some of the rations for dinner, when a three quarter ton truck drives up. They have a keg of beer for us. We unload it and sit it on top of the road marker, beside the table, at the checkpoint. It has a spigot with it and we put the end against the cork in the keg and pound it in. We open the spigot and foam runs out. It takes three cups of foam before the beer starts to flow. I have my canteen cup under it and I get a nice cup of beer with a good head on it. It is only cool, but still tastes good.

And I go dig out one of the rations that can be eaten cold, sit down at the checkpoint table with it, my cup of beer and enjoy my dinner. I will take over the checkpoint for awhile. There is much more traffic here than at Neuhaus and we get to check papers every little bit. The drivers of the trucks hate to have to stop here, because they would rather have a run at the hill. When they stop, it takes them a long time to get up speed.

Each vehicle stops and the driver gets out and comes over to the table to present their papers for our approval. We always look them over, but we seldom can figure out anything about them. After we check them, we tell them they can go on. Some of the vehicles are powered by wood burners. They have a large stove like device in back of the cab, fired with wood chips and they take the gas that is generated and run it through the combustion engine. It does not have near the power of petroleum, but does run. It also makes the engine run very hot and they have a large water tank, mounted on the front bumper, supplying the radiator.

Often, they will take a poker and stir up the fire in the gas generator, before attempting to climb up the hill. Sometimes, they will not be able to make it over the top and they roll back down and then back up the hill, with the lower reverse gear.

I spend some time manning the checkpoint, but it is not hard work. I can reach over and refill my cup with beer and I have one of those German cigars to smoke. There is enough traffic so that it is not boring like before.

The traffic drops off in the evening, with only a few people hurrying to get home before the nine o'clock curfew. Slick fixes supper. He cooks the pike and fixes one of the meals from the 10-in-1 rations. The pike is only big enough so that we each get a taste of it. It is not bad and the rest of the meal is okay, but sure not as good as we had at Neuhaus. We have electricity here too, so we have a light at night. I do not stay up very long and soon go to sleep. I do not sleep long before I have to get up. Too much beer today.

Today we decide to go fishing. Slick, Rich and I go back up to the quarry to see if we can get some more pike. We do not have any fishing tackle, but we do have the hand grenade that I have carried in my pocket. I take the hand grenade, pull the pin and toss it into the water. Five seconds later we hear a muffled thump and water boils up to the surface. Some mud comes up and even a small oil slick, but no fish.

We take turns manning the checkpoint again today. With all the beer you can drink and a bunch of cigars, it is really good duty. We even drink beer for breakfast.

Robbie and Rich take the jeep and go into the town. They say to trade for fresh food, but I have an idea that they are looking for more than food on this trip. While they are gone, Jack says he is going to take the halftrack for a little while. He heads off on the road that goes to Neuhaus. Slick and I man the checkpoint.

Slick likes to joke around, but he has kind of a mean streak too. When we throw down a cigarette butt, it is not long before some German will pick it up. Cigarettes are the best medium of exchange here, so even a butt is worth picking up. Slick will throw a nice long butt out by the road and then he will lay his carbine over his lap and sight it on the cigarette butt. When someone stops and starts to reach down for the butt, he will shoot it out from under their hand. He thinks it is really funny, but I do not see any of the Germans laughing.

In the afternoon, I go up in the woods to see if I can find a rabbit or deer. I do not find any of them, but I do see a squirrel. I am trying to get a shot at him, and I work my way over to the road. Just as I step out of the woods, the battalion commander goes by in the Dodge command car. I do not hear him in time to get back into the woods and I know he saw me.

In the evening while we are eating supper, a sergeant from headquarters comes in. He has been sent out with an order from headquarters that no troops are to be running around by themselves. Looks like I have done it again. I can get into trouble so easily.

We finish our supper. Robbie cooked one of the meals from the 10-in-1 rations. It had beans in it, but I don't think they got done, but I ate them anyway.

I do not feel well, so I go to bed early. I have not been in bed too long before I wake up and I am really feeling bad. My belly is sticking out. I go outside and only go a few feet when I explode. What went down, now comes up with tremendous force and beans fly through the air, but I start to feeling better and go back to sleep.

The next morning, Rich says that he did not feel good last night, but somebody else must not have felt good either, because there are beans all over outside. I tell them about exploding and that I am glad I am still alive, because I thought my belly was going to split.

This morning, the truck comes by to pick up the empty beer keg and drop off a new one. The five of us drank that keg of beer in just two days. While we are standing around, we get to talking about how fast an M1 rifle can fire. Someone suggests that if we filed down the sear, it would fire full automatic. I still have the M1 that I picked up, so I get it out and Slick takes it to work on it.

Right after noon, a couple of girls come looking for Robbie and Rich. The girls stay around with us for awhile and one of the girls says that if we will each give them a bar of soap and a wash rag, they will make something. We each dig out the required items and hand them over. I stay by the checkpoint and man it, while Robbie, Rich and the girls go off into the woods. They are carrying some of the rations, so I guess they are going to have a picnic. They come back late in the afternoon and the girls go back into town.

After supper, Slick says that he thinks he has fixed the M1 so that it will fire full automatic. He says that he wants to wait until nine o'clock and announce the curfew. When nine gets here, he lays the rifle over the hood of the halftrack and aims it at the mountain on the other side of the city and pulls the trigger. It fires so fast, that we have to look in it to see how many rounds it fired. It only fired six of the eight rounds. We load it again and this time it fired all but one. The third time is a charm, it fires them all and the clip comes out with the last shell casing. It fires so fast that it seems to only be one long sound. He says "I bet that they are all in their houses tomorrow night, when it is time for curfew."

The next day is much the same. The girls come back in the afternoon and bring each of us a bath scrubber. They have sewn the bar of soap that each of us gave to them inside of the wash rag. I don't say anything, but I wonder if they made these for the German soldiers. The four go off into the woods again, and after they leave, Jack says that he is going to take the halftrack again. Slick asks where he is going and he says he is going to Neuhaus. Slick tells him to not let anyone see him alone in that halftrack. He says he will be careful and go the back road.

Jack is not gone too long and gets back before Rich and Robbie and the girls. One of the guys asks the girls if they are Nazis. The one girl does not say anything, but the other says that she was. We look at her kind of funny and she says "It was the thing to do at the time." I think that is a good answer. We do not know what we will do until we face the situation. I will be glad to get back to Naila where we can eat at the mess.

In the morning, we get our things together and get ready to go back. It is about the middle of the morning before the other team arrives and we can leave. I had thought we would get back to Naila for breakfast, but instead, we have to eat one of the C rations. At least, we should get back in time to eat dinner.

When we get back, I have to get busy and clean out the hall where they have the theater set up. I do not know who is supposed to do it when I am on outpost , but they have not done a very good job. By the time I get done, it is time for dinner. I have my bed back up stairs and I take a chance that no one will be up there and lay down after dinner and take a short nap.

I get up and walk around to see what has been done since we left. The ball field looks really good. The team has been practicing every day and hopefully they will be ready for the tournament. Day after tomorrow is Memorial Day and we are going to have a service out on the field.

I eat supper and then I get busy and make sure that the room is ready for the movie tonight. I am not planning on attending the movie, but if everything is ready, I will have a chance to get away and go up on the side of the mountain and see what I can find. I walk down the street and then duck under the underpass and get on the path. I do not want to get caught out by myself again and get in more trouble. I walk along the path and see a few girls, but they are all with someone or going to meet someone. I go back down and watch the rest of the movie. I will try again tomorrow night.

The next night, I make another trip up on the side of the moun-tain. I find a young girl walking along the path and ask her if she would like to go for a walk. She says that she would, so we fol-low the path up until I see the narrow path leading off of it. We go until we see the hidden spot on the grove of trees and go in and sit down. She looks young but asks if I have a gummi and this time, I know what it is. I pull a rubber out and show it to her and she nods in agreement. I drop my pants and put the rubber on. As I do, she pulls off her panties, which are made of some coarse material, not at all like those in America. I get ready to lose my virginity. As I pull her dress up, I notice that she does not have any pubic hair. I try to ask her how old she is, but I can't understand what she says. I do not want to be having sex with an underage girl, so I shake my head, stand up, take off the rubber and pull my pants back up. She seems confused by my actions, but puts her panties back on and stands up. We walk back out to the trail and I leave her and go back to the gasthaus.

I go to the movie again and while I am sitting there, I get to thinking about whether she was old enough or not, but then I remember that I do not have pubic hair either.

CHAPTER LXXXV

The Memorial Day service is very impressive. We form up on the grassy field with thirty men from each of the five batteries. The battalion executive officer reads the general's order of the day and the chaplain gives the prayer. There is an eight man firing squad and they fire a three round salute. The shots echo off of the mountain behind us. One man stands right here and blows taps followed by another man playing down the valley. With the mountain behind, it gives a tremendous echo effect. After this, we get dismissed and the rest of the day is a holiday.

The cooks were able to get some hamburger meat and they cook hamburgers for us to eat. Of course, we have plenty of beer to wash them down. The weather is such that we can be outside most of the day.

Today we go back to Neuhaus for outpost duty. I gather up all the rations they will let me have and we move out, going under the underpass and then over the hill to Neuhaus again. We find that the guys that replaced us did not use the cook and she is now working for someone. Grandma is going to cook for us.

We get our things settled in and I take off to the woods to hunt. It does not take long for me to get a rabbit. I take it back and we dress it out and give it to the old woman to fix for dinner. Then I go down to the junction and relieve Jack. While I am there, I get to watch a German farmer cutting hay. He has a mowing machine, pulled by one very old horse and a cow. It is not very efficient, but he is much off better than most of the neighbors, that are using scythes to cut their hay. When it is noon, I make my way back up to the gasthaus for dinner.

The old woman has the table set and the food prepared. We sit down to eat and dish up the rabbit. The first guy to take a bite spits it out and says, "Oh my God." By then I already have a bite in my mouth. I try to swallow it, but can't and I have to spit mine out too. It is enough to gag me. It seems that the old woman did not know about opening the bacon to get grease and used some old fat that had gotten rancid. We got up and went to the rations and pulled out some cans of stuff, that could be eaten cold and ate that.

Rich has the boy go tell the burgermeister that we need to see him. It is not long before he shows up with his hat in his hand. Rich tells him that we need the woman we had before, to cook for us. He argues that she is working and needs the money. Rich tells him that we want her for our cook and the people of the town will have to pay her to be our cook. He says he will see what he can do and leaves. It is not long before the woman shows up and starts to get the kitchen ready to cook again.

I tell her to use the rations we brought for supper and I will try to get a rabbit tonight for tomorrow. I am sure that I will not be able to find one until about evening, when they come out on the grass. Then I go down to the checkpoint to stand guard. Robbie comes down to relieve me and I go back. I am the only one there. The other three are gone someplace. I lay down on my bed and rest for awhile.

When I get up, I go outside and walk around. I am just south of the gasthaus when a woman walks up. She is probably about thirty, but to me, she looks older. She says something in German and I can understand enough to know that she is saying, that she wants to have sex. My heart starts to beat faster and I am having trouble breathing, but I am able to think of enough German words to volunteer for the job. She looks me up and down and then says in German that I am too little and she walks on down the road. I can't get anyone to do it, even when they want it.

In the evening, Robbie and I go out hunting. We look up and see a deer in some tall grass. We both shoot and the deer drops down into the grass. We start walking toward it and see it go running out the other end of the field. We each start firing our carbines but the deer gets away. Around on the other side of the trees, we see a couple of rabbits and I am able to shoot one. We dress it out and take it back for the cook. A few minutes later, Rich and Slick drive up with a deer. We dress it out and give it to her too. We now have a good cook and lots of meat for the remainder of our time here.

The next morning after breakfast, I go down and man the checkpoint. After awhile, Robbie comes down and says that the others have gone to Naila and it is just the two of us here.   A little before noon, we wander up to the gasthaus and wait for dinner. We tell her that the others have not come back and it is just the two of us for dinner. She has fixed a good meal for us and Robbie and I get to enjoy it.

About the middle of the afternoon, Rich and Slim come back. We can tell that they have been drinking. They are feeling no pain. They tell us that they took Jack to the medics. Jack has the clap. They are going to keep him overnight and give him his shots. The medics gave them some alcohol and they have been mixing it with some lemon powder and drinking it. They are really drunk.

About this time, a woman comes to the gasthaus, looking for Jack. I had not seen her before, but Rich and Slick knew her. They start telling her that she gave Jack the clap. I am sure she does not know what they are talking about. Then they decide that she needs to be treated too. They grab hold of her and drag her to the room behind the stage and lock her in. They plan to take her down to the medics and get her treated, but she does not know that. When they go to get her to take her to Naila, she is gone. She climbed out of a window and went across the roofs and escaped.

The next day, Rich and Slim go to Naila to get Jack. It is evening before they get back. The three of them are drunk again. It looks like the medics fixed them up again. Jack is really drunk, with the penicillin and alcohol both, he can hardly walk. He starts talking about a sign and that he is going to shoot it. He picks up his grease gun and walks out the door. In a little bit, we hear the gun going off. He shoots the whole magazine, walks back in drops the gun on the floor and falls onto his bed.

When Jack finds out about his girlfriend, he is really mad. I begin to realize that he really cared for her. He probably never had a girl back home and she was special to him. I really feel bad about what happened.

There are several little boys that hang out in front of the door, where we are staying. I tell them in German to go away, but they do not pay any attention. Slick will stand out there smoking a cigarette, and when he finishes, he will reach out and drop it inside of one of the boys' lederhose or leather shorts. The boy will jump up and down as the hot cigarette makes its way out the bottom. Then he is quick to pick it up before anyone else can get it. The other boys all laugh.

Slick has a German sword that is standing just inside of the door. He picks it up, throws the door open and steps out yelling and swinging the sword. The boys are so scared that they can't get their feet to move. One boy pees his pants. But within fifteen minutes, they are all back, hoping that he will either put a lighted cigarette in their pants or go after them with the sword.

We still have the bicycle that we took from the German soldier when we were here before, so we call the boy that lives here and give it to him. He has never had a bicycle and is really pleased.

We finish out our tour and go back to Naila again. When we get back, we get notice that the whole battalion has been ordered to report back to Naila. The next day, everyone shows up and we are gathered around headquarters. There is a loading dock there and they use it for a speakers platform. The battalion commander says that he wants the chaplain to speak.

The chaplain says that venereal disease is taking a toll on the men of the unit, that the men should save themselves for their wives and sweethearts back home and that it is wrong to be having sex with the women here.

Next the medical officer gets up to speak. He says that if we are going to have sex, we must use a rubber and a pro kit and that they have set up a pro station at the infirmary.

Then the battalion commander gets back up. He says that we have heard the chaplain tell that we should not be having sex and the medical officer telling us what to do if we do have sex, but he is telling us that if we keep getting VD, he will put us so far out in the woods, that we will never have a chance to catch anything. Then we are dismissed.

I keep my regular job at Naila, keeping the theater clean. I notice that after the lecture we got, most of the guys are staying a little closer to where they are supposed to be. The theater attendance has picked up. But it will not last long. The guys, including me, will be out looking again before long.

We are going to a different town for outpost duty this time. We are going southeast a few miles to the town of Rothenburg. We get down there and find that we are to be located at a factory on the west side of the town. The factory formerly made bearings. The allies bombed all of the bearing factories they could find, but this one was so far into Germany, that it was never hit. We are not the only troops here. There are several of us, because they are going to use the factory for a POW camp. The owner or manager of the plant had living quarters here and they have moved him and his family out and we have taken over the quarters.

The first day, I am assigned to go guard a detail of POWs who are being taken to the woods to cut trees for posts to make a fence for the camp. We go out into the forest and they take saws and axes and cut a number of tall poles. They load them onto the truck, we climb on top of the posts and go back to the camp. They unload them and other POWs dig holes and set up the posts. Then they string barbed wire around them making an outdoor compound for the prisoners.

We have prisoners that clean our rooms, make our beds and wash our clothes. Some will cook our food and serve it to us, under the supervision of one of our men. We will have it easy, except for one thing. We are on guard for three hours and off for six hours, night and day, all the time we are here, a lot different than the guard we have been pulling on the other outposts.

CHAPTER LXXXVI

After supper, I go up the hill to the east toward the town. I walk around the town a little bit and run into another guy that is walking around and we decide to investigate together. We are walking along the street and see two girls looking out of a door. They appear to be about twenty and twenty-three years old. We go over to them and start to talk to them as best as we can. Both are very nice looking and seem real friendly. The younger one is named Greta and the older one is Molly. After a little bit, they invite us into the house.

They are living there with their mother and their uncle. Their home is in Cologne and they left when the bombings started there. They have been living in the upstairs of this house. They want to know, what we know, about how bad the damage is in Cologne. But we have not been there and have no idea, other than we have heard that the cathedral has only been slightly damaged.

After we visit with the older people for awhile, we go with the girls out of the room. The other guy goes with the younger girl and they go out in the stairwell, while I go with the older girl and we go to the room that the two girls use for a bedroom. I kiss her and she is more than glad to kiss back. I feel of her breasts and she gets more passionate. Before long, I have her breasts out and am enjoying them, while my other hand is under her dress and my finger finds a warm moist place.

She seems that she is really getting turned on and I know that I am. My heart is pounding and I am breathing hard. The blood is pumping into my loins and my penis is like a board. It looks like this is the time. I ask her if she is ready to have sex and she says no. I keep asking her, but she keeps refusing. I keep hoping she will change her mind, but she does not and I have to get back down to the POW camp to go on guard. I tell her I will see her again tomorrow night if I am not on guard, I kiss her again and then I leave.

I holler at the other guy and tell him that we need to go if we are not going to be late for guard. He says he is ready, he kisses the other girl and we take off. On the way back, he tells me that he has had sex with Greta and it was really good. He asks me how Molly was? Of course, I have to tell him that she would not do it, but I am hoping that she will next time.

The three hours on guard drag by. It seems that it rains on every shift. Mostly just little quick spring showers, but enough that you have to put your raincoat on and of course, you get almost as wet as if you just left it off. Herb Solow had gotten a German P-37 pistol and he let me use it. It is a .32 caliber, made like an miniature .45. I carry it instead of the carbine.

When my guard shift is over, I head for bed. Six hours is not very long for a night's sleep. I have to get up early so that I can eat breakfast, before I have to go on guard duty again. When the next shift is over, I go lay down and take a little nap before dinner. All day, I think about getting back to Molly this evening. I will have all evening off and maybe tonight I will have time to convince her to make love to me.

I hurry through my supper and head back up the hill again. When I get there, Molly is waiting for me. Her sister is with another guy, not the one that was there last night. We go in and visit with the family first and then we go out into the stairwell, because Greta and the other guy are in the bedroom. We spend the time kissing and me feeling of her body. I am holding her close and she can't help but feel my hard penis, pressing against her. I know she is really hot because she is so wet, when I get my finger in her.

In a little while, the other guy has to leave, so Greta comes out of the bedroom and we go in. We get in there, and it is just like in the stairwell, but instead of standing up, we are laying down. I think that if I just forced myself a little, she would give in, but the last thing I need is for her to holler rape. We wrestle around for another hour, before she says I need to leave, because Greta wants to go to bed. I kiss her goodbye and tell her I will try to get back the next night, but will probably be on guard.

The next day seems really long and of course, my schedule is such that I can't get away to see Molly. I work it with one of the other guys and change my schedule so that I am sure to get to see her tomorrow, the last day I will be here. The time goes slow on guard and the time off seems to be used up by sleep and eating.

The last day, I go over to one of the buildings that used to house workers, and take a shower. There is no hot water, but at least I can get cleaned up some. As soon as I get off of guard in the evening, I head up the hill again. Molly is waiting for me. We have the usual visit with the older folks and again, we have to go to the stairwell because Greta is in the bedroom with another guy. I guess I made a mistake in going for Molly instead of Greta. Greta may be trying to make the whole American army happy.

In the stairwell, we kiss and pet, until the other guy leaves and we get to go to the bedroom again. It is a repeat of last time. Lots of kissing and feeling, but no intercourse. I keep telling her that her sister is doing it, and I want her to, but she still refuses. I do not know how I can keep from exploding. I reluctantly give up and head back to the POW camp. The next morning, we load up and go back to Naila.

I get the theater cleaned and straightened up and then have a couple of drinks at the bar. I have accumulated so many drinks on my ration card that I could stay drunk for weeks. One of the guys asks me if I have anything on for this evening. I tell him that I will probably go up on the mountain side and see if I can find something.

He asks if I have had any luck so far and I tell him that I can't have any luck. He says that he has a favor he wants to ask of me.

He has a girl and he told her that he would meet her on the mountain, if he did not have to go on outpost. He is going to have to leave and can't make it. He said that he told her he would try to send someone if he could not be there. He asks if I would go take his place. I try to keep my enthusiasm down, and then say I would be glad to help him out. He says she is real nice and I will like her. I ask if he is okay with me having sex with her and he says sure. He tells me where I am to go to meet her and about what time she will be there.

I go back to the bar and get a couple more drinks. I need enough for my courage, but not so many, that I can't find my way to the right place this evening. I eat dinner and then go try to take a nap, but I can't sleep. I lay there for awhile and then go over to the building beside the headquarters, where they have set up some showers. They have warm water here.

I go back to the bar and have another drink before supper. After supper, I slowly sip another drink until time to leave. I am a little early, but I can't wait any longer. I go out to the street, under the underpass and up the path on the side of the mountain. This time, I turn and go right, then back to the left and up to a little bare spot in the woods. This is just like he described it. I am sure that I am at the right place. I am too nervous to sit, so I stand and wait.

I do not have to wait long. I look up and this nice looking woman is walking right toward me. To me, she seems to be twenty-eight or twenty-nine, but may not be that old. She has a nice smile and pleasant voice. She speaks and I can understand enough to know that she is asking if the other guy had to leave. I use what German I have to tell her that he sent me, to tell her that he would not be there. She asks my name and I tell her. She says that her name is Fran. I stand there awkward, not knowing what to do, but she smiles, takes my hand and leads me along the path.

We go up the path and back right again to a secluded spot and she sits down. I sit beside her and put my arm around her. I lean over and kiss her. Her kiss is responsive and I kiss her again, harder. With the drinks I have today, my courage is up and I start to make my move. I start out by asking about the German words for different things. I touch her lips and ask what they are in German? I kiss her again and then touch her breast and ask what it is called in German. I take that as a sign and ask her in German if I can play with them. She says that I can. I soon have her breasts out and alternate kissing them and her lips.

I move my German lesson on down and soon have her panties off and am fingering her good. By now, she is laying back with her legs spread. I can't wait any longer, I drop my pants, put on the rubber and enter her. I wish it could last longer, but I have been on high alert for so long, that I can't hold back. She is smiling, but I do not know if it is out of gratitude or amusement. But nevertheless, she does not seem angry at my short performance.

We put our clothes back on and walk back down the trail, where we met, she says good bye and we go different directions. I am so excited, that I forget to ask if she will meet me again another time. I bound back down the trail and head to the pro station. I go in, wash and use the chemical pro kit. A couple of the guys see me and immediately start telling everyone "Lovell got laid."

I go back to the gasthaus, get another drink and watch the rest of the movie.

When the movie is over, I go upstairs to my bed, but I am still so excited that I have trouble going to sleep.

Today, the guys are still talking about me. Everyone in the outfit must know about it by now. Tomorrow, we will go back on outpost duty at Selbitz.

We arrive at the Selbitz checkpoint and go into the room where we stay. The room is a mess. The walls have gouges in them and the door leading downstairs is so bullet ridden that you can stick your finger through it about any place. We ask what happened and they say that the supply sergeant, who is nuts, came in when they were all in the room and they asked him, not in a kindly way, what he was doing. He said he was collecting all of the hand grenades to turn in. Then he said he had an extra. With that, he pulled the pin and dropped it on the floor.

He ran out the double doors and slammed them behind him. The five guys in the room ran out behind him and hit the dirt outside. The grenade went off and shrapnel tore gouges in the walls. The supply sergeant left and they went back inside the room. It was not long until they heard the supply sergeant coming back, so they ran down the back stairs and closed the door behind them. As they ran down the stairs, Kazaras turned and fired his .45 pistol back through the door. Since they were down the stairs, it could not hit the supply sergeant, but went into the ceiling of the room instead. When he heard the shot, the supply sergeant fired his grease gun at the door. Unless they got a ricochet, they would neither one hit anyone. They kept shooting back and forth, until they were both out of ammunition. The room and particularly the door, suffered the most.

It was a dumb, dangerous thing to do. They both need to be locked up and the key thrown away. We relieved that team and went about cleaning up the room.

CHAPTER LXXXVII

We clean up the plaster and wood splinters that litter the floor, so that the room is suitable to stay in. Then Robbie and I go out hunting. We find one rabbit and I shoot it. We see a lot of deer tracks and decide to come back in the evening and see if we can get a deer. We dress the rabbit and take it back. Slick says that he will cook it for us. We dig out some things from the 10-in-1 rations and prepare them to go with the rabbit.

I go out to the checkpoint and relieve Jack from duty. I just get there and a three quarter ton truck arrives, with a fresh keg of beer. I fill my cup with beer and it has a good head on it. I get one of the cigars out of the box and light up. It tastes like burning elm leaves, but I puff away on it.

A few vehicles come by and I get to check their papers. I am sure that it makes them mad to have to stop their trucks, get out and bring their papers over to some kid sitting at a table. I know that our purpose is to control illegal traffic, but since none of us can read German and Jack can't read at all, it is all a pretense.

Slick hollers that dinner is ready, so I fill up my canteen cup with beer and go into the building. He has fried the rabbit and we have some macaroni and cheese with it. It tastes real good and I wash it down with beer. After dinner, Rich and Robbie take the jeep and some rations and go to trade for some local food. Slick is cleaning up from his cooking and Jack is back at the checkpoint. I take a walk into the woods north of the quarry. I make sure that I can't be seen from the road.

I am walking up the path away from the quarry, when I meet one of the girls that has been coming to visit Robbie and Rich. She asks if Robbie is there and I tell her that he has gone for a while. She walks with me and then we sit down in a little clearing in the woods. I put my arm around her and then I kiss her. She kisses me back. I put my hand inside of her dress and feel of her breasts. I try to get them out, but they seem to be held in by a bra or something.

Her dress is pulled up and I am rubbing my hand along her thighs. I try to get my hand inside of her panties and can only get one finger under the edge of them. It is enough to finger her and she is getting real wet. She tells me that she is Robbie's girl, but she does not stop me. I try to get her panties down, but I realize that they are not panties, she has a swimming suit on under her dress. There is no way that I am going to get in them, unless she wants me to. When she tells me again that she is Robbie's girl, I give up and walk with her down to the checkpoint.

Rich and Robbie get back and they have traded for some eggs, potatoes and some onions. Robbie's girl says that she has something to tell him. I figure that she is going to tell him that I tried to have sex with her and that he will want to knock my block off. Instead, she drops a bombshell. She tells him that she is pregnant. He says, "That is bad." She says, "No, that is good." It seems that she is thrilled to be having a baby. But I am glad, that I did not have sex with her. This way, she will not be able to say it is mine.

Later in the afternoon, she returns home and Robbie and I go out to see if we can find a deer. We go back to where we hunted this morning and when we get there, we see a deer. We go down in a draw so we can get closer. We agree that Robbie is to shoot first and I will back him up. We come out of the draw and there is the deer about a hundred yards away. We both put our sights on the deer and

Robbie pulls the trigger. All I hear is a click and I do not know what is the matter, so I fire. I shoot over the deer. The deer raises his head and I fire again and hit it in the neck. It drops right in its tracks. It is a nice fat four point buck.

We drag the deer back to the building and hoist it up. Slick comes out and helps us dress it out. We let the deer hang and cool out overnight. I have shot my first deer and we have meat to eat.

Rich has made friends with the woman that lives across the road from us. She is probably in her early thirties and has a daughter about six or seven. The woman is very nice looking and seems very refined. She lives in an apartment above a building. Rich tries to get her to be our cook, but she says she does not want to do that, but would prepare us a special meal we would like.

We gather up some of the rations, a portion of the deer I shot, together with potatoes and onions and deliver them to her. She says for us to come over for dinner the next day and she will have it ready for us. It sounds interesting and we anxiously await the meal.

Today is our special meal. We go over to her house about eleven-thirty in the morning and she greets us at the door. The apartment is not large, but she has a large table set up in the middle of the dining room. The table is covered with a beautiful tablecloth. It is set with fine china and real silverware and crystal. You could not find anything better in the finest of restaurants. On the mantel is a picture of a handsome, young German officer. I do not know German insignia, but I believe he is a major or colonel. I wonder if he brought home all of these fine furnishings, from some other country.

She hands me a pitcher and asks me to go fill it with beer. I walk back across the road to the keg and fill the pitcher. She goes around filling all of our glasses. She is ready to serve the meal. She has roasted the venison with the potatoes and onions and she has also put some carrots in with them. She serves it on a huge platter. She has cooked some green beans that came in the ration and she has baked hot rolls too.

We pass the food and put it on our plates. She and her daughter eat at a small table in the corner. The food is delicious. We have never had anything like it before. We eat and wash it down with the beer. After we finish, she brings out a pot of coffee she has brewed from the instant coffee in the rations. She pours us each a cup and then comes out with dessert. She has baked a cake using the flour, cornmeal and sugar from the rations and some of the eggs we had traded for. She iced the cake with orange marmalade from the rations. It is really an unexpected treat.

When we finish eating, we all light up cigars and smoke them as we finish our coffee. Rich says, "Do you know what would really top off this meal today? If we just tipped over the table now." We all laugh at the outrageous thought.

The next day our tour of duty is over, we return to Naila and I go back to my job in special services. I sweep out the theater and arrange the chairs again. I have so many drinks left on my ration card, that I get a couple and then come back in a little bit and get a couple more. I am not feeling any pain. I eat dinner and then go up to the room where I sleep and lay down on my bed and take a nap. No one bothers me and I get to sleep until almost supper time. After supper, I stay in the bar and drink and I have had so much to drink, that I do not think I better try to go up on the mountain and look for anything. I stay in the bar and watch the movie.

Today, I decide to go easy on the liquor. I do have a couple of beers with my meals, but leave the hard stuff alone. In the evening, I go back up on the mountainside and walk the trails. The only girls I see are either with someone or going to meet someone.

It is time to go on outpost detail again and we will be going back to Rothenburg again. The duty there is hard, but I am anxious to get back there and go see Molly. We get to the bearing factory and go in and pick out our beds.

We are only there a couple of hours, when I have to go on guard duty. There are only two guard posts. One just outside of the wire on the south side and the other on top of the roof of a building, guarding the north side. Actually, you can't see the POW camp from the north post. All you can see is the field to the north and part of the stream that runs down through the field and into the camp. My post this time is up on top of the roof. You have to climb stairs to get up there, but there is a chair to sit in while you stare at the field.

The time passes slow, but at last the three hours are over and I can get something to eat. I only had a snack before I had to go on guard. After I get something to eat, I lay down and take a nap. I have to go back on guard at nine tonight. When I wake up, I go in and wait for supper. The POWs are fixing our rations for us. It is not great, but at least we do not have to cook or wash dishes.

When I finish supper, I head up the hill to the town. I go to the house where Molly lives and she acts like she is glad to see me. I go in with her to visit with her mother and uncle again. They do not speak much English and I do not speak much German, but we use a lot of sign language. Molly's sister, Greta, comes in with another soldier. It looks like she is still entertaining a lot of the troops.

I have not been there very long when Molly says that we should go to her room. I do not hesitate and follow her into the bedroom. This time, she is the one leading the romance. As soon as we enter the room, she grabs me and kisses me. Then she starts to remove her clothes. When I see this, I start taking mine off too. For some reason, I have a feeling that Molly was not alone all the time I was gone.

Molly takes my hand and pulls me down, as she lays down on the pallet, on the floor, that is the bed. Not much foreplay here, she takes hold of my penis and guides it into her. At least, I last longer this time and really enjoy myself. I am content to remain with her for awhile, just like this, but she says we need to go out of the room, so that Greta can use the room.

I get my clothes back on and we go out into the stairwell. We kiss and neck on the stairs and I keep waiting until we can get back to the bedroom. We run out of time and I have to go back, to go on guard. I tell her I will see her the next night and I run back down the hill, so I am not late.

All the next day, I keep thinking about getting back up the hill. When evening comes, I hurry back to Molly's house. She meets me at the door and says I can't come in. They are leaving early in the morning to go to their home in Cologne and they must get to sleep. She kisses me good bye. I slowly make my way back down the hill and go to bed.

CHAPTER LXXXVIII

Guard duty gets old in a hurry, when you have to stand guard for three hours at a time and then get off for six hours. It is so boring. I make it through the day and in the evening, I go up the hill to the town and go by the house, where Molly lives, to make sure that she did leave. When I find out that she is indeed gone, I go back down to the factory and get some rest until the next guard shift.

I get caught in the afternoon rain storm and get wet and muddy. I change into my dry suit of clothes and then go hunt up the POW that takes care of our living quarters and give him my wet, muddy clothes to wash. He is about my age and speaks English fairly well, so it is easy to tell him what I want done. Then I eat and lay down to sleep.

When I wake up, my clothes have dried and I again have clean clothes. The POW that did them tells me about being on the Russian front. He says that he was a machine gunner set up on the west side of the river and was shooting the Russians as they tried to cross. They came so fast that he could not shoot all of them and they began to get across the river. Some of the German soldiers tried to retreat, but the SS officers shot them too. He said that if they stayed the Russians would kill them and if they tried to leave the SS would kill them. Finally, he was able to slip away and make his way to the American lines, where he surrendered.

He says that being a POW is not too bad, but the food is not good. I tell him that they get the same rations that we get and ask what is so bad about them. He says it is because the German cooks do not know how to fix them. I ask him why he doesn't tell them how to fix them. He says that it is because the cooks are sergeants and he is a private. I tell him that I understand. It is that way in our army too.

Today is the last day on guard here and tomorrow we will go back to Naila. I am up on the roof guarding the north side. Some of the guys come up the ladder and want to know if I have seen a German prisoner. I have not seen anyone. It is a German SS officer and he has escaped. He was caught stealing food from the other prisoners and they locked him in the elevator shaft, on the building where I am. When they went to get him, they found that he had climbed the cables in the elevator shaft and got out of the window at the top. He had to have gone right behind me and climbed down the drain pipe to the ground. I am lucky that he did not decide to kill me.

We all spread out and go looking for him, but he has had plenty of time to get away. There is no way I could have seen him, except the brief time he was climbing out of the window and the way they set up the guard post, that was not going to happen. Of course, someone has to be blamed for his escape and they pick me. This is the army way. We will be going back to Niala tomorrow and I will be glad to get away from here.

As soon as our relief arrives, we load up and drive back to Naila and I am glad to get back. Since Molly left, I have no more desire to go back there. I have a lot of drinks left on my ration card and use some of them. I try not to get as drunk as I did the last time.

In the evening, they make an announcement. We are moving to another place. We are to start loading up all of our equipment, so that we can make a road march. Most of the guys do not like the idea of leaving, but since I do not have a girlfriend, it is not a bother to me. But I do admit that Naila is a nice place to be stationed.

We spend the next day loading up our equipment and getting ready to move. The following morning, which is July 4th, we move out of Naila, heading southeast. We go up into some mountains and it starts to snow little pellets of soft sleet on us. At one point, the trailer loaded with small arms ammunition has a white phosphorus grenade go off and it sets off a lot of the other ammunition. You have to be careful in touching any of the contents, because particles of the white phosphorus are still present.

We travel the whole day and end up at the town of Augsburg, right on the Czech border. We pull our vehicles into a courtyard there. The headquarters sets up on the other side of the road and I find a place to sleep in the living quarters above a chinaware place. It is up on the third floor. I assume that the owners of the china factory lived there. This area has seen no fighting and is so far off of the range of bombers that there is no visible damage.

The cooks set up the mess tent in the courtyard, along with the service battery. The motor pool is located back of the headquarters building. There are several of us located in the china building and the rest are located among several of the other buildings. There is a larger room on the ground floor of the building, that I am in and they will use it for a mess hall and theater. I help get the tables and chairs to set it up and help the sergeant get the generator and projector ready for the movie.

We are able to find some beds that are like bunks and some feather ticks for covers. The room that I am in was the kitchen and there is a large cast iron stove in the corner with a water jacket around the side and back. It is warm enough that we do not need the stove.

I go out in the courtyard to help with some of the equipment. The cooks have received a shipment of frozen chickens. They have some POWs that act as cooks' helpers and they are cleaning the chickens. The chickens were processed in the early1930's, so they are over ten years old. They cut their throats and picked most of the feathers off of them, before freezing them. They still have the heads and feet on and the guts inside. It really smells when they are cleaning them.

When it is dinner time, I go into the mess hall and they are serving the chicken. I never cared much for chicken and this is not to my taste, but I take some anyway. The chicken has turned black where it was against the bones. It is tender, but I have trouble getting it down and leave most on my mess kit.

They have not set up a bar yet, so they decide to pass out what liquor they have accumulated. It is mostly wine and I do not care much for wine. However, they have a few bottles of strawberry liqueur. I ask around and soon trade my wine for three bottles of it. I take them up to the room and hide them in the water jacket of the stove. Maybe they will come in handy later on.

I hear that there is a barber down the street where we can go and get a haircut. The last haircut I had was on the Queen Mary, six months ago. I walk down the street until I come to the building. There is one man there and he indicates that I should take a seat in the barber chair. He turns and I notice that he has only a short stub for a left arm. I do not ask, but he probably lost it in the war. He uses a comb and then sticks it under his stub to hold it, while he cuts my hair. He takes a little longer, since he only has the one arm, but he does a good job. I do worry when he lathers my neck, pulls out the razor and starts to shave my neck. I pay him in invasion marks and am well pleased with the service.

They pass around a sheet with a list of subjects that may be taught and we are to sign up if there is anything we would like to take. I sign up for a course in German. The next morning, they post a list of those that will be going to class. I look and it says that I will be attending a class in French. I don't want to take French, so I mark my name off of the list. Later in the day, one of the corporals comes looking for me and tells me that the first sergeant wants to see me.

I go to the headquarters building and find the first sergeant. He wants to know who marked my name off of the list to take French. I tell him that I did. His next question is why. I say because I did not sign up for French and thought he had made a mistake. He informs me that he does not make mistakes and, so that I will remember it, I will spend that weekend guarding the headquarters.

Today we are turning in extra weapons. I turn in the M1 and BAR that I have. Then the armorer asks me what happened to the .50 caliber anti aircraft mount that was on my halftrack. I tell him that it was lost in combat. He says that he was told that I threw it away and therefore, I will have to pay for it. The cost is $750. At my rate of pay, it will take me two years to pay for it. I go find Herb Solow and tell him what happened. He says not to worry, he will take care of it. He goes to the armorer and comes back and says that he took care of it. He signed a slip saying it was lost in combat.

Herb has been working in headquarters. He has won the admiration of most of the guys, even those who say they do not like Jews. Several of the guys have been written up for violations and the paperwork is waiting for action. Since Herb is in headquarters, every time one of the files comes up, Herb just sticks it back on the bottom of the stack. If the file stays out of sight long enough, the guy will be transferred out before any action is taken. However, Herb himself has received orders transferring him out. Before he leaves, he puts all of the files on the bottom of the stack and wishes the guys good luck.

On Herb's last night, we throw a party for him. Someone comes up with an egg and they put it in his beer. Not much of a gift, but it is symbolic of how we feel about him. I give him back his P-37 pistol and thank him for looking out for me.

I find a German who can make me a wooden box, so I can send some things home. I use cloth to pack the box. I put the BB gun in, together with several German things I have picked up, including a Nazi flag and flashlight. I prepare the paper work to ship it and have it inspected and nailed shut. I pay the postage and it is on the way home.

Next door to the barber shop, a photographer has set up a shop. I go down and have my picture taken and mail copies of it home. It is only the third picture I have had taken over here. I am sure that my parents will like it. It is much clearer than the other two that I sent home before. I now weigh about ten pounds more than I did when I came into the army a year ago.

CHAPTER LXXXIX

General Eisenhower has ordered that all of the army troops in Europe receive a short jacket like he wears. We get our shipment in today. They make arrangements with a tailor to fit each jacket to the soldier who is to receive it. We line up at the building where the tailor is working and there is a big stack of jackets there. They have the strong smell of mothballs and have been packed so tight that they all bear the imprint of the jacket next to it.

When it is my time to get fitted, they find a jacket about my size and the tailor has me put it on for the fitting. He takes his chalk and marks the jacket and then has me put my name on it. He will alter them and then we will be notified when we can pick them up.

We get the "Stars & Stripes" paper and it says that some troops are being sent from Europe to the Pacific direct and not through the United States. I figure that with no more time than I have, that I will have to go to the Pacific, but I would like to get to see my folks first. I decide that I will volunteer to go to the Pacific by way of the States. I go to the headquarters building and ask to see the first sergeant. I think this is the first time that I have asked to see him; it has always been the other way around.

When I get to see the first sergeant, I tell him what I have in mind. He is actually civil to me and says that he can understand why I want to do that. He says that he will check on it and get whatever papers I need to carry it out. He says he will let me know as soon as he finds out something. I leave the headquarters building and hope that I am doing the right thing.

This evening, we get on a truck and ride two hours in the rain to Bayreuth to see Jack Benny perform for a USO show. When we get there, the theater is full. When the show is about half over, they let us go inside and stand around the walls. All I can see is the top of Jack's head. I think the show would be good if I could see it. I do get to hear him play something on the violin, besides "Love in Bloom." After the show, we have another two-hour ride in the rain back to Augsburg. If I had it to do over again, I would not go.

Today we are working in the courtyard, when there is an explosion. We all dive for cover. It is easy to see that we are still on alert. When we start looking for what happened, we find that it came from the cook's tent. We go over there and find carbine shells scattered on the ground, together with parts of the carbine. As near as we can tell, the cook hung his carbine on a nail in the tent pole. The nail came out and when the carbine hit the ground, it went off, but the bolt was not closed. The shell blew out through the magazine, tore it to pieces, and scattered the shells and the carbine in several pieces. I put it back together and it seems to be okay.

This afternoon, I get word that the first sergeant wants to see me. I go to headquarters and he says that he has received the paperwork for my transfer. I need to sign the papers volunteering to go to the Pacific by way of the States. There is no guarantee that I will go or that it will be by way of the States, but I will be put on the list and they will notify me if I am to go. I shake a little as I sign. It is a big step. I hope I am doing the right thing.

This morning, there are a half dozen of us just loafing around, up on the third floor of the building where I am staying. We are staying out of sight so that we will not be given some detail. One of the guys says that he wishes we had something to drink. One of the others says that the whole place is dry as a bone. That reminds me of the bottles I hid. I had forgot all about them, with all that had been going on. I tell them to wait right there and I will be back. I go into the other room and reach into the water jacket and fish out the three bottles of liqueur. I take them into the other room and hand them out. We all start drinking. It tastes just like strawberry syrup, that you would put on your pancakes. Sticky and sweet.

In a little bit, everyone is drunk. I am probably the most sober of the bunch and even I am really happy. They get in a contest seeing who can slide the furthest down the banister, without flying off. Guys are crashing into the stairs and walls as they try to go faster down the banister. They get banged up some, but that is not the problem. The problem develops when a couple of the guys climb out on the third floor window ledge and start yelling at people walking down the street. I try to get them back in, but with no luck, until I enlist a couple of the other drunks to help me.

It is too late; they have already been seen by someone in headquarters. It is not a good idea to get drunk and sit on the window ledge across from the headquarters building. Here comes one of the sergeants. He gathers up everyone and tells us to go to bed and not to come out until we are sober. It does not take anything to convince me to get out of sight, but he has to argue with a couple of guys to get them to stay out of sight. I can't understand how we all got so drunk so fast. I get one of the bottles and look at the label and it says that it is ninety proof. I thought liqueurs were about twenty proof. No wonder we got so drunk so quick.

After we all sober up, someone asks one of the guys where we got the liquor. Of course he says, "From Lovell." The next thing I know, I am told to report to the first sergeant again. He doesn't ask me any questions; he just assigns me to guard the headquarters on the weekend. I am the only one that got punishment and I was the most sober of the bunch. Oh well, I was not going any place this weekend anyway.

I get notice that my jacket is ready and I go to pick it up. The tailor makes sure that it fits me and it does look nice. I like it a lot better than the long-tailed ones we have had since basic training. I take it back to my quarters and get out my Red Cross sewing kit, dig in my supply of patches and stripes and sew a set on the sleeves.

In the evening, I get notice that my orders have come in. I will be leaving here on July 17, 1945. I will be going to another division. I write to my mother and tell her to get my room ready, in case I get to come home. I also ask my dad to have the car ready, so I can run around some if I get home.

Today, I turn in my carbine and the watch that I have checked out to me. I also turn in a bunch of other equipment that I will not need, including my gas mask and steel helmet. Maybe since I do not have a weapon, I will not have to pull any more guard duty here.

This evening, I go around and say good bye to a bunch of the guys. Several others are leaving too, so the evening is spent in wishing each other "good luck." We sit around the theater and drink beer. It is late before I finally go up the two flights of stairs and crawl into my bed. This will be my last night as a member of the Ninth Armored Division.

This morning, I go down and eat breakfast, then start hauling my things downstairs and pile them in the street to wait for the truck that will take me away from here. Of course, it is hurry up and wait, but at last the truck arrives and those of us who are leaving throw our duffle bags and packs on the truck and climb in after them. It is a nice sunny, summer morning in Germany. A beautiful day to be traveling.

The truck takes off and we head back the way that we came down here. Right out north of Augsburg we see a halftrack sitting out in a field, all by itself. They were driving it and ran into the back of a "honey wagon," the wooden tank wagon that they use to haul the manure out onto the fields. The halftrack and those in it were covered with fresh manure. They left the halftrack sitting and no one has gone to get it since.

We go through Selbitz and on the road that leads to Hof. At Hof, we are taken to the rail yards. Everyone climbs out with their things and we assemble in the rail yard. There is an officer there that gives our instructions. They will call out our names and tell us what number rail car we will be riding in. As before, they will have places set up along the line to feed us a hot meal every so often and the rest of the time we will get K rations.

As our names are called, we take our things and go to our assigned car. When I get to my car, other guys are arriving too and we help each other get our things into the car. We stack the duffle bags and packs in one corner and put our bedrolls around the sides of the car to sit on. I soon find out that everyone in this car is from Oklahoma. One guy has an envelope with our orders in it. There are seventeen of us. We get him to open the envelope and read our orders. He says that we are to proceed to Camp Chaffee, Arkansas, where we will be given a furlough and then I will proceed to an unknown station, where I will join the 4th Infantry Division. From there, I will be going to the Pacific theater. This is about as good as I could have asked for.

It is different weather now, from what it was like six months ago when I rode this train. We will not need a stove this time. Our bedrolls will be more than enough. Also, with only seventeen in the car, we will have plenty of room to lie down. We are standing alongside of the car, when we see it jolt and we know that the engine has hooked on. In just a few minutes, the whistle sounds twice and we all climb up into the open door. Several of us sit in the open door and a few stand behind, looking out. One of the guys says, "My dad said that if I didn't get busy and finish school, I would end up riding the rails and I guess he was right."

About noon, the train stops and they tell us to get off and get our dinner. We grab our mess kits and climb off the train. We go get in the line to get our food. When we get to the head of the line, we find that we do not need our mess kits; all they have are K rations, and they hand each of us one and they have coffee available. I filled my canteen before I left, so I will just drink water.

The train does not travel very fast and stops often. It often stops because of construction. Almost every bridge on this line was destroyed and they are trying to make the repairs more permanent. It is great to get to slowly ride along and watch the scenery.

In the evening, we stop for supper and they have a hot meal for us. Of course, it is meat and vegetable stew, canned and heated, but it comes with the regular GI bread and some canned peaches. There is coffee if you want it. I pass on the coffee, because I remember what it was like to try to piss out of the car while moving.

We settle down for the night, get our bed rolls laid out and most everyone is laying down. It looks like we are going to stay here for the night. They may not want to take a chance of traveling at night on these damaged rails.

CHAPTER XC

When we wake up in the morning, we are still sitting on the siding. We take our mess kits and go get in line for breakfast. They have corned beef hash, some of the GI bread toasted, grapefruit juice and coffee. Not very imaginative, but is filling. It is not long before the train whistles and we are on our way again.

Each time we stop on a siding, Frenchmen come to the train carrying bottles of wine to trade. Some of the guys have saved enough of their rations that they have some food to trade and it is not long before most of the guys are feeling good. One of the guys on the car is an Indian from Oklahoma and he trades a pair of socks for a bottle of what is supposed to be cognac. Somehow, I am selected to be the tester. Every time they trade for a bottle, they hand it to me, I open it and taste it and give my opinion on whether they should drink it or not.

In the afternoon when it warms up, some of the guys climb up to ride on top of the car. Of course, they are in direct line with the smoke coming out of the engine most of the time and they are soon black. It is not the safest place either, because they have to watch for low bridges, so that they do not get swept off of the car.

We stop in a rail-yard and as we climb out of the car, there is a soldier standing guard there. We can tell by looking at him that he is new. The first thing he says is "You guys stay away from that car," indicating a gondola that is parked nearby. That was the wrong thing to say. We immediately want to know why, so a couple of us climb up on top of the car. There are boards nailed like slats across the top, but underneath are cases of canned goods. I pull out one of the cases and throw it to one of the guys from our car. The guard protests, and even though he has a rifle, we do not think he will shoot us. I keep pulling out cases and throwing them to guys on the ground. The guard runs away to get help, so I figure I better get out of there.

We take the cases to our car and put them under the pile of duffle bags in the corner. We can hear someone shouting to put those boxes back where you got them. We watch as a captain looks into our car. All he can see is a pile of duffle bags in the corner with some guys asleep on them. It is not long before the train whistles and we move out.

As soon as we get to moving, we decide to see what we have. We open one of the cases and it is full of grapefruit juice. We have thirteen cases of grapefruit juice. Probably anything else would be more welcome. At the next stop, we trade some grapefruit juice for cognac. It is more welcome. We soon find that the French do not want grapefruit juice anymore then we do. Then the guys start telling the Frenchmen that they are cans of peaches. They are glad to trade for that. It is not a very honorable trade, but it works both ways, since some of the bottles do not contain cognac either.

One of the guys in the in car back of us is playing with a pistol and it goes off and shoots through the roof. One of the guys riding on the roof of the car is shot through the leg. The guys with him bandage his leg as best they can. It is all they can do, because the train is moving. When it finally pulls onto a siding and stops, they get him down from the roof. There is a mess set up at this siding and they have access to a medical detachment. They turn him over to the people there and then run back in time to catch the train. Maybe he will be able to catch another train and catch up with us later.

Some of the guys are saying that one of the guys did not duck in time and got knocked off of the roof of one of the cars by an overhead bridge. We do not know if the story is true or not, but it could be, because there are a lot of guys on the roof and if someone is not paying attention, they could get knocked off.

After six days on the train, we arrive at LeHarve, France, and get off of the train. The guy with the envelope containing our orders counts us off and we are one short. We do not know what happened to him. He may have missed the train or he might be the guy they said got knocked off of the train. We march out to a camp, called Camp Chesterfield. All the different camps have the names of cigarette brands. We have to carry all of our stuff as we march. The only one that does not mind is the Indian because he only has the clothes on his back. He traded everything else. He even traded a can of GI foot powder for a bottle.

When we get to the camp, we are assigned to tents with cots in them. They tell us where the latrines are, so we can get a shower and clean up. We are all covered with soot from the train and gamy after the six days of travel. They have a laundry and we are urged to send clothes, so that we can have some clean ones to wear. For those guys who do not have a complete uniform, they will have clothes to issue. It looks like the Indian is going to come out fine after all.

As soon as I can, I head out to the latrine and take a shower. They have soap and shampoo there. It feels so good to get a few layers of dirt off. I have one set of clean clothes, so I put them on and send the rest of my clothes to the laundry. Then I go back to the tent and lay down on the cot in just my underwear. It feels good to get to go lie down without having all my clothes on and I am glad to get to rest. As near as I can tell, we will not have details here. We will get processed, so we can get ready to go to the States. It may be awhile, because they say they have a shortage of ships. Many of the ships have been assigned to the Pacific, now that the war is over here.

There are Red Cross workers here to help those who need them. They also have one of the doughnut wagons set up and you can go there and get a doughnut and coffee. I notice one of the Red Cross workers squeezing blackheads out of one soldier's back. He is a fairly handsome guy and I doubt if most of us get such service. The food is better here, almost as good as it was at the 73rd. There is really not much to do but rest. We are out in the country and nothing to see but rows of tents. Like the rest, I turn in early.

Today we get to see what it is like here. Every once in awhile, they will read a list of names over the loudspeaker and tell them to report. After they report, they come back and gather up their things so they can ship out. I ask one guy how long he has been here and he says he has been here for six days.

We get a special treat today. They announce that they have Cokes. We line up and each man gets two bottles of Coca Cola. It would be better if it were ice cold, but it is just air temperature. No matter, we drink them as they are. First I have had for over six months. We are told to return the bottles, because they have a bottling plant set up, but there is a big shortage of bottles.

On the fourth day here, my name is called to report. I go to where we are to assemble and most of the other guys from my car on the train are here too. They tell us to get our things together because we will be shipping out tonight. There is not much to do, because we never really got unpacked. I got my laundry back yesterday, so I have clean clothes to take with me. We spend all day sitting around waiting to go. After dark, they have us assemble and we wait to go. It is after midnight before we get our orders to proceed to the docks.

When we get to the docks, it is hurry up and wait again. At last we board the small ship that is to take us across the English Channel. At four in the morning, the tide is right and the ship pulls away from the dock. A few hours later, we arrive at Southampton, get off of the ship and walk about a mile to the train station and board a train.

We travel all day and at four o'clock in the morning on July 30, 1945, we arrive at a camp north of London. The camp consists of small shack like barracks. The latrine is about a half a block away from the building that I am staying in. I go to the latrine, then hurry back to the bunk and go to sleep. I only get about three hours of sleep before time to get up. We line up for breakfast of powdered eggs and thick bacon. The GI bread has been toasted in ovens. There is coffee to wash it down. It is about the same quality as most of the transient places.

After breakfast, we attend an orientation lecture. They say that they do not know how long we will be there. It depends on when a ship is available to transport us. They say that weekend passes to London will be available for most of us who want them. They instruct us where to go to exchange our money and tell us that we are free to leave the camp and travel locally.

After the lecture, I go to the day room and read some literature about where we are in England. Then I go to the place where we can exchange our money. I have some German and French invasion money. I find that the official exchange rate is about five dollars US to one English pound. The black market rate is about two to one, but we do not have any way to do that. We just have to take what they give us. After dinner, I go back to the barracks and lay down and take a nap. I get caught up on some of the sleep I lost while we were traveling here. After supper, some of the guys say they have heard that there is a pub down the road a ways. They ask me to go along and we walk out of the gate and head east down the road. It is about two and half miles to the pub.

When we get to the pub, we all order a pint and sit at a table to drink. Some of the guys are playing darts, but I am content to just watch. The beer does not taste anywhere as good as that I am used to in Germany, but the locals seem to like it and after a couple of mugs, it gets better. We stay until the pub closes and then we all head out back down the road to the camp. We are not walking as good now as when we came this evening. Fortunately, a bus comes along and we all climb aboard when it stops. It is a double-decker bus and several of us climb up to the top to ride. The bus stops at the camp gate, all the soldiers kind of fall off the bus and stagger back to their barracks. So much for our first night living in England.

The next day, another guy and I decide to go to a local city and see what it is like. We wait at the gate for the bus and catch it into the town. The ride through the English countryside in summer is delightful. We sit up on the top floor of the bus in the open air. The fields are green and livestock is grazing in the meadows. The houses have gardens and the flowers are blooming. When we arrive in the city, we walk around the streets. Things have been tight for the English for several years now, and the stores do not show much in the way of goods for sale. Food is still rationed and we do not have any ration stamps. We are told that about the only food available to us would be fish and chips.

About noon, we find a small stand that sells fish and chips. I am not sure that I want any fish, but I do want some potatoes. I don't know what it costs, but I pull out a one shilling coin and show it to the woman clerk and ask for that many chips. She takes a newspaper and spreads it out and puts a huge mound of what we would call french fries on it. Then she folds it over and hands it to me. We walk around the city the rest of the afternoon and then catch the bus back to camp, for supper.

CHAPTER XCI

The weekend is coming up and I want to go to London. I head over to the orderly room and ask if I can get on the list to get a pass to London for the weekend. The clerk says that I do not need to be on a list, he will just give me a pass. It is good from Saturday morning until Monday morning. He also gives me a few ration coupons that I can use to buy meals while in London. I ask about transportation and he explains how to get there.

Since he is not busy, I ask him about what there is to do in London. He tells me that most things are within walking distance and there are a lot of things to see. I ask about girls. He says that the best place to find a girl is around Piccadilly Circus, and that they charge about ten pounds. He says that the girls in England have the idea that if they do not lay down to do it, they are still virgins. He says that most of them stand up to have sex. This sounds strange to me and I wonder if he is joking.

Friday night, I take my musette bag and put in a change of underwear and my toilet articles. It is too big, but it is the only thing I have that resembles a travel bag. I have everything ready for my trip in the morning.

I get up Saturday morning early, clean up and put on my class A uniform. I have only had my Eisenhower jacket on a couple of times before. I head to the mess hall and am one of the first ones in line for breakfast. As soon as I finish breakfast, I go back to the barracks and get my bag and head for the camp gate.

I wait at the gate with several other guys for the bus that will take us to the town, where we can catch the train to London. The bus arrives, we purchase our tickets and several of us climb up the stairs to ride in the open section on top. It is another beautiful summer day, so it seems natural to want to be outside. The bus goes over the same route that I took the other day to town. It takes us right to the train station.

We line up at the ticket window and I am sure that the clerk gets tired of stamping London on tickets and making change. I get my round trip ticket and go sit on one of the benches to wait for the train. It is not long until the train arrives and we start going along the cars, trying to find an empty compartment. After several cars, I find an empty compartment, open the outside door and climb in. I do not close the door because I know there are several guys behind me. When the third one after me gets in, he closes the door.

I throw my musette bag in the overhead rack and settle back for the ride. The conductor goes along closing the outside doors that are still open and then signals the engine to go. We hear the train whistle and the coach starts to move. It is sure a lot smoother than the box cars we have been used to riding in. It is also a lot quieter. The train speeds along until it gets to the next town. We make lots of stops, but the train still makes good time.

We arrive at Victoria Station in the middle of the morning. It takes us a little time to find the signs that direct us up to the streets. We have the address of the USO, where we can get a place to spend the night. We have been advised to go there the first thing and book a bed, because they fill up fast. The four of us from the compartment in the train decide to go together. We strike out to find the address that we have been given.

We walk for some distance and think we are close, so we stop someone who looks like a business man and ask how to get to our destination. He points out the route and we are on our way again. We get to the USO and check in for the night. We are each given a ticket that entitles us to a bed for the night. It only costs one pound. Much cheaper than anything else we could find.

We split up in pairs and take off to see the city. I am amazed by all of the sights, the big buildings and statues everywhere. We see some buildings that have been destroyed by bombs, but they are already trying to restore things. We go to see Buckingham Palace. It is not open to tours anymore, but we can see the outside. They even have the guards with their bearskin hats. I understand that they were just recently reinstated, after having been eliminated during the war.

About noon, we decide to try to find something to eat. We find a little shop that sells meat pies. We go in and we each buy one. They are expensive in both money and ration points. We take them and go out on the street, where there is a bench and we sit and eat them. They have a few little pieces of meat, some peas, a few carrots, lots of potatoes and gravy inside of a pie crust.

In the afternoon, we walk around some more. We go to Hyde Park and watch people making talks. We can't understand much of what they say and don't know what they are talking about either. It is hard to get used to the cars driving on the other side of the road and we have to be careful when we step out into the street, so that we do not get hit.

In the evening, we start looking for a place to eat supper. We find a small café on a side street and go in. It looks like a place where the local people might eat. The day's special is stew, so I order that. They bring a bowl and a large roll. I did not think when I ordered, but I should have known it would be mutton stew. It turns out to be better than I thought it would. I ask for a glass of water and they bring it to me. I would not have gotten it if I had not asked, as I notice they do not automatically serve it.

After supper, we walk around trying to find Piccadilly Circus. We see a civilian and ask him how to get there. He points in the direction to go and says that we can't miss it. We start walking that way and walk and walk, but do not see anything that looks like a circus to us. We have obviously missed it, so we stop another man and ask him where it is. He points back in the direction we came from and again, says that we can't miss it.

We walk back a ways and then see another soldier and ask him where Piccadilly Circus is. He says right here. I guess he knows from the look on our faces that we have no idea what we are looking for and he explains that Piccadilly Circus is the street, where it goes in a circle, to allow cars to make a turn. I don't know about the other guy, but I feel like an idiot. I thought it was a show or something. So much for the small town boy in the big city.

We are walking along the street and there is a man passing out cards to anyone that will take one. He hands each of us a card and we stop to read them. The card says "THE RED BAR" "8. Green's Court." "Off Brewer Street, W.1." "This card cannot be sold." I am not sure why you would want to sell the card or who would buy it, with the guy giving them away. We ask him where the bar is, since the address does not mean anything to us. He tells us it is just down the street a little way and then turn left at the next intersection and go about fifty feet and it is on the right. We decide to check it out.

We follow his directions and surprisingly, after our previous attempts to find Piccadilly Circus, we go right to the place. The street it is on is very narrow and appears to be a dead end. The place it's self is a dingy front building located between two dingier buildings. We push open the big solid door and find ourselves in a very old bar. It is not real well lighted, but we can instantly tell that almost everyone in the bar is an American soldier. We find a table among the others and a waiter comes over to the table and hands us a menu. We have already eaten, so we are only interested in getting a drink. I look over the menu and pick a drink, even though I do not know what it is.

The waiter comes back and asks what we will have. The other guy orders a drink and then the waiter turns to me and asks what I will have. I tell him the drink I have picked and he says that he can't serve me, because I am too young. The other soldiers around us hear what he says. One big guy with a Ninth Armored patch on his shoulder, stands up and in a very loud voice says "If he is old enough to fight, he is old enough to drink. You bring him a drink or we will tear the hell out of this place." About that time, several of the other soldiers stand up too and start mumbling about not serving me. The waiter decides that maybe I am older than I look and announces that he will be glad to get me my drink.

Everyone sits back down and it is not long before I have a drink in front of me. I figure that it will not have any liquor in it, but I am wrong. We sit drinking and visiting with the other soldiers. My friend and I each have a couple more drinks and then decide to go out and see what is going on. I am not feeling any pain, but I am still able to navigate very well, as we go down the street.

We make our way out of Green's Court and back on to the main street. We see some girls, but do not know what we are supposed to do about getting one. I sure do not want to insult someone. As we walk along, we meet a very nice looking girl about twenty-two, coming towards us. As we get close, she says, "Hi." I answer her with another, "Hi." She stops and asks if I would like to have a good time. And of course, I would. I ask how much and she says that it is ten pounds. I guess that is the going rate. I fish around in my pocket and come out with a ten pound note and hand it to her.

She says for me to come with her and I tell my friend that I will see him later, as I follow her back the way she came. We walk down the street until we come to an alley. The alley is dark and I know I do not have any business going into it, but she has hold of my hand and tells me it is okay, as she leads me back into the dark. I can't see where we are going, but I turn and look back and can see very well back where we came from. We are in the alley about twenty-five feet and she stops and says that this will do.

I unbutton my pants and take out my penis and put on a rubber. She reaches up and puts her arms around my neck and pulls herself tight against me. She looks back out of the alley and sees someone, because she says, "Quick, kiss me." I guess that she thinks it is the police and she wants to appear as lovers, instead of what we are. I kiss her and then she says, "Okay, it is all clear." With that, she pulls herself up and puts her legs around me. I hold her close and she reaches down with one hand, takes hold of me and inserts me into her. She has her arms and legs locked around me and I am holding her close too. I move so that her back is against the wall.

We continue having intercourse until I have an orgasm. Then I release my hold on her and she unwraps her arms and legs from me. She asks me if it was good and I tell her that it was great. I use my handkerchief to clean up, then button my pants and we slowly walk back to the street, while holding hands. She tells me thank you and walks on down the street. I look around for my friend and find him about a half block down the street. He asks me how it was and I tell him it was good. He asks if I think she would go with him. I tell him I am sure she would, if I can find her. We start looking for her and I see a girl that I think is her and ask if she would go with my friend. She says, "Your friend needs to ask for himself." He asks if she will go with him and she agrees. As soon as I said something, I realized that it was not the same girl, but I figured it did not matter. I tell him I will see him back where we are staying, as they walk off.

I make my way back to where I will be spending the night. I think about what all I have done on my trip to London. I have seen a lot of interesting things, eaten a couple of English meals, had enough drinks to not care about much, got rid of some of my sexual tension and left the girl a virgin. I laugh out loud.

When I get to the room, I head for the latrine. I take a shower and scrub real good. When I get out of the shower, I open up the pro kit and use it. I take the soap impregnated cloth and scrub all of my genitals. Then I take the lead tube of ointment, break off the little tip, then stick the end of the tube into my urethra and squeeze one half of the ointment into my penis. I pull the tip of the tube out and massage the ointment as deep into me as I can. Then I take the rest of the tube and squeeze it out and rub it all over my genitals. This pro kit has a small cloth bag in it, that looks like a tobacco sack, to put your genitals in to keep the ointment from staining your clothes. I put it on, put my underwear on and make my way to my cot. I fold up my clothes on the little table by my cot and lay down. It takes a long time to get to sleep, as I think about all that I have done.

My friend wakes me up when he comes in and tells me that I was right, the girl was okay. I tell him that it was not the same girl, but that I think they may be about all alike. I tell him that if he does not have a pro kit, they have some where you check in. He says that he has one and is going to use it now. I tell him I will see him in the morning.

My friend wakes me up again in the morning. We get dressed and go to the other building where they have set up a place for breakfast. It is not much, just coffee and some kind of roll with a spoon of jam on it. We eat and then gather up our things and get ready to leave. We can't leave our bags there because we have to check out before noon. We carry our things with us and go walk around the city. When we get to Hyde Park, it is almost full. Sunday morning seems to be when the most people come here. They have lots of speakers today.

We make our way back to the area around Piccadilly Circus, but it is rather quiet today. We find a food stand and buy cheese sandwiches for lunch. They have sodas too and we each get one. Not very sweet, but they wash down the sandwiches. We still have a lot of time to kill, so we decide to go to the movie. It is an English comedy. We laugh, because we can't understand what the jokes are. We do not stay very long. We decide that we will make our way back to Victoria Station and then head back to the camp. We take our time and slowly walk to the station.

We find that we have nearly an hour before the next train. We find a bench and sit and watch the people coming and going. When our train arrives, we go along the side until we find an empty compartment and then climb in. We leave the door open and sure enough, three other soldiers come running and climb in, just before the conductor closes the door. It is a nice ride back through the countryside. We arrive at our town and go stand at the bus stop to wait for the bus back to the camp.

When the bus comes, I lead the way up to the upper deck. I love to sit up here and look at the English countryside. The weather is perfect. It is a beautiful summer day.

CHAPTER XCII

I wake up in the morning still thinking about my trip to London. I go over and get in the chow line and get my breakfast. After I eat, I go back to the barracks and a sergeant comes in and reads off a list of names, including mine. He says that we will be leaving the camp tomorrow morning to board a ship to the States. We are elated. We thought it would be a lot longer than that. He says for us to get our things together, so that when the trucks come we will be ready.

We spend the rest of the day laughing and joking, happy to be going home. In the evening, a bunch of us go out the gate and walk to the pub down the road. It is our last night in England and we celebrate. We just as well use up the rest of the English money we have and we will not have to exchange it. We are all drunk by the time they put us out.

We start walking back, but the bus comes along and we board it. Several of us go up the stairs to the top deck. One of the guys up there suddenly says that he is not going to ride on a bus without a driver and jumps off of the bus. He hits and rolls. We look back and he is getting to his feet, so we decide he is not hurt too bad. One of the other guys says that he has ridden a lot of bulls without a driver, so he knows he can ride a bus.

We get back to the camp and make our way to the barracks. It is about a half an hour later when the guy that jumped gets there. The whole barracks is full of drunks. A great way to finish off our visit to England.

Right after breakfast, they call us to fall out, to board the trucks that will take us to the train station. It is a special troop train, but it is just like the regular trains and we are in the compartments. With all of our equipment, four to a compartment is enough.

We ride the train to the city of Bristol and then we get off and march down to the docks. Waiting at the docks is a ship with the name of Hilery A. Herbert. It is one of the cargo ships, called liberty ships. They do not have a very good reputation, since they build them so fast, but they are doing a good service.

I expect to have to dump everything I have out on the dock, before I can board the ship, but they do not search us at all. We march across the dock, up the gangplank and onto the ship. They direct us down into the middle of the ship, where bunks are stacked all the way to the top of the hold. A sergeant tells us to pick out a bunk and get in it so that others can make their way in. There is not much room in the bunk after we get our bags in there, but we slide in so we are out of the way.

When this hold is full, they start putting them in other parts of the ship. They tell us that after everyone is on, we will be allowed to go on deck. We only have to wait a couple of hours before they say we can move around. I go on deck as do most of the others and watch as they put supplies on the ship. There will not be too many supplies loaded, because the ship took on most of the things they need before it left the States.

The K ration we received this morning was eaten on the train and I am hungry. I ask the sergeant when they will be serving chow and he says that they will serve the evening meal before long. Several of us go up on the open deck and line up in front of the opening leading down into the hold, where they have set up the kitchen. We are in line for over a half an hour, before the line starts to move. When it does, we have to go through the opening and then climb down the steps leading into the hold. We go through the line and they have hamburger steaks, mashed potatoes that are not made from de-hydrated potatoes, gravy, green beans and a salad. There is peach cobbler for dessert and cartons of milk to drink. The milk has been frozen, so it is not as good as fresh, but it is better than canned.

We move to another part of the hold, where they have some stand up tables. They have raised edges on the tables so that the trays will not slide off. It is nice to get to eat from trays again, in-stead of our mess kits. After we finish eating, we place our trays and utensils where they can put them in the dishwasher and then go up another ladder leading back to the deck.

The tide comes in and they get ready to sail. I watch as we pull out of the harbor and start out into the ocean. I watch until after dark, seeing the lights disappear in the distance. Then I go down below and move things around so I can get in my bunk. I take off all of my clothes except my shorts and crawl into the bunk. With so many men crowded into the close quarters, it is not long before the air gets to smelling. Then as guys go to sleep, there is the snoring. I go to sleep and add my noise to the others.

When I get up in the morning, we are out in the Atlantic some place. It is summer, so it is not real rough, but it is enough that some of the guys are already looking a little green. I go get in line and make my way down the ladder to the mess. Today, they have hot ce-real, which is like Malt-o-meal. They have lots of sugar and there is the milk to put on it. In addition, they have bacon and biscuits, with real butter and some grape jam. I pick up an extra carton of milk and get a cup of coffee too. I go stand at the table and eat.

After breakfast, a bunch of us who have been together since we left Germany, get together on the deck and start talking about some-thing to do on the ship. One of the guys goes and asks the crew if they have any games and he says that there is a volleyball and net we can use. We are not sure where we are to use it, but he says to go to the back of the ship, that the hold in the stern is not being used. We take the net and ball and go to check it out.

The hold is not very big and the floor slopes a lot, but we stretch the net from one side of the ship to the other and then start to play. It is not classic volleyball, but it is fun to bat it back and forth, while running up and down the sloping deck. We spend most of the morning in there and only notice that the ocean is getting rougher by the way the deck falls out from under your feet when you run to make a play.

By noon, the ocean is a lot rougher and several of the guys are getting seasick. But none of us who were playing volleyball have been bothered yet. At noon, we are standing in line on the deck waiting for chow, when one of the guys gets sick and runs to the rail. He picks the windward rail and when he vomits, it goes over the side and then the wind picks it up and takes it up in the air above the ship. We all stand watching it go up and then it moves over the middle of the ship and starts to fall. We are looking up and this big glob of vomit is coming down towards us. The whole chow line scrambles and it lands with a splat, right where we were standing.

The sight of the vomit sends three more soldiers headed toward the rail, with everyone yelling for them to go to the lee side. The line starts to move and we have to hold on to the hand rail as we go down the ladder. We get our chow and go to the stand up tables. Now we know why they have the edge on the tables. As we eat, our trays slide back and forth in front of us. One minute your tray is in front of you and the next, it is three guys down and you are staring at someone else's food.

In the afternoon, we go back down and play ball. It is rougher now and it is fun to try to run across the deck as it moves up and down and side to side. When we go on deck, we see a lot more sick guys. I feel just a little queasy, but I am really thankful that I am not sick, like so many others. I think playing volleyball and keeping active has helped.

By the third day, almost everyone is over the seasickness and things have settled down, even though the ship still has a lot of movement. I go down to the latrine and use the toilet. The toilet is a trough about a foot wide, running across the ship. Water is in the trough and that is designed to take the waste to a holding tank at one side. The water in the trough goes from side to side as the ship rolls. There is a line of guys sitting on the trough. One guy takes a big wad of toilet paper, sets it on fire and drops it into the trough. The motion of the ship and the water do the rest. As the flaming paper moves down the trough, guys yell and quickly stand up. The ones that have been sitting do not think it is very funny, but everyone else thinks it is a riot.

Today is August 6, 1945 and there is an announcement over the loud speakers. The United States has dropped an atomic bomb on the Japanese city of Hiroshima, destroying the city. I have no idea what an atomic bomb is and no one else seems to know either. But we are glad to hear that a Japanese city has been destroyed. It may make it easier when we have to invade Japan.

We are still playing volleyball every day and decide to challenge some of the others to get up a team to play us. This gives us something to occupy our time.

Today they announce that on August 9, they dropped another atomic bomb on Nagasaki and destroyed it too. Everyone cheers that the war seems to be going our way in the Pacific. The ocean is not as rough now and the trip is going better.

I get put on KP. They say that they just do not have enough privates on the ship to handle it and they have had to put some of the others on duty. Another guy from Oklahoma and I are doing the KP chores. It entails a lot of going up and down the ladders to take out and bring in things to the mess hold. But they have lots of cartons of milk sitting there and we can have all we want.

The loudspeakers come on and they announce that Japan has surrendered. It is silent for awhile and then the ship erupts with shouts. After the shouting is over, it gets quiet again as each guy realizes what this means to him. We were all scheduled to be in the invasion of Japan and we know that the chances of surviving that were very slim. It is like we have received a reprieve. When we get off of KP, I tell the other guy to wait there for me. I have two cans of beer stowed in my duffle bag and I go get them and bring them back.

I open them and hand one to him. We sit on the hatch and drink our beers in celebration.

It will be another day before we dock. Everyone is going around in such high spirits. The war is over and we will be going home again. We have lived through the war, but we can't forget those who did not make it.

The ship sails into Boston harbor and we are met by fire boats shooting streams of water into the air. Tug boats come out, attach to the ship and we make our way to the dock. Everyone is on the deck and waving to the people on the boats and on the dock. Many of the people meeting us are suffering hangovers, from the last twenty four hours of celebrating. We get on trucks and they take us to the train station, where a troop train awaits us.

CHAPTER XCIII

As we march from the trucks to the train, little boys line the way saying "Hey Joe, you got a Hershey?" Not too much has changed, when we were in France, they would stand and ask for a cigarette or chocolate and in England there always seemed to be some kids wanting candy. Most of us do not have anything ourselves. It has been a long time since we have been where we could get anything. But surprisingly, some of the guys reach in their pack and pull out a candy bar and hand it to one of the kids.

We climb aboard the train and find a place overhead to put our bags. Then we drop into one of the seats, so that others can get their things put away and seated too. It does not take long for the car to fill and then everyone that gets on is ushered to the next car. This train is much like the one we rode on when we were going to Fort Meade, on the way overseas. There are a lot of coaches for us to ride in and in the middle of the train, there is a car set up for dining.

The train pulls out of Boston Station and heads south down the coast. We can see the marshes along side of the tracks and once in awhile we can get a glimpse of the ocean. We leave Massachusetts, cut across the corner of Rhode Island, through Connecticut and into New York. We go south through New York and down to New York

City. There we pick up several cars of soldiers that have come into the port there.

Now that the train is made up, it heads west into Pennsylvania. The train is traveling fast. We seem to have the green light all the way. I guess getting us home is a priority. At noon, they start feeding us one car at a time. They take a car in front of the dining car and let them go eat and when they have finished, they then take a car from behind the dining car. This way, the ones leaving and the ones going will not run into each other. They keep doing this until all have been served. The food is good and they are not skimpy with it, but they do hurry us to eat it so that they can get everyone fed. There are fresh salads, minute steaks, potatoes, gravy, peas and carrots and sheet cake for dessert. We get our choice of milk, ice tea or coffee. And if you ask, you can have more than one. I get milk and ice tea.

We keep heading west and making good time. I like watching out of the window at the scenery. The USO or someone has put magazines on the coaches and we have Life and Reader's Digest magazines to read.

In the evening, they start feeding again, only in reverse order from the noon meal. It takes a long time to get everyone fed. Tonight, we have roast beef, boiled potatoes, green beans, beets, apple cobbler and of course, milk or coffee to drink. I stick with the milk. It seems that my body has a craving for it, since we just did not get it overseas.

I wake up before daylight and make my way back to the toilet in the corner. I have to wait for a little while, it seems that others have felt the urge too. When I am through, I make my way back to my seat and sit there in the dim light trying to see out the window. Once in awhile I see the lights of a small town as we pass through. When it gets daylight, I can tell that we are going through the midwest. There are fields of tall corn beside the tracks. When we went through here about nine months ago, the fields were covered with snow.

The sun is well up, before it is time for those of us in this car to go to the dining coach. After we eat, we go back to our coach and I pick up a magazine as we return to our seats. When we get to the larger cities, we have to make our way through the myriad of train tracks and then back out on the main line. Sometimes, cars will be removed from the train to go in a different direction. By now, we are traveling more in a southwesterly direction.

As the summer sun heats up, we start to feel the heat and wish that we could change from our winter uniforms to the summer ones. We have the windows open and the smoke from the engine comes into the window, gradually covering us with a layer of black from the burning coal. We are still moving at a good pace, and our stops are usually not very long. We travel down through Illinois and cross the Mississippi River at St. Louis. We are in Missouri now going southwest.

We cross over into Arkansas and on to our destination. We reach Fort Smith forty-five hours after we left Boston. The train drops off our car and then proceeds on to other stations. We unload from the train and climb onto waiting trucks. We are taken out to the post and let off at one of the barracks. They tell us to put our things by one of the bunks and then fall out to go get summer uniforms. It is Saturday and many of the personnel here are off for the weekend. They tell us they will get us out of here as soon as possible. We are marched to the supply room and issued new suntan uniforms. After we have each received our uniforms, we are marched back to the barracks and told to clean up and change before chow.

The shower feels really good and then we get our new uniforms on. We will have to work on our uniforms later. Right now, we do not have any unit patches or stripes on them. I have some extra 9th Armored patches and I also have some T5 stripes for summer uniforms in my duffle bag. I also still have my Red Cross sewing kit. I will fix my shirts when I get back from chow.

We look funny wearing the wrinkled clothes, with no insignia on them. We look something like new recruits, but you can tell that we did not just come into the army. We line up for chow and they feed us very well. After we eat, we head back to the barracks and when we get there, there is a soldier there with an iron. He says he will iron our clothes for a dollar an item. Almost every one of us starts taking off their clothes to have them ironed. He takes a foot locker, puts a blanket on it and then spreads a pillow case over that for a cover and starts ironing clothes. He is making much more than the army pays.

While the others are getting their clothes ironed, I am busy sewing a patch and a set of stripes on my shirt. When I get through sewing, I get in line to have my pants and shirt ironed. The other sets I will take home and have my mother wash and iron them. I look much better after I put on the freshly pressed clothes.

They call out names and when our name is called, we are to go to the building across the street for processing. It takes the rest of the day before we have all been through the process. Of course, we gripe about them holding us up. They are checking our records and figuring out how much travel time we will need, the amount of per diem we will get, the ration stamps we are entitled to and how much back pay we have coming. They also determine what medals we are entitled to.

We spend our time in the barracks waiting for them to finish. We only leave to go to the mess hall or if we are called out. We figure that they will not get through processing us until Monday, but on Sunday, they announce that we will be getting out of there today.

A corporal comes into the barracks and starts calling out names. As each one answers, the corporal hands him an envelope. The envelope contains our furlough orders, food stamps, travel vouchers and meal vouchers. He tells us that as soon as we get our envelope, we are to go to the building across the street and draw our pay. That when we get our pay, we are free to go but to be back here in thirty days.

There is a rush to get to the paymaster. Then we head out the other door and down the street to where there is a bus stop. These are army buses running shuttle to the bus station in Fort Smith.

When we get to the bus station, there is a line waiting to buy tickets. We have plenty of time because the bus does not leave for over two hours. While we are waiting to buy our tickets, a civilian man, about fifty, comes over to the line and asks if I am going to Oklahoma City. I tell him that I am. He says that if he can find four guys that want to go, he will take us for twenty-five dollars each and we will get to ride in a car instead of a bus and get there a couple of hours sooner. I tell him I am interested. He goes along the line and soon he has three other guys who want to go. He tells us to go across the street and wait on the sidewalk and he will pick us up in a few minutes. He says for us to not say anything, because he does not have a license to transport people and the bus company will be after him.

We go to the meeting place and he is there in just a few minutes. We each give him the twenty-five dollars, three of us get in back and the other gets in the front and in less than five minutes, we are on the way to Oklahoma City.

He takes us into Oklahoma City and drops us off at the bus station. One of the other guys lives in Oklahoma City and we agree to get together some time, while we are home on leave. I can't get a bus to Hennessey until morning. In the station, I find a seat and try to sleep, but I am too excited about going home.

They give the boarding call for the northbound bus and I take my bag and go out to the loading dock. The driver puts my bag in the baggage compartment, punches my ticket and I climb on to the bus. I am finally on the last leg home. I watch as we travel the familiar road, and at last we pull up in front of the drugstore in Hennessey.

I get off of the bus and the driver gets my bag out for me. I look up and down Main Street, but don't see anyone. I do not expect a band to be waiting, but I would like to have someone welcome me home. I guess it is too early for the stores to be open yet. I walk around the corner on to Oklahoma Avenue and start the block and half walk to home. I look up and see my mother standing on the sidewalk, in front of our house, looking this way. She is waiting for me. I hurry the rest of the way and hug her. I am home at last. I ask how she knew I would be coming home today, and she said that she just knew. I look at the front window in the house and there are two blue flags in it, one with a gold star, honoring Don, who has died, and one with a silver star, representing my service overseas.

We go into the house. Dad has already gone to work and Tommy is not up yet. She asks me if I have had breakfast and I tell her that I have not had anything but a sandwich at the bus station last night. She asks if I would like to have my usual breakfast of cocoa and toast with jelly. I tell her it sounds wonderful.

She fixes my breakfast and then sits at the table with me and drinks a cup of coffee. She tells me how glad she is to have me home again and that I am all right. I know what she means; she is still grieving Don's loss. She will never get over that.

CHAPTER XCIV

We are just finishing breakfast when Tommy comes down. Mother gets up and gets out the cereal and milk for him. I tell him that I am glad to see him and he says that he guesses that he will have to give up the bigger bedroom now that I am home. Mother changes the subject when she tells him that he needs to hurry up and get ready to go mow a yard, before it gets too hot. I tell them that I want to go to town and see who is around.

I walk the block and a half to the post office and greet everyone there. I thank them for all the mail that they have sent to me. They all tell me how glad they are that I am back safe. Then I cross Main Street to the Safeway store, where I worked before I went into the army. Again, it is good to see everyone. Then I move down the west side of Main Street to the pool hall. It is too early for anyone to be playing, but the owner is sweeping the place and says that he is glad to see me back. The war has only been over for four days, so I am one of the first servicemen home after the war and I attract a lot of attention.

I wave to the merchants as I walk down the street. I stop in the drugstore and buy a bottle of bubble bath. They ask me what fragrance I want and I tell them it does not matter much, but I have dreamed of laying back and soaking in a warm bath with bubbles all around me. I make my way down to the high school. School is not in session, but the superintendent is there getting things ready for school to start. I tell him how much he meant to me and all that I learned in going to school there. He asks me to go to Lions club with him and says that he would like for me to talk to the students after school takes up. I tell him that I would be glad to. Then I start my way back up the east side of the street.

Not much has changed since I left home, except that there are not many of the people my age still left in town. It seems like a long time since I was here, but has only been a few months. I have changed a lot more than the town has. I walk back to the house and am surprised that I have only been gone about an hour and I have covered most of the town. Mother says that Dad is working in the country today, but they called him and told him I was home, so he is coming in for dinner. In this small town, probably most of the people already know that I am home.

Mom has changed the bed upstairs and says that the room is ready for me. I carry my bag up stairs and unpack it. I take the new clothes out for Mom to press and sew my patch and stripes on. She measures the ones I have on to get the right distance. She says she will fix them this evening. Tommy comes back and says that it is too hot to mow and that he will go back this evening, after it gets cooler and finish. I help Mom to get dinner ready and it is almost done when Dad comes in.

I say hello to my dad and we shake hands. He says that I look different. I tell him that I am sure that I do. I have put on over ten pounds and I stand much straighter than I used to. I also realize that I am different and will never be the same again. My experiences will always shape my life.

We sit down to dinner and of course, most of the questions are directed to me. We do not get into my combat experiences, but they do want to know about my trip back from Europe. I also tell them about my visit to town this morning. The noon hour passes quickly and Dad has to go back to work. I tell Mom that I am going to take a bath and then a nap, because I am tired.

I go up to the bathroom and draw a hot bath. I pour some of the bubble bath in it until the tub is filled with bubbles and then I slide in. I lay down as far as I can with just my head sticking out of the thick bubbles. I lay there soaking until the water gets cool and then I add more hot water and soak some more. I stay so long that my skin starts to wrinkle and I climb out. I feel a lot better and feel cleaner than I have for a long time. I put on my shorts and go lay on the bed. I have all of the windows open and there is a slight breeze moving the hot August air.

I wake up and realize that someone is talking to me. It is my uncle. He heard I was home and came to see me. He says that he wants to hear all of my battle stories, the ones that I would not tell the rest of the family. I visit with him for awhile, then dress and go downstairs. He leaves to go back home and I go lay down on the divan in the living room.

Mother comes in and says that she has sewed on my patches and stripes and wants to know if they are okay before she presses them. I thank her and tell her they are fine, much better than the ones I sewed on. She asks me if I will help her get supper ready. I know it is not really my help she wants, but rather my company. I am glad to spend the time with her. I turned over to her my ration stamps and she has gone to the store this afternoon and picked up some things for supper. She used enough meat stamps to fix meatloaf. Of course, we will have mashed potatoes and gravy, home canned green beans and she has, as usual, fixed refrigerator ice cream.

After supper, I visit for awhile and then tell them that I am going to town to see what is going on. Mom said she thought I would. I walk up to the pool hall and the only ones there are some younger guys. They invite me to play a game of snooker and I enjoy it, but I get beat. When it gets almost time for the library to close, I walk the block north and enter the library.

Emma sees me and says that she heard that I was home and thought I would be in. She tells the few kids still in the library to hurry up and put their things away, because it is closing time. She ushers them out the door and closes it and locks it. She turns off all the lights except the little night light they have. I move in and take her in my arms. We kiss for some time and then kiss again. Then she says for me to come and go with her. Her sister is out of town for a few days and she is staying at her apartment while she is gone. We walk down the street and then turn off into the residential district.

When we get to the apartment, she unlocks the door and goes in to turn on the lights. I follow her in. She turns and throws her arms around my neck and we kiss again. I get the feeling that if I want to play house with all the trimmings tonight, I can. But I also get the feeling that if I do, it will not be just for tonight, but will be forever. I like her, but I am not in love with her. I sure am not ready to get married. We sit down on the divan and talk. What is really on our minds, we do not talk about, but we both seem to know what the other is thinking. We have been friends for over a year, even though I have been gone for most of it.

After awhile, I get ready to go and she kisses me good bye. She tells me to stay in touch, and I say I will. But this is where our lives take different paths. I walk slowly home and wonder if I have done the right thing. After I go over everything, I feel that I have. Everyone is in bed when I get home. Mom calls out to me and says that she baked some cookies this evening and there is plenty of milk if I would like some. I tell her that would be great.

While I am having my cookies and milk, she comes out and sits with me. She asks how my first evening home went? I tell her it was okay, I guess. But was a lot duller than what I am used to. We visit a little more and then I make my way back upstairs to my bed. My model airplanes are still hanging from the wire across the room, flying their little circles in the breeze. After my nap this afternoon and the soft bed, it takes awhile to go to sleep.

Tuesday, I stay in bed until after Dad has gone to work and then I get up and go down stairs. Mother wakes Tommy and tells him to come down and eat breakfast so he can get an early start on mowing today. She sets out his breakfast and then fixes me some eggs and toast. I tell her to skip the cocoa and I will drink coffee this morning. She sits with me and drinks a cup of coffee and eats some toast. This gives us a chance to visit about different people. She knows so many of the kids that I am friends with. She tries to fill me in on what they all are doing. Tommy comes down and fixes his cereal and sits at the table with us.

After breakfast, I get the paper and go into the living room to read it. I am really taking it easy. The paper is full of news of the troops returning back home. Maybe some of the ones that I know will be coming in soon. When I finish the paper, I make my morning trip to town. I go into some different stores today and I am warmly greeted at every place. When I get to the barber shop, I decide that I should get a haircut. I do not realize how shaggy I am until I look in the mirror. When I get through, I make my way back to the house. Mom asks if I would like to have a little lunch. Dad is working out in the country and will eat out there. Tommy is already back from mowing and is putting the lawnmower away in the shed.

We have grilled cheese sandwiches and ice tea. It makes a nice lunch. The phone rings just as we are finishing and it is the superintendent calling for me. He asks if I would be willing to make a talk to Lions club on Thursday and then talk to the students on Friday morning. I tell him that I would be glad to. I am enjoying the attention that I am getting, but I am also bored already. I lay down on the divan and doze off.

Mother asks me to help her get supper ready. While we are eating, Dad wants to know what I have done today and I tell him it is a repeat of yesterday, but I did get an offer to speak at Lions club and at the school. He says that is good, that I need the experience.

After supper, Tommy wants to play me a game of dominos. I guess he remembers how he beat me, when I was home after basic. I tell him that we will play chess instead. I have a small portable chess set that one of the guys in the army gave me. We set it up and I show him how to play. I beat him the first two games and he beats me the third. The folks are listening to the radio and I join in. Tuesday night has some of their favorite programs on. I used to listen to them when I was home, but I did not have access to them while I was gone. I stay up and listen to the ten o'clock news and then head up to bed.

CHAPTER XCV

I decide to venture out more today. After breakfast, I ask Mom if I can take the car and drive around a little. She says that it is okay, but that it probably does not have much gas in it. I go get the car out and drive to the filling station. Gas rationing has ended now, so I fill the tank with gas. I bet this is the first time it has been full in four years. The tires are not all that good, but there are none to buy, so I will just have to be careful. I sure do not want to ruin a tire. I do not have a driver's license, but I do not figure that anyone will bother me about it, since I have not been in a position to get one for awhile.

I drive out into the country and look at some of the places that I used to go. Not really that much of a change. I drive by the farm where I used to work and see what is going on. The wheat has all been cut and the ground is plowed. They have some alfalfa that is ready to mow. I guess they are probably still using those work horses to rake it up. I am glad that it is not me doing it.

I am back at the house before dinner and Mom says she will fix us a bite of lunch. She always seems to be able to come up with something in a short time. We visit while we eat and she wants to know what all I did this morning.

When Dad gets home, we have supper. I tell him about driving around today and that I filled the tank with gas. They ask me what I have planned next. I tell them that tomorrow I am to go to Lions club and talk and the next day I am to go to the school. Mom says that she thinks that we should go to Waukomis and have dinner with my grandmother on Sunday, after church. I agree that would be nice.

After supper, I agree to play chess with Tommy again. Of course he beats me. I get bored and decide that I will listen to the radio. I listen with the folks to the rest of the programs and then to the ten o'clock news, before I go upstairs to bed.

Thursday morning after breakfast, I change into a clean uniform, so that I will be ready to go to Lions club. About eleven-thirty, I make my way to the city hall. The Lions meet in a room up above the city hall. I wait down below until the superintendent gets there and he takes me up stairs and puts me with some of the men that I know. He is the secretary, so he will be busy. The meeting starts and then we eat. When most everyone has finished eating, the secretary introduces me and I make my talk.

I tell them about my trip overseas and about some of the things that I saw. They ask about the damage over there and I tell them about it and how the Germans are already trying to get their country restored, but the French are lagging far behind. They ask what is in store for me now and I tell that I do not know, because I was scheduled to go on the invasion of Japan and since that will not be taking place, I assume that in due time I will be discharged. After the meeting is over, they all come by and shake my hand and thank me for my service. It makes me feel very good.

This evening at supper, I tell what happened to me today at Lions club. The folks are anxious to hear about my day. I tell them that I hope my talk to the school goes as well tomorrow. Tonight, I stay home and read and listen to the radio. No use going to the pool hall, since I know that there will not be much doing.

Friday morning, I put on a fresh ironed uniform to go to the school and talk to the kids. It feels good to be able to stand up in front of the whole high school and talk to them, since it was just over a year ago that I was in the same place. When I get through telling about where all I have been and some of the things I have seen, they start to ask questions. Some ask questions that are serious, but after a little while, they start to ask foolish questions, just so they can stay out of class a little longer. The superintendent knows this trick and sends them back to their classes.

I spend the rest of the day doing very little and decide that I would like to go to Oklahoma City next week and visit my friend there. I get on the phone and call his number. His mother answers and says he is out for awhile, but she will have him call me. It is almost supper time when he calls and says that he would like for me to come down Monday and we can run around together. I now have a few days planned, so that I will not be so bored.

Saturday I go to town and it is different scene, more like what I was used to before. The streets are crowded with farmers who have come to town to trade. I go to the drug store, get a coke and sit at one of the stools at the counter. Many of the people coming in stop and talk to me. They remember me from when I used to carry out their groceries. Of course, they ask if I am home for good or not. I tell them I am only home on leave and do not know when I will get out. This is a more exciting day than most I have had since I got home.

I go home for dinner and Mom has fixed some egg sandwiches for a lunch. We have some fresh lettuce and tomatoes on them and some home canned pickles. With the ice tea, it is a fine lunch. She also digs out a few cookies that she baked the other day and we have them for dessert. After dinner, I lay down on the divan for awhile, read the paper and then decide to go back up town again to see what is doing.

It seems that everyone that was there this morning is still there, together with a bunch more people that have come to town since. It is hot in the sun and most people are in the stores or huddled under the awnings in front. The barber chairs are full and there is a long line waiting. This is not wasted effort though, they get to visit while they wait. This is the time that people get to catch up on the news of their neighbors. Some of the kids have been sent off to the afternoon movie. They will get to see a cartoon, serial and then a cowboy movie. It is still ten cents for under twelve and twenty-five cents for over, plus sales tax and war excise tax.

I go back home in time to help Mother get supper on before Dad gets home from the hardware store. He will have to hurry and eat so he can get back to the store for the evening. They will stay open until about nine so the farmers can get what they need. Supper is on the table when Dad gets there and we start to eat, so he can get back. There is not a lot of time to visit this evening.

After supper, I help Mother do the dishes. She is also getting food ready to take to my grandmother's tomorrow. Helping in the kitchen has always been one of my jobs, so I do not mind. When we finish, I tell her that I am going back to town and that I may go to the movie preview tonight and will not be home until late. Then I make the short walk back to Main Street.

The pool hall is full tonight and guys are waiting to play. No kids tonight, the adults have taken it over. One of my friends that is in the navy comes in to the pool hall. I have not seen him since I was home on leave last year. He is on leave, having just finished his boot camp. We have a nice visit. I ask him to go to the preview with me, but he says he told his folks he would be back early. I tell him that I am going to be gone for next three or four days, but want to get with him again while he is home.

Just before eleven, I head toward the theater. It is surprising how many people are lined up to go to the show. I visit in line with them and find a couple that I know and sit by them in the show. The newsreels are showing the Japanese surrender and the troops entering Tokyo. Everyone cheers in the theater. The movie is not very good, but it is something to do. When it is over, I go home. I find some of the cookies, pour a glass of milk and eat them before I head up to bed.

Mom, Dad and Tommy go to Sunday school, but I wait and go to church. The service starts and the minister makes an announcement:

Word has just been received that Jack Stetler, a navy pilot from here, went on a mission the last day of the war and never returned. He is listed as missing in action. Many in the church start crying and turning to others for comfort. Jack was a couple of years older than I am and was a friend from Boy Scouts. The minister asks us all to pray. He asks that Jack be found safe and sound and returned home. He then goes on to acknowledge me being present and thanks God that I have returned safe. I had thought church would be a happy homecoming, but it turns out to be a sad day.

After church, we go home, pack the food into the car and get in. Dad drives the thirteen miles to Waukomis, where my grandmother Shades lives. She is glad to see me. I tell her that I still have the four leaf clover she gave me for good luck before I went overseas, and that I carried it on my dog tag chain, before it wore out and I had to move it to my pocket, and that I think it brought me good luck. They are putting the food out when my uncle and aunt and two cousins arrive. I have never seen the little one before.

We sit down and have a Sunday dinner like I used to remember. This is one of the things I thought about when I was so far from home. They want to know if the food in the army was like this and I assure them that it wasn't. This gives me a chance to thank my aunt for all the cookies she sent to me and to tell her how much we enjoyed them.

After dinner, we all sit around in the living room and I tell them some of the things that I saw. This is one of those times when I have to be very careful what I say. My usual language in the army would not be appreciated here. About four, we pack up and go back home.

We listen to the usual Sunday night radio programs and when the news is over, I head to bed.

CHAPTER XCVI

After breakfast, I pack my toothbrush, paste and clean pair of shorts in a small bag and take it with me, as I walk the short distance to the bus stop. I go in the drugstore and buy a round trip ticket to Oklahoma City. I order a Coke and sit down to wait until the bus gets here. I finish the Coke and look up to see the bus driver coming in the door. I grab my bag and go out to the side street and stand by the bus. The driver comes out, punches my ticket and I board the bus. There are not many people on the bus, so I am able to get a seat next to the window.

The bus moves out and we head down the familiar road. I think about when I rode this way a little over a year ago and all that has happened to me since then. It is a relaxing ride and I enjoy seeing the scenery. When we arrive in Oklahoma City, it is afternoon and I am hungry, so I go into the café in the bus station and sit at the counter. I order a cheese sandwich and glass of milk. That is one of the cheapest things on the menu. It is nothing special, but takes away the empty feeling.

After I eat, I go out on the street and walk a block north where I can catch the street car. If I get on the right one, it will take me to within a couple of blocks of where my friend lives. The street car stops and I ask the conductor if this is the one I want to take me to southeast Oklahoma City. He asks me what address I am going to and when I tell him, he says this is the car and he will tell me when I need to get off. I thank him and find a seat just behind him.

The car starts forward and makes its way through traffic in downtown Oklahoma City. As we go, he keeps ringing the bell trying to get motorists out of the way. It is a noisy ride, but I enjoy it. When we get through the downtown area, he speeds up and the coach sways from side to side and screeches as we make turns. It is not long after that, that he tells me that the next stop is where I get off and that I will need to go to the right. The ride is fun and I would have liked to ridden further, but I get off, wave goodbye and walk down the street.

I keep looking for house numbers and I find the right one in the middle of the second block. I go up on the porch and knock on the door. Ray comes to the door and says he is glad to see me. I go in and he introduces me to his mother. We go back to his room and put my bag away and he shows me the bathroom. Then we go into the living room and sit down and visit. His mother asks if we would drink a glass of tea if she made it and we both say that would be nice.

We sit back and start telling what it has been like to get back home. We both agree that it is great to get home, but not near the excitement that we have been used to. His mother says she will have supper when his dad and brothers get home. She knows we want to get out and run around and she will try to get us fed as soon as she can.

His dad comes in from work and it is only a few minutes later that his two older brothers come in from their job. His mother tells them to wash up because she has supper ready. We all sit down around the big dining room table. They start passing food and it is obvious that she has fixed a lot for this hungry bunch. After the food has all been passed, Ray's brothers start kidding us about going out and finding some girls. One of them says to be sure and take plenty of rubbers and they all laugh. I blush. This is different from my house. Nothing like that would ever be said, especially at the dinner table.

After we eat, Ray and I go out and get in the car and he drives off to the north. We decide to go to Spring Lake Amusement Park and see if there are any girls there. We get to the park and start to walk around through the rides. We get over by the roller coaster and see two girls standing there. They are about seventeen and nice looking. We ask them if they are going to ride the roller coaster. They say they can't make up their minds, that it looks scary. We ask if they would like to ride it with us. They whisper to each other and then say that they guess it would be okay. We buy the tickets and go over and get in line to get on.

We find seats on the roller coaster and we each sit with a girl. The ride starts and of course the first part is very mild. When we go over the top and start down, both girls hang on to us as tight as they can. This is better than we expected. We finish the ride and then we start walking around the park. We have paired off and just make the evening of it. We both know that this is not going to go anywhere, but it is nice to have some female company for the evening.

The girls say that they have to go, it is getting time for them to be in. We ask if we can take them home, but they look at each other and say that they better not, that their parents might not approve. We know what they mean. We say good bye and watch them leave. Then we head to the car. On the way back, we stop at a place Ray knows and go in and he orders a couple of beers. No one asks if we are of age, they just bring out a couple of bottles and glasses. We drink our beers and then head home.

I spend the night there and the next morning. His mother fixes a lunch for us, then I tell them goodbye and walk up the street, where I can catch the street car back downtown. I sit on the bench and wait for it to arrive. The same man is running the coach and remembers me from yesterday. He asks if I had a good time and I tell him that I did. I ride to the bus station and I only have fifteen minutes to wait until my bus leaves.

I spend the next few days mostly at home. I lay back on the divan and read or take a nap. I am bored. There is not much that I can do and I begin to get lazy. I work around the place some. I build new roosts and nests in the chicken house and clean it out. That was a job I used to hate, but now it does not seem so bad. I even pull some weeds in the garden.

The next week, I run into Don, the sailor who is home on leave. He tells me about the great girl he had a date with Saturday night. She lives in Waukomis. He says he has another date with her this coming Friday night. I ask him to see if she has a friend that I could go with. He says he will call her tonight and see.

I go to the pool hall tonight and Don is there. He says he called Wilma and she said she would let him know if she could find someone to go with me. This sounds more promising. I hope something works out.

Today I take a hike. I walk all the way out to Turkey Creek and visit some of the places where we used to play. It is quiet and peaceful along the creek. The cottonwoods are starting to turn yellow on the very tops. I circle around and take a different way back to town. It is a nice walk and I needed to get out and move around more. In the evening, I go to the pool hall and Don is there. He says that she is to let him know tomorrow night if she has found anyone to go with me. We play three games of snooker and then we go home.

I keep wondering all day if I will get to have a date this week. I spend the day doing about what I have done most of the other days since I have been home. After supper, I head to town to the pool hall. I am waiting when Don walks in. He is smiling and says, "It is on."

"You mean I have a date?"

"Yes, they will meet us at the drugstore at seven tomorrow night."

"That's great. Can you get the car?"

"Yes, the folks said I could use it, since I have to start back to California, early Sunday morning."

We will pick up the girls and then go to Enid to a movie. It sounds great. Then I get to thinking, what if she is ugly or has a bad disposition? I realize that I need to forget those things. Just accept whatever happens. We shoot a couple of games of snooker and then we both go home.

Friday passes slower than usual. I am anxious to be going out. I tell my mother that Don and I have a date with a couple of girls from Waukomis and she says that is nice. Early in the evening, I get cleaned up and put on clean uniform. After supper, I walk to town and wait on the street for Don to come. He drives up and we head for Waukomis. It is only thirteen miles, so it does not take long to get there. He parks in front of the drugstore and we get out and start into the store. Don holds the door for me and I step in first. In front of me is this pretty, young girl with brown hair. I turn to Don and say, "That is the one I want."

We go in and there are two girls, the shorter one that I first saw and a taller redhead. The tall one says, "Hi Don."

He says, "Hello Wilma." Then he introduces me to her.

She says, "This is Dolores Bullard."

We stand there talking for a few minutes. Dolores says that she knows my cousins that live in Waukomis. That she lives just down the street from them. We go out and get in the car. Don and Wilma in the front seat and Dolores and I in the back seat. Don drives to Enid and we go to the movie.

During the movie, I am bold enough to put my arm around her shoulders. She seems to just fit under my arm. I watch the movie, but my mind is not on it. I am more interested in the person beside me. After the movie, we go to a drugstore in Enid and get Cokes. When we finish our Cokes, we get in the car and head back toward Waukomis.

A couple of miles north of Waukomis, Don turns off on a county road. We go about a mile and then he pulls over and parks. I have my arm around Dolores and I lean over and kiss her. She seems as eager to kiss me as I am her. I hold her close and we talk to each other. I find out that her name is really Billie Dolores Bullard, but she goes by Dolores. She is fifteen years old. I am nineteen, so I am not too comfortable about her being so much younger, but I am already in love.

We neck awhile in the car and then we drive the girls back to their homes. We take Dolores home first and I walk up to the porch with her and kiss her goodnight. Then we take Wilma home and Don walks her up to the house and kisses her. It is a long kiss because he will not see her again for several months. After that, we drive back to Hennessey. Don asks how I liked my date and I tell him that I am already in love. The date could not have been better. I can hardly wait to see her again.

CHAPTER XCVII

I am excited about my date. I will be looking forward to seeing her again. I told her I would try to get to Waukomis next Friday night. She said that if I can, to come to the skating rink and she will be there. A week seems a long time to wait, but since she is in school, she can only go out on Friday or Saturday nights.

More of the service men are coming home now. Some on leave and the older ones for good. The whole feeling of the town seems changed. I am glad to get to see the other guys.

The days seem to be all the same now as I wait for Friday night and going back to see Dolores. At last the day arrives and I have permission to use the car. My mother warns me about watching for the Rock Island Rocket, the high speed passenger train, that goes through both here and Waukomis. Several people have been killed by the train when they drove out in front of it.

I drive to Waukomis and park in front of the café with the skating rink in back. I go through the café and when I get in the back room, I see her. She is skating around the rink. As she comes around, I wave and she backs up and comes over to where I am standing. She says to wait a few minutes, she wants to make a few more turns around the floor before she leaves. I watch as she gracefully skates away.

She comes off of the rink and sits down to take off her skates. She has her own shoe skates that she uses. She tells me that she is glad that I came and that she has been looking forward to it all week. We go out and get in the car and I drive to Enid to go to the show. When we get to the theater, we go up in the balcony. There is an understanding that the balcony is for couples. I put my arm around her shoulders and she moves as close to me as she can. The feel of her body next to me and the scent of her perfume is wonderful.

When the show is over, we look for a place where we can go and get something to drink, but it is too late, all of the places have closed. We drive around Enid looking, but decide that we should start back towards Waukomis. When we get north of the town, I turn off on the county road, where Don turned off last week and I drive to where he parked before. We stop and when I shut off the car, I turn and she is turned toward me, so I lean over and kiss her.

I take her in my arms and hold her close and we kiss some more. Then we sit and talk. She tells me about things at school and about her family. I tell her about some of the things that I have seen and about my family. She knows a lot about my family, since she is friends with some of my cousins. I tell her that I will have to leave Monday and report back to the army at Camp Chaffee, Arkansas. But I am going to ask if I can use the car tomorrow night again, since I do not have much time left. That if it is okay, I will meet her tomorrow night again. She says she would like that.

We kiss some more and then she says that she needs to get home, before it gets too late, if she is to be able to go out tomorrow night. I drive her home and walk up to the door with her. I kiss her good-night and then head for home.

Saturday morning, I ask if I can have the car tonight again, that I have a date. Mom says that she guesses so, since I do not have much time left before I go back. I go to town and the town is busy today. I find a lot of people to visit with. I go back home at noon and Mom says that I got a telegram from the army. I open it up and it says that my leave has been extended another fifteen days. I am delighted, but not sure how my mother feels. She may have had all she wants of me for awhile.

I go to Waukomis and meet Dolores. She too is delighted that I have another fifteen days at home. We spend some time at Waukomis tonight instead of going to Enid. I get to meet several of her friends, as they come into the skating rink. After awhile, we slip away and go back out to the parking spot. I can't seem to get enough of her kisses. When it is time to take her home, I tell her I will see her again on Friday night.

The next two weeks are very much like the last week. I get to see Dolores three more times. The last night, the necking moves into the petting stage, but with her being so young, it does not go any further than that. I tell her that I am in love with her and she says that she loves me too. She promises to write to me just as soon as I send her my mailing address. I take her home, walk her up to the door and we have a long goodbye kiss. Then I make the lonesome drive back home.

Sunday, the others go to Sunday school, but I wait and join them at church. After church, Mom has fixed a nice meal, for my last dinner at home for awhile. In the afternoon, I gather up all of my things, get them packed and ready to go. I will have to leave early in the morning in order to get to Camp Chaffee by evening.

Monday morning, Mom is up early and fixes breakfast for Dad and me. Then I kiss her goodbye and Dad and I walk up to the bus stop. He will wait with me until the bus comes and then he will go on to work.

The bus comes and again I shake hands with my dad and climb on the bus. I really do not know what is ahead for me. I sleep a lot on the bus, waking up every so often to see where we are. I have an hour wait in Oklahoma City, before the bus leaves for Fort Smith, Arkansas. I go into the café in the bus station and order a piece of pie and cup of coffee. The pie is nothing like what my mother makes, but it will have to do. I take my time eating it, because it is more comfortable in here than out in the waiting room.

I go back out into the waiting room and there are several soldiers there, and I assume that some of them will be going to Fort Smith on the same bus. At last they give the first boarding call for the Fort Smith bus. I gather up my bags and go out to the dock. I am third in line to get on.

There are other soldiers getting on and some civilians. The bus is filling up, but is not quite full. So far no one is sitting next to me. Then I hear a voice say, "Is this seat taken, soldier?" I look up and it is Ray. I am glad to have him join me. I ask him what he has done with his time. He tells me that he got bored sitting at home and when his brothers asked him why he did not go to work with them, he said that he decided he would. They work as carpenters building and repairing houses. So he joined them, kept busy and made some good money. He is also assured of a job, when he gets out of the army.

Ray asks what I did and I tell him that I really did not do much of anything all the time I was home, but that I did meet a girl and fall in love. He asks if we are going to get married and I tell him not for a long time, because she is only fifteen and still in high school. But it is nice to have someone back home, that I can look forward to seeing again.

When we get to Fort Smith, we get our things and then go around to the other side of the bus stop where the shuttle buses from Camp Chaffee stop. It is not long before one of the buses comes and we board it for the post. They take us back to the transient area where we are to report. We go to the orderly room and report back in. They assign us to a barracks. Ray and I are in different barracks. We say goodbye and each head for our assigned barracks.

I get in the barracks and there are hardly any bunks occupied. I pick out one, get out the things I will need and put the rest at the head of the bed. I unfold the mattress, put on the mattress cover and blankets, put a pillow case on and my bed is ready. I put the lock back on my duffle bag, since these transient places are a good place to have things stolen. You do not know anyone yet, so you can't trust anyone.

It is supper time, so I get to looking for the mess hall. I see some guys going down the street and figure that they are going to chow, so I follow them. I get in line and have to wait for them to open the doors. While I am waiting, Ray comes up, so I drop out of line and go back and stand with him so we can eat together. We get in and go through the serving line. The food is not anything special, but is better than usual for a transient mess. I notice that the non-coms are eating at a different table, but since Ray is only a PFC, I stay with him.

After supper, we walk back and then separate to go to our barracks. When I get to mine, I see that a few more guys have checked in. Then I decide to go get my shower before everyone else decides to. I get my shower and go ahead and get ready for bed. It seems that I am the only one in the barracks that was in the Oklahoma car on the train coming from Germany. It has been a long day and I go to sleep long before lights out.

Today, we are just sitting around waiting for something to happen. Some of the guys have already been called to ship out. We are down to thirteen guys left in the barracks. I think that Ray has shipped out, because I have not seen him at chow. One of the sergeants comes by and we ask him when we will be shipping out. He says that as soon as they can get us connections, that we will be going too. We spend the whole day waiting and then late in the evening, decide that we will not be going anywhere today.

A couple of guys say since we are not going to leave today, they are going to go to town. They do not have any passes, but they say that they do not think anyone is checking the gate very close. We wish them good luck and they head out. It is late at night when they come in. It is obvious that they have had plenty to drink. I am sure they do not care.

We still do not have orders to ship out and it is after dinner. The two guys that went to town last night bring out a bottle of whiskey and start drinking. Then they pass the bottle around. Soon, everyone of us is drinking. We finish that bottle and they bring out another. They say that they bought it for the trip, and since we are drinking it up now, we will have to get some more for the trip.

Along in the evening, we get the word to fall out with all of our things. We are shipping out. None of us are feeling any pain, as we load into the truck that is to take us to the train station. One of the guys says he hopes that we have time to get some more whiskey, before we get on the train. The truck keeps going and we go right through Fort Smith and over to Van Buren, Arkansas.

The truck stops beside the train tracks and they tell us to get out and board the rail car sitting there on the siding. We get our things and climb on to the rail car. It is a compartment car, with two of us to each compartment. This would be a deluxe car if we were traveling in civilian life. We put our things in place and then the sergeant that is in charge of the group and one of those that went to town last night, says that we need to send out a party to get some whiskey. Four of us volunteer to go get the whiskey.

We get off of the train car and walk down the street toward the center of Van Buren. We do not see a liquor store, so we ask a guy where one is located. He says there are not any. Van Buren is in a dry county. But then he tells us where the bootlegger is. We go to the building that he points out and the guy says he is out, but he has a load coming in a little bit. We tell him that we have to ship out on the train, so he tells us to go back to the rail-yard and he will have the driver meet us there.

We stop in a grocery store and each of us gets a quart of ginger ale to use as a mixer. Then we walk down to the rail-yard. We are just walking into the rail-yard when this car pulls up beside us. He asks if we are the guys that wanted the whiskey and we tell him that we are. I hand him my money and he hands me a pint of whiskey. The next guy does the same thing. We have not noticed, but another car has pulled up behind us. The last two guys buy their whiskey and just then, two policemen get out of the second car.

They arrest the bootlegger for selling the whiskey and take the last two guys as witnesses. I notice that they do not care much about the whiskey itself, because they tell the two guys, that they are taking as witnesses, to give us the bottles. Then they drive off with one officer with the bootlegger and the other with the other two soldiers. I wonder if we will ever see them again, and wonder why they let us go.

We each stick the two pints of whiskey into the pockets inside of our Eisenhower jackets and carry a quart of ginger ale in each hand. We walk to where our rail car is and it is not there. We go on to the depot and ask where our car is. The agent says that they have pulled it out to the east yard. We ask how we can get to it. He says that the train that will be pulling it will be coming in shortly and that if we climb on it, we will be able to make our way to the car, when they hook it onto the train. He seems to know we are not in the best of shape, so he cautions us to get right on, when it comes, because it will not stop long.

The train pulls in and we run up to the entrance of the nearest car and climb into the train. It is a troop car; full of new recruits. We can tell by their uniforms. There is one second lieutenant with them. He gives us the eye, but does not say anything. He can tell that we are combat veterans and we can tell that he is not. But there we stand, with a quart of ginger ale in each hand and bottles of whiskey sticking out of our jacket pockets.

When the train stops to hook on to our car, we make our way back to the car. We turn over the whiskey and ginger ale and then tell them what happened, that the other guys were taken as witnesses and we are lucky that they did not take us too.

The trains starts to move and we can hear a siren. Then the train stops again. The police car pulls alongside and the two guys climb into the car. As soon as they are on board, the train moves out again.

CHAPTER XCVIII

The train is moving now and we are all present and accounted for. The porter comes back to our car and they send him back to get some ice. One of the guys becomes the bartender and we move through the car from one compartment to another. It becomes our own club car. We drink and tell jokes until one by one, we head back to our own compartments to sleep.

We wake up in the morning and wonder how we are going to eat. The sergeant with our papers says that he has some meal vouchers and we can go to the dining car on the train. We start moving toward the front of the train and find that the cars of the recruits have been taken off of the train. We are still the last car. We only have to go through four cars to reach the dining car.

It is still early, there are not many in the dining car, so we can each find a seat. Someone asks the sergeant what we can have to eat. He says he does not know, but he will find out. He calls over the waiter and asks him. The waiter says that most items on the menu are too expensive for our vouchers, but he points out some of the things that we could afford. I pick the pancakes and bacon with coffee to wash it down. It seems that most of the other guys are ordering something similar.

It takes awhile to get served, but when we do, it is good, even if there is not the quantity that we are used to. The coffee is good and there is real cream to put in it. We take our time eating and can tell that they would like for us to hurry up and get out, so that they can feed other people. When we have finished, we go back to our car. None of us know where we are. But we think we are heading east. By noon, we have all had another drink.

Some of the guys have set up a table and are playing cards. They only have room for four at a time to play. A few are reading and the rest seem to be milling around through the car. I go back to the compartment and raise the shade and sit and watch the scenery go past. We spend the time just taking it easy and drinking.

On the fourth day, we are sitting in the rail-yard in Birmingham, Alabama. I know, because I can see a sign. We are about out of whiskey again, so I leave the car, walk through the rail-yard until I come to a street running alongside of the tracks. I follow it a couple of blocks and find a little liquor store. The guy does not say a word about my age, just sells me a bottle. As soon as I get it, I head back to the rail car. If I were left behind, I have no idea how I would get to where we are going.

On the evening of the seventh day, we arrive in Durham, North Carolina, but not without incident. One of the guys is drunk and gets in an argument with the conductor. He takes a swing at the conductor and hits him. The conductor calls the cops and they arrest the guy. The rest of us go to a Chinese restaurant to eat supper, before we go out to the base. When we finish eating, the sergeant gets ready to pay with the meal vouchers and since we have not eaten all of our meals, there is money left over. He talks the Chinaman into giving him the balance in cash.

The sergeant and another guy leave us to wait at the bus station, while they go to the police station. They use the extra meal money to post the other guy's bail and then bring him back with them. I am not sure what they told him, but he is acting real peaceful now. When we are all together, we go to catch the next bus to Camp Butner, home of the 4th Infantry Division.

We arrive at Camp Butner and report in to the headquarters. The sergeant in charge has a private show us to the transient housing. We will get our assignments in the morning. The private leads us to a barracks a couple of blocks away. It is much like the barracks we had in basic training. I find a bunk, throw my things on the floor, unfold the mattress, put on the cover and a couple of blankets, put on the pillow case and then head for the showers.

By the time I get out of the shower, I am sober, but tired and sleepy. I head for the bed and dive under the covers. That is the last thing I remember until I wake in the morning. When I get up in the morning, I start looking for the mess hall. I see some of the guys from the other barracks heading down the street, so I decide to follow them. I end up in line at the transient mess.

We have some of that thick army bacon with some powdered eggs. They have toasted the bread in the oven and they have some black coffee. It is very much like the transient mess halls I have been in before, but it would have to rank near the bottom. I hope that the food will be a lot better when I get to my unit.

About nine o'clock, a sergeant comes into the barracks and calls out all of our names and tells us to get our things together and fall out in fifteen minutes. It does not take us long, because we never had unpacked. We are standing in the street in front of the barracks and a truck arrives. We help each other climb in with our things. The truck drives down a street, stops and the sergeant in the cab hollers out a couple of the names. He tells them that this is where they go. A few more get off at different locations and then it is my turn. I am the only one getting off here.

I am standing in front of an orderly room. The sign says Hq. Co. 3rd Bn. 12th Inf. Regt. 4th Inf. Div. Unless there is some mistake, this will be my new address. I walk into the orderly room and there is a first sergeant sitting behind the desk. I hand him the copy of my orders. He looks at them, stands up, extends his hand and welcomes me to the outfit. He calls out to the other room and says, "Captain, one of the new men is here." The captain comes out of the other room and I come to attention and salute him. He returns my salute and asks my name. I tell him my name and he says, "We are glad to have you Lovell." So far, this is the best welcome I have had since I got in the army.

They sit down and then tell me to sit down too. They ask what my specialty is and what I have been doing. I tell them that I have been a radio operator. The captain says that they do not have need of radio operator right now, but probably will later. The first sergeant is looking at my papers and he turns to the captain and says, "He can type."

The captain says, "You can type?"

"Yes, sir. Not very fast, but I can type."

"Would you mind working here in the orderly room? We need a clerk really bad."

"No sir, I would be glad to help out."

"Good. As soon as you get settled in, come on back here and the sergeant will show you what needs to be done. Sergeant, why don't you show Lovell where he is to bunk?"

I follow the first sergeant back through some barracks until we come to the one on the far corner away from the orderly room. He leads me in and tells me to take any of the bunks that are not being used. That gives me a lot of choices, because most are empty. Then he tells me that when I have my things put away, to come on back to the orderly room and he will show me what needs to be done. I have only been in the outfit for fifteen minutes and I already have a job and a place to stay.

I figure that I will be here for awhile, so I take my time and hang up my clothes and arrange my foot locker. Then I make my bed. When everything is in order, I go back to the orderly room. When I get there, the first sergeant says that he would like for me to put all of the army regulations away. The whole set came in boxes and he says he is tired of falling over them. He would like for me to put them in order on the shelves.

I start going through them and I soon see that the army seems to have a regulation covering just about everything. I sort them by number and then put them on the shelves. I thought it would only take a few minutes, but it is going to take hours to do them all. I work on them until noon and then the first sergeant says for me to come with him and we will go to the mess hall. I ask how the chow is here and he says that it is not very good. The cooks they have are not very experienced and the rations they get are very skimpy. This does not sound very good.

We get to the mess hall and he says for me to come with him. We go past the guys lined up and go in and sit at the non-com table. He says that as soon as the others get through the line, we will get our food. The line moves through and when there is a clear place, he says that we should get our food now. We go through the line and they put the food on our trays. It is some kind of meatloaf, mashed potatoes and gravy, with green beans. They have plain Jell-O for dessert.

We sit down to eat and about that time the supply sergeant comes in and joins us. The first sergeant introduces us and tells him that I will be helping out in the orderly room for awhile. I start to eat and the food is not good. The meatloaf has a funny taste to it. I think it is mixture of beef and mutton. The potatoes are made from pow- dered potatoes. I eat, but I do not finish everything. I pour myself a cup of coffee and put a lot of sugar and milk in it and drink it. If the food does not get better, this may be a long tour of duty. When we finish, we go back to the orderly room and I get back to work.

I work for fifty minutes and then I take a ten minute smoke break. No one told me to do that, but that is what we used to do and I think that I will keep doing it until someone tells me different. A little before seventeen hundred, the captain leaves and says he will see us tomorrow. The first sergeant tells me to go ahead and go, that he will wait for the CQ (charge of quarters) to show up. I head back to the barracks and find that the other guys have returned from their details. One of the guys is getting ready to go on CQ, the rest are laying around, waiting for supper. I tell them who I am and that I am working in the orderly room. I see a couple of the guys have on PFC stripes, but all the rest are privates. This outfit is sure under strength.

I never went upstairs in the barracks, so I did not know that the switchboard for the phone system is up there. A couple of guys man it all day. At seventeen hundred, they plug all lines together, so that it is a party line and then the switchboard is not in service until morning. I visit with the guys and find out that they have all been out on details, that they never seem to have enough people to take care of all the jobs that are assigned to the outfit. I am sure glad I had typing in high school, because it has landed me one of the better jobs here.

No one falls out for retreat. They do not even change uniforms, but keep on their fatigues. I have been wearing my class A uniform while I work, so at least I am dressed. When it is time for chow, I fall in with the others and make my way to the mess hall. When we get there, I go ahead and go sit at the non-com table. The first sergeant is there, and a corporal comes in and joins us. He has been on some detail and is still wearing his fatigues. The first sergeant introduces me to him. We wait until the others have been served before we go through the line. They have some kind of meat in a gravy and they are serving it over rice. They have some peas and carrots and a sheet cake for dessert. It does not look very good.

We take our trays back to the table to eat and the meal tastes better than it looks, either that or I am really hungry. I ask the other two if there are things that I need to know and they say that things should get better when we get more troops in here. I ask if more troops will help the food and they both laugh. The first sergeant says that the only way the food will be better is to shoot the cook and go rob a grocery store. After we finish eating, I head back to my barracks. The other two are living in a barracks across the street from the orderly room.

I go take my shower and get ready for bed. I spend my first night as a member of the 4th Inf. Div.

CHAPTER XCIX

This morning, I get up, dress in my class A uniform and am ready to fall out for reveille, but I see that no one else is getting ready. They are all putting on fatigues to go on details. They start out to the mess hall and I fall in behind them. When we get there, they line up and I go ahead, go in and sit down at the non-com table. I am soon joined by the first sergeant, the corporal I met yesterday and the supply sergeant. The food does not look very good, but I see that they have boxes of bran flakes. I get three of them, a big bowl and eat cereal with lots of sugar and milk on it.

After breakfast, I go back to the barracks and make sure that all of my things are in order. Then I make my way to the orderly room. I still have a lot of the army regulations to put away, so I go to work on that. The first sergeant comes in and a few minutes later, the captain arrives. They tell me that they need some papers typed, so I go to the desk and start work on them. I can always file the army regulations. I spend the whole morning working in the orderly room and then the first sergeant and I go to eat dinner.

After dinner, I go back to the barracks and lay down until time to go back to work. The work is not hard and it allows me to know what is going on. When I get a chance, I ask the first sergeant about falling out for reveille and retreat. He says that when we get more troops in, we will probably have to start having to fall out, but for now, everyone is busy and he does not see any need for it.

The days are all the same for the rest of the week. It is like I have a regular job to go to. I open one dispatch and see that we will be able to go to a college football game this weekend if we want to. It sounds good to me. I pass the word around to the rest of the troops and on Saturday morning at eleven, we load up in a truck and are driven to Chapel Hill, North Carolina to watch the University of North Carolina play Duke.

We have a great time at the game and get back to the camp in the evening. We are too late for supper, so I stop off at the PX and get something to eat before I go back to the barracks. Sunday, I spend the day lying around the barracks and reading.

Monday I am in the orderly room when we get a dispatch saying that every unit is to send one man to report to headquarters the following morning. The person is to be a member of the general's new drum and bugle corp. The first sergeant says that we do not have anyone to send because everyone is already working. He says for me to go and tell them that we do not have anyone to send and then to come back.

Tuesday morning, I go to the headquarters to tell them that we do not have anyone to send. The colonel who meets with us says that not having anyone to send it not valid reason, and whoever showed up is it. I do not want to be in a drum and bugle corp. But he goes on to say that the only way you can be excused is by the general himself. I am in, whether I want to or not.

They have a T/5 to teach us. He tries to make it sound like it is a good deal for anyone involved. He even says that we will all get to be T/5's. Since I am already a T/5, it is not much of an advantage to me. They do not have any drums or bugles yet, but they do have a whole box of drum sticks. We will be practicing with the drum sticks. Since we do not have the drums, we will use the back of a bench for our drum. He shows us how to hold the drum sticks and how to beat the drum. The sticks hitting the back of the bench sounds like a group of giant woodpeckers at work. I not only look stupid hitting that bench, I feel stupid.

When we get a break at noon, I go back to the orderly room and tell the captain what happened. He says that they need me there, but he can't go against the general and he guesses I will have to stick it out.

The next day I am back at headquarters pecking away on the back of the bench. I know that I have to do something. In the evening after we are dismissed, I go back to the orderly room and get the captain and first sergeant together. I ask them if it is okay for me to get out of the drums, if I can. The captain says that it is okay with him. Then I ask him not to give me away, if I try something.

I get to drum practice and I tell the T/5 in charge that I am not going to be able to do the drums. He wants to know why and I tell him that the constant pecking is driving me crazy. He agrees to go to headquarters and tell them that I am having trouble. He comes back in a little bit and says that I need to go see the colonel that is in charge of getting the drum and bugle corps. set up.

I am really shaking when I go in to the colonel's office. He asks me what is the matter and I tell him that overseas I had to listen to code day after day and the constant dots and dashes got to me. That now I am listening to the drum sticks hitting the bench and it is driving me crazy. That all night long I hear the constant clacking sound and that I can't sleep. He sees how I am shaking and after talking to me for a few minutes, he says he can see that I will not be able to do it. He is going to go ahead and dismiss me without going through the general. He says for me to go back to my outfit and tell them to send someone else.

I thank him and then head back to the orderly room. When I get there, I tell the captain that they need to send someone else to be a drummer. He wants to know how I got out and I tell him it is better if he does not know. We go over the roster and pick another guy to take my place. I go find him on a detail unloading supplies and tell him that the next day he is to go to drum and bugle corp. He is delighted and I am back at work in the orderly room. Too bad we did not send him in the first place.

We are getting some more men in now. Among them is a first lieutenant. I meet him when he reports. The next morning, he comes into the orderly room and says that he fell out for reveille this morning and he was the only one that showed up. We also get in a guy that had trained as a company clerk. He moves in to take over my job and they put me in the communications section. We only have a few men in the section, but we have the responsibility for the switchboard, connecting all of the daytime phones. Since there are so few of us, I have to take a shift on the switchboard too.

I am now getting regular letters from the brown headed girl in Waukomis. It is nice to have someone to get mail from. Almost every weekend I leave the camp, if not to a football game, just to spend time in Durham or Raleigh. There is a great USO in Durham and I go there a lot. The captain gives me a blank signed pass in case I have a problem getting back to base. I can just fill in the date and be covered until I can get back.

It is getting closer to Christmas and I want a furlough home. I go to the train station and check on the cost of a round trip ticket home. The agent says that it is twenty dollars. I then go to the orderly room and put in my request for a ten-day furlough. The captain says I am in luck because they just got orders to let anyone who does not have essential duties to have leave over Christmas. I sit at the typewriter and type out my own orders and he signs them. I go call my mother and ask her to send me twenty dollars for my train fare.

I spend most of what money I have for presents, so I will need the money from home. I will not get paid until I get back from leave. My mother wires me twenty-five instead and it is a good thing because the station agent did not tell me about the tax on the ticket. When I get my ticket, I only have two dollars left. I notice that the porter is putting bags on the train before we are allowed on. He is using them to reserve seats for people. When I get on the train, there are no seats left. It is standing room only.

The aisle is full of people, mostly soldiers. We lean against the seats and shift our weight to keep our legs from going to sleep. After awhile, one of the soldiers next to me, looks up at a cabinet in the corner at the top of the car. He reaches up and pulls the door open. Inside is the broken arm from one of the seats. He closes the door. I tell him to let me over there. I reach up, open the door and take out the broken arm. I slide it under the seat. I take my overcoat and lay it on the floor of the cabinet and put my duffle bag in the corner of the cabinet. I climb up on the back of the seat and slide into the cabinet. There is just room for me to curl up. I ask the other guy to please close the door.

I go to sleep and sleep for several hours. When I wake up, I push open the door and look out. It is early morning. I climb out of the cabinet and there are a bunch of surprised people. They got on the train after I got in there and they had no idea anyone was up there. I stand and try to get the kinks out of my body. It is not long before we get to Birmingham and have to change trains.

This train is standing room only, too, but I find a place in the corner where I can put my duffle bag down and sit on it. It is better than standing and makes the trip to Memphis a lot easier. I get into Memphis in the early morning, but the train to Oklahoma City is full and I will not be able to get out until evening. They do say that I can put in for the Rock Island Rocket and if they get a cancellation they will put me on. The Rocket is the high speed passenger train that only stops at major cities. It takes a lot less time to get to Oklahoma City.

While I am waiting, I go to the USO to wait. The USO has doughnuts and coffee that are free, so at least I have something to eat. I do not have enough money left to buy much. In the middle of the afternoon, they page me to go to the ticket office. The woman there says that they have not had a cancellation, but that she is going to put me on any way. She says that when I get on, to go to the last car on the train, which is the club car and ride there. I keep saying thank you and she says that I better hurry up or I will miss it.

I go out to the shiny metal train and show my updated ticket to the conductor. He has me climb on and I make my way to the club car. I find one of the big easy chairs and settle back in it. There are people sitting around smoking and having soft drinks. No alcohol served on this train. I look out of the window and we are flying across Arkansas. The train runs ninety miles an hour, only slowing to eighty when they go through a town. We only have a couple of stops before we get to Oklahoma City.

It is only a few blocks from the train station to the bus station. I do not have to wait long before the bus leaves for home. The folks have the Christmas tree up and I can see the lights through the window. What a great welcome home. Of course, when I get in the house, Mom fixes me a snack for supper and I get to sample all of the Christmas candy she has made. After my supper, I call Waukomis and tell Dolores that I will be up to see her tomorrow night. It is a school night, but I am sure her folks will not care, since I just got home.

CHAPTER C

This morning, after breakfast, I make my way to town. More veterans are home for good. They are mostly the married men and some of them have been gone a long time. I make it home for dinner and Mother makes us a small lunch.

As soon as supper is over, I borrow the car and head for Waukomis. I go by and get Dolores. She has me come in and see her folks. We visit for awhile and then Dolores and I go to Enid to the show. After the show, we find a place that is open and go in and get a Coke before we start home. Of course, we pull off the highway and find a place to park. Her kisses are wonderful. We neck for awhile and then I take her home. I will be back in a couple of days.

After the first day, things at home are rather boring, but my trips to see Dolores are the most important thing about my leave. We go to church on Christmas eve and enjoy the service. The next day, we have Christmas dinner at our house. We have a big dinner, share gifts and then everyone goes back home. In the evening, I go to Waukomis to see Dolores again.

The next day, my dad runs into the superintendent of schools and he says that he is wanting to go quail hunting, but his wife has the car, so he does not have any way to go. Dad says that he knows where there is a boy who has a car and would love to go quail hunting, but he does not have a gun. The superintendent says he has the gun and to have me come by and get him.

He has some good places to hunt. There are a lot of quail, because there have not been many young men around to hunt them. We have a good time and get our limit of quail. We dress them and I take half of them home and Mother fixes them for supper. It was a good break in my leave. I only have a couple of days left, so I spend my evenings with Dolores.

I pack up and leave a day early so that I will be sure to get back in time. I do not have any trouble getting back, but some do. They have had heavy rains and much of the South is flooded. The train travels for miles with water on both sides of the tracks. I get into Durham, go to the USO and get a bed. I stay in Durham the whole day and then go out to the camp on the day I am scheduled to return. I report in and tell the captain about my trip.

The next day, one of the others, who went home for Christmas reports in two days late. I am in the orderly room when he reports. The captain tells him that he is late. He says that he could not get back because of the flood. The captain then tells him he is in luck, because I had already told him about the flood, so his story is backed up. He keeps telling me, thank you. I tell him that he has to make up those two days and he can start by being latrine orderly. He is really relieved and takes off at a run toward the barracks.

While I am in the orderly room, they get orders to send one man to recoiless rifle school. It will be his job to learn all about them and then to teach the rest of the company. I ask the captain if I can be the one to go. He reminds me about the drum and bugle corps., laughs and then says that if I want to go, to go ahead. I have to report the next morning to the ordnance section.

The next morning after breakfast, I walk to the ordnance building. The class is interesting. I go everyday for the rest of the week. The last day, we go to the range. They demonstrate firing both the 57mm and the 75mm. Then we each get to fire one round from the

57mm. I fire my round and am just a couple of yards short of the target. I wish we could fire more, because I am sure I could hit it the next shot. I just did not allow for enough distance.

At the end of the week, we get notice that we will have to furnish a detail to guard prisoners. The captain calls me in and tells me that I will need to pick four other guys to go with me for the next week. Not what I want to do, but I am stuck. I go back to the barracks and pick out the four guys who have the least important jobs and tell them they are going to be prison guards for the next week. They do not seem any more delighted than I am. We will have to draw weapons.

We go to the supply building and tell them that we are there to draw weapons to guard prisoners. They ask if we have all qualified with the .45 pistol. Four of us have, one has not. Then they ask if we have all qualified with the M1. Everyone has. They pull out five M1's and hand them to us. I ask about getting a pistol instead. Sergeant says that they have to issue all the same. I do not have any desire to carry an M1 for a week, but I have no choice.

Monday morning, we march over to the stockade. They give each of us a M1 clip with seven rounds. We load our rifles with the chamber empty. Our job is to go with a prisoner detail and to see that they do not escape. There are four prisoners on the detail, one truck driver and one guard. Their job is to load coal onto the truck and then haul it to any barracks that needs it and to fill the coal hopper. All I have to do is to stand there with the rifle and see that they do not run off.

Most of the guys are in the prison because they went AWOL (absent without leave). They are not dangerous, just guys like the rest of us. They are out working and one of them asks me if I would shoot him if he tried to escape. I tell him that it is my understanding that if I let him escape, I have to take his place and I am not going to shovel coal. He nods that he understands what I am saying.

The week goes so slow, just standing and watching them shovel coal. The rifle gets very heavy. I feel like handing it to one of the prisoners and telling him to let me shovel for awhile. When the week is over, the other four guys and I go to the PX to celebrate and get drunk on beer.

Monday morning, I get notice that the captain wants to see me at the orderly room. I wonder what I have done now, but the captain and I have been friends, so I do not think it is anything too bad. When I go in to see him, he says that he is making me head of the communications section. That in addition, he is promoting me to T/4. I do not particularly want to be head of the communications section, but I do like the idea of being a T/4 and getting sergeant's pay. He says that we are getting more men in and we need to be more organized. I ask if that means that we will be standing reveille and retreat. He says that we are not that organized yet. I thank him and ask if he has any special orders. He says that he would like for me to set up a schedule of switchboard operators and train them to properly answer the phone. I tell him I will get right on it. But first I need to go to the PX and get me some T/4 stripes. Those guys will not believe me, unless they see the stripes sewn on my sleeve.

I take off for the PX and get six sets of T/4 stripes. I go back to the barracks and find a place out of the way, where I can sew the new stripes on my shirt and field jacket. I will sew them on my other clothes later. I put on my shirt and jacket and walk up to the room where the switchboard is located. There are two guys there, the operator and one of the other communication section guys. I do not say anything about my promotion. I just sit down and visit with them for awhile. The guy on the switchboard turns around to talk to me and after a little bit, he notices the stripes. He asks who's jacket I have. I tell him it is mine. He says, "Oh Yeah, when did you make T/4?"

"About an hour ago."

"How come?"

"I got promoted when the captain made me chief of the communications section."

"No shit, you are our boss now?"

"I guess so."

"That is great. It is about time we had someone to go to bat for us."

"One of the first things I want to do is to work out a fair work schedule for all of us. I hope you guys will help me do it. I am going to go check on some things now. I will see you all later.""

I know they will pass the word along about me being the new boss. I am sure some will resent it, but I think most will be glad about it. I go back to the orderly room and the captain says that it did not take me long to get my stripes on. I get some paper and make a form for setting work schedules. I will let the men have some say on it.

When everyone is back to the barracks from their details, I have all the members of the communications section meet in the room with the switchboard. Word gets around fast, because everyone already knows that I am now the head of the section. I show them the form that I have made up for the work schedule and ask for any suggestions. Several of them ask that some changes be made, but mostly they agree on what I have already prepared.   One of them remarks that I have assigned myself to some of the shifts. I tell them that I will not ask them to do anything that I will not do. This seems to satisfy everyone.

We get a new cook in the mess hall and instead of getting better, the food gets worse. We have already had horse meat and it was one of the best meals we have had. But that was with the old cook, who got shipped out. The new cook is Mexican and he loads everything with red pepper. The men ask me to talk to the captain about it. I tell them that I want a couple of them to go with me and we will see if anything can be done.

I get permission to speak to the captain and take two of the men with me. We tell him what has been going on. One of the guys says that the food is so hot, that it is a wonder that the beds do not catch on fire when someone farts. The captain says that he knows there is a problem. In fact, he has received notice that the general is going to address the entire camp about the food tomorrow afternoon. But that he will talk to the cooks and see if he can get them to go easier on the pepper.

The whole division forms up on the parade ground. They have erected a stage at one end for the general to use. They have loud-speakers around the grounds. The men are all standing on the field when they call attention and the general takes the stage. He says that the reason that the food is not very good, is because they did not plan on us being sent here and they have not moved any supplies in this direction. Someone shouts "BULL SHIT!" Soon, men are shouting all over the place. Some are yelling "LET US GO HOME!" The general is drowned out and leaves the stage. Another officer takes the stage and shouts in the microphone "DISMISSED!" I am sure that we will all be punished over this.

The food does not get any better. Our punishment is that we have to eat it, but the cook does cut back on the red pepper. The PX is getting more business as guys go to buy what they can to eat, but the PX has little in food other than cookies, candy and beer. The beer seems to win out. More than one guy comes into the barracks loaded and falls into his bunk.

CHAPTER CI

Suddenly we receive orders to start closing the camp. We are to start turning in all equipment. I receive orders to turn in all of the batteries that the communications section has in its storage. I do not know of any batteries. I check in the orderly room and find that in the upstairs of the vacant barracks next door is a supply of batteries. I am given the key to the front door of the barracks and told to get the batteries out and deliver them to the supply building. They will dispose of them, probably through surplus sales.

I pick out four men from my section, give them the key and tell them what to do. I do not think it will take them long. After all, how many batteries could we have anyway? When they have been gone for over two hours, I decide to go check on what is holding them up. When I get to the other barracks, I see the two wheeled cart from supply parked in front and it is loaded down with wooden cases. I look at the stencils and see that they are cases of all kinds of batteries. I hear a loud crash from inside the barracks and go to investigate.

At the bottom of the stairs is another of the wooden boxes. I guess I should say at the bottom of what used to be the stairs. The steps are all gone. All that is left is a mass of splintered wood and

577

the stringers against the wall. I yell up and ask what is going on. I see a couple of heads sticking out. One of them says to watch out. I step back just as another case of batteries comes flying down what is left of the stairs. I yell up to hold it and ask how you get up there. They tell me to put my feet on the stringers next to the walls and climb up.

I get up stairs and they still have several cases of batteries left. They tell me that the cases were too heavy to carry down the steps so they just rolled them down. Soon there were no steps left, so they just continued to throw them down. I decide it is too late now, we just as well throw down the rest of them. When all of the cases have been removed, we climb down by holding tight to the walls. I help them load the last cases on the cart, then I close the doors and re-place the lock. I take one of the splinters of wood and stick it in the key hole in the lock and break it off. They will have to cut this lock off to get in. Maybe no one will see this until after we are gone.

We are ordered to move out of our barracks and to go to the area across the street from the orderly room. Some of the troops are already there. This will consolidate the living quarters and take less utilities. This means that we have to remove the switchboard and check it in. All of the lines leading from it will have to be taken down and turned in. The switchboard is easy. I take my wireman's pliers and cut all the wires leading into it. I pull the plug to the power, we carry it downstairs, load it on a cart and haul it to the supply building. The lines are a bigger problem. They go out of the building and are tied to the top of high line poles, all over the area.

I check out a couple of sets of climbing tools and ask how many in the section know how to climb a pole. Everyone of them says they have never even seen climbing tools, let alone climb a pole. I have at least seen them, and I used to use my dad's safety belt to play around in trees, but I have never had the spurs on or attempted to climb a pole.

The next morning I strap on the climbers and belt and stand by the pole in front of the orderly room. I grab the pole and start up it. I get about half way up and the captain comes out of the orderly room. He says, "How much insurance do you have, Lovell?"

"Ten thousand dollars, sir, why?"

"I don't think it is enough." Then he goes back inside. But I am sure he is watching from inside to see if I make it to the top. I get up to the top, fasten my belt around the pole, lean back and take loose the wires and let them go crashing down. Then I unhook my belt and make my way back down the pole. One down and a whole bunch more to go. The others in the section are rolling up the wire. After a few more poles, I get one of the other guys to try to climb a pole, but he chickens out about half way up. I climb twenty-seven poles by evening. I grab a bite of supper and lay down on my bunk, with my clothes on.

I wake up in the morning and some of the guys are standing around my bunk. I can see them, but I can't move. When they see that I can't get up, they take hold of me and lift me up onto my feet. I try to move my legs and they refuse. I tell them I need to go to the latrine and a couple of the guys, with one on each side of me, help me get there. I drop my clothes off and make my way into the shower. After twenty minutes in the shower, I can move better. I get dressed and make my way to the mess hall.

After breakfast, we go back to finish our job. I only have fifteen poles to climb today. My body screams as I start up the first pole. After five or six, I start to loosen up, but I am still tired from the day before. We are almost done, only two to go. I get to the next to the last pole and I have to climb up the front side to be able to get the line loose. This is not the safest way to do it. When I take the line loose, it drops down on my belt, and is between me and the pole. Then I have to take my belt loose and let it drop down on my feet. Any pull on the line will pull my feet away from the pole and knock me off of the pole.

I take one spur out of the pole and just stick it back in above the wire when my other foot is yanked off the pole. I am hanging by one arm and one spur. I missed being knocked from the pole by a fraction of a second. I get my spur back in pole and look to see what happened. One of the crew got in a hurry and let the line down across the road, before I was clear of it and a truck hit it.

I climb down and I am still shaking. By the time I get to the guy, I have had time to settle down. I point out to him and the others that his carelessness nearly cost me my life and from now on, to pay attention to everyone around. Then I go to the last pole and climb it. When I get down I tell them to finish up, that I am through for the day and if they want me I will be in the PX drinking beer.

The orderly room and supply building are the only occupied buildings in that block now. All of us are in the barracks across the street from the orderly room. Guys are getting orders almost every day to ship out.

Three of the guys have received their orders ship out, so they are packing their things. One of the guys has a can of lighter fluid that he does not want to take with him, so he is playing around with it. He takes it and makes a large circle on the floor of the barracks. He lights it and then jumps in and out of the circle of fire, while chanting like an Indian. We stomp out the fire. About five minutes later, a couple of guys come into the barracks and yell that the barracks is on fire.

The lighter fluid has run through cracks in the floor and the floor is on fire under the barracks. We grab the fire extinguishers and a couple of guys crawl under the barracks and put the fire out.

Several of us get notice that we will be shipping out, including me. We will find out tomorrow where we will be assigned. There are twenty of us on orders. We go ahead and pack up all of our things except one class A uniform to wear as we travel. We are excited about getting out of here. We all go to the PX and celebrate our leaving tomorrow.

The first sergeant comes into the barracks and starts handing out our orders. Everyone is quick to open theirs and see where they will be stationed. It could be any place in the United States. We are not likely to be going overseas. I open mine and quickly scan for the destination: Fort Sill, Oklahoma. I will be going back to Oklahoma.

I shout it out. Others are telling their assignments. There are only three of us going to Fort Sill.

I go over to the orderly room and tell the first sergeant and captain goodbye. They have both treated me very well while I have been here. I ask if they were responsible for me getting to go to Fort Sill and they both say they had nothing to do with it, that I am just that lucky.

There are about a dozen of us that board the same train in Durham. We will be together at least until Birmingham, Alabama. We even get seats on the train this time. Most everyone is in a good humor, even the guy from New York that is going to Fort Sill with me and the other guy.

We keep losing guys along the way and by the time we get to Memphis, only we three, who are bound for Fort Sill, are still together. We arrive in Memphis early in the morning and will not be able to get a train out until evening. I tell them I have been here before and to follow me. We go to the USO and get coffee and doughnuts for breakfast. Then we decide to see some of the city while we have to wait.

On the way, we see a bar. We go in and the owner is just cleaning up from the night before. It is still early in the day, but we each order a beer. He does not ask any of us our ages, but brings the three draft beers. Then he goes back to cleaning up. By the time he is through cleaning, we are ready for another beer. After the fourth beer, we decide that we better head back to the train station.

In the train station, we each order a hamburger with fries. The food helps soak up some of the beer in me and I am moving better now. I find a bench to sit on and settle in to wait on the train. I ask the other guys to wake me in time to get on and I go to sleep.

The train pulls in and we climb aboard with all of our things. The train takes us to Oklahoma City and then we have to change to the bus to go the rest of the way. When we arrive at Fort Sill, we report to the building on our orders. They split us up there and I get to ride in a jeep to my new station. I still remember the old wooden barracks that I stayed in, when I came into the army. It is different this time. I will be staying in a big brick building, located on the south side of the parade ground. They are still the same beds, but there is not another one on top of it. We each have a tall locker to hang our clothes in and a foot locker for our other things. The floors are covered with some kind of linoleum and are waxed and polished. It is by far the nicest place I have been in the army. There is a PX about a block away and across the parade ground is the post theater, next to the officers club.

I meet the other guys who I will be working with, when they come in from their details in the evening I ask about the unit and what we will be doing. They tell me that it is a demonstration unit. They have all kinds of artillery. When they need to show what some kind of artillery can do, they demonstrate it. I will be in the communications section. There is a staff sergeant in charge, but I will be expected to work under him and to be in charge of small parties of communications workers.

Most of the guys in the outfit have been here for some time. They seem glad to have me join them. They show me to the mess hall, which is located in the next building, which looks much like the one I am staying in. The food is army fare, but really good after what we had in Camp Butner. Tomorrow, we will be going out to fire a problem with 105mm howitzers. They have already laid the wire for the mission. All we will have to do is to hook on field telephones and we will be ready.

We fall out for reveille and then go to breakfast. When breakfast is over, we load up in trucks and head out to the firing range. I will be on the phone by the cannons and be connected to the forward observer. It will be my job to relay the fire mission to the gunners and then to let the forward observer know when the cannons have been fired. It is not hard work and it is fun to watch the cannons fire, even if it is hard on the ears.

The day goes fast. When the firing is over, we take the wire trucks, wind up the lines and take them back to the storage. Tomorrow is Saturday and we have to stand inspection in the morning. They tell me that if I have all of my things in order, there is nothing to it. After the inspection, we will be free for the weekend. I have already written to my folks and to Dolores that I am going to Fort Sill, so they will probably expect me to come home.

The inspection goes well and we are dismissed by ten o'clock. I catch the post bus to the gate on the highway and start hitch hiking. It is not long until a GI comes along and asks where I am going. I tell him Hennessey and he says to get in, he is going right through there. I am home by noon. When he drops me off, he says that he will pick me up Sunday evening about six.

CHAPTER CII

My folks are not surprised to see me. They said that they knew, when I said I was going to Fort Sill, that I would be home shortly. They start asking what I am going to do, when I get out of the army. They want me to go to college. No one in our close family has ever gone to college. I tell them that it is my intention to go in the fall. My dad says that if I do not know what I want to study, that he would suggest that I enroll in pre-law. It would at least give me a basis for other things.

In the evening, I drive to Waukomis and see Dolores. It is good to get to see her again. I tell her that I will come home every chance that I get. With any luck, I can be home nearly every weekend.

The next day I attend church with the folks and afterwards we have a good Sunday dinner. I take a nap in the afternoon and then we visit for awhile before an early supper of leftovers. About five-forty, I head to town and wait for my ride back. I expect him to be a little late, but he is there at six-ten. He takes me back to Fort Sill and says that he will probably be going home again next weekend and that he will be looking for me. I thank him for the ride and offer to help with the gas, but he refuses. He laughs and says he is running on tractor gas from the farm.

The next week is busy. We have a different fire mission about every third day here. That means one day to get ready and string wire, one day to shoot and then the third day to gather the wire back up. We do get quite a bit of time off. We get Wednesday afternoons, Saturday afternoons and Sundays.

The guys like to tease me. We go out to gather up the wire. When we have finished rolling up the wire, we start back to the storage building. We are on the main road on the post and it happens to run straight into the City of Lawton. When we get back to where we are supposed to stop, they keep on going down the road, right out through the main gate and into the city. I am hollering at them to turn around, before we get in trouble and they say that I am in charge, so I am the one that will get in trouble.

I guess they know that the security at the gate is very lax and no one says a word either time we go through the gate. The second time, they do drive to the storage building and we deliver the wire. They all laugh and say that they are glad that I did not get in trouble, making them go off of the post and into Lawton.

We have a party in the evening. We get several guys together and go to the PX. We are not allowed to take beer out of the PX, but can drink it in the beer garden outside. The beer garden is surrounded by a tall fence and the only way into it is through the PX. Some of the guys go into the PX, buy several bottles of beer and take them to the beer garden. A couple of the other guys go to the outside of the fence and they each have a gallon pickle jar. The guys inside pass the bottles of beer through the fence and the ones on the outside fill up the jars with them. At the same time, other guys are in the PX buying a bunch of steak sandwiches. We all head back to the barracks and we eat the steak sandwiches and wash them down with beer out of the jars.

Today we are firing a mission, using 155mm cannons. I have seen them many times and have even been close to the firing when we were in Germany, but today I am right with them, relaying the commands from the forward observer. They fire one gun and there is a terrible screaming noise. I dive toward the ground. The others all just stand there and laugh. One says that it was just a rotating band that came loose. The shells for this gun have a copper band around them that engages the rifling in the barrel and as I found out, it sometimes comes loose when it is fired and screams as it goes through the air.

I get to go home again on the weekend and the same GI picks me up, takes me home and brings me back. I really appreciate getting to ride this way. He says we will plan on doing it again next week.

This week we are practicing for an important night firing mission. They are going to have forty-nine generals come to Fort Sill, from several different countries, to observe artillery fire. Our unit is to fire 155mm illuminating shells over the target area and when it is lighted, the other units will start shelling the targets. We run the wire from the observation area to the firing area, so that all we will have to do is to hook the phones on, when we are ready to shoot.

We go out for a practice firing session tonight. The guns are all in place and I get the order to have the first gun fire an illuminating shell. I give the order and they fire. I speak into the phone and say "On the way." In a little bit, I get call that they are waiting. I tell them that it was fired some time ago. They say they did not see anything, to fire another shell. I pass on the order to fire another shell. Again I tell them that it has been fired and again they say they did not see anything. The shells are not exploding over the target and are going out and landing somewhere.

They send a lieutenant back to the guns to set the fuses on the shells. The lieutenant sets a fuse and they fire the shell. The result is the same. It appears that we have received a batch of defective fuses. While we are waiting to see what they will want us to do next, one of the gunners says "Lieutenant, I know what we could do.'"

"What is that?"

"We could catch some of these fireflies, put them in a jar and throw them over the hill."

The lieutenant does not think it is the least bit funny, but the rest of us like the joke. They decide to call off the shoot for that night and we head back to the barracks. We will see what happens next week, when we shoot for the demonstration.

I get my usual ride home on the weekend, but he tells me that it will be his last week. He is to go to the separation center the next week and get discharged. I will have to find another way home.

This week we are firing the demonstration. We have not practiced again, so I hope the fuses work. Tonight we are going to do it for real. I pass on the command to load all guns with illuminating shells and get ready to fire on command. I report that all guns are ready and they tell me to standby. Then the command comes to fire and I shout it to the gunners. Instantly the entire battery of guns fires and in the dark the fire shoots out of the muzzles of the four guns. In a moment we see the lights floating down.

With the light on the targets, the other artillery opens fire. As the light fades, I get the command to fire another volley of shells and again they light the sky. It should be an impressive sight to the generals sitting in the bleachers, where they can see the targets.

This weekend, I go down to the highway and start hitchhiking home again. It takes longer since I am unable to get a direct ride. I decide that I better take the bus back on Sunday night, because I do not want to be late getting back and the hitchhiking is just not that dependable.

I enjoy the weekend home and with Dolores, then on Sunday evening, I catch the bus south.

This week, one of the guys in the outfit asks me to go to Oklahoma City with him on Wednesday afternoon. He is engaged to a girl who lives in Oklahoma City. I agree to go with him. We get off duty at noon on Wednesday and we go to the highway and start hitchhiking. We catch a ride with another GI to Norman, Oklahoma, about twenty miles south of Oklahoma City. When we get there, we catch the interurban coach to Oklahoma City.

We get to downtown Oklahoma City and go to the phone office, where his girlfriend works. I wait in the lobby for him and he goes in to tell her that he is in town and will meet her when she gets off work in the evening. He comes back out and says that we have some time to kill, because she does not get off until five. We walk around the city. I want to go to the Planter's nut store. I remember it from when I was little and my aunt took me there to see "Mr. Peanut." We find the store and we each buy a big sack of peanuts. Many of the nuts that I like are no longer available, since the war stopped their import.

Then we make our way to a little bar. We go in and each order a beer. We sit and drink our beers until time for him to go to meet his girlfriend. I drink a couple more beers and then go to the bus station to wait for him. I eat supper at the bus station café. It seems that I have eaten a lot of meals here. At least, they do have reasonable prices and the pie is not too bad.

Ranson shows up just before time to catch the bus. His girl is with him and he introduces us. We get our tickets, he kisses her goodbye and we get on the bus. It is soon obvious that the bus has a problem. The driver starts it and the gears grind as he take off. He is shifting without the clutch. By the time we get out of Oklahoma City, we can tell that the clutch is out. The driver tries to stop each time on a down slope, so that he can start the bus in gear. At one stop, he can't get started, so all the passengers, who are mostly sol- diers, get off and push the bus to help get it started.

We finally get to Fort Sill, all the local buses have stopped run- ning and we have to walk a couple of miles to the barracks. It is four-thirty by the time we get back. We try to be quiet as we get out of our dress clothes and get ready for bed. I sit down on my bunk to get in bed and the lights come on. Then a voice says "Everybody up. Breakfast is at five, we fall out at six to go to the field." I stand back up and put my fatigues on and get ready for breakfast.

We get out in the field doing a fire mission and the lieutenant looks at Ranson and I and asks what is the matter with us. He says that we look like hell. I tell him that we went to Oklahoma City yesterday and did not get in until four-thirty this morning. He says "Lovell, you are a sergeant, you ought to know better than that and Ranson, you are older, you ought to know better too." I explain about the bus and he tells us both to crawl up in the truck and sleep for awhile. He will wake us up when he needs us.

This weekend we are participating in the "Armed Forces Day" parade. We are riding in a prime mover, pulling one of the 155mm howitzers. We ride out of the camp and down the main streets of Lawton and then return to the post. When we get everything put away, it is still not noon yet, so I decide to go home again this weekend. I hurry and get my few things together, catch the bus to the gate next to the highway and then start hitchhiking.

I spend the weekend as usual and then catch the bus back to Fort Sill on Sunday night. Monday I check the duty roster and see that I am to be sergeant of the guard on the following weekend. I write letters to my mother and Dolores and tell them I will not be home the following weekend. It will be the first time since I got here that I have not spent the weekend at home.

I make it through the week and on Friday evening, I clean up, put my class A uniform on and report to the guardhouse. I am issued a pistol belt with holster, .45 pistol, whistle and an MP arm band. The guards show up and they are lined up for inspection. After we inspect them, we assign them to shifts and then they are taken to where they are to stand guard. I will be in the guardhouse, except when I go out to check on them.

Most of the guards are located near the PX, in case the beer garden gets rowdy. I hope for a nice quiet weekend. Fortunately it is nice weather and most of the soldiers have gone. The few that remain are relatively quiet. I try to go out during every tour just to see that everyone is in their place. The rest of the time I spend reading in the guardhouse. It is quiet enough that I get my sleep too.

Monday morning, I dismiss the guards and we go back to our own barracks. Since I was on guard the whole weekend, I am off duty today. I go to the service club and spend most of the day.

CHAPTER CIII

We have some excitement this week. Yesterday, some of the guys were playing ball on the parade ground and when they finished, they hid the bat and ball in the barrel of the old cannon that sits at the corner of the grounds.

The cannon is the one they fire each evening at retreat. The crew for the cannon, goes out, opens the breech and shoves in the blank shell. When they fire, the bat goes across the parade ground and lands right in front of the officer's club, while the ball goes over the top of the post theater and into the trees behind it.

The next day, the guys admit that they put the bat and ball in the cannon, but insist that they did not know it was used. They were not punished, but a new order comes down from headquarters, that the crew firing the cannon will make a visual inspection of the barrel before loading. Most of us think that the guys really knew that the cannon was fired each evening and wanted to see what would happen.

I celebrate my twentieth birthday this week. The guys help me celebrate by holding on to my feet and shaking me over the stairwell. My money falls out of my pocket and they add it to the rest of the contributions and head to the PX, to get the beer and steak sandwiches for a party. I really feel honored.

Saturday afternoon, I hitchhike home again. Saturday is like usual, but Sunday it turns cold and starts to drizzle. In the evening I go to the drugstore and get my bus ticket. While I am waiting, three guys from the country drive up in a pickup. One of them is going to Fort Sill too. We keep waiting on the bus and it does not show. If it does not come soon, we will miss our connection in El Reno. The phone rings in the drugstore, the owner answers the phone and then announces that the bus has broken down and it will be about forty five minutes before another can get there. We can't wait that long, we will miss all of our connections and be AWOL.

The boys from the country decide they are going to drive to El Reno. They tell me to climb in too. There are four of us in the cab of the pickup. They take off down the highway. I look at the speed-ometer and it shows that we are going forty-five miles per hour. We will never make it at this speed. I ask if we couldn't go a little faster. One of them says that we better not, that this pickup has oversized truck tires on it and we are already going seventy-five. Sure enough, we arrive in plenty of time.

Monday morning, I am called to the orderly room. They hand me my orders. I am to leave tomorrow and go to Camp Chaffee, Arkansas, where I will be separated from the service. It is the word that I have been waiting for, but at the same time, I am rather sad to be leaving. I know that I am not the type to stay in the army, but it has been interesting.

I go back to the barracks and start packing my things. I have some money saved up and will be getting more when I get out, so I decide to throw a party to celebrate my leaving the outfit. When evening comes and the guys come in from their details, I tell them that I am getting out, but before I go I want to have one more party. After supper, I dig out the money and we send a detail to the PX to get beer and sandwiches. I furnish the money. They think that is really good. They had thought that I was expecting them to pay for it.

The party is a great success. We have beer and sandwiches in the barracks and do not get caught.

This morning, I take all of my things, a copy of my orders and catch the bus for the trip to Fort Smith. It is a beautiful spring day, May 7, 1946. I ride the bus and sit by the window watching the scenery, as I go across Oklahoma. It is evening, when I get to Camp Chaffee and I check in at the separation center.

They assign me to one of the usual wooden barracks and tell me to stay close enough so that I can hear my name when it is called, as they do each step of the separation process, they will have me report to a different place. That will start tomorrow. They point out the mess hall and tell me that if I hurry, I may still be able to get supper before they close.

I take my things to the barracks and put them on an unoccupied bunk. Then I walk to the mess hall and get in just before they close. They have ham with pineapple, fried potatoes, green beans, rolls and a peach cobbler for dessert. They must be feeding us well so that we will consider enlisting. I fill my tray and find a place at one of the closest tables. I can tell that the KP's would like for me to hurry and eat.

Back at the barracks, I decide to take one of the upper bunks on the other side of the barracks, so that I get more of a breeze. I make my bed, store my things and then I go take a shower. When I get back, I climb into my bunk and read a "Life" magazine. More guys keep coming into the barracks and of course they are griping because they missed supper. Some of them throw down their things and then head for the PX. It is not long before I go to sleep.

After breakfast, I wait for what will be my next step. I get my first call just before nine o'clock. I am to report to one of the buildings across the street. I go in and take a seat. There are about a half dozen of us waiting. When my name is called, I go into the office. The sergeant there makes sure that I am the right one and then he goes over my file with me. I guess this is to see that they have the right one and do not separate the wrong guy. It takes about ten minutes and then I am on my way back to the barracks.

Like everything else in the army, it is hurry up and wait. I do not get called out again all morning. I go to dinner and after dinner, I lay down on my bunk. I doze off and am awakened by my name being called. I miss where I am to report, but one of the other guys remembers what they said, so I hurry off to my next meeting. This must be my physical. A corporal asks me questions about if I was ever wounded or injured or had an illness. I tell him that the only thing was getting my feet frozen. He wants to know if they still bother me. I tell him that if they get cold, they start to ache again. He makes a note on my record and dismisses me. That takes care of the first day.

This morning after breakfast, several of us get our names called to report to one of the buildings across the street. We hurry over to the building. When we get there, there is a sergeant waiting for us. He has us take a seat and then begins his lecture. His job is to try to get us to keep our GI life insurance. Some of the guys do not want anything to do with the army, including the insurance, but I know that I want to keep mine. He starts out telling us that the life insurance is a bet. The government is betting $10,000 that you are not going to die this month against a little over $6 that you will. You don't think you are either, but those are the best odds that you will ever get. I think every guy there signed up to keep their insurance.

As soon as we get signed, we go back to the barracks to wait for the next call. I figure that we are probably through until after dinner, but it is only a few minutes before I am called to report again. There are a bunch of us this time. The lecture is on the GI Bill of Rights. This lecture takes the rest of the morning and when we get out, we hurry to the mess hall and get in line.

In the afternoon, I go again for a one-on-one interview with a corporal. He goes over my service record to make sure that the jobs I have had are listed and checks to see what decorations that I am entitled to receive. I will receive the World War II Victory medal, American Theater medal, European Theater medal with two battle stars, the Army of Occupation medal, Presidential Unit Citation and the Good Conduct medal. He also goes over my pay record to see if I have any outstanding pay. He calculates how much pay I have coming and how much travel pay and per diem is due me, until I get home. This is one of the more interesting sessions.

The next thing is to check over my clothing. If I have any worn out clothing, I can get it replaced. A lot of the guys could care less, but I have outgrown all my clothes at home and will need to wear parts of my uniform for awhile. Most of my clothes are in good shape, but I do trade in a couple of pair of pants and a shirt for new ones.

If everything goes okay, this will be my last day in the army. I eat breakfast and then go back to the barracks and put my things in my bag, so that I will be ready. Then I lay down on my bunk. I am laying there looking up at the big wooden beam that runs across the barracks, just above my head. Someone has written on the beam. It says: "What to do with your mustering out pay? Stand on any street corner in any city and count it. This is known as muster's last stand." I laugh and laugh because I am sure that is true.

I wait all morning and do not hear anything, so I go eat dinner. This should be my last meal in the army. It is nothing outstanding, but we have pork steak, mashed potatoes and gravy, beans , corn, rolls and a berry cobbler for dessert. When I finish eating, I go back to the barracks. At one o'clock I get called out. They must have gone to dinner and I am first one of the afternoon.

They hand me a big envelope to put my things in. They have a check list and go over it with me. As they hand me things, they check them off of the list. I have my medals, my separation order, my discharge and pamphlets about veterans rights. They hand me a cloth patch and a small gold pin, both show an eagle on a circle, denoting a veteran. These are also known as a "ruptured duck."

I then move to the next room where the paymaster is set up. They pull out my sheet and show me what I have coming. I have the balance due on this month's pay, my travel expense to home, my per diem for getting home and the first $100 of my mustering out pay. The balance will be sent to me later. I sign for the money, move over and count it and then walk out of the building.

I am out of the army, but I am still under army jurisdiction until I return home. I have been in the army twenty-two months and twenty-five days. It seems much, much longer than that. I go back to the barracks, pickup up my bag and walk out to the bus stop, to catch the bus to Fort Smith.

I go to the bus station in Fort Smith and buy my ticket to Hennessey. While I am waiting for the bus to leave, I see other guys that I can tell have just got out too. Many of them are so drunk they will miss their bus. I can see why they do not give us all of our mustering out pay here.

The bus is loading and I climb aboard. I have been over this road several times the last few months. It is late when we get to Oklahoma City and I will have to wait until morning to get a bus home. I do not want to spend the night in the bus station, so I walk a few blocks down the street to an old hotel and get a room. When I check in, the man at the desk asks if I am in the army. I point at the small gold pin on my collar and say "Not now."

I make my way back to the bus station the next morning. Once again I am eating in the bus station café. I finish my breakfast and walk out on the dock to board the bus. I hand the driver my bag to put in the baggage compartment underneath and then I find a seat next to the window. The bus is not crowded, because it is early Saturday morning. The bus travels out of Oklahoma City along the familiar road; along Highway 66 over to El Reno to Highway 81 and then north to home.

I get off of the bus, get my bag and turn the corner at the hardware store and start down Oklahoma Avenue to home. I look up and I see my mother standing on the sidewalk in front of the house looking this way. I can see her smiling as I get closer. She says "I thought you might be home this morning. Welcome home, Robert."

CHAPTER CIV

It is almost a week, before I get a job. They are building a plant on the north side of town to dehydrate alfalfa for feed. My job is to work on the furnace. They have a huge steel drum that will be the heater. It has to be lined with clay. The special clay comes in boxes. We take the clay out of the boxes and then using a hammer, we pound it into the sides of the drum. This gives it the density that it needs, when they fire it up. I spend most of the week inside of this drum, pounding with a hammer. After the first fifteen minutes, the job is extremely boring. The last afternoon, we finish with that and then help hook up some drive belts. The job lasts the one week. I get my pay check and it is $20.46 after deductions for taxes, not the best job that I ever had.

The following week, I get a job helping a farmer just outside of town. He is not all that easy to work for, but his wife is nice and feeds very well. His equipment is old and during the war, parts were not always available. We have to make do with what we have. I do some mowing with the tractor and mower to start with and some odd jobs while we are waiting for the wheat to ripen.

When harvest starts, it is my job to haul the wheat to town. He has an old pickup truck to use. The brakes are out on it, so you have to make plans ahead of time to stop. You hope that no one will get in your way. He fills the pickup so that it is overloaded and then tells me to hurry and get back. When I get to the elevator, I put it in the lowest gear and ease it onto the scales and then up on to the lift. I always tell the workers that I do not have brakes, so that they will not get in my way.

The third time, I have come close to having a wreck and I tell him I will not drive it anymore until he gets the brakes fixed. He gets someone to work on them enough so that I have some brakes, but I never do trust them and only use them when I have to.

After harvest, there is not much work around. So many guys are returning from the service that there is plenty of labor. I sign up for unemployment benefits. This is known as the 52-20 club, since you can draw $20 for up to fifty two weeks. For me, this is better than working. I make as much and do not have to do anything.

I get a call from Ranson, who was my friend at Fort Sill, wanting me to be his best man at his wedding in Oklahoma City. I travel to Oklahoma City and meet with him, his mother and aunt. They have all come down from their home for the wedding. It is only the second wedding I have ever attended and certainly the first one that I have been a part of. Fortunately, there is not much to do. The wedding is a simple affair. They do not even have a reception after the wedding. The couple is going to spend the night in Oklahoma City at a hotel and the next day, they will be going to Pennsylvania where they will make their home. After the wedding, I go to the bus station and catch the bus back home.

My friend, Jack Wells, gets out of the navy and comes back to Hennessey. His parents have moved away while he was gone, but he stays with relatives. Jack has a relative that has a 1926 Star automobile stored in a barn. Jack talks him in to selling it. Jack also has a girlfriend, Barbara Martin, in Waukomis, so we get in that old car and make the trip to see the girls.

Each trip is an adventure in itself. We use all kinds of methods to keep that car running. It is necessary to stop every six miles and drain gas out of the tank and pour it into the small tank under the hood to keep the engine running. The starter does not work, so we park it on a slope or we have to push or use the crank to get it going. It blew the head gasket and we use homemade gaskets, until he can get one from the engine manufacturer. These homemade gaskets only last about twenty miles and we keep a supply in the back seat. We can pull the head and change the gasket in about fifteen minutes and it is good for another twenty miles. The girls like riding in it better than the newer cars and never complain about having to help push to start it.

One of the boys I graduated with, Nathan Armstrong, had gone to Tulsa University on a football scholarship. I decide that I would like to go there too. I check into the university and find that they have a law school. I send into them and receive an application for admission. They notify me that I will have to take entrance exams before I will be admitted. On the day before the entrance exams, I catch the bus to Tulsa and spend the night at a downtown hotel. The next morning, I am very nervous as I take the tests. I am afraid that I will not get in the school. After the exams, I catch the bus back home to wait for their reply.

In a week, I get notice from the university that I have been accepted in the pre-law program. The summer passes quickly and the next thing I know, I am over at Tulsa again, finding a place to stay. Housing around any college is at a premium. People are living in about anything they can find. I ask at the university about housing and they give me the name of a woman who says she has a room to rent. I go to see her and rent a sleeping room from her for $20 a month. Then I go back home and get ready to move to Tulsa. Jack and a couple of other friends are going to go to Oklahoma A & M College at Stillwater. It is break up time again.

I take the bus to Tulsa again, carrying everything that I think I will need. I get moved into my room and the next day I enroll. I get a huge stack of books. I am glad the GI bill is paying for them. The following day, I attend my first class. I am sure that my parents think they are free of me for awhile, but after my last class on Friday, I set out to hitchhike home. The little brown haired girl at Waukomis is too much of an attraction.

The GI bill pays me $75 a month to live on. After the rent is taken out, I only have $55 for everything else. My insurance is $6.40. No more free cigarettes, I have to buy them now. I eat breakfast at the school cafeteria, where I can get a cup of coffee and a roll for fifteen cents. I eat most of my other meals at a little greasy spoon restaurant a block from where I am staying. I just do not have money for anything that is not necessary.

After football starts in the fall, I do not go home as much, but instead stay in Tulsa to watch the games. But I do not usually go more than two weeks without a trip home. Of course there is the Thanksgiving holiday and then the next month it is Christmas. I go home before Christmas and do not have to be back until after New Years.

After the Christmas vacation, I realize that it has been ten years since our family arrived in Hennessey. Things have changed a lot since then. As Lee Hart, the superintendent said after Pearl Harbor, "Your life will never be the same again."

EPILOGUE

June 13, 1948, Robert C. Lovell and Billie Dolores Bullard were married at Waukomis, Oklahoma. They lived in Tulsa until Robert graduated from the University of Tulsa Law School in 1953, and they moved back to Hennessey. Robert went to work at the Farmers & Merchants National Bank. He worked there for twenty years before leaving to go into private law practice. In 1978, Robert was elected judge and served for four terms before retiring at the end of 1994.

After their children got old enough, Billie Dolores went to Phillips University and earned a teaching degree. She taught school for twenty years before she retired.

They have three sons, Donald R., William R., and John B.; two grand-daughters, a great grand-son and numerous extended family.

Robert and Dolores still live in Hennessey and keep up an active retired life.